KARGIL: THE TABLES TURNED

KARGIL

The Tables Turned

Edited by
MAJ. GEN. ASHOK KRISHNA AVSM (Retd.)
P.R. CHARI

MANOHAR
2021

First published 2001
Reprinted 2007, 2008, 2021

ISBN 978-81-7304-368-0

Published by
Ajay Kumar Jain *for*
Manohar Publishers & Distributors
4753/23 Ansari Road, Daryaganj
New Delhi 110 002

Printed at
Ganpati Enterprises
Delhi 110 052

Contents

Illustrations

Acknowledgements

From May to July 1999, India fought an intense localised conventional war in Kargil against Pakistani regulars who had intruded across the Line of Control. The Institute of Peace and Conflict Studies (IPCS) discussed the conflict on a regular basis during this period, issuing weekly operational up-dates on its website, holding weekly seminars and bringing out bulletins. This endeavour was maintained throughout the war and each member of the IPCS contributed to it. This book is the outcome of these efforts. It was, however, felt that, rather than rushing into a quick publication, a deliberate venture would be more rewarding. Consequently, this book is an amalgam of analyses and deliberations extending for over a year.

The editors in grateful acknowledgement, thank all those officials who provided intellectual inputs that have gone into the making of this book. These comprised serving and retired military and civilian officials. We would like to respect their anonomity. We are also thankful to Lt. Col. B.D. Maitra and Maj. D. Das of the Directorate General of Public Relations (MoD) for providing us with the photographs that have been used in this book. Needless to add, the editors and authors of the various chapters of this book are responsible for the analyses made and conclusions drawn.

Special mention is made of Sushil Aaron, former Research Fellow in the IPCS, who read through some of the chapters and made valuable suggestions. To Arpit Rajain, who helped in organising the IPCS seminars, Mallika Joseph and Suba Chandran, Research Officers, who kept the web-site updated, and the office staff of the Institute—Vermani, Swapna, Vijay Singh and particularly Surendar Singh, we owe a special debt of gratitude.

The editors would also like to thank the authors of the chapters for taking a balanced view of the issues discussed in their chapters. No attempt has been made to modify the opinions expressed. Inevitably there is some repetition of information as the authors, at times, have chosen to explore the same issues. We have respected their different perspectives.

Lastly, we would like to thank Ramesh Jain of Manohar Publishers & Distributors and especially Bhola Varma for accepting the responsibility for bringing out this book in the least possible time frame.

PRC
AK

Introduction: Some Preliminary Observations

P.R. Chari

An Overview

In terms of the prevailing theology, democracies do not fight each other, and countries with nuclear weapons refrain from direct conflict. The Kargil conflict between India and Pakistan is unique precisely for this reason: it took place between two democracies and putative nuclear weapon powers, and could have escalated to reach the nuclear level. Three events strengthened these perceptions in the international community.

First, a report appeared in the *Washington Times* claiming that the Indian Army was making defensive preparations along the border with Pakistan: armoured units (which could be used for offensive operations) were leaving their garrisons in Rajasthan. Pakistan, too, began counter-operations by moving its armour. The danger of Pakistani forces being overwhelmed by the larger Indian Army 'could tempt them [Pakistanis] to play their last and most devastating card'.[1]

Second, acting on a tip-off, Indian customs officials searched a North Korean ship bound for Pakistan in Kandla. Some '148 containers listed on the cargo manifest as "water purification machinery" destined for Malta turned out to contain missile parts, machine tools, and blueprints of a Scud missile, all allegedly bound for Pakistan'.[2]

Third, the shooting down of a Pakistani maritime reconnaissance aircraft by an Indian fighter aircraft in early August, *after* the defusing of the Kargil conflict, revealed the fragility of the uneasy

[1] John Lancaster, 'Kashmir Crisis was Defused on Brink of War', *Washington Post*, 26 July 1999, p. A01.

[2] Steven Mufson, 'Losing the Battle on Arms Control: Pakistan-India Nuclear Race is Just Part of a Disturbing Trend', *Washington Post*, 17 July 1999, p. A01.

truce that had been effected. The agreement reached between India and Pakistan on Prevention of Airspace Violations and for Permitting Overflights and Landings by Military Aircraft[3] clearly stipulates in Clause 2 (a) that 'Combat aircraft (to include fighter, bomber, reconnaissance, jet military trainer and armed helicopter aircraft) will not fly within 10 kms of each other's airspace. . . .' The claims and counter-claims of both countries need not detain us. But this incident prompted the United States to 'urgently call on both sides to reinstitute this [Prevention of Airspace Violations] agreement in order to avoid further loss of life and further escalation and heightening of tensions'.[4]

The anxieties raised in the international community by these events were further exacerbated by threats of condign nuclear punishment held out during the Kargil conflict. The Kargil conflict closely followed the sequential nuclear tests conducted by the two South Asian adversaries in May 1998, and their boastful claims to have become nuclear weapon powers. This might have been expected to stabilize their relations, but it did not happen. There are two other disconcerting facts about this Indo-Pak nuclear stand-off.

First, the nuclear era has not witnessed any direct conflict between the nuclear states despite periods of high tensions and instabilities between the US and the Soviet Union at different periods during the Cold War. The sole exception to this empirical rule is the sporadic border clashes that occurred in 1969 between the erstwhile Soviet Union and China along the Ussuri river. Therefore, the Kargil episode was unique in itself.

Second, the historical record informs us that the earliest nuclear interactions between the US and the Soviet Union in the late 1940s and early 1950s were extremely dangerous since 'nuclear equations are most unsettled and tension-producing at the outset of any such pairing'.[5] In this situation, the alarm evoked in the international community by the Kargil conflict cannot be dismissed as exaggerated,

[3] Text of Agreement available in Michael Krepon and Amit Sevak (eds.), *Crisis Prevention, Confidence Building, and Reconciliation in South Asia* (Manohar, New Delhi, 1996), pp. 257-8.

[4] 'U.S. Urges Both India and Pakistan to Honor their 1991 Pact', *USIS Backgrounder*, 12 August 1999.

[5] Michael Krepon, 'South Asia: A Time of Trouble, A Time of Need', in Jill R. Junnola and Michael Krepon (eds.), *Regional Confidence Building in 1995: South Asia, the Middle East, and Latin America*,The Henry L. Stimson Centre, Report No. 20, December 1995, p. 5.

despite palliative statements regularly made by leaders in India and Pakistan that international fears of a nuclear conflagration between them were unfounded, and that their restraint in past Indo-Pak conflicts was commendable in comparison to the destructiveness of European conflicts in the twentieth century.

The enunciation of a nuclear doctrine by India shortly after the Kargil conflict makes clear that it intends to follow through on the logic of the nuclear tests and develop a triadic nuclear force, reinforced by adequate C^3I (Command, Control, Communications, Intelligence) arrangements and early warning systems. Although it was later sought to be soft-pedalled as only a draft nuclear doctrine meant to elicit views and engender a public debate,[6] the commitment of the government to its various facets, like developing and deploying longer-range missiles, is apparent. It could be reasonably expected that Pakistan might follow suit to declare a doctrine in spite of the parlous state of its economy. Would it then economize on its C^3I arrangements by adopting a hair-trigger launch-on-warning nuclear posture? A possible Indo-Pak conflict in future, therefore, portends great dangers from the use of nuclear weapons, not in anger, but through misperceptions and inadvertence.

The Kargil conflict marked a qualitative difference in the pattern of hostilities that have continued intermittently along the LoC after its establishment in 1972. An escalation in cross-border firings occurs each year with the onset of spring and the melting of the snows, allowing infiltration through the mountain passes. This seasonal increase in border incidents could be occasioned either by the shifting of boundary markers in winter, or by troops deployed along the LoC seeking to improve their ground positions or to assist infiltration/intelligence operations. The Kargil episode falls into an altogether separate category. It was marked by the surreptitious intrusion of regular Pakistani troops across the LoC, interspersed with mujahideen of both Pakistani and foreign origin; they succeeded in occupying and fortifying a large number of posts on the Indian side of the LoC. This was qualitatively different from the other border incidents that have occurred over the years but did not involve the physical occupation of territory.

This much is clear. The Kargil conflict succeeded in derailing the Lahore peace process. It would take determined statesmanship in

[6] Cf. interview given by Jaswant Singh, Minister of External Affairs, to C. Raja Mohan in *The Hindu*, 29 November 1999.

both countries to continue this process of dialogue and mitigate the bitter hostility that presently distinguishes their mutual relationship. It needs greater appreciation that the military coup in Pakistan, designed to counter the attempted civilian coup by Nawaz Sharif, was a direct offshoot of the Kargil conflict and the efforts of its civilian and military leadership to shift responsibility on each other for the debacle. By a quirk of circumstances the military leaders in Pakistan who planned and executed the Kargil adventure now constitute its ruling elite.

Pakistani Calculations

In retrospect, there was little prospect of Pakistan succeeding in its audacious but reckless attempt to seize Indian territory in the Ladakh region. The infiltrators could not have continued their illegal occupation of isolated mountain posts at altitudes over 4,000 m in the Kargil/Dras sector for long: this required assured logistical support, including continued supplies of food and ammunition. But their lines of communication could be easily observed and were vulnerable to interdiction by Indian troops in their territory with the artillery and air support available to them. This would have left Pakistan in an invidious position, facing the Hobson's choice of either escalating the conflict by using its air power to provide air defence against Indian air strikes, or extending the ground conflict to other sectors of the LoC for relieving pressure on its occupied posts. Both these options contained the germs of a general conflict between India and Pakistan that could only have ended in the defeat of the weaker conventional power. In theory, that would have required Pakistan to raise the stakes to the nuclear level for supporting its aggression, with its unpredictable consequences. In truth, Pakistan has been very cautious in the past in avoiding escalation of its proxy war in Kashmir, whilst providing moral and material support to militancy in Kashmir and exacerbating this ulcer in India's body politic. It is surprising that Pakistan did not take this possible scenario into account.

Pakistan's adventurous Kargil policy also required the indulgence, if not the overt support, of the international community for its success. This further presupposed that the international community's fears of a nuclear exchange destabilizing the situation would translate into activism to discover a solution to the Kashmir problem that would be to Pakistan's advantage. It remains unclear how the course of events that actually transpired—like the use of air power by India and the disapproval of the United States—was not war-gamed by Pakistan's military and political leadership into their calculus of how the Kargil situation could evolve. In the event, the intruders were left unsupported in their occupied posts, except by artillery fire from across the border. This shelling disrupted Indian attacks to an extent, and caused the major number of Indian casualties, but it could not halt the methodical Indian recapture of these posts or alter the flow of events in the Kargil conflict. International support was not available to Pakistan. Indeed, the international community unequivocally condemned it for its unprovoked and dangerous aggression. What, then, might have been Pakistan's calculations in launching this offensive remains a mystery, although educated surmises are possible to unravel it. Some four reasons may explain its motivations.

First, a purely military calculation obtained that the militancy in Kashmir had not succeeded in creating sufficient turmoil in the state to permit an interventionary force to deliver the final *coup de grace*. Heavy shelling to disrupt traffic along the vital Srinagar–Leh highway over the preceding two years had activated the LoC in the Kargil sector. An interdiction of this highway would have isolated Leh, which is the support base for the Indian troops located on the Siachen glacier, and enabled Pakistan to evict Indian troops from this disputed area.

Second, a politico-military intent might be discerned. Infracting the LoC, it could have been surmised, would invite a violent Indian reaction, alarm the international community and precipitate its mediation efforts, possibly through the UN. The Siachen dispute would, thereby, also get activated. This inexorable course of events would internationalize the Kashmir dispute to Pakistan's advantage.

Third, a domestic political component to Pakistan's motivations is possible. It might have estimated that a foreign enterprise, despite its inherent dangers, would deflect attention from Pakistan's increasingly difficult financial and internal political situation. It remains uncertain at what stage and to what extent the political leadership was informed of this operation. Conventional wisdom holds that Prime Minister Nawaz Sharif must have known of the Kargil intrusions planned by the military, but the question remains unanswered whether he knew its full implications, specially its chances of success and the consequences of failure.

Fourth, the presence of a large number of armed and trained

mujahideen, apart from foreign mercenaries, who find themselves unoccupied in Pakistan, required utilization in some fashion, or else they could further exacerbate the law-and-order situation within the country. These elements joined hands with the religious militias in Pakistan to become a grave danger to its internal stability. The Kargil intrusions provided an opportunity to Pakistan for deflecting their energies against India whilst simultaneously serving Pakistan's larger strategic purposes.

Why Kargil?

The issue arises as to why the Kargil sector was selected for these intrusions in the first place. It was undoubtedly suitable on military considerations, but the historical context needs better recognition. Briefly, Kashmir has been either the prescient reason or the major theatre of operations in all past Indo-Pak conflicts, and the Kargil sector has always been the scene of fierce engagements.

During the 1947-48 conflict, Pakistani troops occupied the heights that could threaten Kargil town and disrupt the Srinagar–Leh highway. Following the cease-fire, India was left in a disadvantageous tactical situation in this area.

Aware of its tactical vulnerabilities here, India seized important strategic areas north of the Kargil–Dras sector across the cease-fire line in the1965 Indo-Pak war; this enlarged the area under its control for protecting the Srinagar–Leh highway. But this captured territory had to be returned to Pakistan in terms of the Tashkent Agreement which envisaged that 'all armed personnel of the two countries shall be withdrawn . . . to the positions they held prior to . . .' the commencement of the hostilities.

The Kargil sector was the scene of fierce fighting in the 1971 Indo-Pak war, which resulted in the capture of several Pakistani posts across the cease-fire line. In terms of the Simla Agreement, 'the line of control resulting from the ceasefire of December 17, 1971, shall be respected by both sides without prejudice to the recognized position of either side'. So, the areas captured across the new line of control remained in India's possession to its tactical advantage. These areas were the theatre of operations in the recent Kargil conflict.

Intermittent firing and artillery exchanges across the LoC in Kashmir had been taking place. In fact this collective violence has been described as an interstate conflict by SIPRI since 1996. Significantly, it also remains the only case of interstate conflict in the world, the others being described by SIPRI as cases of intrastate conflict.[7] These firings and artillery exchanges were seen in India as largely intended to infiltrate militants into the state, and reaffirm the distinction between the temporary LoC and the permanent international border between the two countries. Such incidents were especially frequent in the Kargil area. Consequently, Pakistan's choice of this area for its intrusions is entirely explicable on strategic considerations.

Its choice of this sector is explicable for another reason: the local population was getting disaffected with Srinagar and New Delhi, which had refused to grant autonomy to the entire Ladakh region but only conceded a titular autonomous council status to the Buddhist-dominated district of Leh. This converted the Shia-Muslim-dominated Kargil district into a separate region; it included a Sunni-Muslim pocket in Dras that had cultural and linguistic affinities across the LoC in the Skardu region of Pakistani-held Kashmir. 'The Buddhist-Muslim rift in Ladakh was perhaps being better monitored by Islamabad than by New Delhi. Pakistan synchronised its intrusion of the mujahideen in Kargil when the State Government proposed its separation from Leh as an administrative and political unit.'[8]

The Kargil episode highlighted Pakistan's deep-rooted hostility towards India; this anti-India syndrome provides grist for its two-nation theory, whilst sustaining the *raison d'être* for Pakistan's creation and existence, apart from providing the glue to cement its internal polity. The basic structure of that polity is based on the four pillars of Punjab's dominance over Pakistan's governance; the control of the Army over its governance processes; the steady Islamization of the country's polity; and the influence of Saudi Arabia, the US and China over its governments, irrespective of their different political persuasions.

To imagine in this milieu that Prime Minister Vajpayee's 'historic' bus journey to Pakistan and the ensuing promulgation of the Lahore Declaration would initiate a peace process and to believe that the Kargil intrusions were unthinkable, and to complain of a breach of trust when they occurred, compounded naivety with fecklessness. International relations are about promoting national interests, hence

[7] Margareta Sollenberg and Peter Wallenstein, 'Major Armed Conflicts', SIPRI *Yearbook 1998: Armaments, Disarmament and International Security* (Oxford University Press, Oxford, 1998), p. 17.

[8] Balraj Puri, 'Kargil in the Perspective of Indo-Pak Conflicts', *Mainstream*, 31 July 1999, p. 2.

neither pessimism nor euphoria have any place in its practice.

The failure to discover and frustrate the intrusions, which then needed to be vacated at a high human cost and the intercession of the US, is obvious to all except the most obtuse observers. This needs a plausible explanation. Had the area been regularly patrolled by ground troops or surveyed by helicopters/aircraft, they could not have remained undetected. Further, the extensive preparations in Skardu that preceded these intrusions and included the training of militants, building up of ammunition stocks, constructing tracks up to and beyond the LoC, and transportation of stores to the posts occupied and so on remained either undetected or not realistically assessed.

The failure of intelligence occurred therefore at both the tactical or local level, but also the strategic or command level.[9] The evidence is slowly emerging that the concerned ministries and high political personages in New Delhi were informed by the various intelligence agencies of the increasing hostile activities across the Kargil sector in Pakistan-Occupied Kashmir. They were ignored because of a sense that after obtaining nuclear parity with the sequential nuclear tests in May 1998, the chances of a conventional conflict were remote, besides the unwillingness to derail the Lahore peace process by taking counter-measures that might have been deemed provocative.[10]

A 'review', as distinct from an 'inquiry', with its censorious connotations, was ordered into the failure to detect and counter these Pakistani intrusions: it was also to suggest measures to safeguard the country's future security in the light of this experience.[11] The members of the committee were former officials and non-officials, but its secretary was an official, who was also the member secretary of the National Security Council. The Review Committee thus had a curious structure. More important, it had no statutory authority. Consequently, it could not either summon official witnesses or official records, although these were made available to the Committee by the Government.

It was reasonably expected that the 'review' of the Kargil conflict would comment on the failure of the local armed forces/paramilitary personnel charged with defending the LoC in the Kargil-Dras sector to acquire tactical intelligence and act with celerity upon

[9] P.R. Chari, 'After Kargil, What?' *Deccan Herald*, 23 July 1999.

[10] Nitin A. Gokhale and Ajith Pillai, 'The War That Should Never Have Been', *Outlook*, 6 September 1999, p. 26.

[11] Special Correspondent, 'Kargil: Govt. Orders Probe', *The Hindu*, 25 July 1999.

it. This has been done in passing, but the intelligence agencies were primarily indicted. The remit of the committee did not enable it to pursue the larger failure of the political leadership to act on the strategic intelligence that must have been available to it regarding the steady build-up of forces and equipment across the border, the infiltration of intruders, and their establishment of posts in Indian territory over the several months preceding their detection. In other words, this 'review' exercise was restricted to chronicling the failures of the local commanders and other authorities, without examining the failings of the higher national security decision-making echelons in New Delhi: that would have been embarrassing to the Government.

Rationale/Structure of Study

This study by the Institute of Peace and Conflict Studies attempts to analyse the Kargil episode from both the military and political perspectives, and derive appropriate conclusions of relevance to the turbulent Indo-Pakistani relationship. The institute had arranged a series of weekly seminars during the conflict to discuss the military operations as they were proceeding: the invitees included knowledgeable civil and military officials who had occupied sensitive positions in the government, apart from concerned scholars and media-persons. A gist of the discussions in these seminars was published on the institute's web site, along with a weekly update of the conflict, a daily update relating to press reports/comments, and short articles by specialists dealing with the technical and general aspects of the operations as they were proceeding. This extensive database provided an online source of primary information that was of invaluable assistance in writing this book. The facts contained in this database could be questioned by later revelations; so could the conclusions reached on their basis. But they will remain relevant to future studies of the Kargil conflict, despite their embellishment by later sophistication.

The following chapters seek to establish a backdrop to the Kargil conflict. This is followed by speculation on Pakistan's political and military objectives in pursuing a policy of blatant irredentism. A large part of the subsequent section describes the military operations in some detail (including the air operations), besides detailing India's political and diplomatic response. The external dimensions of this conflict, viz., the role played by the United States, China, the G-8 countries, Russia and Japan is thereafter described. Finally, the implications of this crisis, and the lessons to be learnt therefrom are discussed. The concluding chapter speculates on the future of Indo-Pak relations and highlights the unique aspects of this South Asian conflict.

This brings us to the expected charge that this book is too near the events that it portrays to be either comprehensive or analytical. The academic community has, perhaps rightly, an abiding suspicion regarding the value of such writings. In fairness, 'quickies' can project a biased account of events since they are premised on a limited corpus of current knowledge. It is, therefore, arguable that historical accounts improve in veracity with the passing of years, as they would have access to the reflections and reminiscences of participants in these events. The argument could also be made that the government could make public the official records relating to the conflict, which could be relied upon to lend authenticity to the narrative; hence it is arguable that such histories should only be attempted after some years have elapsed to improve their accuracy.

However, as mentioned above, this account has relied upon the extensive database and contemporary analysis available to the institute. This has been supplemented by the relevant observations made by the Kargil Review Committee in its report. The efflux of time might actually work to the detriment of politico-military accounts relating to the Kargil episode. No doubt, the passage of time would allow the participants in this conflict to speak out after they retire from service, as they would no longer be inhibited by the prohibitions of the Service (Conduct) Rules, although they will remain constrained by the provisions of the Official Secrets Act. But memory has a strange way of blurring the distinctions between fact and opinion, accurately recollecting the chronology of events, projecting one's own role without exaggeration, and rising above strongly-held biases and prejudices about other participants in the crisis. I have encountered all these problems in interviewing the *dramatis personae* involved in the Brasstacks crisis (1987) and the Kashmir-related Spring crisis (1990):[12] these required difficult judgements about facts and conclusions to be frequently made.

[12] Cf. Kanti P. Bajpai, P.R. Chari, Pervaiz I. Cheema, Stephen P. Cohen, Sumit Ganguly, *Brasstacks and Beyond: Perception and Management of Crisis in South Asia* (Manohar, New Delhi, 1995); and P.R. Chari, Pervaiz I. Cheema and Stephen P. Cohen, *The Complex Crisis of 1990: Politics, Proliferation and Insecurity* (forthcoming).

The empirical evidence also informs that it is most unlikely that the records relevant to the Kargil episode will ever be deposited in the official archives, which has been the experience regarding files pertaining to earlier conflicts. More disconcerting is the fact that the official histories of the conflicts in the post-Independence era (1962, 1965 and 1971) have yet to be published despite their having being written several years ago, and at considerable expense. They are with the Ministry of Defence, but have not been published on the entirely recondite grounds that the facts contained in these official histories may not be complimentary to the Government, and that their revelation might affect India's relations with other countries. It would be naive to imagine in this milieu that official documents will ever become available to scholars for analysing the Kargil conflict. Apropos, the Kargil Review Committee Report is replete with security deletions and its supporting appendices and annexures have not been made public and perhaps, never will be.

There is another reason why an early publication of this account of the Kargil conflict, despite its reliance on openly available unclassified information, might be useful. I hesitate to point out the likelihood of official records being either destroyed or rewritten to improve them. There are valid grounds for making this observation. Maj. Gen. Palit has provided a wholly unedifying account of what happened to the official records pertaining to the Sino-Indian border conflict. Apparently, a senior research officer of the Historical Section in the Ministry of Defence sought to interview Palit to discuss the events preceding the Sino-Indian war, since Army Headquarters had informed him that the General Staff files of that period had been eliminated. Palit observes that:

> It is unusual, to say the least, for the General Staff to destroy operational records of a critical period of military operations. At the same time, having been only too aware of government attempts at a cover-up immediately after the end of the Sino-Indian war, I was not overly surprised.[13]

The Bourbons in French history, they say, learnt nothing and forgot nothing. So do other governments. As this account will establish, there are several comparisons possible between the Kargil conflict in its early phases and the debacle of 1962. Finally, one must appreciate that an area of the 'unknowable' will always remain

[13] Maj. Gen. D.K. Palit, VrC, *War in the High Himalaya: The Indian Army in Crisis, 1962* (St. Martin's Press, New York, 1991), p. vii.

despite the publication of a plethora of reminiscences and accounts regarding this conflict. What went into the calculations of the political leaders and the decision-making elite on both sides? What were the operational plans of the two militaries? How and why were they modified? Was a nuclear dimension configured into these plans? These are some vital inputs for writing a history of the Kargil conflict that may never come to light. The passage of years may do little, consequently, to improve the database for attempting this exercise.

Undoubtedly, the Indian Army succeeded, with the support of the Indian Air Force, in reducing a large number of posts that were established by the Pakistani intruders before the American intervention succeeded in ensuring their total withdrawal. This was achieved by the heroism of young officers and jawans. Nearly five hundred of them laid down their lives for the country: several hundred more suffered grievous injuries that will handicap or disfigure them for life. It is to the sacrifice of these young officers and jawans that this book is dedicated in all humility.

1

Why Kargil? Pakistan's Objectives and Motivation

D. Suba Chandran

When the news of infiltration around Kargil by Pakistan-supported forces broke in the second week of May 1999, many in India thought it was part of the perpetual border clashes between the two countries. But during the second half of May, as the extent of infiltration came to light, many questions were raised in India and elsewhere. Why did Pakistan abet the militants' infiltration, especially after Indo-Pak relations had improved following the Lahore Declaration? What was the motivation underlying Pakistan's venture in Kargil? Was it the handiwork of the Pakistan Army, attempting to sabotage the political rapprochement between the two countries? In the process, were they trying to score a point over its own political leadership? Was it really an incursion by 'freedom fighters' as Pakistan claimed? Was it a desperate attempt by then Prime Minister, Nawaz Sharif to divert attention from the snowballing internal crisis in Pakistan? Or was it part of a bigger plan aiming to internationalize the Kashmir issue?

Before looking into the motivation of Pakistan, it is essential to clear certain misperceptions regarding the coup that took place in October 1999. There is a widespread belief that the Washington declaration and subsequent withdrawal of Pakistani troops from the Indian side of the Line of Control (LoC) were a great blow to the Pakistan Army, hence this resulted in the coup. The coup was in reaction to developments that took place in the aftermath of the Kargil misadventure rather than due to differences between the Prime Minister and the Army. Elsewhere in this chapter, it would be shown that the Pakistan Army played second fiddle to the political objectives of the civilian government during the crisis period. After the withdrawal of Pakistan's support to the infiltrators, civil-military relations underwent a dramatic change in Pakistan.

Before discussing the motivation of Pakistan, it is necessary to clear certain myths and misperceptions about Pakistan that are prevalent in India. The failure to understand Pakistan, its internal dynamics and policies among Indian analysts, academics and policy-makers complicates Indo-Pak relations. There are at least two erroneous assumptions in India about Pakistan, which are based on the latter's historical evolution. First, that the Pakistan Army is the real boss and the democratic polity in Pakistan plays second fiddle to the Army in regard to Pakistan's policies towards India in general, and Kashmir in particular. The second assumption is that Pakistan, created on the basis of the 'two-nation theory', is an Islamic state and is increasingly becoming a fundamentalist country. These assumptions create an impression in India that three societies exist in Pakistan, civil, military and fundamentalist, and civil society is subjugated to them. This assumption undermines the significance of the Pakistani polity and its policies. Whenever there is a crisis between the two countries, everybody looks into the 'military factor' and the 'Islamic factor' in Pakistan. True, they do exert pressure on the polity, but an overemphasis on these two factors clouds the 'political factors'. In the current crisis, too, there has been an overemphasis on the Army and Allah factors.

Kargil Crisis: An Independent Initiative by the Pak Army?

The Pak military exercised control over the civilian leadership in the past, even if it was not ruling the country directly. After the death of Zia, the Army continued to influence political happenings in the country such as the rise of the Pakistan Muslim League (PML) and Nawaz Sharif's coming to power in the 1990 elections, his resignation in 1993, the removal of Chief Justice Sajjad Ali Shah in 1997 and so on. In the post-Kargil period, the Pakistan Army overthrew the Nawaz Sharif government on 12 October 1999, after the latter removed Gen. Pervez Musharraf from the post of Chief of the Army Staff. These events might suggest that the Kargil adventure was an independent initiative of the Pakistan Army.

However, an in-depth analysis would prove the above assumption wrong. In the pre-Kargil period, after Sharif returned to power with a two-thirds majority in the 1997 elections, there was a gradual change in civil-military relations in Pakistan. During this period, the Pak Army seemed to be under the total control of the civilian leadership, and Sharif was able to assert the supremacy of Parliament over the other institutions including the Judiciary and the Army. Thereof, he succeeded in freeing the polity of the Army's control, if not bringing the Army under its control.

It should be recalled that in October 1998 Nawaz Sharif sacked then Chief of Army Staff Gen. Jahangir Karamat for suggesting the formation of a National Security Council as a solution to 'the destabilising effects of polarisation, vendettas and insecurity driven expedient policies'.[1] Though, in a democracy, military personnel are not expected to comment publicly on problems facing the country and lecturing the democratically elected leadership on how to govern, given the role of the Army in Pakistani politics, what Gen. Karamat had suggested did not amount to any grave misdemeanour. There was, in fact, widespread support for Gen. Karamat's suggestion in the media and opposition parties.[2] Though Gen. Karamat had only three more months to retire in January 1999, that did not prevent Sharif from sacking him because, according to him, the 'supremacy of the parliament and democratic principles should not be undermined at any cost'.[3] This, despite Gen. Karamat expressing his wish to continue till his 'retirement in January 99, Inshaallah'.[4] According to many analysts, 'The exit of Gen. Jahangir Karamat has ended an era in which it was generally believed that the real power rests with the GHQ and parliament is just a façade for democracy. The politicians in [the] wilderness would no more look towards the GHQ for their rehabilitation. It is now the responsibility of the politicians, but more so of the Prime Minister, to demonstrate that this nation has moved another step towards unadulterated democracy.'[5] This was proved wrong by the October coup in 1999, but during this interregnum, there was a widespread belief that the

[1] 'COAS Stresses Internal Stability', *Frontier Post*, 6 October 1998.

[2] The support for Gen. Karamat's view can be seen from the various editorials, news reports and opinion articles published in the leading dailies of Pakistan. For example see *Dawn*, 7 October 1998, *Frontier Post*, 7 October 1998, *Frontier Post*, 11 October 1998.

[3] Shakil Shaikh, 'Supremacy of the Parliament at all Costs, says PM', *News*, 9 October 1998.

[4] 'COAS Stresses Internal Stability', *Frontier Post*, 6 October 1998.

[5] Mir Jamilur Rahman, 'End of an Era', *News*, 10 October 1998.

supremacy of Pakistan's Armed Forces over the civilian leadership had ended.

Sharif did not stop with sacking the Chief of the Army Staff. To prove his control over the Army he handpicked the next Chief of the Army Staff, Gen. Pervez Musharraf, superseding two more senior generals, Lt. Gen. Khalid Nawaz and Lt. Gen. Ali Quli Khan. Besides the COAS, Lt. Gen. Ziauddin, the Director General of the much-dreaded Inter-Services Intelligence (ISI) was also handpicked by Sharif. Besides, in April 1999, Sharif appointed Gen. Musharraf as the Chairman of the Joint Chiefs of Staff Committee, a post that should have gone to the Chief of Naval Staff, Admiral Fasih Bokhari on a rotation basis. Unless Musharraf commanded Sharif's loyalty, he would not have been appointed to this post. Besides, Musharraf was initially appointed for a period of one year, instead of the normal three years. Later, in the post-Kargil period, Sharif extended his tenure as the Chairman of the JCSC till October 2001.

The second misperception regarding civil-military relations in Pakistan was that the Army kept Sharif ignorant about the preparations for the Kargil infiltration. Many in India continue to believe that a divide existed between the two on Kargil. Defence Minister of India Mr. George Fernandes holds this view. According to him, 'In this entire episode, the Pakistan Army has hatched a conspiracy to push in the infiltrators and the Nawaz Sharif Government did not have a major role. The ISI which we know initiate such activities has not played any role.'[6] However, many in Pakistan are not willing to believe that the Army acted independently, keeping Sharif in the dark. 'There is no reason to believe that decisions, at any point, were taken without the government's consent. If the Prime Minister did not want to go along with the army's strategy, he could have expressed his reservations.'[7]

Musharraf himself has stated that Sharif 'had full details of what was happening on the LoC . . . from the very start', and had approved the Army's operations 'absolutely',[8] hence this assumption is no longer valid. Besides, the Armed Forces were in complete agreement with the government on all major decisions taken during the crisis, which were taken by the Defence Committee of the Cabinet (DCC). The DCC, besides the Prime Minister and other political leaders,

[6] 'Sharif, ISI Uninvolved, by George!', *Hindustan Times*, 29 May 1999.
[7] Jalees Hazir, 'Civil Society Shares the Blame', *News*, 21 July 1999.
[8] 'Nawaz Approved Kargil Operation: COAS', *News*, 17 July 1999.

also included the Chairman of the Joint Chiefs of Staff Committee, Army Chief Gen. Pervez Musharraf, Adm. Fasih Bokhari (Naval Chief), Air Chief Marshal Pervez (Chief of Air Staff), Defence Secretary Lt. Gen. (retd) Iftikhar Ali Khan, and the chiefs of the intelligence agencies.

According to Gen. Mirza Aslam Beg, former Chief of the Army Staff, the Prime Minister was briefed about the mujahideen operation in the GHQ and ISI HQ in January 1999.[9] There were at least seven meetings thereafter during the crisis, in which major decisions were taken.

1. On 22 May, the Prime Minister had a meeting at Chaklala air base with the Chief of the Army Staff to discuss developments along the LoC. It was decided in this meeting 'to give a befitting response to India if New Delhi launched any misadventure at the Line of Control'.[10]
2. On 25 May, Sharif chaired a high-level meeting in Islamabad. This was attended by: Foreign Minister Sartaj Aziz; Kashmir Affairs Minister Lt. Gen. (retd) Abdul Majid Malik; Defence Secretary Lt. Gen. (retd) Iftikhar Ali Khan; acting Army Chief Lt. Gen. Saeeduz Zafar (Corps Commander, Peshawar); Commander of 10 Corps Lt. Gen. Mehmood Ahmed; Director General Military Operations (DGMO) Lt. Gen. Tauqir Zia; and some senior civil officials.[11]
3. On 2 June, there was a one-to-one meeting between the Prime Minister and the Chief of the Army Staff for forty-five minutes, followed by a three-hour meeting which included Foreign Minister Sartaj Aziz, Defence Secretary Lt. Gen. (retd) Iftikhar Ali Khan, Chairman Joint Chiefs of Staff Committee and Army Chief Gen. Pervez Musharraf, Foreign Secretary Shamshad Ahmed, Chief of the General Staff Lt. Gen. Mohammad Aziz, and Corps Commander Lt. Gen. Mehmood Ahmed. In this meeting, the proposed visit of Foreign Minister Sartaj Aziz to India and other initiatives taken by the Prime Minister and his telephonic conversations with world leaders were discussed.[12]

9 Gen. Mirza Aslam Beg (retd), 'The Kargil Denouement', *Frontier Post*, 14 July 1999.

10 Shakil Shaikh, 'PM, COAS Discuss Indian Build-Up at LoC', *News*, 23 May 1999.

11 Shakil Shaikh, 'Pak Armed Forces Put on High Alert', *News*, 26 May 1999.

12 Shakil Shaikh, 'Pakistan Vows Not to Allow LoC Violations', *News*, 3 June 1999.

4. On 1 July, in a meeting held at Islamabad which was attended by the COAS along with others, it was decided to convene the Defence Committee of the Cabinet (DCC) to take important decisions. The visit of Niaz A. Naik was also discussed during this meeting.[13]
5. On 2 July, the first meeting of the Defence Committee of the Cabinet was held, which was attended by ministers of the Interior (Shujaat Hussain), Finance (Ishaq Dar), Religious Affairs (Raja Zafarul Haq), Minister of State for Foreign Affairs (Siddique Kanju), Chairman Joint Chiefs of Staff Committee and Army Chief Gen. Pervez Musharraf, Naval Chief Adm. Fasih Bokhari, Chief of the Air Staff Air Chief Marshal Pervez Mehdi Qureshi, Defence Secretary Iftikhar Ali Khan, Foreign Secretary Shamshad Ahmed and some other senior officials. It was in this meeting that all eventualities, including the withdrawal of the mujahideen, its implications on the morale of the nation and Armed Forces, its impact on the liberation movement and the mujahideen inside Kashmir were discussed.[14] Nawaz Sharif's visit to the US was also discussed during this crucial meeting.
6. On 8 July a meeting of a 'Group of Four', including the Prime Minister, the COAS, the Defence Secretary and the Chief of ISI was held in Islamabad.[15]
7. On 9 July the DCC meeting was held in Islamabad, in which it was decided to appeal to the mujahideen 'to help resolve the current Kargil situation and to provide an opportunity to the international community to play an active role for realisation of the legitimate aspirations of the Kashmiri people and to promote peace and development in South Asia'. This meeting was attended by the Minister for Foreign Affairs, Sartaj Aziz, Finance Minister Ishaq Dar, Interior Minister Shujaat Hussain, Kashmir Affairs Minister Majid Malik, Religious Affairs Minister Raja Zafarul Haq, Chairman Joint Chiefs of Staff Committee and Army Chief Gen. Pervez Musharraf, Naval Chief Adm. Fasih Bokhari, Chief of the Air Staff Air Chief Marshal Pervez Mehdi Qureshi, Defence Secretary Lt. Gen. (retd) Iftikhar Ali Khan,

[13] Shakil Shaikh, 'DCC to Approve Final Strategy Today', *News*, 2 July 1999.

[14] Shakil Shaikh, 'India Warned Against Wider Conflict', *News*, 3 July 1999.

[15] Shakil Shaikh, 'Concrete Steps for Mujahideen Pullout Likely in Three Days', *News*, 9 July 1999.

Foreign Secretary Shamshad Ahmed, chiefs of the Intelligence agencies, and a couple of other senior officials.[16]

It is, thus, clear that all the major decisions during the crisis were taken by the civilian government and the military together, and decisions taken by the Government were approved by the Army. The Pakistan Army at no point seemed to have an independent plan in Kargil or acted against the wishes of the government. Even after the Kargil crisis, there were no signs of the Pakistan Army planning for a military take-over. This was despite fundamentalist parties like the Jamaat-e-Islami expecting the military to continue its policy vis-à-vis Kashmir regardless of the outcome of Sharif's visit to the US and the subsequent Washington declaration. Opposition parties belonging to the right wing felt that, since the Sharif government betrayed the liberation movement, it was the responsibility of the military to continue its Kashmir policy. Syed Munawwar Hasan of the JUI expected the 'armed forces to remain consistent on their standpoint regarding the Kashmir issue and prevent the government from persuading Mujahideen to withdraw from their positions held in Kashmir'.[17]

Apart from the COAS, Nawaz Sharif chose Lt. Gen. Ziauddin to be the Director General of the ISI, Lt. Gen. (retd.) Javed Nasir as his Principal Adviser on Intelligence matters, and Brig. (retd) Imtiaz as Principal Adviser for Internal Security.[18] It is inconceivable that these handpicked men who were manning key posts would conceive of such a large operation without informing their political patron.

Hence, it is totally incorrect to believe that the Pakistan Army functioned independently and kept Sharif uninformed about the infiltration. Sharif knew from the beginning what was happening along the Line of Control. The plan could have been drafted by the Pakistan Army in detail, but without a green signal from Sharif, it could not have gone ahead. According to Gen. Mirza Aslam Beg, former Chief of the Army Staff, in January 1999 the Prime Minister, was briefed about the mujahideen operation in GHQ and ISI HQ.[19] It is also possible that such a plan had existed for a long time in

16 Shakil Shaikh, 'Pakistan Appeals to Mujahideen to Help Resolve Kargil Crisis', *News*, 10 July 1999.

17 'JI's Country-Wide Rallies Against Washington Accord', *News*, 7 July 1999.

18 B. Raman, 'The Pakistan Hand in Kargil', *Business Line*, 28 May 1999.

19 Gen. Mirza Aslam Beg (retd), 'The Kargil Denouement', *Frontier Post*, 14 July 1999.

Pakistan and Sharif activated it since it suited his political objectives. This would be discussed later in this chapter.

Appeasing the Fundamentalists?

Another misconception about Pakistan is that it is increasingly becoming a fundamentalist country and fundamentalist forces have strengthened their hold over civil society. It is true that fundamentalist forces in Pakistan are anti-Indian and support the 'jihad' against India. Jamaat-i-Islami chief Qazi Hussain Ahmad and leaders of other parties were highly critical of the Indian Prime Minister's visit to Lahore and the Lahore Declaration. However, Nawaz Sharif was not under any pressure from them. It should be understood that the fundamentalists in Pakistan do not constitute a monolithic entity. There are vast differences among their various parties and groups. For example, there are three major fundamentalist parties: the Jamaat-i-Islami (JI), founded by Maulana Abul Ala Maududi in the 1940s; the Jamiat-e-Ulema-e-Pakistan (JUP), which was part of the Jamiat-e-Ulema-e-Hind and comprises the Barelvi ulema; and the Jamiat-e-Ulema-Islam (JUI), which is a faction of the Jamiat-e-Ulema-e-Hind, formed by the pro-Muslim League Ulema in the mid-1940s and comprises the Deobandi ulema. These parties do not share a common platform and always contest elections separately.

While accusing Pakistan of becoming increasingly fundamental, what one fails to understand is that the support base for these fundamentalist parties has been on a steady decline. Out of the total number of 207 seats, the fundamentalist parties hold only 6 seats in the current National Assembly.[20] All these 6 seats are held by the JUI (F) and out of these, it had won 5 from Baluchistan and one from NWFP. This is less than the number of seats which the fundamentalist parties were able to get in the 1988 elections held after the death of Zia. In the 1988 elections, the Jamaat-e-Islami and the JUI (F) were able to get 7 seats each, with the JUI (D) getting 1 seat.[21] The support base for these fundamentalist parties has been steadily declining since the 1988 elections.

Again, by passing the 15th Amendment, Sharif wrested the initiative from the fundamentalists. Hence, it is totally incorrect to

[20] *POT Pakistan*, 7 February 1997, vol. 25, no. 33, p. 318.

[21] *POT Pakistan*, vol. 16, no. 209, pp. 4649–50.

believe that it was pressure from the fundamentalists that forced Sharif to undertake the Kargil adventure.

Next, it is unlikely that there was a deliberate plan hatched by Pakistan to sabotage the positive steps taken by both countries preceding Kargil, like issuing the Lahore Declaration. Many believed that 'after the Lahore declaration, there was considerable criticism in Pakistan that Mr. Sharif had given too much. And that his policies would lead to putting the Kashmir issue on the back burner',[22] hence, Sharif had to revive the Kashmir issue. This was not accurate because the Lahore declaration says that both government had agreed to 'intensify their efforts to resolve all issues, including the issue of Jammu and Kashmir'.[23] Sharif could have put the declaration to use to discuss the Kashmir issue rather than ruin the Lahore process. Therefore, it was not in the interest of Nawaz Sharif to wreck the ongoing dialogue or the Lahore Declaration.

It was also believed in certain quarters that the objective of the Kargil infiltration was to divert attention from the internal problems faced by Pakistan. It was unlikely that problems such as the arrest of Najam Sethi and external criticism would have made Nawaz take such an initiative for the reason that this operation would have been thought out well in advance. Besides, the attention of the nation had already been diverted by the floods in Sindh, which killed thousands of people, and the government's decision to celebrate 'Yaeem-e-Takbeer'—the first anniversary of Pakistan's nuclear tests. Also, it is unlikely that Sharif would take such a step for internal reasons as he was well aware that the BJP government in New Delhi, then facing the elections, would take strong measures to help it during the elections. Moreover, the opposition to Sharif inside Pakistan had only strengthened during April 1999. The fact that the infiltration process started much earlier disproves this internal chaos thesis.

The next misconception is that political conditions prevailing in India made Pakistan calculate that June-July was the ideal time to create trouble in India. With the forthcoming elections, and the BJP government being a caretaker, it is arguable that Pakistan felt that to be the right time. Inside Pakistan, there was a view that 'if the Vajpayee government had not been unseated, negotiations between India and Pakistan would have commenced under the Lahore process

22 C. Rajamohan, 'Retrieve Kargil, but Remember Lahore', *The Hindu*, 30 May 1999.

23 See The Lahore Declaration on web-site www.ipcs.org/statements

and in that case the Kargil operation might not have taken place.'[24] The Lok Sabha was dissolved on 26 April. The first observations of the infiltrators were made on 3 May. It was not possible for Pakistan to undertake an infiltration of this magnitude at such short notice. It should be clear, consequently, that the reasons underlying the infiltration were neither pressure from the Pakistan Army nor from the fundamentalist groups. There was internal criticism against Sharif, but it was not grave enough to require a war with India.

What else could be the reason(s) underlying the infiltration? Given the circumstances, the main reason seems to be the desire to internationalize the Kashmir issue. The statements and efforts by Pakistan immediately after the crisis unfolded proves this point. The Pakistani leaders at various levels repeatedly called for outside intervention as if they had rehearsed this event.

INTERNATIONALIZATION OF KASHMIR

On 26 May 1999, replying to a question accusing Pakistan of sending infiltrators into Kashmir, Tariq Altaf said: ' It is an unfounded charge. We would like a neutral force to be deployed to check the facts. We will welcome the UN Military Observers Group in India and Pakistan (UNMOGIP) to send its observers. We will welcome if the UN Secretary Gen. Kofi Annan sent other observers.'[25]

On 27 May 1999, Sartaj Aziz requested UN Secretary Gen. Kofi Annan to send a special representative. He said, '(the special representative) being here, he can . . . reduce the ongoing tension and this could also lead to an increase in the presence of United Nations military observers'.[26] Altaf, by the end of May 1999, claimed that: 'Kashmir today is a nuclear flashpoint. The solution of the issue does not lie in escalation of brutal repression or in provocative military action but in recognising the wrong done to the Kashmiris and honouring the commitments made to them by India.'[27] Altaf made the same point again. He said, 'We call upon the international community to recognise the serious implications in [*sic*] continued impasse in the Kashmir dispute on account of the Indian intran-

[24] Afzal Mahmood, 'Seeing Kargil in Perspective', *Dawn*, 18 July 1999.

[25] Anwar Iqbal, 'Pakistan Reserves Right to Retaliate: Foreign Office', *News*, 27 May 1999.

[26] 'Sartaj for UN Special Representative in Kashmir', *News*, 28 May 1999.

[27] Iqbal, op. cit., n. 25.

sigence and to engage meaningfully with the process of finding a just and final settlement of the dispute.'[28]

On 28 May, Sharif released a letter that Pakistan had sent to UN Secretary Gen. Kofi Annan, which said, 'India not only refuses to accept any role by the UN in the resolution of the Kashmir dispute but also rejects any third party involvement which is against the global trend for mediated settlement of conflicts and disputes'.[29] Later, Aziz, while remarking that the LoC was not clearly marked, said, 'We must first ascertain whether somebody has at all crossed the Line. We have to look at all aspects and in our view the role of United Nations observers is also critical. If India maintains there is no real problem in Kashmir, why don't they allow the UNMOGIP to visit the area?'[30]

The above statements encapsulated the following line of Pakistani reasoning:

First, with India and Pakistan acquiring nuclear status, Kashmir had become the 'nuclear flashpoint' in the South Asian region. If this issue was not solved, it would lead to nuclear war.

Second, the international community should understand the nature of the threat in South Asia, which had grave implications for regional and global stability and security. India should be pressurized by the international community to arrive at a just and final solution on Kashmir.

Third, there was need for a third neutral force to ascertain whether there had been any violations of the LoC. Pakistan expected the UNMOGIP to ascertain this violation or expected Kofi Annan, the UN Secretary General, to send a special envoy to the region to look into this matter.

Thus, the primary objective of the infiltration was to internationalize the Kashmir issue. The second part of this strategy was embedded within the first one—provoke India to retaliate, so that the issue would automatically get internationalized. The fact that the militants were supplied with Stinger missiles proves that Pakistan had anticipated air strikes by India. If internationalizing the Kashmir issue was Pakistan's objective, why did it choose a particular period to do it? Why not earlier, when militancy in Kashmir was at its

[28] Ibid.
[29] 'Pakistan Calls for UN Intervention', *News*, 29 May 1999.
[30] 'Sartaj Slates India for Violating LoC', *News*, 5 June 1999.

height? Why at all, specially when Kashmir was not an issue during the previous elections in Pakistan? In fact, Sharif, during his election campaign, told the nation that he would improve relations with India.

At least three factors could be cited to understand the reasons underlying Pakistan's attempt to internationalize the Kashmir issue: the internal situation in Kashmir, the general global attitude towards Kashmir, and improved Indo-Pak relations with its implications for Kashmir.

First, the internal situation in Kashmir. Despite occasional violent events, life in Kashmir was returning to normalcy after the elections. By the second half of 1998, normalcy was fast returning to Kashmir so far as the day-to-day affairs of the people were concerned.[31] After nine years, cinema halls were opened for screening movies in Srinagar by the beginning of August.[32] Tourism was slowly reviving. More than one lakh (one million being equal to 10 lakh) tourists had visited Jammu and Kashmir by the end of August 1998, compared to only 16,138 during the whole of 1997.[33] The big industrial houses of India started showing interest in investing in J&K as a result of the decline in insurgency. By the end of September 1998, State Industries Minister Bodh Raj Bali noted that proposals for investment of Rs. 1,700 crore (one crore being equal to 10 million) had been received by the state government, and letters of intent for investment of Rs.154 crore had been issued.[34] Besides, realization was growing among the displaced Kashmiri Pundits that the situation in Jammu and Kashmir was returning to normalcy. Panun Kashmir, an organization of the displaced pundits, released a 'module for the safe and dignified return of the community to their homes in Kashmir valley during December 98'.[35]

The central Government's efforts also contributed to restoring normal life in Kashmir. Elections were conducted in 1996. An economic and political package to strengthen the economy and

[31] See the following articles: Prem Shankar Jha, 'Kashmir Then and Now', *The Hindu*, 24 July 1998; 'Turnaround in J&K', *Pioneer*, 11 August 1998.

[32] Zafar Meraj and Sunil Narula, 'Line of No Control', *Outlook*, 17 August 1997, vol. 4, no. 32, p. 16.

[33] Elisa Patnaik, 'Tourism Slowly Picking up in Kashmir', *Asian Age*, 13 September 1998.

[34] 'Kashmir Takes a Step Toward Industrial Revival', *Economic Times*, 5 October 1998.

[35] 'Plan to Help Kashmir Pandits Return the Valley', *Statesman*, 26 December 1998.

security of the region was implemented. During July 1998, the central Government announced an assistance of Rs. 250 crore to tide over its financial crunch.[36] The BJP Government decided to follow a 'proactive' policy in Kashmir comprising a four-tiered strategy:[37]

1. Defeat the ISI's designs in J&K.
2. Gear up the intelligence network for better coordination between the Army, state administration and the paramilitary forces.
3. Economic development of the state.
4. Rehabilitation of the Kashmiri pundits.

Besides, the nature of militancy in Kashmir had changed greatly over the preceding couple of years, which further affected change in the internal situation in Jammu and Kashmir. During 1998-9, the majority of militants came from outside the region rather than from inside. According to the Indian Government, out of the 1,874 militants killed in Kashmir, 43 per cent were foreign militants (since 1996).[38] The support of the local people to the terrorists hit an all-time low by the end of August 1998.[39] The changed nature of militancy in Jammu and Kashmir clearly indicated that the people were losing faith in terrorism and violence as a solution to their problems. This also indicated that neither the people nor the extremists were looking towards Pakistan as their saviour. When Shamsad Ahmed, Pakistani Foreign Secretary, said that he would represent the Kashmiri people in his dialogue with India, the pro-independence as well as the POK group rejected him. The JKLF said: 'Only the people of Kashmir have the right to choose who will represent them and decide their future. Pakistan's role in Kashmir is that of a occupier and has no locus standi.'[40] With normalcy returning to Jammu and Kashmir and Pakistan losing its grip, it felt

[36] 'Bailout Package for J&K', *The Hindu*, 6 July 1998.

[37] 'Advani's Active Policy Showing Results', *Economic Times*, 25 August 1998.

[38] 'Pak Hand Visible in Kashmir Insurgency', *The Hindu*, 15 July 1998. Also see the following articles on this subject: Shujaat Bukhari, 'Where the guns boom again', *The Hindu*, 9 August 1998; 'Foreign Mercenaries Hijack J&K Secessionism', *Hindustan Times*, 17 September 1998; Ajith Pillai, 'The Jihad Spill Over', *Outlook*, 7 September 1998, vol. 4, no. 35, pp. 12-18.

[39] 'Local Support to J&K Ultras at an All-Time Low', *The Hindu*, 6 October 1998.

[40] 'Pak an Occupying Force: J&K Groups', *Pioneer*, 12 October 1998.

that internationalization of the Kashmir issue would receive less support, unless something was done.

THE DECLINING GLOBAL SUPPORT FOR KASHMIR

At the international level, the support to Pakistan on the Kashmir issue was declining. Pakistan expected, with both India and Pakistan becoming nuclear weapon powers, that the international community would play an active role in resolving the Kashmir issue. Contrary to its expectations, all major countries expected India and Pakistan to resolve the Kashmir issue bilaterally. Consider the following statements made by different countries in different forums in the post Pokhran-Chagai period.

Laurent Fabius, Speaker of the French National Assembly and former Prime Minister on a visit to India said, 'All of us want a resolution of this (Kashmir) dispute peacefully and bilaterally. France has no wish to internationalise the issue.'[41]

China also made it clear that the Kashmir issue should be resolved bilaterally. Zhou Gang, the Chinese Ambassador to India said in September 1999 that Kashmir 'should be solved bilaterally on the principles of the Shimla agreement'.[42]

Preferring status quo on Kashmir, Vladmir Lukin, the Chairman of the Russian Duma Committee on International Affairs, on his visit to India in September 1998 said: 'I don't think we will convince India to give up Kashmir or Pakistan to liberate the part of territory it occupies in the historically foreseeable future. . . . If both the countries could negotiate, without external interference, a long-lasting agreement on the maintenance of status quo, even if not a direct border, it would be [a] fine and more realistic way.'[43]

However, more than others, it was the US attitude towards Kashmir, specially the failure of Sharif to force Clinton to interfere in the Kashmir problem, during his visit to the US in the beginning of December 1998 that forced Pakistan to redefine its strategy on Kashmir. Prior to his departure for Washington, Sharif announced that 'Pakistan would welcome mediation by the US, or for that

[41] *Times of India*, 17 September 1998.

[42] 'Kashmir Issue Should be Resolved Bilaterally: China', *The Hindu*, 15 September 1998.

[43] *The Pioneer*, 13 September 1998.

[44] 'Nawaz Urges US Role in South Asia over Kashmir', *News*, 2 December 1998.

matter, mediatory efforts by any other country or international organisation to resolve [the] Jammu and Kashmir dispute.'[44] However, Clinton made it very clear that, unless both parties requested it, the US would not interfere in Kashmir. Clinton informed him that 'The US can be effective . . . only if both parties want us to do so. . . . There is no place we have injected ourselves in a dispute in the absence of an agreement on both sides. Otherwise it does not work.'[45] Besides, the US also emphasized during Sharif's visit in the first week of December 1998 that both India and Pakistan should place greater emphasis on the dialogue between them. It was this US attitude towards India-Pakistan conflicts in general and Kashmir in particular that would have made Sharif realize that unless something dramatic was done, Kashmir would become a dead issue.

THE NUCLEAR CAPABILITY AND THE CHANGED STRATEGIC ENVIRONMENT

Besides the return of normalcy in Kashmir and the declining international support for Pakistan's Kashmir policy, the changed strategic scenario in South Asia could have been another reason for the Kargil venture. Both India and Pakistan became nuclear weapons powers in 1998, making the conventional military superiority of the Indian military irrelevant, if not obsolete. 'Buoyed up by a sense of power conferred by the nuclear capability, the government and its friends, may have thought that they could now take on India in occupied Kashmir without the threat of a full-scale war.'[46]

India's response to earlier attacks during November 1998 and February 1999 would have strengthened Pakistan's above-noted convictions. During the last week of September 1998, Pakistani troops resorted to firing along the LoC, in which three Indian soldiers were killed—two near Kaksar in Kargil and the other in the Uri sector.[47] During 1998, the number of artillery/mortar shells fired by Pakistani troops along the LoC was more than twice the number during 1996 and 1997, and Kargil sector alone was pounded by around 2,00,000 shells.[48] During the second week of February 1999,

[45] Quoted in *Dawn*, 3 December 1998.

[46] M.B. Naqvi, 'Looking Beyond Kargil', *News*, 19 July 1999.

[47] 'Tension on Border as Pak Resumes Firing', *Hindustan Times*, 1 October 1998.

[48] Vikram Jit Singh, Pak's Artillery Blitz on LoC, Siachen Puts Wars on Shade', *Indian Express*, 14 February 1999.

Pakistani troops again resorted to firing along the LoC.[49] India's response on both occasions was feeble, as it did not want to escalate tensions and did not want to upset the ongoing talks with Pakistan.

Thus, the return of normalcy to Kashmir, declining international concern regarding the Kashmir issue, and the changed strategic scenario in South Asia, in which India was hesitant to respond strongly, provided the reasons for Pakistan to go ahead with its Kargil adventure to internationalize the Kashmir issue.

[49] *The Hindu*, 8 February 1999.

2

On the Military Dimensions of Kargil

Maj. Gen. Ashok Krishna

INTRODUCTION

India and Pakistan have been fighting against each other in Jammu and Kashmir (J&K) since 1947. None of these battles and wars ended decisively. It is said that a decisive battle ends in a clear victory of one party over the other, thereby stopping the hostilities and their recurrence, and shifting the direction of human affairs away from the battlefield. An indecisive battle, on the other hand, stops hostilities only temporarily. The battle may resume based upon the political calculations of the adversaries, their relative strengths, range of weapons, intelligence and several other factors. The decisiveness of a battle, therefore, rests on its end results. It is possible to posit, therefore, that the recent Kargil conflict is a continuation of an unresolved problem.

It is a matter of some interest as to what the recent Kargil episode should be called, a conflict or a limited war. Considering the scale of the aggression, the nature of weaponry used and the involvement of regular Pakistan Army troops, it can be accurately termed a 'limited war'. (For the purposes of convenience, it will hereon be referred to as the Kargil war.)

In analysing this war, it is necessary to briefly trace the origins of the J&K problem and take a fleeting look at the Indo-Pak wars that have been fought since the partition of India in 1947. This chapter endeavours to do so, and in the process, reviews the general topography of the state of J&K with special reference to the area of the recent Kargil war. It assesses the causes and broad military conduct of the first war of 1947-8 which was confined to J&K, and the two general wars of 1965 and 1971 which were fought by the two sides with their full military might; it touches upon the Siachen conflict and thereby locates the recent limited Kargil war within the politico-military context that has arisen out of the past bloodshed.

TOPOGRAPHY: JAMMU AND KASHMIR

The undivided state of J&K extends from Punjab and Himachal Pradesh in the south to the trans-Himalayan and trans-Indus regions of Ladakh, Baltistan and Gilgit. The old trading route, the Silk Road, lies to the north. Linking Central Asia with China by way of Tibet, this route was often utilized by successive caravans and conquering armies. J&K has been the halting place of caravans travelling between the plains of India and Central Asia.

Bound by the river Ravi in the east and the river Jhelum in the west, this state of 84,471 sq. miles (2,22,236 sq. km) is contiguous with the Indian Union for about 250 miles (402.25 km), Pakistan for about 350 miles (563.15 km), Afghanistan for about 100 miles (160.9 km), Tajikistan (across the Pamirs) for about 100 miles (160.9 km), and to Xinjiang and Tibet for approximately 300 miles (482.7 km) each. Historically, culturally and economically, J&K has been an integral part of India over the centuries.

Topographically, the state can be divided into three well-defined regions. The first is the sub-mountainous and semi-mountainous region stretching from the Punjab plains to the Pir Panjal range of the Himalayas (the peaks of this range rise to over 4,538 m or 16,000 ft). It covers the south-eastern part of the state and forms the basin of the river Chenab. The next geographical region is Kashmir Valley, surrounded by the high Himalayan ranges (heights of 5,500 m or 18,000 ft) with one natural outlet along the course of the river Jhelum. This river takes the waters of the Kishen Ganga at Domel near Muzaffarabad and then forms the western boundary of the state for about 150 miles (241.25 km). It drains the waters of Kashmir Valley, as also of the western districts of Muzaffarabad, Poonch and Mirpur. The region thus forms the basin of the river Jhelum. The third and most extensive geographical region of the state is the trans-Himalayan plateau comprising the frontier regions of Ladakh, Baltistan and Gilgit. The river Indus flows through this region forming deep ravines, narrow gorges and fertile valleys. These areas are sparsely populated. The climate, specially in winter, approximates arctic conditions.

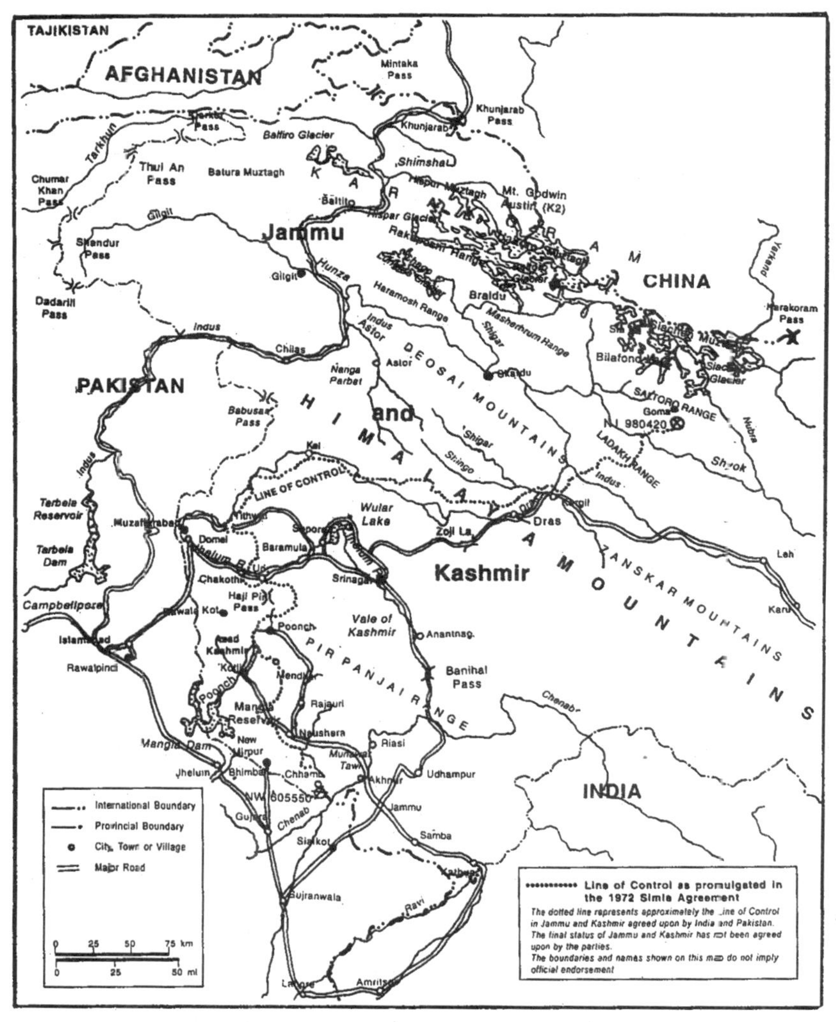

MAP 1: JAMMU AND KASHMIR SHOWING THE LINE OF CONTROL.

Thus, the Pir Pinjal range divides the Jhelum basin from the Chenab basin and the Great Himalayan range divides the Indus basin from the Jhelum basin. For administrative convenience, the state was divided into four administrative units as follows.

1. *Jammu Province.* It includes the districts of Jammu, Kathua, Udhampur, Riasi, Poonch and Mirpur. Its total area is 31,541.02 sq. km (12,178 sq. miles).
2. *Kashmir Province.* This is also referred to as 'Kashmir Valley', or just 'the Valley'. It includes the districts of Anantnag (including the city of Srinagar), Baramula and Muzaffarabad. Its total area is 22,116.01 sq. km (8,539 sq. miles).
3. *The Frontier Region of Ladakh.* It includes the whole of Ladakh and Baltistan. It forms one administrative district subdivided into the tehsils of Leh, Kargil and Skardu. Its total area is 1,18,523.58 sq. km (45,762 sq. miles).
4. *The Frontier Region of Gilgit.* It includes the Gilgit district and the tributary states of Hunza-Nagar, Chilas, Ishkuman, Yasin, Punial, Kuh and Ghizar, together known as the Gilgit Agency. Total area 50,055.12 sq. km (19326 sq. miles).

On 1 January 1949, after the first Indo-Pak war, a cease-fire came into effect under UN supervision. A negotiated Cease-Fire Line was drawn up on an actual holding basis pending future settlements. It starts from a few kilometres east of Munawwar and follows a northerly course. It passes close to Chhamb, Naushera and Rajouri, and leaves Poonch proper at a distance of three kilometres; it then reaches Uri from where it intersects the river Jhelum and goes northwards towards Tithwal. From Tithwal, it generally follows the river Kishen Ganga: it bypasses Trehgam and approaches Kel to the north; it then takes an easterly course and crosses Kanzalwan and Gurez from where it separates Skardu Tehsil from Kargil and Ladakh. From here it enters Ladakh and proceeds north-eastwards and leaves the whole of Gilgit to Pakistan.

At present about 78,932 sq. km of the state is under Pakistan. This area is referred to as 'Pakistan-Occupied Kashmir' (POK) by India, but 'Azad Kashmir' by Pakistan. China is in occupation of 4,855.9 sq. km ceded to it by Pakistan and 37,879.1 sq. km is with them since the 1962 war. The total area with China is thus 42,735 sq. km. India retains an area of only 100,569 sq. km out of the total area of the J&K state of 2,22,236 sq km.

POK consists of Mirpur district, Bagh and Palandri tehsils of Poonch district, a major part of Muzaffarabad district, Gilgit

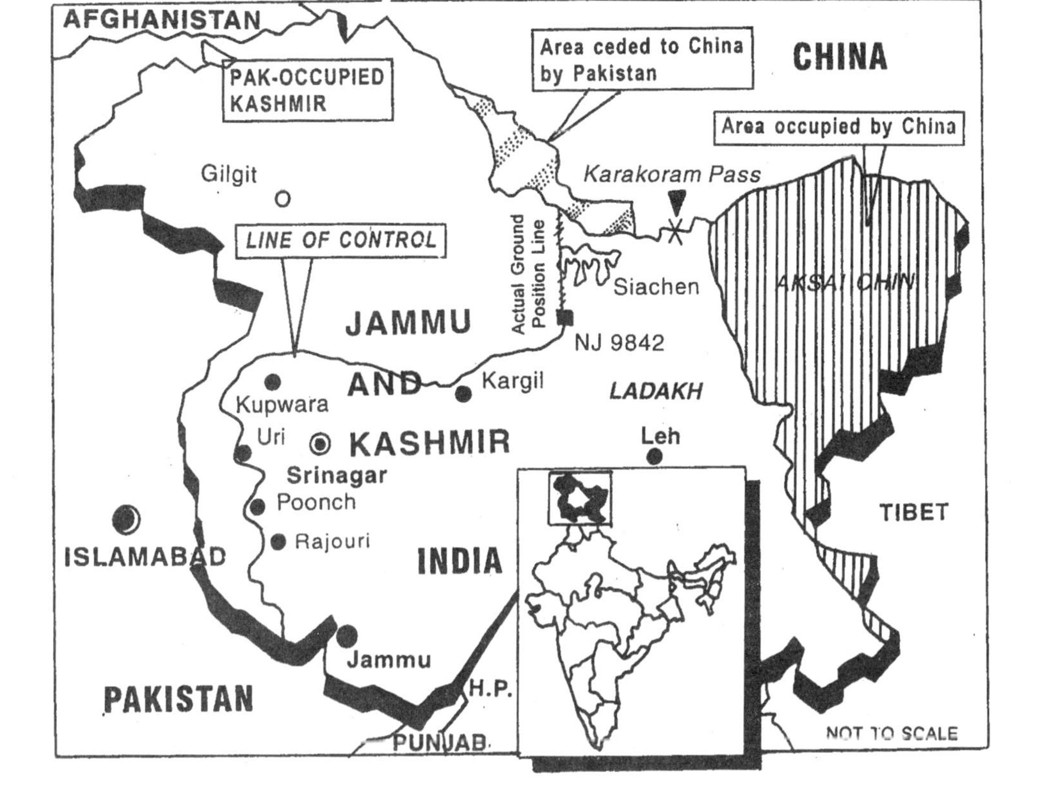

MAP 2: JAMMU AND KASHMIR SHOWING AREAS OCCUPIED AND CEDED.

Agency, and Skardu tehsil of Ladakh. The area is administered by the POK Government, which is located in Muzaffarabad and has its own president, cabinet and flag. However, POK is governed and financed by the Pakistan Ministry of the Interior. The Karakoram Highway which runs through Gilgit and Hunza provides a direct road link between China and Pakistan, hence, these areas assume great strategic importance.

The population of POK consists predominantly of Kashmiri Muslims in southern POK and tribals in the Kagan, Indus, Gilgit, and Hunza valleys. Baltistan is mainly peopled by a mixture of Tibetan and Indo-Europeans. The Baltis profess the Muslim faith of the Shia sect, but there are some villages which still profess the Buddhist faith. The Kishen Ganga valley (the Pakistanis call it the 'Neelam valley') and the Lipa valley are inhabited by a mixed stock of Mongoloid, Baltis and Aryan Kashmiris. In addition, there are a large number of ethnic Gujjars or graziers (on both sides) who keep large herds of sheep and milch cattle.

On the Indian side, the Jammu region is peopled by Hindus, Sikhs and Muslims and the Kashmir region by Muslims, Kashmiri Pundits, Sikhs and Hindus.

Ladakh comprises the three *tehsils* of Leh (also referred to as Ladakh), Kargil and Skardu. The Kargil war involved all the three *tehsils* of Ladakh. The whole region is mountainous. The elevation of Ladakh varies from 2,440 to 4,570 m above the sea level. The mountains vary in height from 5,180 to 7,620 m. The Aghil ranges form the northern boundary of Ladakh. To the south lies the Ladakh range, and further south the Zanskar range, the two being intersected by the river Indus. To the west are the areas of Kargil, Suru and Dras on the road to Srinagar. The climate of Ladakh is rigorous. The nights are very cold and the days hot. The position of the mountains is opposite to the direction of the winds and hence little rainfall occurs.

Three major rivers flow through Ladakh:

1. *Indus River*. The Indus river springs from the north-west of the holy lakes of Mansarovar and Rakas on the south-western slopes of the Kailash mountains at an estimated height of 5,180 m. At Nimu, just 40 km below Leh, it is joined by the Zanskar river, a dark and turbulent torrent of equal or perhaps greater size. The Dras river joins the Indus near Kargil and the confluence of the Shyok river with the Indus takes place east of Skardu. At Makpoui-Shang Rong, the Indus cuts the Deosai

chain of mountains by a sudden sweep southwards where it receives the waters of the Gilgit river. The length of the mountain course of the river is about 1,450 km. The river forms a major lifeline of the Ladakh region.

2. *Shyok River*. It is the principal mountain tributary of the Indus and rises in the Karakoram mountains to the north-west of Leh. Its upper course is turbulent down a narrow glen, but its middle course is broad and divided into numerous channels. The whole length of the Shyok river is 640 km and the total fall 3,200 m. It is often blocked by glaciers that cause severe floods which are felt even in the Indus.
3. *Nubra River*. It is a tributary of the Shyok river and originates from the Siachen glacier in the Karakoram mountains. It flows south-east and joins the Shyok river at Tirit at an altitude of 3,715 m. The Nubra valley is the most beautiful valley in Ladakh.

Segregating Kashmir Valley from Ladakh is the Great Himalayan Range with the 16,427-ft Zoji La (Zoji Pass) being the only route across it. Zoji La marks not only a geophysical, but also an ethnic and linguistic divide. The people of Dras, the first major village over the pass, are Dards, an Indo-Iranian stock akin to the Kashmiris, but as the road continues towards central Ladakh, there is increasing evidence, in the people's features, of the quite different racial elements represented by the Tibetans. Similarly, the Dard language, spoken at Dras, which belongs to the same language group as Kashmiri, gives way to the Ladakhi language, a dialect of Tibetan. The Ladakhis are Buddhists and Muslims.

The Great Himalayan Range forms a barrier to the entry of moisture-laden clouds coming from the direction of the Valley to the rest of Ladakh, but at Zoji La they find a way through the gap and the resultant heavy snowfall (some 9 m or 30 ft at the pass) renders the area entirely inaccessible from October to May. Dras is the coldest permanently inhabited place in the world outside Siberia. At Dras village, the valley opens out into a series of alluvial plateaux at different levels. The road follows the Dras river for a two-hour journey, passing its confluence with another major stream, the Shingo. As the valley narrows, the vegetation diminishes and the landscape grows starker. The meeting of the Dras with the Suru river coming from the south-east is then reached, followed by Kargil town, the second-largest city in Ladakh with a population of about 91,000, and a natural halting place for the night. It is situated at a height of about 2,750 m. The winter snowfall here is much less than that near Zoji La. There is almost a perpetual traffic jam in its streets and alleyways. The town occupies a strip of land which is too narrow for the construction of a bypass, consequently, the Srinagar-Leh highway runs through its main bazaar. The Kargilis hold fast to their traditional faith, a strict and puritanical form of Islam's Shia sect.

Although Kargil is only about 20 km south of the Indus as the crow flies, the road continues on a course roughly parallel to it, crossing two passes higher than Zoji La, and then making a southward curve to join the Indus at right angles at Khalatse, 100 km down river from Leh. About an hour's drive from Kargil, the road emerges into the pasture land around Mulbekh—the first predominately Buddhist area on the route to Leh. From Leh, the road crosses the Ladakh range at Khardung La (5,440 m), on to Siachen and Turtok.

There is another line of communication from Himachal Pradesh along the Beas valley, over the very high passes of Rohtang and Barachala to Leh.

Jammu town in the plains is connected to the rest of India by rail; there is no other railway line in the state.[1]

Political Background

THE GILGIT EPISODE

The dismemberment of J&K started with Gilgit. When the Soviet Union took over virtual control of Xinjiang in 1935, the British government and the Maharaja of Kashmir executed an agreement whereby Gilgit was given on a 60-year lease to the British. The ostensible purpose of the lease was to guard against the USSR's expansion into Central Asia. There was also an unstated desire to isolate Kashmir from any significant international frontiers. The British, thereafter, raised an irregular force, the Gilgit Scouts, officered exclusively by them. With the announcement of the Mountbatten plan on 3 June 1947, Gilgit was handed back to the Maharaja amid much jubilation, and the Gilgit Scouts became a part of the State Forces.

The Maharaja dispatched a Governor and the Chief of Staff of the

[1] Details about topography have been taken from various professional papers and from the book: Balraj Madhok, *Kashmir Divided* (Rashtra Dharam Prakashan, Lucknow, 1949), pp. 6–15.

J&K State Forces, Maj. Gen. Scott, to take over Gilgit. When they arrived in Gilgit on 30 July 1947, they were informed that all the British officers of the Gilgit Scouts had opted to serve Pakistan. The Governor stayed back and Gen. Scott returned to inform the Maharaja. After the tribal invasion of Kashmir commenced, the Gilgit Scouts surrounded the residence of the Governor, and a provisional Governor was installed. On 4 November, the British Commandant of the Gilgit Scouts hoisted the Pakistani flag in the unit lines and on 21 November, a political agent arrived from Pakistan. Thus, Gilgit was taken over under the garb of a popular uprising, and the Maharaja was able to do nothing about it.

The strategic value of Gilgit was appreciated in 1935, hence the 60-year lease. By 1947, its importance had enhanced due to the vastly increased power of the Soviet Union. India, it was realized, would never have agreed to Gilgit being used for spying on the USSR. It is evident that the retrocession of the area to the Maharaja in June 1947 was merely a gesture, and Gilgit was firmly designed to become part of Pakistan, ostensibly as a result of a piratical action. These events indicated the involvement of certain British officers in Pakistan's plans; clearly they were pawns in a much larger game.[2]

PARTITION AND J&K

At the time of Partition in 1947, Kashmir was ruled by an autocratic monarch, Maharaja Hari Singh, even though he had a Council of Ministers since 1939. Opposition to his rule took the form of the All Jammu and Kashmir Conference, founded in October 1932, and led by a young Muslim, Sheikh Mohammad Abdullah. Because of the diverse character of Kashmir's population, Abdullah made a concerted effort to make the movement secular in character, particularly after 1938, when the organization changed its name to the National Conference, and adopted an explicitly secular political orientation. This shift in political orientation did cause one section of the party to leave in 1939. Nevertheless, secularization of the party continued apace, and in 1940, Sheikh Abdullah invited Nehru to visit Kashmir. Abdullah's own political sympathies accorded with Nehru's; consequently, the evolving political orientation of the Kashmir National Conference assumed an increasingly socialistic and secular character.

[2] Maj. Gen. Ashok Krishna, *India's Armed Forces: Fifty Years of War and Peace*, (Lancer Publishers, New Delhi, 1998), p. 8.

Jinnah and the Muslim League saw that the growing secularization of politics in Kashmir boded ill for the fortunes of the League. The success of the National Conference in uniting both Hindus and Muslims against a common adversary, the federal Hindu monarch, thwarted Jinnah who sought to create a rift between the two religious groups in the state. Abdullah and Jinnah split permanently when Abdullah realized that Jinnah's strategy would only undermine his support among Kashmiri Hindus and weaken his party. At that time, out of a population of four million, 77 per cent were Muslims and 20 per cent Hindus.

Meanwhile, the League started to argue that the state should accede to Pakistan. Abdullah rejected this suggestion as premature; only after the Conference overthrew the Maharaja would it consider the question of accession. The Maharaja had his own plans and wanted to head a completely independent state, an aspiration that turned out to be short-lived. The rulers of the princely states had been given till 15 August to decide which Dominion they wanted to join. Maharaja Hari Singh chose to join neither. He did, however, sign a Standstill Agreement with Pakistan and offered to sign one with India. According to V.P. Menon, the Secretary of the Indian States Ministry, the Indian government did not accept his offer because the States Ministry wanted to study the situation further.

There is considerable evidence that the Pakistan government honoured its agreement in the breach. For example, Pakistan interrupted the flow of essential commodities to Kashmir. The Kashmir government protested on several occasions but to no avail. The 'economic blockade', however, failed to ensure Kashmir's accession to Pakistan.[3]

THE 1947-48 INDO-PAK WAR

The 1947-48 Indo-Pak war was fought not for the mere possession of territory nor for its strategic value alone. There was a strong ideological component to the motives of the two states. For Pakistan, the possession of Kashmir was crucial to its ideology, namely, that religious philosophy could serve as the cornerstone of a state. To India, Kashmir, quite apart from its strategic significance, represented two fundamentally important issues. It demonstrated that even a Muslim-majority state could live within a predominantly Hindu India, thus validating the concept of a secular, democratic

[3] Ibid., p. 9.

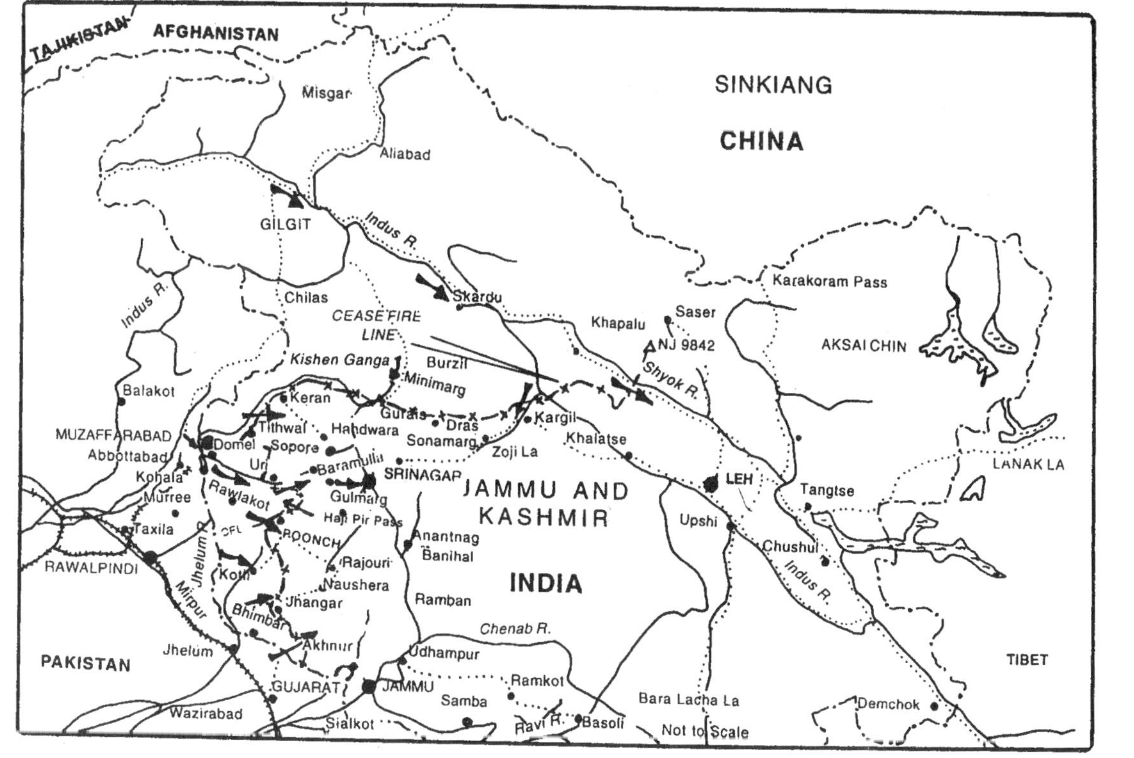

MAP 3: INVASION: JAMMU AND KASHMIR (1947).

state. Additionally, its integration had considerable psychological import for key members of the Indian elite, many of whom feared a precedent being established that could lead to the eventual 'Balkanisation' of India.

Finally, the lack of institutional arrangements by the British to ensure an orderly transfer of power was also one of the causes of the war. Having failed to secure accession by economic coercion, Pakistan now resorted to naked force. In order to exert even stronger pressure, a series of raids against the border posts of the State Forces was organized by Pakistan and launched into Jammu in early October 1947. Strange as it may seem, neither the deployment of the State Forces nor the strength of their garrisons was known to Army Headquarters. Therefore, the intercepts reaching Delhi about the Pakistani invasion could not be correctly interpreted nor was there any outward indication that Pakistan was involved. Pakistan precipitated a crisis in J&K on 22 October 1947 when it launched Operation Gulmarg with tribesmen from the North-West Frontier Province (NWFP), bolstered by Pakistan soldiers on leave masquerading as tribesmen, to coerce the Maharaja into acceding the state to Pakistan.

On 23 October, Brig. Rajinder Singh of the J&K State Forces hastily assembled a group of 200 men, reached the steel girder bridge at Uri in the face of the raiders, and blew it up. On 24 October, Sir Hari Singh appealed to India for help. Mountbatten, who was Governor General, took the line that the Maharaja must accede to India before India could intervene and that his state's accession must be subject to his agreement that a plebiscite would be held to decide the wishes of the people after the rebellion had been suppressed. Sir Hari Singh eventually acceded to India on 26 October 1947. His letter to Mountbatten is worth reading (Appendix 2). At this time, the tribesmen were at Uri, a mere 100 km (62 miles) from Srinagar. Lord Mountbatten then ordered the Indian Army to contain the raiders instantly.

When Jinnah heard (on 27 October) that Indian troops had landed in Srinagar, he ordered Gen. Gracey, the officiating Commander-in-Chief of the Pakistan Army, to rush troops into Kashmir. Gracey contacted FM Auchinleck [on the telephone] who was still presiding over the problems of partitioning the former Indian Army troops and assets between the Dominions, having informed Jinnah that he must have the approval of the Supreme Commander before issuing such an order. On 28 October, Auchinleck flew to Lahore and informed Jinnah that, as Kashmir was now a part of India, if Pakistan troops moved into it, every British officer serving in the Pakistan Army would immediately be withdrawn. This would have crippled the Pakistan Army, which could not function without the British officers. Jinnah stormed, but had no option but to rescind his order.

An ad hoc Indian brigade, hastily assembled and operating on light scales, managed to hold and thereafter beat back the tribal main body thus giving the campaign an excellent start. That the Valley was saved must be put down to two factors: the gallantry of the Indian soldiers, and Pakistan's error in choosing frontier tribesmen for this task.

After reaching Uri the Indians did not head for Domel and Kohala, but diverted their efforts southwards to link up with Poonch over the Haji Pir Pass. Efforts to go beyond the heights of the Uri bowl did not succeed, and with the onset of winter, the Indian effort now switched to the Jammu sector to clear the province and ensure the security of communications which was politically imperative. Here, the operations were largely aimed to relieve the beleaguered State Forces garrisons and helpless non-Muslims surrounded in them. The Pakistanis, too, concentrated on this sector. Their emphasis was on tribals and irregulars as the Pakistan Army was still being reorganized.

In November 1947, Pakistan considered going to the UN but abandoned the idea as, legally, it had no standing in J&K, and politically, it was not sure of the outcome. At about the same time, a similar suggestion was made by Lord Mountbatten. India went to the UN on 1 January 1948. Pakistan, most likely, inferred the following from India's complaint:

1. India was not politically prepared to enforce a military solution and to accept the accompanying hard options to evict the intruders.
2. India did not want to enlarge the conflict beyond J&K.
3. The reference to the UN also indicated a desire for early cessation of hostilities which in turn meant that India was unlikely to apply military effort to regain areas under Pakistani occupation, either because these areas were pro-Pakistani, viz., the narrow western and south-western tracts, or were inaccessible, like Baltistan and Gilgit.

Throughout the winter, the road from Jammu through Akhnur

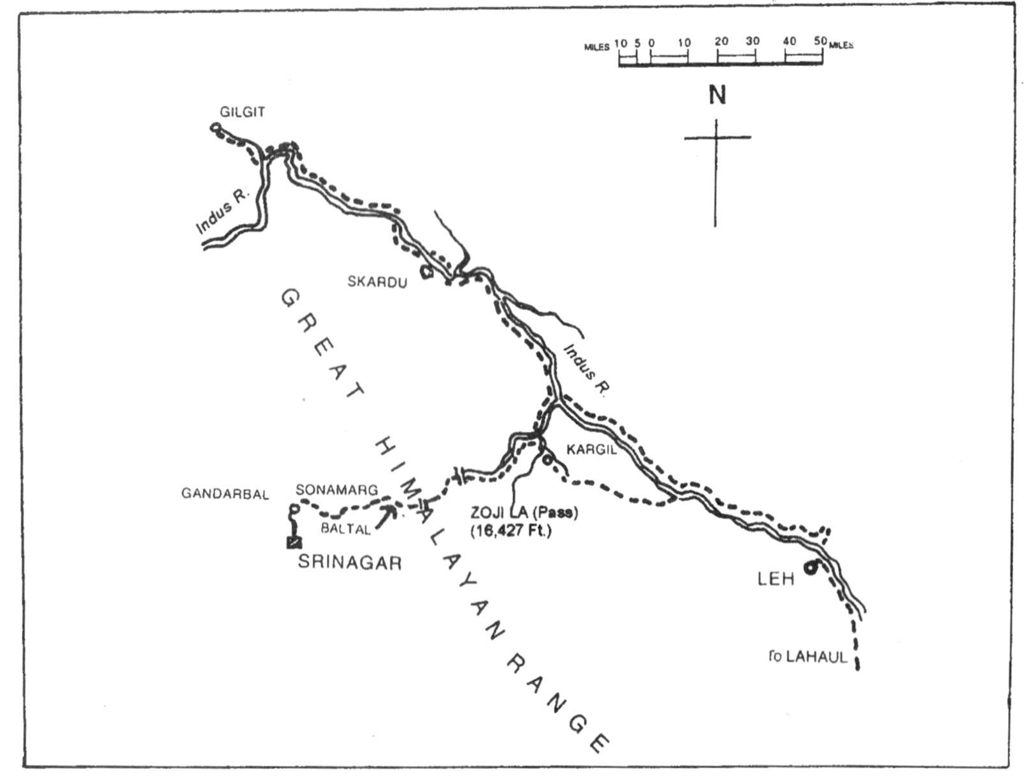

MAP 4: SKETCH SHOWING THE ROUTES FROM GILGIT TO LEH AND SRINAGAR TO LEH.

and Naushera to Jhangar was the target of Pakistani irregulars. A fierce battle took place at Naushera on 6 February 1948, in which the Pakistani attacking force was estimated at 15,000. By this time Pakistan had moved its 7 Division up to the frontier as a backstop in case the Indian Army drove the 'Azad Kashmir' force back over it. Some personnel of the Pakistan Army had crossed over to support this operation. They were also in action in Poonch in March.

By April 1948, the Indians resumed operations in right earnest and with greater coordination. Gen. Gracey, C-in-C Pakistan, sensing that India was planning an offensive to capture Bhimbar, Mirpur and Poonch (under siege) in the south and Muzaffarabad and Kohala in the north, advised his government that the Indian Army not be allowed to advance beyond the general line Uri–Poonch–Naushera.

Initial Indian moves were followed by a counter-offensive (forces in J&K having increased to two divisions) and by the end of May, Maj. Gen. K.S. Thimayya, who commanded the troops in Kashmir, had captured Tithwal on the Kishen Ganga river and his forces were only 18 miles from Muzaffarabad. This threat to Azad Kashmir's capital brought more Pakistani forces into action, and the armies of the two countries were now firmly face to face. On 23 November 1948, the besieged garrison in Poonch was relieved, a full year after its siege. This meant that a firm grip had been established, all the way from Pathankot, over the major portions of Jammu province.[4]

SKARDU, KARGIL AND LEH

The recent Kargil war encompassed the area of Skardu on the Pakistan side and Kargil and Ladakh on the Indian side. Hence, it would be appropriate to review the military operations conducted in these areas in 1948. Commencing in February 1948, Pakistan launched a subsidiary but complementary offensive from Gilgit through the Northern Territories with the aim of advancing up the Indus river. A weak State Forces battalion barred its path at Skardu. The target was Leh, the capital of Ladakh. The force employed consisted of a strong element from the Gilgit Scouts, defectors from the Jammu and Kashmir State Forces, and tribals. The plan involved a movement of 300 miles over inhospitable terrain. But it was by no means a pioneering effort. Fur dealers and other traders had used

[4] Ibid., pp. 10-21.

the route for many decades, and all that was expected was minor skirmishes against weak opposition.

After neutralizing Skardu, the Pak force was to move unimpeded along the road, attack Kargil on its right flank, held by a weak State Forces detachment, and move on to Leh. The people of Leh were unarmed and incapable of offering more than token resistance. There was no airstrip at Leh. Its reinforcement with troops, even if they were available would have been extremely difficult because of the adverse flying conditions during winter. Success was, therefore, assured even if the rate of advance was maintained at about 10 miles (16.09 km) per day.

Skardu came under enemy pressure in end-February. The invading force split here, one group investing the town, with the main body continuing towards Kargil and another group spreading into the Shyok river valley.

The Commanding Officer of the weak 6th Battalion, the Jammu and Kashmir State Forces, soon found that his best chance of survival, if he remained in the Skardu area, lay in evacuating his lightly held outpost positions and concentrating his unit within the fort. He also accommodated a number of women and children within the fort and placed everyone on a minimum ration scale to conserve the available foodstuff. Attacks against the fort were delivered at periodic intervals, but a steady and firm defence repulsed them, the casualties inflicted imposing caution on the enemy. However, the overall situation in Kashmir was such that no aid could be expected by the garrison at Skardu. The enemy's next step would be to lay siege to Skardu. It was in these circumstances that Skardu Fort asked Headquarters 161 Infantry Brigade for permission to slip away. The brigade headquarters concurred and signalled Headquarters J&K Force that as Skardu had neither strategical nor tactical value (this was the perception in those times), the garrison should be permitted to withdraw to Kargil where it could present a much bolder front together with the detachment there. Since the enemy lines of communication were stretched, it would not only survive but also be a thorn in the enemy flank. Headquarters J&K Force did not agree and issued an order that the Skardu garrison fight to the last man and the last round.

After fifteen days, Skardu sent a signal to the effect that the enemy had occupied every vantage point around the fort, and that as any movement drew fire, which was resulting in casualties, patrolling outside the fort was no longer possible. The inevitable had happened—Skardu was besieged. An attempt was made to relieve the siege of Skardu in late May 1948, but the State Forces troops that moved out made very little progress against determined enemy opposition and withdrew. An air effort was then mounted to drop ammunition and supplies, but this proved too costly in casualties sustained by the defenders, who had to battle with the enemy to recover the stores that landed in the area outside the fort. In early September, their last round of ammunition fired and their ration store empty, the Skardu garrison was forced to surrender. The women and children that it had striven so desperately hard to safeguard, met a fate equalled only by the rape and massacre of Baramula on 28 October 1947. Consequent upon the surrender at Skardu, the strategic areas of Gilgit and Baltistan passed out of Indian hands. It is the largest portion of J&K under Pakistan's control.

On 3 March, a few days after it had been encircled by the enemy, Skardu Fort reported by signal that about five hundred armed men and about two hundred porters had arrived from the direction of Gilgit. They had camped for the night in the vicinity of Skardu town, and had set off the next morning in an easterly direction, presumably heading for Kargil. There was deep anxiety at the prospect of Leh being attacked. Had the monastery at Leh been ransacked, it would cause serious repercussions in the Buddhist world. The small State Forces garrison at Kargil could not be expected to arrest the move of the raiders towards Leh. To get to Ladakh from Kashmir Valley was considered to be an impossibility at that time of the year, as the Great Himalayan Range divided the two and was an insurmountable barrier.

Lt. Col. G.G. Bewoor, Commanding Officer of 2 DOGRA, mentioned that 2 DOGRA, during its service as a Territorial Battalion, had enlisted, among other classes, a number of Lahaulis. Many of them were still serving in the battalion, including two officers, Capt. Prithi Chand and his cousin Capt. Khushal Chand. Lahaul, situated to the north of what is now the state of Himachal Pradesh, has a contiguous border with Ladakh, and over the centuries there has been close affinity between the Lahaulis and the Ladakhis. Having explained the situation, he told the two young officers that the only available route was via Zoji La, which was covered by snow to a depth of about 30 ft. Local experts, he said, were emphatic that no one had attempted to negotiate it under such conditions and to do so would be courting disaster. He asked them to consider the matter very carefully, assuring them that no adverse opinion would be held against them if they decided not to undertake the task. Without hesitating for a second, the officers said, 'We'll go to Leh.' It was then decided to send a strong platoon with a signal detachment, a total strength of forty personnel.[5]

Basing his column at Baltal, Prithi Chand moved forward with a few men to prepare Zoji La for the assault. It was necessary to create avalanches, and this was done by beating drums in the stillness of the night. This procedure continued over three nights and then Prithi Chand signalled that he was ready to make the attempt to cross the pass. There was no contact with the column for the next forty-eight hours, and then came a signal that the crossing had been accomplished successfully without a casualty, and that the column was setting out for Kargil on its way to Leh. Prithi Chand and his men reached Leh without encountering the enemy. The rifles and ammunition they carried were distributed among suitable young men and they were given hasty training in their use. Defensive positions, based on a bridge, were taken up and the arrival of the enemy awaited. It arrived in due course and was surprised to meet stubborn opposition. Every attempt to overrun the defences met with a serious reverse, until eventually, finding that his attacks were proving to be too costly, the enemy abstained from attempting to proceed to Leh. In May, Air Cmdre Mehar Singh flew Gen. K.S. Thimayya, who commanded the troops in Kashmir, in a Dakota to Leh. They landed on a hastily constructed bumpy airstrip after flying at 23,000 ft without oxygen. Consequent to this visit, more troops were inducted in stages.

Prithi Chand and his determined band of men were later joined by two companies of the 2nd Battalion, the 8th Gorkha Rifles on 10 July. They carried out an equally prodigious march 320 km from Manali over heights of 4,500 m (15,000 ft), through Lahaul on to Leh.[6] That Leh was held, and the aggressors prevented from sacking and looting it, was the outcome of boldness and enterprise in the face of adversity.

Zoji La was occupied by the main column of the raiders who could not be evicted as they were occupying heights and were well entrenched. Therefore, adequate forces had to be built up. The

[5] Lt. Gen. L.P. Singh, *Slender was the Thread* (Orient Longman, New Delhi, 1969), p.165

[6] Col. R.D. Palsokar, *Red Pompons: History of the 8th Gorkha Rifles* (Commandant 58 Gorkha Training Centre, Shillong, 1993), pp. 68-70 .

assault on the pass was launched successfully on 1-2 November 1948 in a snow storm by 77 Infantry Brigade supported by 7 Cavalry (Stuart tanks). At approximately 3,500 m, this was the highest altitude that tanks had operated in the history of warfare.

On 1 January 1949, a cease-fire came into effect under UN supervision. A negotiated Cease-Fire Line was subsequently drawn up on an actual holding basis pending future settlements. This meandering, and at places militarily illogical line, ran some 700 km from Chhamb in the south to a map reference point (NJ 9842) in Ladakh in the north. The latter reference point lay beyond the Shyok valley and was situated on the lower slopes of the Saltoro Range—an offshoot of the Karakorams. It was added to the agreement that the line thereafter went north to the glaciers, of which there was a surfeit in the region. Here lay the seeds of a future conflict between India and Pakistan, the battleground being the highest glacier region in the world (Siachen).

The northern borders of India remained unconsolidated. It meant full-time manning of an active defensive line for the Indian Army. Pakistan's boldness in precipitating a situation in J&K allowed it to retain 12,950 sq. km (5,000 sq. miles) of territory west of the cease-fire line and nearly one million people under its control, apart from Gilgit and Skardu (called the Northern areas by Pakistan). It imbibed valuable lessons with regard to the use of irregular troops and the need to have them controlled and commanded by and through the regular army. Infiltration was used and psychological warfare tried out in a rudimentary manner. However, they underestimated the fighting qualities of their opponents, resulting from blind faith in their martial superiority, and were humbled on this count. Consequent upon the J&K war, security and the Armed Forces were to become significant factors in the evolution of Pakistan. Further, an obsession with Kashmir was to afflict the political, military and even intellectual establishments henceforth.

The first Indo-Pak war ended indecisively and this led to more conflicts in future. It is necessary to emphasize the real issue here. It is not the status of J&K or the question of its accession to India; the issue is Pakistan's aggression on Indian territory. This aggression, which was committed in 1947, continues till today. If the UN wishes to discuss Kashmir at all, it should discuss the question of Pakistan's aggression, and find ways and means of getting Pakistan to vacate that aggression. During the years when the Kashmir question was before the Security Council, its members turned a blind eye to this patent fact. It was this attitude, together with the indulgence of

Pakistan by its allies in the Security Council, which has been the greatest obstacle to the solution of the J&K question. It has bedevilled relations between the two countries.

UN Resolutions: 1948

Based on India's complaint, the UN took up the J&K issue in the beginning of 1948. The Security Council passed four resolutions on 17 January, 6 February, 21 April and 13 August 1948. By the Security Council resolution of 17 January 1948, the United Nations Commission for India and Pakistan (UNCIP) was set up. It was authorized by another resolution of 6 February to investigate the situation, get India and Pakistan to restore law and order and then conduct a plebiscite to determine the future of the state. On 21 April 1948, yet another resolution strengthened the UNCIP by raising its strength to five and it was asked to make specific recommendations. This resolution also required Pakistan to arrange the withdrawal of the tribesmen and troops in Kashmir, and that India reduce its troops to the minimum needed for maintaining law and order. Thereafter a yet-to-be appointed administrator would be asked to conduct a plebiscite.[7]

The 13 August resolution was the most important as it was the basis for the cease-fire which came into effect on 1 January 1949: every problem had to be examined thereafter within its ambit. This resolution is in three parts and is given at Appendix 3. The UNCIP reached India in July and on 13 August produced a detailed plan of action to implement the UN resolution. This was the time that the Pakistanis formally admitted that their troops were committed against the Indian Army. Somewhat reluctantly, India went along with this plan. But the Pakistanis rejected it. However, by the end of the year, the two sides agreed to proceed further.

Following the cease-fire, beginning 1 January 1949, the UNCIP sent a letter on 2 July inviting Indian and Pakistani representatives to meet jointly in Karachi under the auspices of the Cease-Fire's Truce Sub-Committee to establish the Cease-Fire Line (CFL). The letter clarified that the meeting would be 'for military purpose; political issues will not be considered'. The military representatives of India and Pakistan met together in Karachi from 18 to 27 July 1949 under the auspices of the Truce Sub-Committee of the United

[7] Study Group Headquarters Northern Command, *Soldiers Role in Jammu and Kashmir*, p. 118.

Nations Commission for India and Pakistan. The Indian delegation was led by Lt. Gen. S.M. Shrinagesh and comprised Maj. Gen. K.S. Thimayya and Brig. S.H.F.J. Manekshaw, Mr H.M. Patil and Mr Vishnu Sahay, Defence Secretary and Secretary (Kashmir Affairs) respectively. The Pakistani team was led by Maj. Gen. W.J. Cawthorn and among its members were Maj. Gen. Nazir Ahmed, Brig. M. Sher Khan and Mr Ayub and Mr Khan. There were also four members of the Truce Sub-Committee of the UNCIP.

After ten days of hard bargaining, the Karachi Agreement was finalized on 27 July 1949. A negotiated CFL was agreed upon. The agreement also stipulated that the CFL would be drawn on a one-inch map and then be mutually verified on the ground by local commanders of each side with the assistance of the United Nations Military Observer Group in India and Pakistan (UNMOGIP) personnel 'so as to eliminate any no man's land'. This document was signed by Lt. Gen. Shrinagesh, Maj. Gen. Cawthorn and Hernado Samper M. Delvoie, Chairman of the Truce Sub-Committee. Thereafter the two sides ratified the agreement, and clarified the line on the ground. After this process, the Commission's Military Adviser issued a map marked with the definite CFL.

Other salient points of the Karachi agreement were:[8]

1. no troops shall be stationed or operate in the area of Burzil nalla from the south of Minimarg to the CFL;
2. any dispositions that may be adopted in consequence of the present Agreement, [it shall be ensured that] troops will remain at least 500 yards from the CFL except where the Kishen Ganga river constitutes the line;
3. both the sides shall be free to adjust their defensive positions behind the CFL subject to no wire or mine being used when new bunkers and defences are constructed;
4. no additional military potential will be introduced into the state of J&K by either side;
5. the United Nation commission will station an observer where it deems necessary.

From the outset, Pakistan was alive to the prospect of altering the CFL. For example, while there had been no hostile troops south of the Burzil pass on 1 January 1949, but when the snows melted, the Pakistani forces occupied the heights overlooking Kargil town well

[8] Ibid., pp. 118-19.

after the cease-fire. As the Indian official history of the war notes, 'A greater alertness on the part of junior Indian officers on the spot could have prevented these illegal encroachments.'

The Indian side had another disadvantage. They had been ready to accept the cease-fire for several months since the passage of the August 1948 resolution in the UN. But Pakistan dragged its feet, hoping till the end to improve its position. The cease-fire came suddenly, as soon as Pakistan indicated its willingness to throw in the towel. But the Indian commanders had little forewarning and were not able to adjust their operations towards occupying better post-cease-fire tactical positions.

NON-IMPLEMENTATION OF THE 13 AUGUST 1948 UN RESOLUTION

This resolution visualized the settlement of the Kashmir problem in three phases: cease-fire, truce, and determination of the status of J&K in accordance with the will of the people. The last part was conditional and contingent on Pakistan vacating its aggression and this condition has not been complied with till today. The resolution was violated, both in letter and spirit, right from the date of signing. Important violations are:[9]

1. continuing presence of Pakistani personnel in Kashmir;
2. introduction of additional military equipment into the occupied territory;
3. construction of airfields in the occupied territory;
4. consolidation and incorporation of the occupied areas of J&K into Pakistan;
5. sustained organising and financing of subversion and sabotage in J&K; and
6. Pakistan negotiating Kashmir's border with China, thus disrupting the territorial unity of the state of Jammu and Kashmir.

The 1965 War

PRECEDING EVENTS

Periodic border skirmishes took place between India and Pakistan from 1949 to 1964, but a full-scale war did not break out. Efforts to resolve the J&K issue through UN mediation and bilateral

[9] Ibid., p. 119.

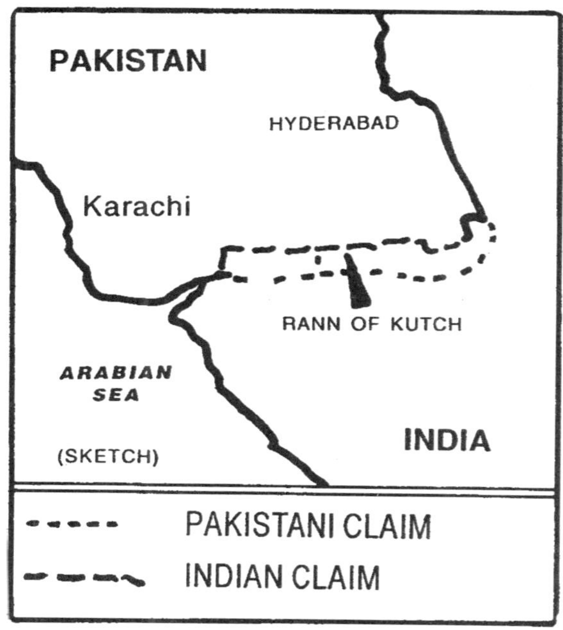

MAP 5: THE RANN OF KUTCH: BORDER CLAIMS.

negotiations did not succeed. This period showed the continuing relevance of the two related factors (ideology and irredentism/anti-irredentism) that animated the conflict between India and Pakistan.

At the domestic level, both governments sought to weld their nations into unified states. Both sides solidified their positions in Kashmir by concrete measures. By 1960, the Pakistan government had built the Mangla Dam in POK and had sought to integrate this part of J&K into the rest of the country. Similarly, India had finalized the process of integration of Jammu and Kashmir in January 1960, when the Supreme Court assumed jurisdiction in the state.

Because of its perceived military weakness, Pakistan tried to involve other regional and global powers in support of its quest. It joined the Baghdad Pact and the South-East Asia Treaty Organisation (SEATO) which resulted in the influx of substantial quantities of US arms. India sought to fend off what it perceived as the interference of external powers in an essentially bilateral conflict. But the forces which had triggered the Indo-Pak war of 1947-48 remained in the state.

In early 1965, the Pakistani leadership engaged in a classic 'limited probe' operation in an area of apparently no importance to either country (although a disputed one), the Rann of Kutch, an almost uninhabited region east of the mouths of the Indus, mud flats in the dry season, and covered with water when the south-west monsoon starts blowing in May. The attack was contained with considerable casualties to Pakistani troops. Subsequently, a cease-fire was arrived at. During the Commonwealth Conference in London in June, an agreement on the Rann of Kutch was reached between Shastri and Ayub Khan under which both parties agreed to revert to the status quo ante.

As part of its continued pressure on the cease-fire line in Kashmir, Pakistan planned to interdict the Indian lines of communication to Ladakh in the Kargil area. On 16 May 1965, Pakistani forces launched a series of attacks against Indian positions in the Kargil sector calculated to disrupt the tenuous land route to Leh. There were in all fourteen incidents in the Kargil area between 16 May and 7 June 1965, in which 60 Pakistanis were killed, 40 injured and 3 captured. The Indian Army, forced to take defensive measure in this sector, attacked and ousted the Pakistani forces from two dominant hill features, Point 13620 and Black Rocks, that overlooked the road to Leh and had allowed the Pakistanis to interfere with this vital line of communication. These two positions in Kargil were, however, voluntarily relinquished by India following the Kutch Agreement and an assurance from the UN that the Pakistanis would not be permitted to cross the cease-fire line and menace the road to Leh. (These heights had to be captured again during the September war).

India's perceived inability to coordinate plans and develop a coherent defence strategy must have been evident to Pakistan, particularly after the Kutch episode. This lends support to the thesis that the Kutch affair emboldened the Pakistani leadership and provided the necessary margin of confidence for an attack on Kashmir. The episode led to the development of Operation Malta and the Gibraltar Force. Operation Malta was the overall strategy for the invasion and eventual seizure of Kashmir, while the Gibraltar Force was the code name given to the invading forces, composed of both the Pakistan Army regulars and Azad Kashmir guerrillas. The entire Pakistani strategy according to Air Marshal Asghar Khan, was based on three important premises:

It was assumed that widespread support existed within occupied Kashmir to make such a guerrilla campaign a success. It was also considered unlikely that, as a consequence of this action, India would be inclined to attempt a large-scale military offensive against Azad Kashmir territory. Lastly, the possibility of India crossing the international frontier in East and West Pakistan was ruled out.[10]

PAK OPERATIONS IN J&K

The 1965 war consisted of five main actions: the infiltration of guerrillas; the Pakistani advance to Chhamb; the Indian drive on Lahore and the Pakistani counter-offensive in the Khemkaran sector; the Indian attack on Chawinda; and the war in the air. This narration is confined to the operations in J&K.

The subversion campaign in J&K was entrusted to Maj. Gen. A.H. Malik, GOC (General Officer Commanding) 12 Division of the Pak Army. His force of about 30,000 men was divided into ten 'forces' each of six units of five companies each. The commanders were regular officers of the Pakistan Army; lower echelons of command were provided by the Azad Kashmir Forces and the rank and file were recruited from Mujahid and Razakar irregulars. On 5 August Maj. Gen. Malik's force infiltrated across the cease-fire line on a wide front in four main areas; one near Kargil where Pakistan had tried to cut the road to Leh in May 1965; the second on the approaches to Srinagar on a broad front; the third in the Poonch region where they succeeded in capturing Mandi; and the fourth aimed at the road through Jammu—this force was supported by Pak artillery fire from across the border.

The Pakistani radio and press were giving fantastic reports every day of their exploits. In addition, a radio station styled 'Sada-i-Kashmir' ('Voice of Kashmir') had been set up under the command and control of the Pakistani authorities, at a place called Khari, 6 miles from Muzaffarabad in POK to broadcast distorted news. The people of Jammu and Kashmir, however, saw through the game. They gave the lie to the lurid accounts of a 'popular uprising' put out by 'Sada-i-Kashmir' and echoed by the Pakistan press and radio, by cooperating with the authorities and giving valuable information which helped the security forces to trace and round up the infiltrators. In some cases, the villagers captured the infiltrators themselves and handed them over to the police. While the people in Kashmir were busy tracking down and mopping up the infiltrators,

[10] Air Marshal M. Asghar Khan, *The First Round* (Vikas, Ghaziabad, 1979), pp. 75-6.

India's armed contingents fanned out to guard important points of entry into the country. Wherever necessary, they had taken positions on strategic points commanding the infiltrator's lines of communication and reinforcement.

Almost within a week of their crossing the cease-fire line, the first 3,000-5,000 infiltrators were liquidated by the Indian security forces with the cooperation of the local people. Some were killed and wounded, some taken prisoner and the rest had to flee in to the ravines and jungles where they passed helpless days without food and shelter. Ultimately, they found their way back across the cease-fire line through unfrequented paths. But in their first rush and before the security forces could be alerted several groups of infiltrators had sneaked into the interior of the Valley and had even reached the suburbs of Srinagar.

The Government of India approached the UN Observers Group to prevent these incursions by the Pakistani armed personnel in civilian clothes. But they were helpless. As the UN Secretary General reported to the Security Council on 4 September 1965, he had been unable 'to obtain any assurance from Pakistan that the cease-fire agreement and the cease-fire line in Kashmir would be respected henceforth or that efforts would be exerted to restore conditions to normal along the line'.[11]

The Indian Army had, under these circumstances, no other choice except to take action to plug the entry routes used by Pakistani raiders for infiltrating into J&K. When fresh attacks were resorted to by the Pakistanis on the Srinagar–Leh road near Kargil, the Indian forces had to reoccupy the two Pakistani posts vacated earlier by them on the assurance from the UN Observers that no fresh trouble would be created by the Pakistanis there.

DEFENSIVE ACTION BY INDIA

On 24 August 1965, the Indian forces crossed the cease-fire-line in the Tithwal sector and occupied the 2,750 m high Pir Sahiba post. It was in this sector that the infiltrators had entered the valley in strength and fanned out towards Kupwara and Gurais. By 13 September, the Indian forces were dominating Mirpur and all areas east of the Kishen Ganga river in Pakistan-Occupied Kashmir. Thus, they controlled the strategic Muzaffarabad–Kel road, which

[11] Note 6, p. 162.

served as the supply line to the infiltrators operating from the Gilgit sector.

Another crossing, this time in the Uri sector, was made on 26 August. The operation was quick, efficient and successful. The Indian forces captured the strategic posts of Sankh, Burjipathri, Kuthnar-ki-Gali in quick succession and finally the 3,965 m high Bedore, 14 km south-east of Uri. The next objective was the Haji Pir Pass, the strategic gateway to the 520 sq. km 'bulge' in the cease-fire line. The capture of Haji Pir Pass was a prelude to the operations to link up Uri and Poonch; this was completed on 10 September 1965. In these operations the Indian Army had to clear more than thirty posts of the Pakistanis. It was a success they could be proud of. The link-up completely changed the strategic position in this vital area and denied Pakistan the use of the shortest route to Kashmir Valley for subversion or outright aggression.

Pakistan's strategy for the defeated subversion campaign was flawed in three important ways: Pakistan grossly overestimated the support of the local populace; it overestimated their attachment to notions of Islamic brotherhood; and it underestimated the language barrier between the infiltrators and the Kashmiri population.

There were now only two alternatives to follow before the rulers of Pakistan. Either they had to completely write off the guerrillas and admit the failure of Operation 'Gibraltar', thereby becoming the target of their own people's wrath, or to take a more daring and adventurous 'Third Step' and commit their country to an all-out war with India. As was to be expected from a military dictatorship, they chose the latter course.

The Pak attack on Chhamb on 1 September was mainly carried out from across the international border, with a subsidiary thrust from across the cease-fire line to the west. From the trend of past operations, the Indians had not expected Pakistan to attack across the international border. The Pakistanis were able to capture their objectives in this sector without much difficulty, and subsequently their newly raised 6 Armoured Division penetrated up to Jaurian, only six miles from Akhnur. This led to India deciding on the following strategy.

1. In Punjab, to advance and secure the line of the Ichhogil Canal and thereafter pose a threat to Lahore by crossing over at selected places.
2. From the Jammu side, to advance and cut off Sialkot from

Lahore by driving a wedge in the area north of Gujranwala. This would remove the threat to the vulnerable lines of communication based on the Pathankot–Jammu road, which runs parallel to the border and quite close to it.

3. An offensive-defensive in the mountainous sector of J&K, Rajasthan and Kutch. Against East Pakistan, remain on a purely defensive posture.

After twenty-two days of intense fighting in the Punjab (Amritsar–Lahore axis, Khemkaran–Kasur axis and the Sialkot sector), India and Pakistan agreed to a cease-fire which came into effect at 3.30 a.m., Indian Standard Time on 23 September. The two parties finally met in Tashkent on 4 January 1966. On 10 January 1966 India and Pakistan declared that 'all armed personnel of the two countries shall be withdrawn not later than February 25, 1966, to positions they held prior to August 5, 1965, and both sides shall observe the cease-fire terms on the cease-fire line'. (Text of Tashkent Declaration, 10 January 1966.) The status quo ante was thus restored everywhere. The 1965 war had ended indecisively.[12]

The importance of the Tashkent Declaration lay in that it represented important concessions by both sides. The Indians gave up the strategic positions captured in the Azad Kashmir region, and the Pakistanis agreed to withdraw from the territory across the Munawwar Tawi river in the Chhamb sector that they had seized in the conflict. The Indians backed down from their original position that Pakistan acknowledge responsibility for guerrilla infiltration. Shastri had to concede the strategic positions of the Haji Pir Pass and the Mirpur–Bugina Bulge in Tithwal in J&K and this led to considerable domestic discontent. Ayub also faced domestic discontent over the end result of the war.

The 1971 War

The effect of the 1965 war had been to strengthen the right-wing elements in the Congress party and to reinforce those who supported the strengthening of India militarily. The embargo on arms supplies imposed by the US and UK during the 1965 conflict had encouraged Pakistan to turn to China for arms. It led India to accelerate its indigenous production and also to seek arms from the Soviet Union.

[12] Note 1, p. 71.

In 1965, Pakistan had been on the crest of a wave militarily and economically, but less so politically, based primarily on the results of ten years of military and economic aid from the US, the great bulk of which was applied for the benefit of West Pakistan. The failure of its attempt to solve the Kashmir problem and the estrangement from the US which this brought about, produced a reaction against Ayub and his government particularly in East Pakistan, which saw its interests, including good relations with India, sacrificed to Ayub's military ambitions and obsession with Kashmir. For twenty years, out of the total revenue expenditure of Pakistan, only one-third was spent in East Bengal and of the total foreign aid received, about 80 per cent went to the west. There were glaring disparities in social services and in the industrial field. The tensions resulting from a combination of these factors led to Ayub's succession by Gen. Yahya Khan in 1969, and to the mounting popularity in East Pakistan of Sheikh Mujibur Rahman and his Awami League, which demanded a greater degree of independence from Islamabad.

Yahya Khan promised general elections and held them in December 1970. The Sheikh won an overwhelming victory in East Pakistan giving his Awami League a majority in the Pakistan National Assembly. Bhutto's Pakistan People's Party was second and secured a majority in West Pakistan. The Sheikh was entitled to become the Prime Minister of Pakistan but this was prevented, which led to violent demonstrations in East Pakistan. Yahya's reaction was to declare martial law and suppress the agitation using the Pakistan Army, which came down on the population with a heavy hand.

In pursuance of his strategy to convert the Bangladesh problem into an Indo-Pak conflict, Yahya Khan ordered large scale mobilization in September. By October, 80 per cent of the Pak Army was massed along India's borders from Gujarat to Jammu and Kashmir. These moves clearly indicated that Pakistan was getting ready to launch a war. The Indian strategy at this time was to ensure the earliest possible return of refugees to their homes in the erstwhile East Bengal, to keep the defence forces ready to meet any contingency, and in the event of a war, to hold a defensive posture in the west and carry out swift operations in the east. The war strategy employed in East Pakistan was the achievement of air supremacy in the shortest possible time, a naval blockade in the south, multi-pronged thrusts by the Army from the west, north and east into East Pakistan, integration of Mukti Bahini operations, timing of the offensive and early seizure of Dacca.

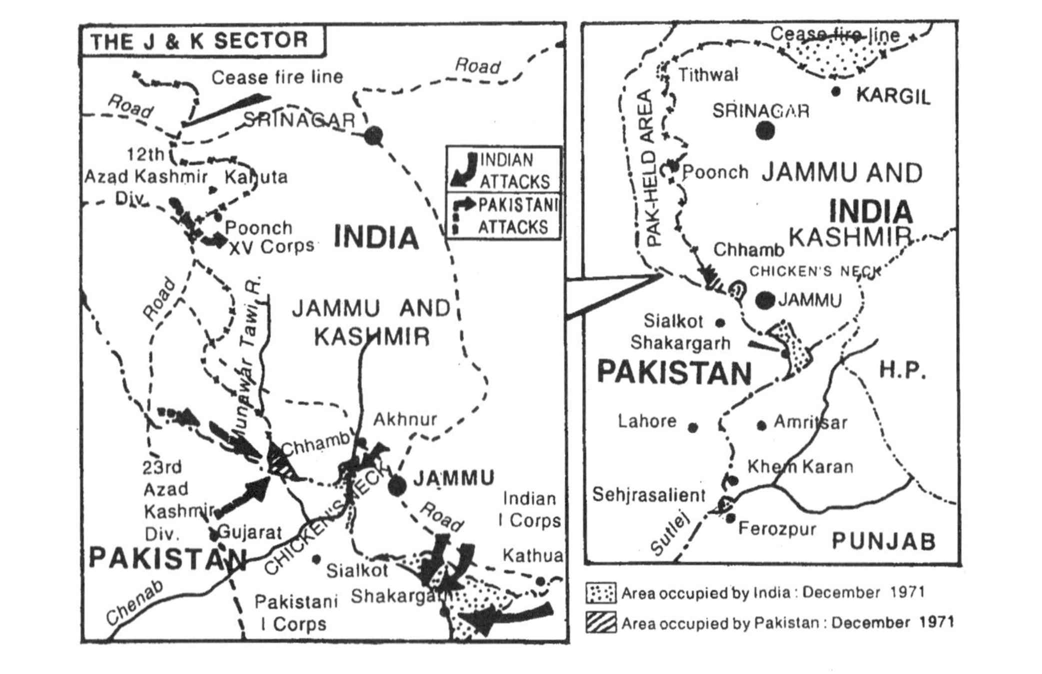

MAP 6: THE NORTHERN FRONT: DECEMBER 1971.

Yahya Khan's reaction to Indian support for the Mukti Bahini and the deployment of Indian forces in areas surrounding East Pakistan was to strengthen his Army in the Punjab, and embark on a repetition of threats to the Indian position in J&K. At 5.45 p.m. on 3 December, the Pakistan Air Force (PAF) made a number of ineffective attacks on seven Indian airfields in north-western India, thus providing the rationale for direct Indian intervention. Mrs Gandhi proclaimed a state of emergency because 'the war in Bangladesh has become a war on India'.[13]

The 1971 war was fought with speed and ferocity on both the eastern and western fronts. It is, however, outside the scope of this work to discuss these operations leading to the liberation of Bangladesh, except insofar as they relate to J&K, and particularly to Ladakh and Kargil.

THE WAR IN J&K

At the same time as it launched its air attacks, a force of two Pakistani brigades crossed the cease-fire line on 3 December and attacked Poonch with a view to capturing it and developing operations to secure all the territory up to the Pir Panjal range. The attack on Poonch failed after gaining some initial success on the approaches to the town. Subsequent Indian attempts to improve their defensive posture were also not successful.

On 3 December, Pakistani forces also attacked in the Chhamb sector and by 10 December they had succeeded in establishing a bridgehead across the Munawwar Tawi. However, vigorous counterattacks by Indian troops inflicted very heavy losses on the Pakistanis and they were thrown back across the river. The situation thereafter stabilized in this area. (As part of the Simla Agreement, India lost the territory west of the Munawwar Tawi.)

In order to eliminate any threat to Akhnur and Jammu town from the Pakistani salient known as 'Chicken's Neck', Indian forces attacked and captured it. In addition to this area, the Pakistani posts of Chhota Chak, Chumbian and Peeli were also captured, but under the Simla accord, all these areas were returned to Pakistan.

In the Ladakh and Kargil sectors India had, by 17 December, captured 36 Pakistani posts and secured about 110 sq. km of territory. These gains were retained. In the rest of J&K, local actions

[13] See note 1, pp. 53-80 and 81-100.

to improve the defensive posture were launched by both sides but these were not of much consequence. Details of the operations conducted in these two sectors are given below.

Ladakh and Kargil (3 Infantry Division)

The area opposite the Partapur sector was held by Pakistan with one company of Karakoram Scouts, who were later reinforced by one or two companies of mixed Karakoram and Gilgit Scouts. Pakistan had one wing of Karakoram Scouts reinforced by two additional companies in the Kargil sector. It later transpired that Pakistan had hastily mustered some reservists and pensioners to make up the manpower of some posts. The entire sector had about three 75 mm guns, a section of 3.7 inch howitzers and six 3 inch mortars. Most of these weapons were deployed singly for opportunity-firing. The Pakistani posts were held in varying strengths from a section upwards. The defences were well prepared and likely approaches were mined. Being located in inhospitable terrain, both sides vacated their posts in winter except for a minimum presence required for security. The Karakoram Scouts, a paramilitary organization, had a low defence potential, specially as they were ill-equipped with snow clothing to brave sub-zero temperatures.

One company of the Ladakh Scouts under Maj. Rinchen attacked and captured the posts of the Karakoram Scouts who were blocking the entrance to the Shyok valley under Pakistani occupation. He followed this up by advancing towards Turtok. Emboldened by his initial success, he collected resources and porters to rout the hastily retreating enemy in fine style. However, due to problems of maintenance in this terrain, Rinchen's advance had to be halted at Turtok. He had advanced about 20 km in all and captured several square kilometres of area.

In the Kargil sector, the Indian offensive to provide greater security to the Srinagar–Leh road opened with a two-pronged thrust on either side of the Shingo river. These thrusts were supported by two Vampire aircraft, a regiment of 120 mm mortars and a field battery. In spite of fierce resistance by the Pakistanis, Indian troops advanced systematically and cleared post after post. They again captured the critical heights of Point 13620 and Black Rocks which had been captured earlier in 1965 but were returned to Pakistan after the Tashkent agreement. By 17 December 1971, India had captured 36 Pakistani posts and secured about 110 sq. km of territory. It was significant that in these operations, India lost 2 officers and 2 JCOs (Junior Commissioned Officers) killed, 12 officers and JCOs wounded, 1 officer and 1 JCO missing, 7 officers and 6 JCOs frostbitten, while the only leadership casualty on the Pakistani side was a solitary JCO. Later, under the Simla Agreement, India retained its gains in Ladakh and Kargil.[14]

SIMLA SUMMIT

An Indo-Pak summit meeting was held at Simla on 28 June 1972 and an agreement was hammered out and signed on 2 July 1972. The significance of the Simla Summit lay in the fact that this meeting was aimed at laying down a fresh structure of peace in the subcontinent based upon the new and demonstrated power-realities in South Asia. With the signing of the Simla Agreement, the Karachi Agreement became defunct. The Cease-Fire Line gave way to the Line of Control (LoC), and India did not thereafter deal with UN observers in connection with Pakistan. Sector and subsector commanders dealt directly with Pakistani commanders, on a geographical basis, as under.[15]

1. Northern Sector: Dhulang Glacier to Keran.
2. Central Sector: Keran to Madarpur Bridge (Poonch sector).
3. Southern Sector: Madarpur Bridge to Chenab river.

The Line of Control (LoC)

The LoC came into being as a result of the Simla Agreement of 2 July 1972. It replaced the Cease-Fire Line established by the Karachi Agreement (1948). India sought this terminological change so as to deny the United Nations Military Observers Group for India and Pakistan (UNMOGIP) any future role in J&K by urging that the new LoC was distinct from the old Cease-Fire Line which UNMOGIP was charged with monitoring.

Clause 4 (ii) of the Simla Agreement states that:

> In Jammu and Kashmir, the line of control resulting from the cease-fire of December 17, 1971 shall be respected by both sides without prejudice to the recognized position of either side. Neither side shall seek to alter it unilaterally, irrespective of mutual differences and legal interpretations.

[14] Note 6, pp. 190-1.
[15] Ibid., p. 200.

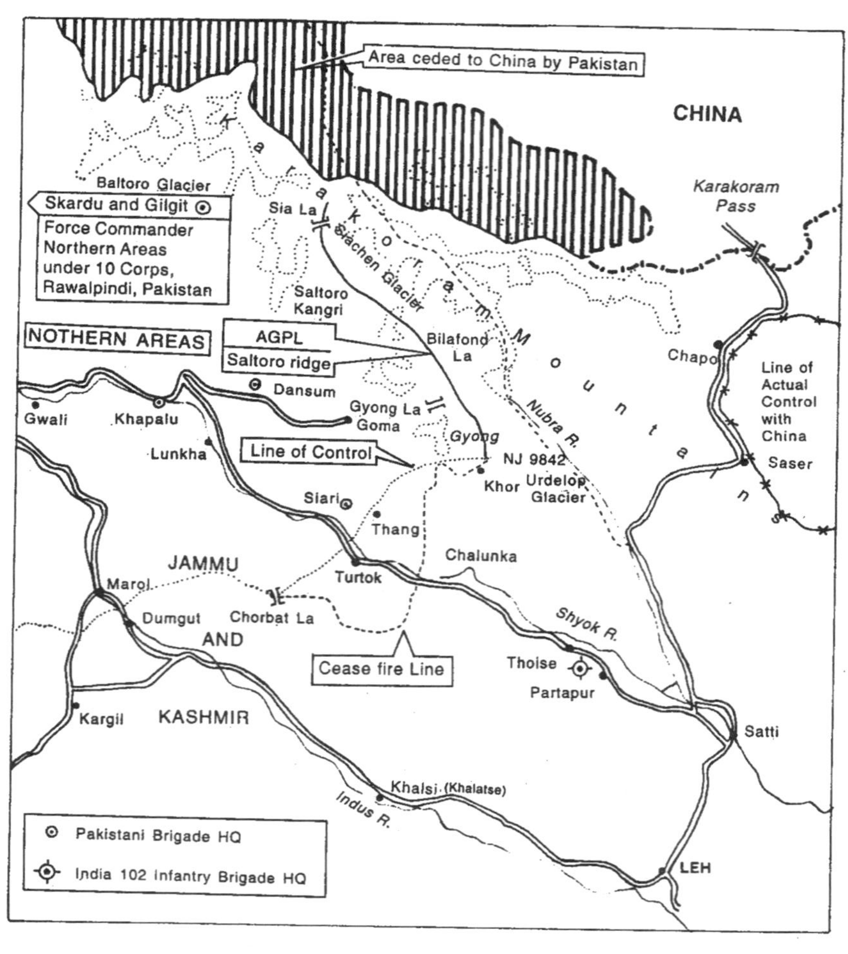

MAP 7: SKETCH OF THE AREA OF THE SIACHEN GLACIER.

Both sides further undertake to refrain from the threat or use of force in violation of the line.[16] [Pakistan has steadily eroded these provisions over the years by promoting militancy in Punjab and Kashmir.]

Army Headquarters of India and General HQ of Pakistan were given the responsibility for delineating the LoC as envisaged by the Simla Agreement. Their representatives (Lt. Gen. P.S. Bhagat for India and Lt. Gen. Abdul Hameed Khan for Pakistan) met on 10 August 1972. An agreement was quickly reached that it need only be re-demarcated in stretches where the old Cease-Fire Line was disturbed following the hostilities, and to demarcate it by recognizing the physical occupation of territory by both sides on the date when the hostilities ended, viz., 17 December 1971. Several problems, however, arose.

First, India linked its withdrawal of forces from across the international border to delineation of the LoC in Jammu and Kashmir. This was unacceptable to Pakistan, which argued that the Simla Agreement had separate clauses governing these distinct segments of the Indo-Pak border. However, on India's persistence, Pakistan finally conceded this demand.

Second, identification of the LoC became problematical in places like the Lipa valley in Tithwal sector where some posts changed hands after the cease-fire came into force.

Third, a breakdown of talks occurred on the Thako Chak issue. Pakistan captured this salient in the Jammu sector: a part lay across the international border and another across the Cease-Fire Line. The Simla Agreement required this minor salient to be divided between India and Pakistan. This seemed pointless to India, but became a matter of principle for Pakistan. Talks dragged on endlessly. Ultimately, India resolved this problem by compensating Pakistan elsewhere along the LoC.

Thus, the LoC resulting from these negotiations was inscribed on 19 mosaics and 27 maps and verbally described. These documents were signed by military officials of the two countries, and formally exchanged on 11 December 1972. The decision not to exchange captured territory and revert to the status quo ante as occurred under the Tashkent agreement had important military implications for both sides. India lost its enclave in the Chhamb sector across (west of) the Munawwar Tawi river, which provides Pakistan with a contiguous and formidable defence line along the obstacle. India

[16] Ibid., p. 203.

gained strategic territory across the Cease-Fire Line in Kargil to defend its communications between Srinagar and Leh, which was the scene of Pakistan's present aggression. Both sides, therefore, accepted the LoC with its military advantages and disadvantages.

The LoC's precise location is well recognized by usage. Sector commanders have resolved disputes pertaining to the LoC through flag meetings over the years. Pakistan's General Headquarters (i.e. Army) HQ knows all this. Hence, its assertion that 'the LoC has many areas where the interpretation of either side is not what the other side believes' reveals an easy propensity to verisimilitude that will make future negotiations with Pakistan very difficult. This specious logic could obviously apply to other segments of the LoC and convert it into a live and unstable border. Pakistan's disputation of the LoC in truth questions the Simla Agreement. By breaching its provisions Pakistan has exhibited aberrant international conduct.

As Brian Cloughley (a writer sympathetic to Pakistan), points out in his book on the Pakistan Army, the delineation of the Line of Control in Jammu and Kashmir resulting from the cease-fire of 17 December 1971 in accordance with the Simla Agreement of 2 July 1972 is an 'unambiguous' document. 'Its territorial precision is remarkable', writes Cloughley, whose book reflects the access granted to him by the Pakistani Army. According to Cloughley, it contains these descriptions:

> The Line of Control runs from NR 313861 to NR 316865, thence to NR 319867, thence EAST to NR 322868, thence NE to NR 331872, thence to a monument on ridge line at NR 336874 approximately 500 yards SE of point 10008 (NR 3387), thence to a point NR 338881 on the Nullah such that point NR 336874 and point NR 338881 are connected by a counter clockwise arc with a radius of 500 yards, thence NE to junction. . . .

Cloughley admits that the only point that was not precise was what happened after NJ 9842. At the time of delineation, Indian and Pakistani officers agreed that 'anyone who wanted to lay claim to ice and rocks was welcome to them'.[17]

CONSEQUENCES OF THE WAR

The 1971 war between India and Pakistan ended decisively in the east but not so in the west. The creation of Bangladesh freed

[17] Brian Cloughley, *A History of the Pakistan Army: Wars and Insurrections*, (Oxford University Press, Karachi, 1999), pp. 254-6.

Pakistan from a host of problems, including having to defend both its eastern and western wings. It was, however, no longer possible for Pakistan to tie down Indian forces in the eastern sector. So far as India was concerned, the new state caused some unanticipated problems, such as smuggling and immigration. Notwithstanding a period of contentious relationship, stable links are bound to emerge between Bangladesh and India in the long run. The attenuated size of Pakistan has made the Pakistani governments look increasingly towards Afghanistan since 1971. Resentment against India for its part in the 1971 war and the dismemberment of Pakistan reinforced long-held animosities and feelings of strategic vulnerability, which has fuelled its desire to acquire nuclear weapons.

India, in its largesse, did not want to seem to impose a solution of the J&K dispute on Pakistan. Consequently, the Simla Agreement of July 1972 left loopholes which Pakistan was quick to exploit. Tacit understandings are best recorded in definitive terms. This would perhaps have prevented the misery and bloodshed which the people of J&K had to face in subsequent years. On the other hand, there was no guarantee that a firmer accord would have buried the differences. A realization that the present status quo cannot be altered, would accrue with the efflux of time.

The Siachen Conflict

The seeds of the Siachen conflict lie in the 1949 and 1972 Indo-Pakistan agreements on delineation of the Cease-Fire Line and the Line of Control between the two countries. In both cases, the northernmost end of the military line was vague, since it was felt that neither country could send military forces into this area. Hence, the peace settlement separating the two armies was drawn up without any delineation northwards beyond a map reference point (NJ 9842), and was vaguely worded to the effect the line went thereafter 'northwards to the glaciers'.

Over the years, Pakistan interpreted this to its advantage to mean that the line continued in a generally north-east direction across the ranges and valleys to the Karakoram Pass on the frontier with China. They licensed international mountaineering expeditions to this region, which were accompanied by Pakistani personnel. In the early years of the 1980s, Indian mountaineers discovered evidence of these activities and they also learnt that Pakistan was buying special clothing and equipment in Europe with the aim of occupying this region. In a pre-emptive move, on 13 April 1984, the Indian Army occupied the Saltoro range (to the west of the Siachen glacier) of the Karakoram mountains.

Pakistan's objections were met with the logical argument that this was the natural watershed and their interpretation of the line was untenable as being impractical in that it ran against the grain of the country. The principle that the boundary runs along the watershed is important to India because this conforms to its reasoning with China in their border dispute. The Pakistani objection that occupation of the Saltoro range by Indian troops violates the proviso in the Simla Agreement prohibiting the use of force was rejected by India, and this led to several unsuccessful Pakistani attempts to dislodge the Indian troops occupying the watershed heights. Had India not occupied these heights, Pakistan was all set to do so with its army.

It needs to be noted here that an area north of the Saltoro range was seized by Pakistan in 1947-48 and subsequently ceded to China. This illegal transfer assuaged China's concerns to protect its lines of communication to Xinjiang, viz., the military road clandestinely constructed by China through the Aksai Chin which was one of the causes of the 1962 war between China and India. China recognizes this illegality because a clause was inserted in the treaty to the effect that the transfer was subject to renegotiation with the dominant power in the region in the future.[18] The Saltoro range and the Siachen glacier are linked to the area ceded, at their northern end. Hence, these areas are vital for India.

Pakistan is a de facto client of China and is linked to it through the Karakoram Highway. The capture of Ladakh will mean that they will be directly linked to China by much easier routes. The severing of the lines of communication to Leh in the area of Kargil would make it intolerably costly for India to maintain its military garrison in the Siachen sector.

[18] Lt. Col. Nandan Nilakanta, 'Tracing the Genesis of Operation Vijay', *The Hindu*, 13 July 1999.

3

The Kargil War

Maj. Gen. Ashok Krishna

General

This chapter deals with certain conceptual aspects of the Kargil war pertaining to Pakistan, the formulation of Pakistan's strategy for mounting insurgency and terrorism in J&K, and the Kargil aggression. Terrain analysis, the Pakistan Army's outline plans for the intrusions and India's determined response are included. It also covers the important battles fought in the area from Turtok in the north to Mushkoh in the south based on available inputs, as well as air and naval operations, and attempts to illuminate the heroism of the Indian officers and soldiers amid the smoke and flame of battle.

Pakistan's Concepts

Pakistan's overall strategic objective quite obviously remains unchanged since Zulfikar Ali Bhutto articulated it in a memorandum to FM Ayub Khan in the mid-1960s.[1] Pakistan's national survival and unity, said Bhutto, depended primarily on keeping India on the defensive and destabilizing it. Apart from agitating on bilateral issues like Kashmir, Pakistan's policy against India should be closely coordinated with China and countries like Nepal. Pakistan should also endeavour to cut off links to India's north-eastern states from mainland India. All this, Bhutto felt, would ensure the erosion of Indian power, dismemberment of its territory, and the consolidation of an anti-Indian geostrategic nexus. Nuclear blackmail now stands added to this list.

Pakistan's operational concepts have flowed from this objective

[1] 'Square up to Perfidy', *Indian Express*, 19 August 1999.

and have also been evolved from a deep fear that Indian hegemony aims at undoing the very concept of Pakistan. This perception may undergo change in future, but it has till now dictated its political and military strategy towards India based on fostering or supporting separatist movements, specially those of a religious nature, thereby creating a political-cum-social problem that would facilitate its military operations. In addition, it would attempt to internationalize the Kashmir issue to receive political, and covert and overt military support to achieve its aims. Hence, in Kashmir—and possibly Punjab—Pakistan will always do its utmost to psychologically subvert the population and materially encourage separatism.

The thinking in the higher echelons in the Pakistan Army is to regard tension, and strained relations with India, as economically and militarily beneficial, and, therefore, the creation of crisis situations, specially in the border areas of J&K, follows as a natural corollary. This is also reflected as a main theme in all its war games. The creation of communal disturbances in areas close to the border is an addition since 1988.

Under these conditions, Pakistan's political aim, as assessed, continues to be to capture maximum territory in J&K with the ultimate aim of merging the state into Pakistan. It feels that, regardless of all other considerations, being a predominantly Muslim-inhabited state, it should have gone to Pakistan at the time of the partition of the subcontinent in 1947, and that India is illegally occupying a part of the state. Consequently, its military aim (as derived from the foregoing) is: to capture maximum territory in J&K and elsewhere along the Indo-Pak border; to isolate the state from the rest of India; and be in a position of advantage to bargain to settle issues subsequently. In doing so, it must not lose any territory of significance to India.

Pakistan's highest ground force's headquarters is their General Headquarters (GHQ) located at Rawalpindi. It acts as a static, coordinating and resources-allocating HQ to lower formations depending upon the overall tactical situation in the country. The Pakistan Air Force (PAF) and Pakistan Navy (PN) join at the GHQ's level to coordinate and allocate their resources to support the Army's plan. It is seldom that the PAF or PN are allowed to dictate or formulate their overall plan at the national level, presumably due to the vast differences in the strengths of these two services compared with that of the Pakistan Army. Thus, they merely contribute to the overall plan conceived by the GHQ. It will, therefore, not be wrong to deduce that Pakistan's ground forces' operations dictate their national strategy for the conduct of aggression against India.

The Pak Army views with concern any action that would diminish its prime importance in Pakistan. Its officers have acquired land, property and business assets over the years, and they control most aspects of civil life in Pakistan. If Indo-Pak hostility were to reduce, so would their importance. This explains the escalated firing that has always coincided with every high-level bilateral political exchange between India and Pakistan.

All Pakistani operations against India have been conceived and launched on the basis of one common assumption: that the Indians are too cowardly and ill-organized to offer any effective military response which could pose a threat to Pakistan. The 1947-48, 1965 and 1971 wars were started on this premise (and so was Kargil).[2] The above concepts, aims and facts are well known to India, though it cannot be said that, in the last five decades, Indian governments in power have taken adequate measures to counter Pakistan, or to adequately prepare the Armed Forces and paramilitary and police forces to deter the adversary.

Formulation of Pakistani Strategy under Gen. Zia

Gen. Zia-ul-Haq, upon becoming the President in 1977, redirected the discourse of Pakistan's politics by using the Islamic metaphor with a new vigour with the object of Islamizing the polity, society, and economy. He was emphatic and persistent that Pakistan was an ideological state. These Islamization policies of the Zia regime not only consolidated the influence of religious groups, quite disproportionate to their actual strength on the ground, but also the authority vested in religious institutions both in terms of value orientation and social control. Under the Zia regime, the military expanded its role in the civilian sectors. The successful conduct of the Afghan resistance movement by the ISI (Inter-Services Intelligence) against the Soviets led to its politicization and it became assertive in defining how politics should be managed and controlled in Pakistan.

Zia was successful in consolidating a new ruling coalition of religious groups, trader-merchants, industrial groups and feudals. In the military and bureaucracy, he encouraged the advancement of

[2] 'Kargil Intrusion was Scripted in 1987', *Times of India*, 13 August 1999.

like-minded officers. At the institutional level, he sought to inoculate Islamic values among the young officers [See Appendix 4]. As a ruler, however, Zia failed to promote the politics of consensus building. He left Pakistan turbulent and rife with sectarian and ethnic tensions. Political parties were left weak and divided. In such a divided polity, the military was not merely the hegemon, but also the only institution that had grown, expanded and emerged as the arbiter in defining power relations among various contending power groups.

Pakistan's retaliatory impulse against India came to the fore after 1971 when it started developing nuclear weapons, which it finally acquired by 1987. The Afghan crisis erupted in the late 1970s and this gave Pakistan the opportunity to play the role of a front-line state against the spread of Soviet influence into West Asia. In the process, it received massive consignments of American arms for the mujahideen (freedom fighters), but these did not reach them in full. About 40 to 50 per cent of the weapons were stored in Islamabad and Rawalpindi for use in the Punjab and J&K at the opportune time in future.

Ever since its inception in 1949, the ISI has been working for the dismemberment of India. Pakistan is not comfortable with an India seven times its size and would like India's northern, eastern and southern wings to be severed, so that what remains of India approximates Pakistan's size. Prior to 1971, the ISI aided and abetted insurgencies in eastern India, and, in the post-1971 period, it enlarged its activities to encompass Punjab and J&K and later Tamil Nadu. [For further details about the ISI and its goals, see Appendix 4.]

The Situation in Kashmir

As early as 1982, almost immediately after Sheikh Abdullah's death, Gen. Zia had initiated a plan to train Kashmiri youth to launch an 'armed crusade' in the Valley. But it did not meet with much success and it was not until the mid-1980s that the plan was revived. Gen. Zia's official stand towards India on Kashmir was openly conciliatory:

> 'Pakistan's point of view is: let us talk. You can claim the whole of Kashmir,' he said in an interview with Indian journalist Rajendra Sareen in 1983. 'But may be there is a via media. So let us talk at least. We are not in favour of resorting to force. But we are not in favour of being browbeaten by the

Indian point of view that since there is a Line of Control, there is therefore no issue involved.'[3]

Almost at the same time, India made some serious mistakes in J&K. The dismissal of the Farooq Abdullah government in 1984, and the installation of a defectors' government under G.M. Shah was a most unpopular measure. Although Mrs Gandhi's assassination in October 1984 removed the architect of Farooq's dismissal, the memory of betrayal remained, not necessarily because of what happened to Farooq Abdullah, but because of what his dismissal signified for Kashmir.

Instead of ordering fresh elections in the state, Rajiv Gandhi insisted on a National Conference–Congress alliance. This time Farooq Abdullah, who had spurned the alliance with Mrs Gandhi five years earlier, agreed, because he felt Kashmir would never prosper unless he had the backing of Delhi. In November 1986, Rajiv reappointed Farooq as Chief Minister. The election was scheduled for the following year. Overnight, Farooq was transferred from hero to traitor in the Kashmiri mind. He was charged with betraying his father's legacy of pride. There was now a vacuum where the National Conference had existed, and extremists stepped into it. *Kashmiriyat* or Kashmiri way of life (a secular outlook characterised by lack of bigotry, and above all, generosity in the spiritual sense) had become vulnerable to the votaries of violence and Muslim hegemony, both injuring Kashmir and perverting *Kashmiriyat*. Abdullah was to later admit that the 1986 alliance was his most serious political mistake.

The accord with Rajiv Gandhi, the 1987 elections, the alleged corruption of his government, and subsequent inability to control the situation had all lost Abdullah popular support. There was an alienation of the people because funds for development were not reaching the grass-roots level. Irresponsible talk about abrogation of Article 370 led to more dissatisfaction. Under these circumstances, Governor Jagmohan dissolved the State Legislative Assembly in February 1989. It was not realized that by dismissing the government, even friendly parties like the National Conference would be alienated. By strengthening the duly elected government, which had more than three years to go, the problem could have been dealt with more effectively. Thus, Kashmir may not have been an issue if the Valley had not exploded on its own due to Delhi's misguided policies. As the

[3] Victoria Schofield, *Kashmir in the Crossfire* (Viva Books, New Delhi, 1997), pp. 234-5.

decade of the 1980s drew to a close, the Valley of Kashmir became 'the explosive situation' of which Sheikh Abdullah had so often warned.[4]

THE FORMULATION OF PAKISTAN'S STRATEGY FOR J&K

Pakistan could not be unaware of events in the Valley. It was a tempting scenario, another chance to make up for the failures of 1947 and 1965, coupled with the desire to take revenge for the loss of Bangladesh in 1971.

In 1984, Pakistan was pre-empted in Siachen, and at about the same time, a Movement for the Restoration of Democracy (MRD) headed by Benazir Bhutto was launched in Pakistan directed against Gen. Zia's military dictatorship. To divert attention from this military setback and domestic problems, Zia chalked out a strategy to create trouble in Punjab and J&K. Although Zia planned the strategy for insurgency in J&K in 1985, it could not be put into operation then as Pakistan was deeply engaged in Afghanistan and its soldiers were fighting side by side with the mujahideen. But before Zia was killed in a plane crash at Bahawalpur on 17 August 1988, he had set his plan in motion, and it continued unimpeded under the new administration of Benazir Bhutto. It is estimated that about 15,000-20,000 persons exfiltrated from J&K to POK/Pakistan for arms training in 1987-8.

One of India's top defence specialists, K. Subrahmanyam, maintained that Operation Topac named after Topac Amin, an Inca prince, who fought a non-conventional war against Spanish rule in eighteenth-century Uruguay, was planned in Pakistan in April 1988 to nurture an indigenous insurgency. Published in the *Indian Defence Review* of July 1989, including reports of alleged instructions from Gen. Zia to his army officers, Topac was denied by the Pakistani authorities. They alleged that it was an invention by the Research and Analysis Wing (RAW) of the Government of India. But subsequent events were to prove beyond doubt that Operation Topac was very much a reality, and the insurgency in J&K had its origins in Pakistan.

The aim of the operation was to annex the state of J&K through a proxy war by infiltrating militants to foment trouble in the state under the garb of a jihad, take militancy to uncontrollable levels, and at an opportune time, strike with regulars, if necessary, to finally integrate J&K with Pakistan. Broadly, the first phase of Operation

[4] Ibid.

Topac involved indoctrination of army personnel and militants; the second, sabotage by fifth columnists; and the third, a major thrust by the Pak Army to consolidate.

The essence of the detailed plan could be summarized as follows.

1. Establishment of terrorist training centres and camps from where recruits would be regularly sent on jihad missions to J&K (and other parts of the world). Some 37 camps were set up in Pakistan and 49 in POK. In addition, there were 22 Pakistani-run terrorist camps in Afghanistan. These figures may vary marginally.
2. Chosen men were to be planted in key positions: they were to subvert the locals, the police forces, financial institutions, the communications network and other important organizations. Sabotage was to be carried out by fifth columnists. Anti-Indian feelings were to be whipped up among students and peasants, preferably on religious issues. Pakistan was to achieve some success in its endeavours before the people became disenchanted with the militants. They did succeed by the mid-1990s in subverting an element of the Shia population in the Dras-Kargil area, as also some Buddhists in the Turtok area.
3. The campaign was to start as a low-level insurgency against the J&K regime, so that it came under siege, but did not collapse, resulting in the imposition of President's Rule. The intention was then to inspire a popular uprising against India by inducting trained militants belonging to fundamentalist Muslim organizations. Kashmiri youth were to be enticed with money and false promises to go to Pakistan for training and induction. The Pak Army had contacted the J&K Liberation Front (JKLF), which agreed to cooperate on the condition that Kashmir would be granted independence soon after Indian control ceased over the state.
4. The next step was to organize and train subversive elements and armed groups with capabilities to deal with the police forces located in the Valley.
5. Further, an endeavour would be made to cut off lines of communication between Jammu and Srinagar and within the Valley and Ladakh by stealth, without recourse to force. The road over Zoji La up to Kargil was to receive special attention.
6. Furthermore, to carry out ethnic cleansing of Hindus and Sikhs along the spine of the Pir Pinjal range and in the Valley and also Jammu.

7. Establish virtual control in those parts of Kashmir Valley where the Indian Army was not located.

The next phase was designed to exert pressure on Siachen, Kargil, Rajouri and Poonch sectors and force the Indian Army to deploy reserve formations outside the main Kashmir Valley. In the third and final phase, detailed plans for the involvement of the military were to follow.

Here there is a need for a correct understanding of the term 'jihad'. One does not find the word in the Koran in the sense it is being used, i.e. 'holy war'.[5] The word in the Koran for war is '*qital*'. 'Jihad', in its literal sense, means 'to strive, to assert or to make efforts'. In Koranic terminology, it means 'to assert oneself or to make efforts to promote what is right and prohibit what is evil'. In the Koran, *qital* is permitted against persecution and to establish justice, not for territorial aggrandizement. Even if the word 'jihad' is used, it is for the defence of the faith and not for the annexation of territory or to solve territorial disputes. Also, to kill innocent civilians as the extremists are doing in J&K, cannot be defined as jihad: it is against all principles of Islam. Kashmir is a territorial dispute to be resolved between India and Pakistan and there is no question of religious persecution. The Kashmiris have fought against the intruders from Pakistan and checked their further advance. It is really ironical that the intruders are described as 'mujahideen' (i.e. those waging a jihad). Are they defending Islam in Kargil? In fact, the people most affected by jihad are the Muslims. Relentless shelling in Kargil and other places has destroyed their homes and hearths.

The Pakistani plan for insurgency did meet with a measure of success in the initial stages. Pro-Pakistan supporters celebrated Pakistan's Independence Day on 14 August 1988, but India's Independence Day on 15 August was called a 'Black Day'. On 27 October 1988—the anniversary of India's airlift into Srinagar in 1947—there was a complete strike due to what the protesters were now calling 'Occupation Day'. Whereas in 1947, the Pakistanis were deemed to be 'invaders' whilst the Indians were greeted as 'liberators', by 1988 these roles had been psychologically reversed in the minds of the militants. The insurgency continued to gain in intensity till 1992. In a mass exodus, the Hindus left the Valley for camps located around Jammu and in Delhi.

As insurgency picked up, the Pak Army engineered a split in the

[5] 'Pakistan, Jehad and Ethnicity', *The Hindu*, 24 August 1999.

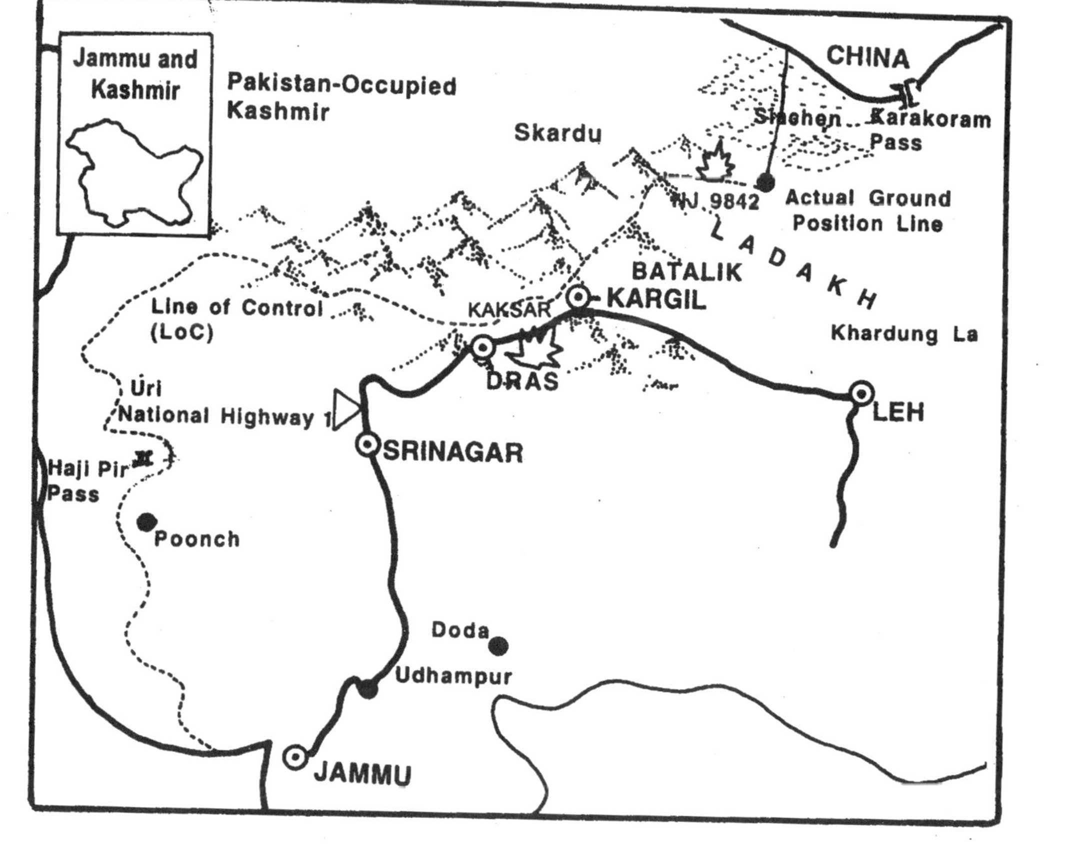

MAP 8: OVERVIEW OF THE AREA OF THE KARGIL WAR.

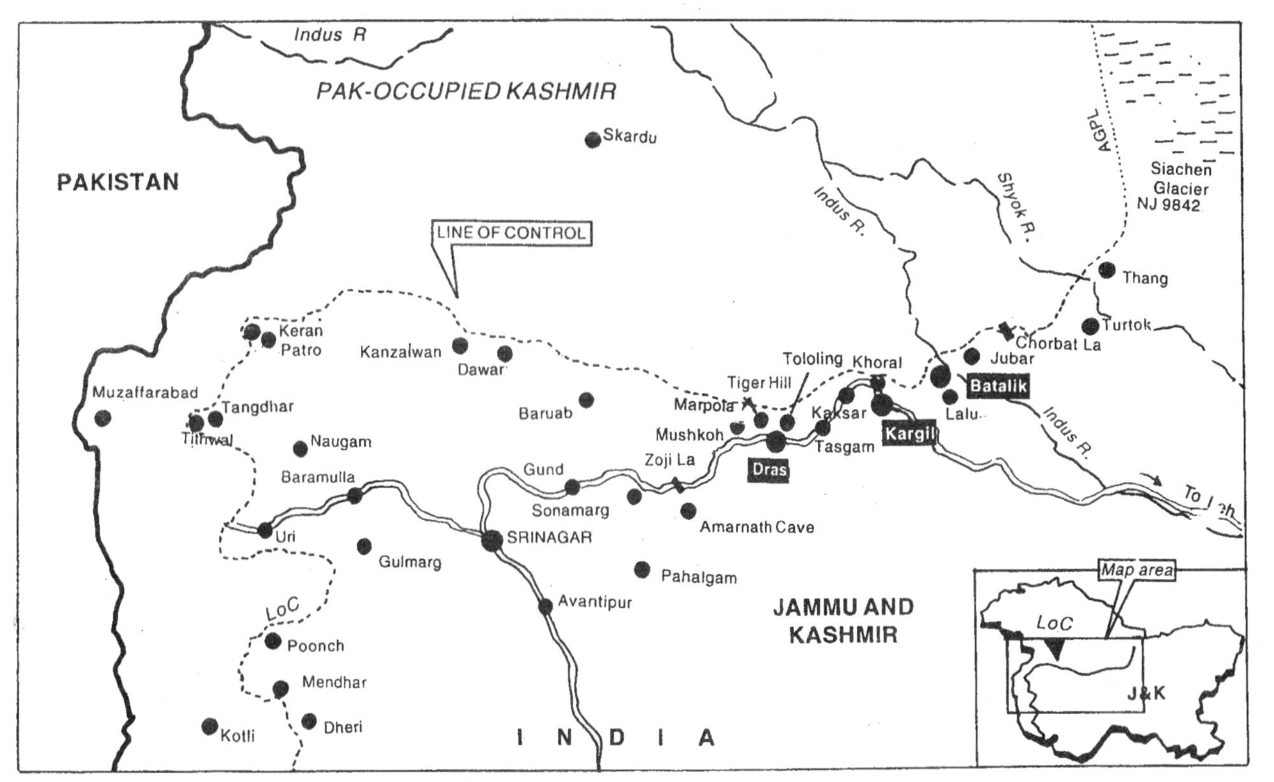

MAP 9: ANOTHER OVERVIEW OF THE AREA OF THE WAR.

JKLF, and went back on its commitment to an independent Kashmir. The control of anti-Indian operations later passed on to pro-Pakistan elements which made it a pro-Islamic movement and raised the slogan of Kashmir's accession to Pakistan. The Kashmiri youth saw through Pakistan's deceit and disassociated themselves from it. It was the population of J&K, imbued as it has always been with the spirit of *Kashmiriyat*, that defeated Pakistan's plans. By 1997, the situation was well under control to enable the Government to hold elections.

Operation Topac was effectively foiled through a well-orchestrated and synergized effort by the Indian security forces. Consequently, the militancy lost its steam on account of heavy attrition inflicted on various militant outfits. Since 1990, 8,253 militants have been killed and 23,357 weapons recovered. In 1999 alone (till July), 464 militants were killed and 789 weapons recovered from them.

May 1998 saw the nuclear tests and pressure on both India and Pakistan not to escalate tension. Some Indian defence analysts believed that nuclear weapons would preclude a conventional war and lead to settlement of the J&K issue along the existing LoC. In the last two or three years, it had become clear to Pakistan that, in the part of J&K with India, a mere 5 per cent of the population wanted to join Pakistan, the rest would opt for autonomy within the Indian Union. What was worse for Pakistan was that the Kashmiris in Pak-Occupied Kashmir (POK), having been denied political and economic freedom for fifty years, wanted to break loose.

Thus, the Pakistan Army had to do something quickly to redress the situation. It consequently shifted to a military approach. The essence of this strategy was to use the Pak Army to occupy important heights in the Dras–Kargil–Batalik–Turtok area and thus cut off the Ladakh division and the Siachen brigade. It was calculated that this critical situation would force the Indian Army to divert troops from the Valley and elsewhere in J&K to meet the challenge. This would enable Pakistan to induct some 2,000 to 3,000 mercenaries all over J&K and whip up a fresh wave of insurgency. Initial success would provide the impetus for the Pak Army to breach the LoC at other points. The overly stretched Indian security forces, unable to thwart this two-pronged invasion, would continue to lose control and Pakistan would be able to internationalize the J&K issue.

Altaf Gauhar, the once-powerful Information Secretary to President Ayub Khan in the 1960s, writes in the *Nation* that the Kargil intrusions were first authorized by Gen. Zia-ul-Haq (along with

Operation Topac) in 1987.[6] But at the formal war committee meeting at which Zia was to approve the Kargil plan, then Foreign Minister Gen. (retd.) Sahibzada Yakub Khan opposed it on the plea that as a former general he knew the posts that Pakistani soldiers would occupy: these were totally covered with snow almost throughout the year and it would be extremely difficult to have communications with them and meet their day-to-day needs. He said some soldiers had died there and they remained untraced so far.

Second, he said, as the Foreign Minister he would find it extremely difficult to justify the Pak military action. According to Altaf Gauhar, Gen. Zia was impressed by this assessment and decided to shelve this plan. As per a *Nawa-i-Waqt* story, this plan was revived and placed before Mr Nawaz Sharif, but the then Army Chief Gen. Jahangir Karamat was not willing to endorse it. Whether or not this was one of the reasons for his 'resignation' in October 1998 is not clear, because there was the larger issue of his suggesting the setting up of a national security council that would give the Army a greater say in the running of the government, which Sharif could not countenance.

Altaf Gauhar states that the same plan was put up before Mr Sharif in 1998 (after Gen. Pervez Musharraf took over as COAS on 7 October) assuring him that the Indians were totally unaware of the strategy and would not be able to offer any adequate response to the Pak offensive. Through this operation, he was told, he would have a military victory to his credit after his courageous decision to explode the nuclear bomb despite international pressure, Gauhar writes. It is believed Sharif gave the go-ahead to this plan before signing the Lahore Declaration with his Indian counterpart in February 1999. 'The assumption that the Indians would not offer an effective military response turned out to be a complete hoax', he writes. Mr Sharif's government just looked on helplessly 'while the soldiers were starving on the heights of Kargil and we did not have enough fuel to carry on the war'.

Terrain Analysis

The Kargil war encompassed the area from Turtok in the north to the Mushkoh valley in the south [see Maps 8 to 14 and particularly Maps 11 and 12]. Important aspects pertaining to the terrain are analysed below.[7]

[6] 'Kargil Intrusion was Scripted in 1987', *Times of India*, 13 August 1999.

[7] The maps illustrating the sphere of operations outlined in this chapter have been taken from the web-site http://armedforces.nic.in/kargil/armyupdate.htm

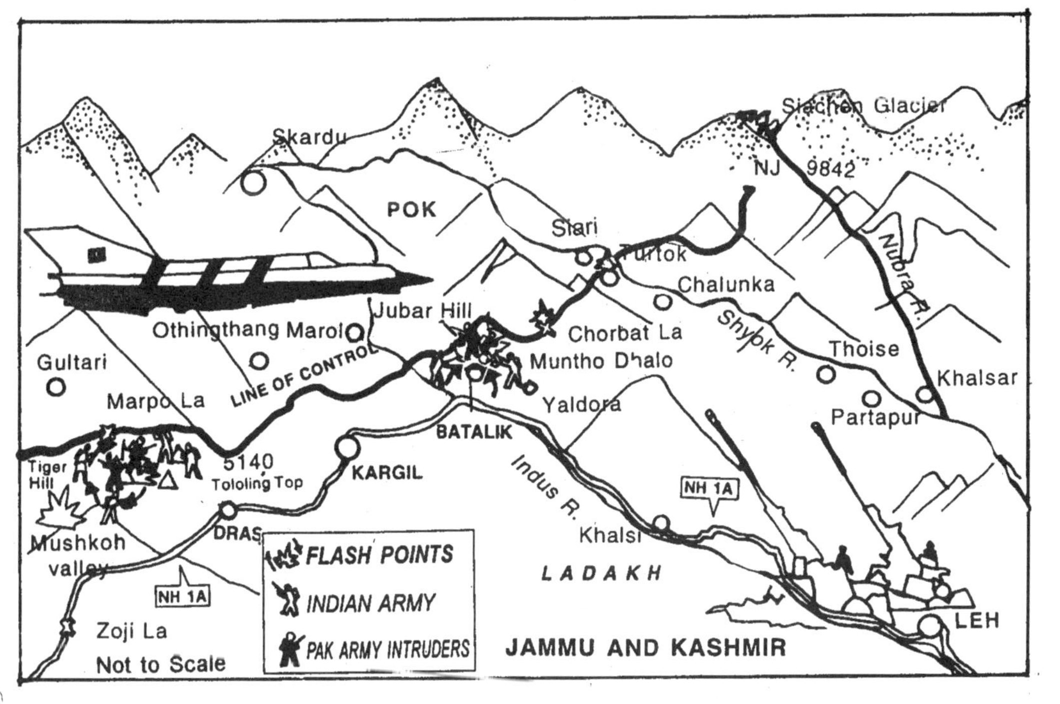

MAP 10: FLASH POINTS.

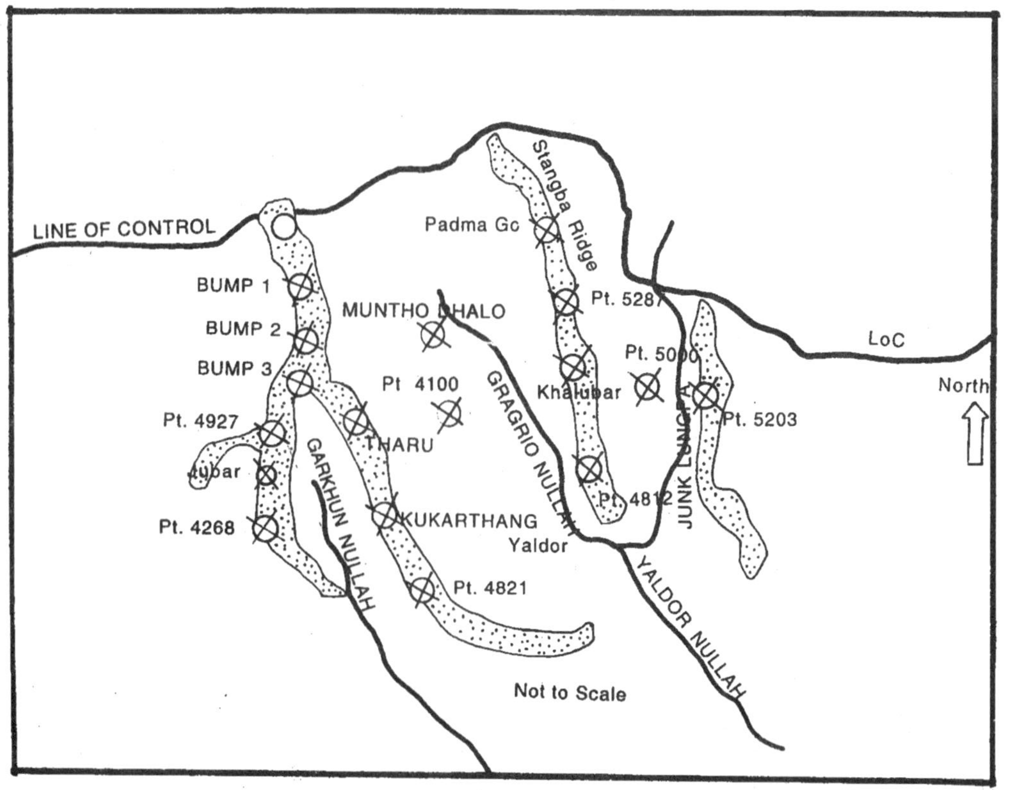

MAP 11: THE BATALIK SECTOR.

Turtok

Turtok lies on the Shyok river and has a population of about 1,500. The last Indian post beyond Turtok is at Thang and beyond it is the village of Prahnu in POK. While other sectors of the conflict are approachable from the Srinagar–Leh highway, to reach Turtok Indian troops have to travel up to Leh from where they are trans–ported across the 18,380 ft (5,800 m) high Khardung La (pass). Thereafter, the route lies along the Shyok valley. Over two-thirds of the route to Turtok is the same as that for Siachen. Any Pakistani advance up the Shyok valley would put pressure on the flanks of the route to Siachen and make the 3,000 m high Thoise airbase vulnerable. Furthermore, it would open up the approaches to Leh.

Chorbat La

Leh is connected with Skardu by a road running along the banks of the Indus. During the summer months, due to melting of the snows, the waters of the Indus flood its banks, hence travellers generally preferred ascending the heights as far as Chorbat La 17,000 ft (5,200 m) and then descending towards Skardu. The Baltis who carried dried apricots, which were in great demand in Ladakh and Tibet, frequently traversed this route. Zorawar Singh took the Chorbat La route when he conquered Baltistan in 1839-40.[8]

Access to Chorbat La from the Indian side lies along the Hanuthang valley which leads up from Hanuthang to Handangbrok to Gol Tekri and then to Chorbat La. The valley is drained by the Hanu Lungpa. The area of Chorbat La is part of the Batalik sector for operational purposes.

Batalik

This sector lies to the north of the Indus River. Important villages along the river, from east to west, are Dah, Garkhun, Urdas and Batalik on the Indian side, and Marol on the Pakistani side. Marol is situated on the junction of the Shingo and Indus rivers.

On the Indian side, three major *nullahs* (streams) draining south from the LoC broadly dissect the sector. The farthest to the west is

[8] C.L. Datta, *Ladakh and Western Himalayan Politics: 1819-1848* (Munshiram Manoharlal, New Delhi, 1973), pp. 11-12.

the Grugurda, in the centre is the Garkhun Nullah, and in the east the Yaldor Nullah which draws its waters from two mountain streams coming from the north-west (Yaldor West or Gragrio Nullah) and the other from the north-east (Yaldor East or Junk Lungpa), both joining at Yaldor village in a Y-shaped layout. These three streams join the Indus at Batalik, Garkhun and Dah respectively. A minor drain, the Urdas Langpa, lies between the Grugurda and Garkhun Nullahs. The Grugurda descends from the Pakistani position at Shangruti Top (5,343 m) from where almost the entire area can be observed.

The Jubar hills rise to the west of the Garkhun Nullah and comprise the features Point 4268, Jubar (4,924 m), and Point 4927. To the east of the Garkhun Nullah are the heights of Point 4821, Kukarthang and Tharu. These two ridges merge at Bump 3; thereafter one main ridge line continues towards the LoC. Important features on this ridge are Bump 2 and Bump 1.

Running north from Yaldor village, between Gragrio Nullah and Junk Lungpa is the Stangba ridge on which Point 4812, Khalubar, Point 5287 and Padma Go are located. Point 4100 and Muntho Dhalo lie on the western side of this ridge, across Gragrio Nullah. Point 5000 is located on a ridge to the east of the Khalubar ridge. To its east is Junk Lungpa and to the east of this stream is another ridge line on which Point 5203 is situated.

Batalik's ridges are less steep from the Pakistani side, an advantage that helped the intruders breach the LoC and occupy heights at 16,000 to 18,000 ft (4850 to 5480 m) without their movement being noticed. On the Indian side, these positions had to be approached from heights of 10,000 to 12,000 ft (3500 to 3650 m), a Herculean task entailing massive logistics.

Kargil

Kargil town lies at the junction of the Shingo and Suru rivers. Going northwards from Kargil along the Shingo, one comes to the villages of Gangam, Bielargo, Olthingthang and Marol; all of them lie on the Pakistani side of the LoC and were used as logistics bases. Beyond Marol is a well-developed road, which follows the course of the Indus to Skardu.

Point 4151 (also known as Point 13620) dominates Kargil town; it lies 4 km north east of Kargil and about 3 km from the LoC on the Indian side. It is the key to the town's safety from Pakistani guns: artillery observers located here can dominate the entire area on the

Indian side. Likewise, Indian artillery observers can watch deep into Pakistan enabling their detachments to fire on Pakistani targets, including the Pakistani base at Olthingthang. This height was captured by India in the 1965 war, but after the Tashkent agreement, it was returned to Pakistan. Indian troops recaptured it in 1971.

Kaksar

To the west of Kargil at a distance of approximately 30 km is the village of Kaksar. It is located on the southern bank of the Shingo river. Point 5299 dominates Kaksar, which is near the LoC. Other dominating heights in the area are Points 5108 and 4000; the former lies due west of Kaksar on the LoC. There are no clear ridge line routes to these features.

Dras

The Dras sector is dominated by the Tololing heights to the north and the Tiger Hill complex to the north-west. The two are separated by the Sando nullah. The Tololing complex virtually sits on the Srinagar–Leh highway. One can observe all movement on the road with a pair of binoculars. The Tololing ridge lies to the north of Tololing village. The main heights on the Tololing ridge are Point 4590 (lower summit) and Point 5140 (the highest point). Spurs from this complex reach behind Kaksar. Between this ridge and Sando nullah to the west, there is another complex of hills. Important heights in this area are Knoll, Three Pimples, Lone Hill and Point 4700.

The Tiger Hill complex is divided into two by the Tingel nullah. To the *nullah's* north-east is the ridge on which Tiger Hill and Helmet are located, and to its west is the ridge leading to Point 4875. Tiger Hill is a single peak dominating the Srinagar–Leh highway from where accurate artillery fire can be directed. It is not the highest peak in the area; at 4,965 m, it is 175 m lower than Point 5140, the tallest peak. It stands all alone and rises steeply into a conical shape with few spurs or ridges on either side. Tiger Hill is a very difficult objective to assault. A few men sitting atop the peak can hold much larger forces at bay.

A track running along the Sando Nullah goes right up to Marpo La on the LoC. Beyond, on the Pakistani side, is the road to Gultari, one of their important bases. Tracks from Gultari lead to Faranshat (in POK) and on to Shaqma.

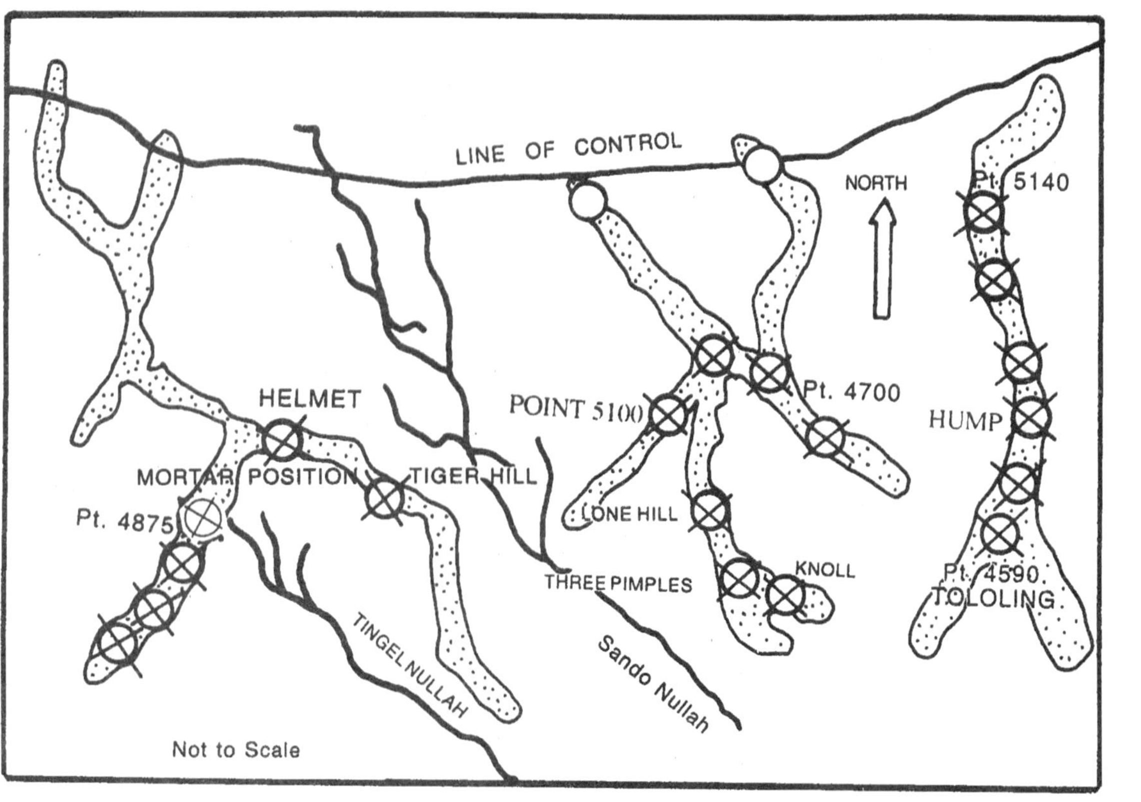

MAP 12: THE DRAS SECTOR.

Mushkoh Valley

From the Pak side the Mushkoh valley is reached through the 5,353 m high Marpola Pass. There is no other pass in the vicinity, hence, control of this pass cuts off access to the Mushkoh valley. At its western end, the Mushkoh valley empties through the Kaobal Gali and the Tillel valley into Gurais. Spurs from Tiger Hill dominate the Mushkoh valley.

The Kargil sector over which the Indian 121 Infantry Brigade (of 3 Infantry Division) had jurisdiction extended over a frontage of 168 km from Kaobal Gali to Chorbat La. (This brigade at the time of the intrusions was commanded by Brig. Surinder Singh.)

Pakistan Army's Plan for the Kargil Intrusions (Operation Badr)

GENERAL

The genesis of the Kargil war lies in Pakistan's repeated failures to annex J&K. Conventional wars, fifteen years of fighting in Siachen and twelve years of militancy had led to exasperation.[9] In the period from 1995 onwards, militancy even in Kashmir Valley was on the decline and this was a cause of concern to the Pakistani political and military establishments.

AIMS

Strategic policy is a blend of aims and capabilities reacting with each other. Hence, Pakistan planned a big operation this time, to strike the Indian Army's centre of gravity in the northern part of Kashmir. Its strategic and diplomatic aim was to bring back the J&K issue into focus because global attention had been flagging, and draw India into a negotiating position wherein it would be forced to accept the international community as mediators and observers in the J&K dispute. Tactically and geostrategically, Pakistan thought that by choking the road to Leh and by turning the Indian defences, it would inflict a demoralizing reverse on the Indian Army, and by gaining territory and freezing the situation it would erode the concept of the LoC and the Simla Agreement. Thus emboldened, it would be able

[9] The narrative of the operations in Kargil is based on media reports, briefings and interviews, with additional inputs from web-sites http://www.vijayinkargil.org/features/feature5.html and armedforces.nic.in/kargil/armyupdate2.htm

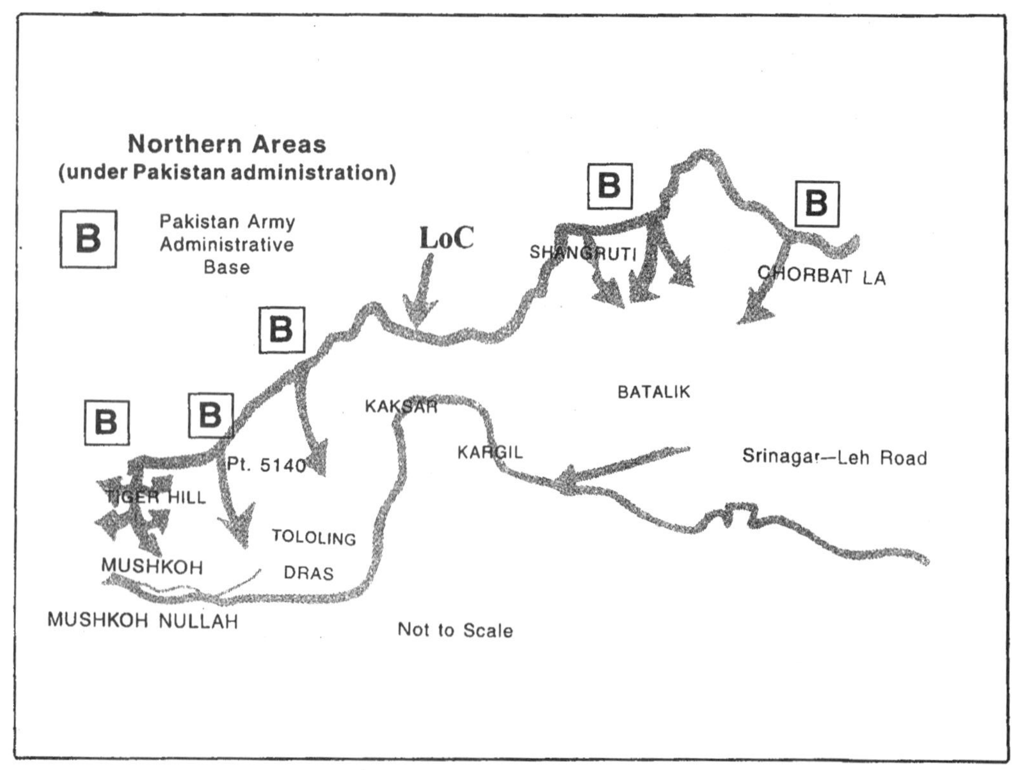

MAP 13: PAKISTAN ARMY PLAN FOR INTRUSION.

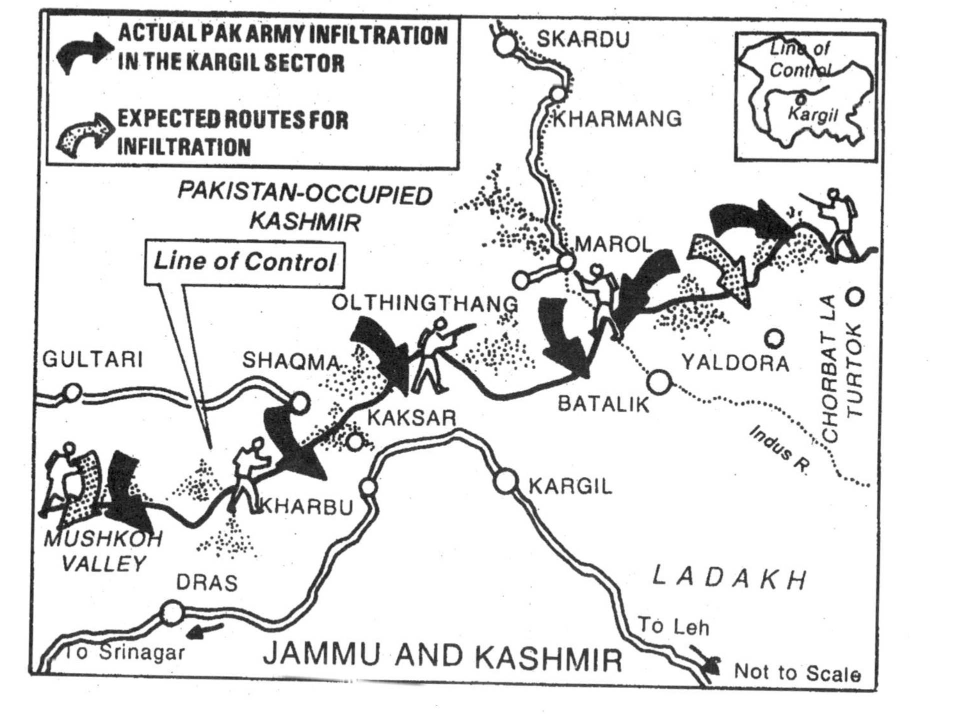

MAP 14: PAKISTAN ARMY INFILTRATION.

to repeat its tactics elsewhere in J&K, and combine aggression with large-scale infiltration and militancy.

OBJECTIVES

In specific terms, Pakistan's offensive had five main objectives, as follows.

1. Choke the strategic road linking Srinagar with Leh and prevent vital supplies for the ensuing winter reaching Indian troops in Ladakh.
2. Occupy Dras and Kargil and open up the LoC issue.
3. Capture heights in the Batalik and Turtok areas to initially sever the southern Siachen Glacier, and later, choke access to both the northern and southern glaciers along the Nubra river, and force India to back down on Siachen.
4. Control the Mushkoh valley near Dras and use it as a major route for fresh infiltration.
5. Spread insurgency in Kargil district of Ladakh to ease the heat unleashed on militant groups in the Valley.
6. To bury the Simla Agreement by altering the LoC and bring the Kashmir issue back on the international stage.

PARAMETERS

The intrusion plan was reportedly the brainchild of Pakistan's Chief of Army Staff (COAS) Gen. Pervez Musharraf and Lt. Gen. Mohammed Aziz, Chief of the General Staff (CGS). They obtained an 'in principle' concurrence, probably without any specifics, from the Prime Minister, Nawaz Sharif. Recovered documents and recent intelligence inputs reveal that the following two essential parameters were laid down at the conceptual stage.

1. The plan was to be kept top secret. The very minimum number of persons were to have knowledge of it, and there was to be no unusual activity opposite Kargil, which might give away Pakistan's operational plans.
2. There had to be a cover plan to obfuscate the aggression to bring about a defusion of the situation in an early time frame. This brought in the façade of the 'mujahideen' and 'freedom fighters'.

With these terms of reference in mind, the plan evolved by the

Pakistan Army was reportedly kept confined to only their COAS, CGS, Director General of Military Operations (DGMO), GOC 10 Corps, and GOC Force Commander Northern Areas (FCNA) who was made overall in-charge of operations in the Kargil sector. The other corps commanders, who are normally taken into confidence, were not kept informed about the plan, its motives and its execution. This was to cost Pakistan dearly after the Indian response got under way. The genesis, motives and implementation of the plan have been substantiated by the taped telephonic conversation between Pakistan's COAS and CGS.

PREMISES

The plan was based on the following premises.

1. Exploitation of the large gaps that exist in the defences in the Kargil sector, both on the Indian and the Pak side of the LoC. The terrain is extremely rugged and there are few tracks leading from the main roads towards the LoC. During winter, the area gets heavy snowfall, making movement virtually impossible. To give an example, the gap in the Indian defences between Kaobal Gali and Mushkoh (Marpola) was 36 km, between Marpola and Bhimbat LC (north east of Dras on the LoC) 9.5 km, between Bhimbat LC and Kaksar 9 km, and between Kargil and Batalik 9.5 km. The gap between Batalik and Chorbat La was about 25 km, and a similar distance obtained in the defences between Chorbat La and Turtok. (These gaps had no force allocation. However, after 1993 when Pakistani-supported militants made an abortive bid to infiltrate through the Mushkoh valley, the Army had been allotting two additional battalions to 121 Infantry Brigade during the summer months, one each to patrol the gaps in the Mushkoh/ Dras and Batalik sectors.)
2. Zoji La Pass normally opens by the end of May or beginning of June. Movement of reinforcements by road from Srinagar is not possible till then. The Pakistan Army assessed that even if the intrusions were discovered in early May (as they were), the Indian Army's reaction would be slow and limited, thereby allowing time for the effective consolidation of territorial gains. In 1999, on account of the unseasonal melting of snow, Zoji La was opened for the induction of troops in early May itself.
3. The intrusions, if successful, would enable Pakistani troops

to secure a number of dominating heights from where the Srinagar–Leh National Highway 1A (NH 1A) could be interdicted at a number of places. The intrusions would naturally draw in and tie down the Indian Army reserves.

4. Pakistan would gain control over substantial tracts of strategic territory across the LoC, thereby enabling Islamabad to negotiate from a position of strength. The intrusions would irrevocably alter the status of the LoC.

SURPRISE AND DECEPTION

Apart from keeping the plan top secret, the Pakistan Army also undertook certain steps to maintain surprise and maximize deception. There was no induction of any new units or any fresh troops into the FCNA for the proposed operation: any large-scale induction of troops would have drawn the attention of the Indian Army. (Post-Kargil information, however indicates that Pakistan had increased the number of infantry battalions in the FCNA from 13 in 1998 to 15 in the period prior to the launching of Operation Badr. Two infantry battalions already part of FCNA were also moved up from rear locations during late 1998/early 1999.) Pakistan Army artillery units, which were inducted into the FCNA during the heavy exchange of fire across the LoC from July to September 1998, were not deinducted. Since the exchange of artillery fire continued thereafter, though on a lower scale, it did not arouse suspicion.

There was no movement of reserve formations or units into FCNA until after the Indian Army's response. No new administrative bases were created. Stocks were moved and stored from the existing defences. The logistic lines of communication were to follow ridge lines and *nullahs* well away from existing positions of the Indian Army.

OUTLINE PLAN

Simplicity was the keynote of the plan. Four independent groups were created from four Northern Light Infantry Battalions (for characteristics and organization see Appendix 5) and two companies of the Special Services Group (SSG), which were already located in the FCNA. These were:

1. 4 NLI Battalion, the FCNA reserve, located in Gilgit;
2. 6 NLI Battalion from 62 Infantry Brigade, located at Skardu;

3. 5 NLI Battalion from 82 Infantry Brigade, located at Minimarg; and
4. 3 NLI from 323 Infantry Brigade, located at Dansam.

(Scrutiny of various captured documents, interrogation reports and signals intelligence, however, indicate that the intrusion plan was initially based on 5 NLI from Hamzigund, 6 NLI from Buniyal, 8 and 12 NLI Battalions located at Skardu and Gultari respectively, and the fourth group had comprised elements of 3, 4, 7 and 11 NLI Battalions.)

Special Services Group (SSG)

Two companies of SSG were to be allotted in teams varying from thirty-two to ninety-four personnel among the groups.

Additional Resources

1. The groups were allotted shoulder-fired air defence missiles of the Stinger variety and ANZA anti-aircraft missiles. This, coupled with the 12.7 mm Air Defence (AD) machine guns integral to the NLI Battalions, gave them a modicum of air defence capability.
2. Puma and Lama (MI-17) helicopters.
3. Gas masks, Passive Night Vision Devices (PNVDs) and snow scooters.

Artillery Support

A total of eighteen to twenty batteries of the Pakistan Army's artillery in the area were to provide fire support to the intruding groups from Pakistan's side of the LoC. This ensured that each intrusion had the support of three to four batteries. Artillery Observation Post officers from the Pakistan Army's artillery corps with telephone and radio communication equipment were also grouped with the infiltrating troops.

Infiltration

The main groups were split into a number of smaller subgroups of thirty to forty each for carrying out multiple intrusions along the ridge lines and occupying dominating heights. To start with, the strength of the intrusions in the four main subsectors were:

1. Batalik: 250 approximately.
2. Kaksar: 100 approximately.
3. Dras: 250 approximately.
4. Mushkoh Nullah: 200-300 approximately.

(Various agencies have indicated that a total of 1,500 troops, both regular and irregular, were deployed. As per estimates of the Indian High Commission in Islamabad, about 1,700 NLI troops were deployed in Kargil. The Indian Army fought Pakistani regulars who were supported by some fighting porters.)

Logistics

Logistics support was carried out by personnel of the Bajaur and Chitral Scouts, who functioned as fighting porters, besides supplementing the posts suffering from deficiencies. The routes for supplies were along ridge lines and *nullahs*. Build up forward of main bases, over mule and foot tracks was very difficult, hence, logistics was a weakness of this plan.

Reserves

After the plan had been implemented and the Indian response got under way, further accretions were effected in the FCNA region. These were: brigade headquarters 2; infantry battalions 13 (to reinforce the intrusions, to occupy defensive positions along the LoC and in depth areas); SSG companies 2; artillery fire units 15; engineer battalions 2; and signal battalion 1. The deployment of troops in the FCNA region along the LoC opposite the Kargil sector in July 1999 was 2 brigades plus.

Timing

At the top level in GHQ, this plan was always at the back of the Pakistani mind. Pakistan had infiltrated its agents into the Turtok–Batalik–Kargil–Dras areas in the early 1990s to subvert the population and win it over. During the prime ministerial tenures of Deve Gowda and Gujral, India was perceived as a weak and divided nation and these plans were most probably reviewed then to carry out the aggression. Further, Gen. Musharraf made a pronouncement on 29 October 1998 while addressing troops of the Kharian–Mangla garrisons stating, 'Do not be carried away by the rhetoric of the

Indians whose armed forces are totally exhausted and whose morale is at its lowest.'

The development of roads, tracks and helipads may well have been done in depth in 1997 and, or 1998 as part of normal military activity. Logistics and artillery build-up commenced in 1997 and was completed in 1998. Pakistani artillery was very active in these two years and there were heavy exchanges of artillery fire between the two sides. Artillery reconnaissance parties were sent for reconnaissance to the areas earmarked in end-1998: in January and February 1999, these parties occupied ground on the Indian side. Regular Pakistani troops occupied ground on the Indian side of the LoC from February to April 1999.

OBFUSCATION ATTEMPTS BY PAKISTAN

There has been a systematic and consistent effort by the Government of Pakistan to portray a confusing picture. As directed by the Pakistani COAS, Foreign Minister Sartaj Aziz spoke in different languages at different times. The shifting stand of Pakistan since then has been on the following lines.

1. 'The LoC is delineated but not demarcated.' This is the most brazen attempt towards obfuscation. The line, while not marked on the ground, is clearly identified by both the armies and has remained so for the last twenty-seven years.
2. 'The Pakistan Army has been in occupation of these heights for a long time.'
3. 'The intrusions across the LoC are not by the Pakistan Army, but by militants, over whom Pakistan has no control.'
4. 'The Pakistan Army is fighting in the Dras and Kargil sectors.'

These statements were consistent only in their contradictions. The bodies of Pakistan Army soldiers with identification papers and other documents clearly brought out these lies. The LoC is also marked on Pakistani maps just as it is on Indian maps. Some captured maps showed that an attempt had been made to obliterate the line by using white chalk or correcting fluid.

ASSESSING THE SITUATION

Three residents of Garkhun village were the first to spot the Pakistani intrusion on the morning of 3 May. They had moved up some 5 km along the Jubar Langpa when one of them scanned the mountains through a pair of binoculars, and saw groups of men in Pathan attire digging bunkers. Some were armed, although at that distance their precise numbers and equipment was difficult to detect. They quickly made their way to a local detachment of the Army (3 PUNJAB) and informed them: the best guardians of the border are its people.

On 6 May one of the first Indian Army patrols to go out, a group of eight, stumbled on a camp of about ten Pak personnel on the Kukarthang ridge in the Batalik sector and lost one soldier in an ambush. Taken by surprise at the audacity of Pakistan's action, the Indian Army hastily sent up patrols to gain more information and evict the intruders. Soldiers of a second patrol sent out the next day were injured in a skirmish, and on 9 May a third patrol was ambushed. Operation Vijay was then launched to evict the intruders from Indian territory—it covered all actions from 1 May onwards. The aggressors had achieved complete surprise, and, therefore, the extent and strength of the intrusion was not known at that time. On 9 May forward observation posts established by the intruders directed accurate artillery fire on a stretch of the Srinagar–Leh highway and settlements around Kargil and Dras and destroyed the main Army ammunition dump outside Kargil town. (For sectorwise details of the initial Indian response, see Appendix 6).

The next few days were a trying period for the Indian Army. A patrol of 16 GRENADIERS operating in the Yaldor area was fired upon from three sides and suffered heavy casualties. Another patrol led by Maj. Rohit Gaur was mown down on Jubar ridge. A column of 8 SIKH on a mission to assess the enemy's strength in the Dras sector returned after suffering heavy casualties. A patrol operating in the area north-east of Dras was ambushed and wiped out. The Pakistanis had given each section four to five automatic weapons and this had considerably boosted up their firepower. An Army helicopter was also engaged by the intruders in the Dras sector.

A six-man patrol of 4 JAT under Lt. Saurav Kalia went missing on 14 May while patrolling in the Kaksar area. When their bodies were received back on 9 June, it was a gruesome sight. The men had been tortured and put to death. Their bodies had been mutilated and disfigured, with their eyeballs gouged and genitals cut off.

The Army's initial assessment in early May was that Pak Army regulars and trained mujahideen had infiltrated across the LoC and were occupying certain remote and unheld areas. Their numbers at this stage were unclear, estimated at about 200 to 300. The Defence Minister, George Fernandes, visited the forward areas on 12-14 May.

He was accompanied by the General Officer Commanding-in-Chief of Northern Command, Lt. Gen H.M. Khanna, and the 15 Corps Commander, Lt. Gen. Krishan Pal, who briefed him on the developments in the region. Meanwhile, Prime Minister Vajpayee, too, was given a detailed briefing about India's plans to deal with the intruders.

Some Pak positions were sighted in the Mushkoh valley on 14 May and a Pakistani helicopter was seen on 19 May in the same area heading back to POK. By 18 May, the Army had gunned down 52 heavily armed Pak soldiers and injured many others in different areas. It was by now clear that about 600 to 800 Pakistani regular soldiers (not mujahideen) had intruded and occupied ground on the Indian side of the LoC. On 21 May, one Canberra reconnaissance aircraft was hit by a surface-to-air missile, but it limped back safely to Srinagar.

The initial aim of the Indian forces was to establish contact, assess the extent of intrusions, and contain the enemy. Consequently, a series of attacks was launched in the ensuing days on features held by the Pakistanis. In the face of heavy enemy fire and opposition, the troops established viable firm bases and carried out intensive patrolling from these bases to find out precise details of Pak deployment and strength. As reports came in, it became abundantly clear that the enemy was well entrenched and his eviction would require very deliberate measures. At this stage, HQ Northern Command and HQ 15 Corps made their request for the use of air power.

In New Delhi, the Vice Chief of the Army Staff, Lt. Gen. Chandrashekhar (officiating in place of the Chief who was away on a week-long visit to Poland) consulted his staff and decided to process the request for the use of air power with the Indian Air Force (IAF) and the Government. The Air Chief maintained that if air power was to be used, the country should be prepared for a Pakistani response, and, therefore, the relevant Air Commands had first to be activated. Hence, on the recommendation of the IAF, the Cabinet Committee on Security (CCS) which had been brought into the picture by then, initially deferred the Army's request to use air power to evict the intruders.

On 21 May, the Army Chief, Gen. V.P. Malik, returned and rose to the occasion. He was briefed about the situation through the following day and visited the forward areas on 23 May to get a feel of the situation. By this time, the Army acknowledged that 600-800 Pak infiltrators were lodged in the Dras, Kargil and Batalik sectors. On 24 May, the COAS invited Air Chief Marshal A.Y. Tipnis for a briefing and discussed the situation with him. This convinced Tipnis that the IAF had to go in. On the morning of 25 May, Tipnis and Malik made their case to the CCS. In that meeting, Vajpayee was clear that there was no way he was going to allow Pakistan to occupy Indian territory, especially in a strategic area like Kargil, and ordered the Armed Forces to take any action necessary to evict the intruders.

The Prime Minister chose an unusual modality to signal his determination to take on the Pakistani challenge. In the afternoon, he flew to Pondicherry to inaugurate a power plant. There, he told stunned local reporters keen on eliciting his views on the BJP's break-up with Jayalalitha's AIADMK that the country was facing 'a new challenge in Kargil' from militants bent on occupying territory and staying there. The infiltration was backed by the Pakistani Armed Forces. Vajpayee warned: 'The situation is totally unacceptable to us.' He even revealed that he had called Sharif the previous night and told him that 'all possible steps will be taken to clear our territory of intruders'.[10]

On 26 May, the Indian Air Force joined Operation Vijay and Indian air strikes began in Kargil. At first light that Wednesday morning, Air Force MiG-21s, swing-wing MiG-27s and Mi-17 helicopter gunships flew out of Srinagar and Awantipur airfields to strike at two sub-base camps of the intruders near Dras. Significantly, these were the positions closest to the Leh–Kargil road. Later, just before noon, another round of strikes took place in the Batalik area. That Pakistan had anticipated the Indian reaction, including the air strikes, is evident from the fact that its troops were fully equipped with surface-to-air missiles (SAMs), weapons that had not figured in the Kashmir conflict so far. Srinagar airport was closed to civilian traffic on 26 May.

On the second day of the air strikes, one of the MiG-27s suffered a serious mechanical problem, and the pilot, Flt. Lt. K. Nachiketa, had to eject. He was taken prisoner of war. His flying buddy, Sqn. Ldr. Ahuja, remained in the area to look for the first pilot. In the process his MiG-21 was shot down with a surface-to-air missile. Pakistan later claimed that Sqn. Ldr. Ahuja had died, but when his body was returned to India, it became clear that the Pakistanis had shot him after he had ejected.

[10] *India Today*, 7 June 1999, p. 22.

The next day, the IAF lost a Mi-17 helicopter after a very successful attack on Tololing in the Dras sector. Intruders using a shoulder-fired surface-to-air Stinger missile hit the chopper when it veered close to their hideout. Sqn. Ldr. Rajeev Pundir, Flt. Lt. Subramaniam Muhilan, Sgt. P.N.V.R. Prasad and Sgt. R.K. Sahu died in the incident. Mi-17 helicopters were not used in the war zone thereafter. These were to be the last losses suffered by the IAF, and, as a spokesman said on 28 May, 'We have been operating in a very self-restrained manner and using air power in confined and difficult terrain.'

On 26 May, an eighteen-man patrol from a Grenadiers unit ran into heavy concentration of infiltrators in the area of Tiger Hill. Suddenly, machine guns started firing from three sides. The exchange of fire continued for ten hours. Four Indian soldiers were killed.

INITIAL ATTACKS

Between 29 May and 2 June, initial attacks launched against enemy positions and special missions and patrols sent out from firm bases encountered stiff opposition and suffered some reverses. In Batalik sector, 1 BIHAR undertook a daring operation on 29 May to get behind and encircle one of the intruder positions north of Point 4927 on Jubar ridge. While the enemy was initially surprised, an intense fire-fight ensued. Maj. M. Saravanan (who was leading the group of thirty) engaged the enemy in a long gun battle. On reaching Point 4268, Saravanan went ahead of the patrol and engaged the enemy in hand-to-hand combat. Four men from the enemy side were killed before he and ten soldiers fell to bullets. The officer was posthumously awarded the Vir Chakra for his daring.

Commencing on the night of 22-3 May, an 18 GRENADIERS company had crawled up three ridges from the Indian side, led by Lt. Col. R. Vishwanathan and Maj. R.S. Adhikari. Creeping behind boulders and covered by artillery fire, they took seven days to reach the Tololing feature, where they established a firm base. (Even with no enemy on top, it takes seven hours for a mountaineer to reach the top.) On 29 May, a company led by Maj. Adhikari attempted an assault in the Tololing area. They were stopped just 15 metres short of their objective. Adhikari and two others died in hand-to-hand combat. The intruders rained fire on the attacking troops and pushed the company back 30 m, then more, and then some more distance away. This forced 23-year-old Capt. Sachin Nimbalkar and his men to perch behind a large rock fronting on a tiny ledge on a sheer cliff-face for three days, till they were extricated. Maj. Adhikari was awarded the Maha Vir Chakra (posthumously) for his bravery.

On 2 June, Lt. Col. R. Vishwanathan, Second-in-Command of 18 GRENADIERS, led another group of men towards the enemy positions. Vishwanathan made good progress despite inclement weather. A heavy exchange of gun and mortar fire ensued. In the fierce combat, he and his patrol were gunned down, but not before killing three of the enemy. The officer was posthumously awarded the Vir Chakra.

Capt. P.V. Vikram of 141 Field Regiment (Col. John George Commanding) was on duty at a forward post located at 16,200 ft (4935 m) in Kaksar. On 2 June, he along with his observation party tried to move ahead to another location. The intruders began firing. After almost an hour of gunfire, the enemy began artillery shelling which hit their position. He and three others succumbed to injuries.

In the same vein, many other subunits and patrols attacked enemy positions to inch forward, and to probe for information. This concerted effort all along the war zone yielded vital inputs.

OPPOSING FORCES

By the beginning of June, intelligence inputs indicated that some 160 Pakistani soldiers had been killed in fighting with Indian troops; reports in Rawalpindi acknowledged that the figure was around 125. By 3 June, the Indian toll stood at 57 killed including 4 officers and 3 JCOs, and 203 wounded. Indian troops recovered the first clinching evidence of the Pakistan Army's presence in the area of intrusions. An identity card of Sep. Abdul Ayub, 4 NLI, his rucksack and personal weapon were recovered from one of the positions in the Batalik sector.

By this time, patrolling and subunit actions had yielded more precise information about the Pakistan Army deployment in the area of the intrusions. Important heights were held in company and platoon strength in rudimentary fortifications, and the approaches to them were guarded by groups of section or half-section strength in *sangars* [improvised bunkers of local stones/rocks]. All told, some 130 such positions were established. Identifications revealed the presence of one brigade in the Batalik sector and another in the Kargil–Dras–Mushkoh valley sector. Each brigade initially comprised 2 battalions of the Northern Light Infantry (NLI),

2 companies of the Special Services Group (SSG), along with 600-700 Frontier Corps troops (the Chitral and Bajaur Scouts) for carrying supplies and stores. High altitude warfare consumes a large number of troops in administrative duties, hence, the effective strength in the positions manned was about 1,200 to 1,400. They were backed by well co-ordinated military planning and leadership, which had anticipated much of the Indian response. They were willing to fight hard for the heights they had occupied and withstand sustained Indian attacks. Their firepower was accurate and included heavy artillery. Their eviction obviously needed very deliberate preparation in terms of movement of troops, acclimatization and build-up.

As the battle progressed, two more battalions of the NLI were identified. Therefore, by the end of June, the units known to be involved in the intrusions were 2, 3, 4, 5, 6, and 7 NLI. Due to the attrition caused to 4 NLI, Pakistan planned this unit's relief by 8 NLI. Also identified in the area were 11, 12 and 13 NLI, and 19 and 33 Frontier Force battalions. Thus, in the entire aggression, including the SSG commando battalion, Pakistan used a total of about 13 battalions. They were supported by 15 artillery fire units, 2 engineer battalions and 1 signal battalion.

INDIAN CONCEPT OF OPERATIONS

The Indian concept of operations was to evict the enemy from those areas from where he was effectively dominating NH 1A, and then from the other areas. The priority for the capture of objectives was as under.

1. *Priority 1*: Dras sector.
2. *Priority 2*: Mushkoh valley sector. This sector was initially to be encircled.
3. *Priority 3*: Batalik sector.
4. *Priority 4*: Kaksar area. This area was not held by the Pakistanis in strength and such areas as were occupied did not have domination over the Indian lines of communication.

Since Pakistan had initially planned to outflank India's defences from the south in the Turtok and Chalunka sectors (to sever the southern Siachen Glacier) and in a later time frame to choke access to both the northern and southern Glaciers, there was considerable fighting in the Siachen sector. As these operations are outside the scope of this study, it would suffice to state that 102 Infantry Brigade (Brig. Prakash Katoch Commanding) was to thwart all Pakistani attempts to improve their positions, and in the process they suffered severe losses in men and equipment as also lost some territory. Brig Katoch was awarded the Uttam Yudh Seva Medal (UYSM) for conducting operations in a bold and imaginative manner.

On the Indian side, 8 Mountain Division (under its cool and dashing GOC Maj. Gen. Mohinder Puri) comprising its two integral brigades (56 and 192) and 79 Mountain Brigade (ex corps reserve) was given the task of evicting the Pakistanis from the Kargil–Dras–Mushkoh sectors. Initially, this entire sector was with 56 Mountain Brigade (Brig A.N. Aul). Later, Dras was with 56 Mountain Brigade and Mushkoh with 79 Mountain Brigade (Brig. R.K. Kakkar). Finally, 56 Mountain Brigade was between Sando and Bhimbat Nullahs, 192 Mountain Brigade (Brig. M.P.S. Bajwa) between Tingel and Sando Nullahs, and 79 Mountain Brigade west of Tingel to Mushkoh valley (which included the area of Point 4875).

Brig. Devinder Singh's 70 Mountain Brigade of 3 Infantry Division (GOC Maj. Gen. V. S. Budhwar) was to evict the Pakistanis from the Batalik sector.

During the conduct of actual operations, units were moved from one sector to the other to achieve concentration at the point of attack. The Indian Army employed 16 to 17 battalions to evict the intruders—a clear illustration of the principle of concentration of force at the point of decision, step-wise. It would be worth noting that these units were inducted from outside the area of operations, and, therefore, had to be properly acclimatized before being committed to battle. The process of acclimatization is lengthy. The minimum is 6 days at 9,000 ft (2,750 m), three days at 12,000 ft (3,650 m) and three more days at 15,000 ft (4,570 m). Even then, not everyone is fit to function at optimal level. Movement of troops and dumping of ammunition, rations, fuel, clothing and stores takes time, particularly along a single line of communication subjected to artillery shelling and the vagaries of weather. The Army correctly assessed that it needed time for all these activities as well as for planning and rehearsals, hence, it could not give any specific time frame for the completion of the eviction operations.

The heroic nature of the Indian counter-attack cannot be overstated. It must be remembered that the genius of the Pakistani offensive lay in the conception of the entire plan, the surprise achieved, and the preparations made to make their positions and

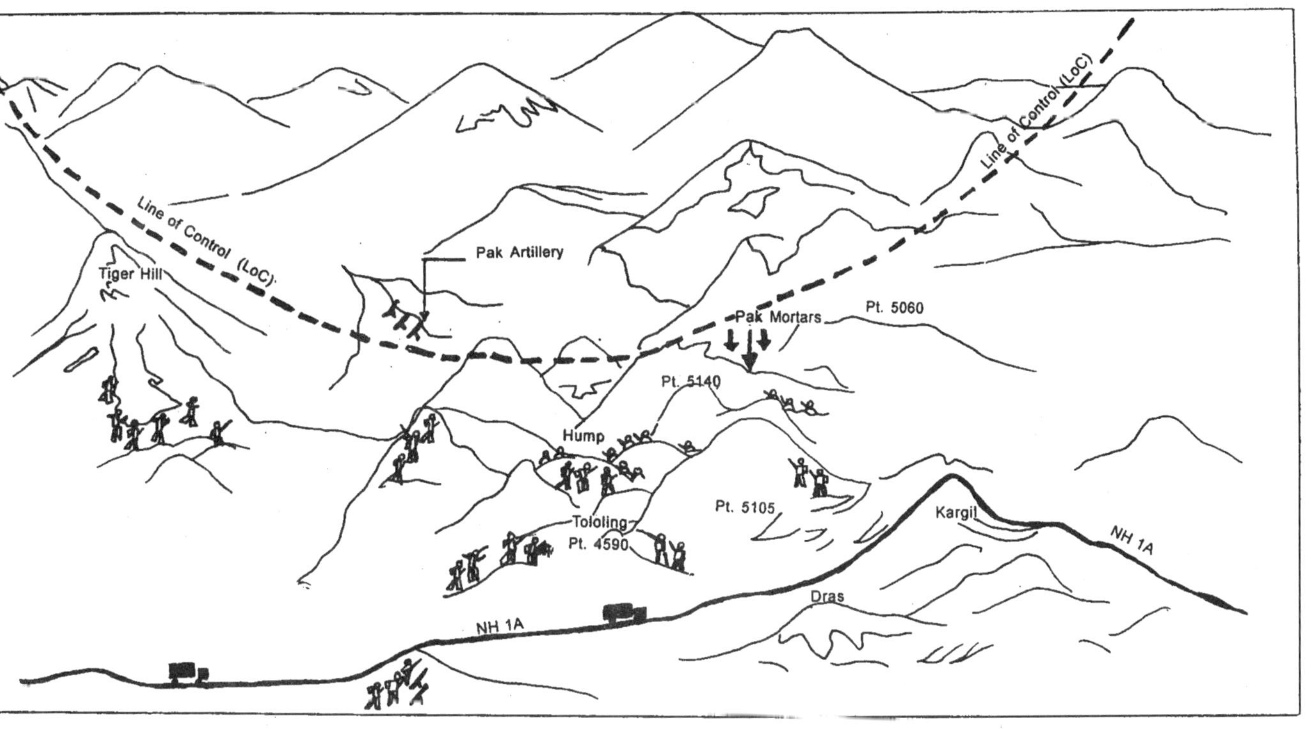

MAP 15: BATTLE OF TOLOLING.

defences as impregnable as possible in the time available. During the execution stage they fought extremely well throughout. The Indian onslaught launched in the teeth of adversity, initially in a hurry, faltered at the outset in the face of overwhelming odds and the heavy fire brought down from higher altitudes. But as the battle gained momentum, the heroism of the Indian soldiers and their commanders came to the fore and they carried all before them.

THE BATTLE OF TOLOLING

Due to Tololing's domination over NH 1A, it was vital to capture this complex as early as possible, not only to prevent interdiction of the highway, but also to provide a launch pad for further operations. To emphasize the point, the enemy had to be evicted from the entire Tololing ridge extending from Point 4590 to Point 5140, as also from features west of this ridge—Knoll, Three Pimples, Lone Hill and Point 4700. See maps on pages 94 and 111.

On 20 May, 18 GRENADIERS (CO Col. Kushal Thakur, YSM), a unit raised in 1976, was tasked to recapture Tololing. The complex can broadly be divided into Tololing Top, Area Flat, Point 4590 and Barbad Bunker. The battalion commenced its operations on 21 May with a view to closing in on Tololing. A three-pronged assault was launched to achieve this. With virtually no cover and intruders entrenched all across the ridges in their defences fortified with iron girders and corrugated iron sheets, the advance was stopped even as it began. Things were so bad that 18 GRENADIERS were pinned down by effective enemy fire for many days.

Movement was only possible during bad weather or on moonless nights. The wind screamed along with gunfire, and temperatures were hovering between –5 and –10 °C. From the base, it takes at least 11 hours for a fit, acclimatized soldier to climb to battle positions. But crawling up, inch by inch, along the steep, smooth incline in the face of blanket firing by the intruders made the task of the troops extremely hazardous. Maj. Adhikari and Lt. Col. Vishwanathan had already been killed leading their men in daring actions.

On the night of 2 June, the 18 GRENADIERS led their fourth courageous assault against the intruders. The expected 'softening' of enemy positions by blasting them with artillery and mortar fire appeared only to harden the resolve of the well-fortified, do-or-die Pakistani regulars. Every move against Tololing was met with deadly

Plate 1: Air Chief Marshal A.Y. Tipins, CAS, is being briefed. To his left is Maj. Gen. Mohinder Puri, GOC 8 Mountain Division.

Plate 2: General V.P. Malik, COAS, viewing captured weapons. On the extreme left of the photograph is Lt. Gen. Krishan Pal, GOC 15 Corps.

Plate 3: Tololing Top.

Plate 4: Snipers seen engaging Point 5140 from the slopes of Tololing.

Plate 5: Guns in action in the Dras Sector.

Plate 6: Tiger Hill.

Plate 7: Soldiers of 13 JAK RIF atop Point 4875 after its capture.

Plate 8: The Jubar feature was the first to be recaptured in the Batalik Sector.

crossfire from adjacent heights where the intruders were entrenched. Faced with heavy resistance from all directions and incessant artillery shelling, the unit nevertheless moved forward, creeping up from boulder to boulder along razor-thin ridges. It had taken the battalion 7-10 days to reach near the Tololing feature and establish a viable firm base by end May on the slopes of three ridges about 30 m below the Pak positions. This firm base was used by 2 RAJ RIF on 12 June for the assault on Tololing.

By 3 June, the Indian death toll had reached 98, with over 317 wounded in the entire area of operations. About 250 intruders had been killed. It became clear to the higher commanders that the Indian Army had lost too many men. More deliberate measures would be required in future. For the next nine days, the army bolstered its artillery firepower by bringing in more guns. Some 42 fire units were built up in the area of operations, half of them medium and heavy guns. Approximately 250 guns were now available to support the troops. Fresh assault plans and logistics were worked out.

In order to capitalize on the determined pressure mounted by 18 GRENADIERS, 2 RAJ RIF (CO Col. M.B. Ravindarnath, VrC) was ordered to continue the attack from the firm base established by the Grenadiers. Meanwhile, the hard lessons learnt by the Grenadiers were absorbed by the Rajputana Rifles. For a week before the final assault on 12 June, the battalion conducted mock operations on a nearby ridge similar to Tololing. They chalked out their assault techniques on a mud and stone model they had designed after reconnaissance of the Tololing heights from different directions.

The weapons and ammunition were test-fired, an exercise that eliminated a defective lot of hand grenades. Everyone—washermen, cobblers and barbers included—physically carried ammunition up the slopes below Tololing. It takes 4 persons to support 1 soldier on the battlefield. The battalion was by now primed for the attack. A team of about 90 was handpicked by the Commanding Officer from an endless number of volunteers. Among them were the battalion's sportsmen, mostly athletes. (They wanted to prove that they were good not only in peacetime, but also in war.) On 11 June, letters were written and left behind with friends to post in case someone did not return.

The 2nd Battalion of the Rajputana Rifles launched a multi-directional attack on Point 4590 with 1 company each on the south-east and south-west axes. The 2 attacking companies were each backed by a reserve of 1 company. The attack was launched at 23.00 p.m. on 12 June. The advancing troops came under intense automatic fire from light, medium and heavy machine guns and heavy artillery shelling from the Pakistan side. Undeterred, the troops pressed home their attack. Fierce hand-to-hand fighting ensued, and by the early hours of 13 June, resistance had crumbled and Point 4590 had been captured. Soon thereafter, the unit recaptured Barbad Bunker, a position 100 m south-west of Point 4590.

In these operations, Maj Vivek Gupta along with 2 JCOs and 5 OR (Other Ranks) laid down their lives, displaying exemplary courage. The officer was awarded the Maha Vir Chakra for his gallantry. The fleeing Pakistanis left a number of their dead behind. The recovery of weapons included rocket launchers, machine guns, automatic grenade launchers, mortars, anti-personnel mines, assault rifles and forty-five boxes of belted ammunition.

This success was to bring 18 GRENADIERS into the fray. Moving with speed and dexterity, they captured Hump on 14 June, located about 3 km north of Point 4590. Thereafter, 13 JAK RIF (CO Lt. Col. Y.K. Joshi, VrC) which was the reserve was moved up for the capture of Point 5140—the highest feature on the Tololing complex. Point 5140 was a strongly fortified position held by a company plus, heavily reinforced with automatic weapons. It has treacherous approaches. Two attempts at capturing it met with limited success. 18 GARHWAL (CO Col. S.K. Chakravorty, SC, SM**), 13 JAK RIF and 1 NAGA (CO Col. D.A. Patil) were then tasked to capture Point 5140. The operation was planned meticulously. Simultaneous multidirectional attacks were launched by columns from these three battalions. The operation began around 8.30 p.m. on 19 June. The moment the companies started to climb, they came under intense fire. Every five to six steps they had to take shelter.

Capt. Vikram Batra of 13 JAK RIF had prevailed upon his CO to let him lead the battalion attack. In an audacious move, this young company commander decided to approach the Pak position from the rear along a sheer rock face. As 'D' Company neared the top, a machine gun nest opened up, trapping the troops on the precipitous slopes under its murderous fire. Undaunted, the officer climbed on followed by five of his men. Being the first to reach the top, he crawled towards the machine gun nest and hurled two grenades. Thereupon, three of the enemy rushed out of their *sangar*. He single-handedly engaged them in a close fire-fight and killed all of them.

Inspired by this display of extraordinary leadership, his company fell upon the enemy and annihilated them, finally capturing Point 5140 by 0335 hours on 20 June.

The recapture of Point 5140 set in motion a string of successes. West of the Tololing complex and east of Tiger Hill are a series of heights which had to be taken if Tiger Hill—the next objective—was to be successfully isolated. These were: Point 4700, Three Pimples and Lone Hill complex.

Point 4700 was held by well-entrenched troops. 18 GARH RIF was tasked to capture it. They launched multipronged attacks on enemy-held positions on the night of 28 June. What followed was the fiercest battle to date in this sector. The attacking troops had to engage in hand-to-hand combat braving bullets and mortar fire, till they ultimately reached the top after ten hours of intense fighting. Although 40 Pakistanis were killed, the casualties on the Indian side were also high. All weapons, ammunition, radio sets and other warlike stores recovered from the position bore Pakistan Ordnance Factory (POK) markings.

Equally difficult and costly in human terms was the recapture of Three Pimples and Lone Hill complex. These features were to be captured by 2 RAJ RIF. On the night of 28/9 June, Col. Ravindranath sent three columns across terrain that allowed only two ways to go up. The enemy sat perched well on top, dominating both the routes. Yet, all three columns climbed under consistent artillery and small arms fire. The valour of Capt. Neikezhakou Kenguruse, an intensely religious young Naga officer, typifies the indomitable spirit the unit displayed. His citation reads, 'Despite being injured in the abdomen and bleeding profusely, the officer kept on approaching the bunkers. At a steep climb, he took off his shoes to get a better grip, scaled the cliff face, fixed the climbing rope and took up a rocket launcher to fire at the enemy bunker. Unmindful of his personal safety, he charged to the top and personally killed two men with his rifle and two others with his knife before succumbing to his injuries.' The officer was awarded the Maha Vir Chakra for his gallantry.

The unit also recounts with pride the brave act of Nb. Sub. (Naib Subedar) Sunayak Singh in holding on to his post for four hours while being vastly outnumbered. 'What Sunayak did is the perfect example of what this unit is all about—once given a task, we only know that it has to be done, whatever the cost', says Col. Ravindranath. Sunayak, of course, does not look at it as anything exceptional.

'*Yeh to hamara farz tha*' (This was our duty), he says. In the battle for Three Pimples and Lone Hill complex, the battalion lost three of its best officers. Maj. P. Acharya was awarded the Maha Vir Chakra posthumously for displaying exceptional courage during the battle of Three Pimples. By 30 June, the Pakistanis had been evicted from nearly all the ridges north-east of Sando Nullah.

The Chief of the Army Staff, in recognition of the meritorious and gallant performance of the 2 RAJ RIF in the battle of Point 4590 and Three Pimples area in the Dras sector on the nights of 13/14 June and 28/9 June, respectively, awarded them the coveted Unit Citation. In these operations, 4 officers, 2 JCOs and 17 OR of 2 RAJ RIF were killed and 70 were wounded. Of the wounded, 6 lost their limbs and 20 were so badly incapacitated that they would no longer be able to serve their unit for which they had given their all.

For their outstanding performance, 18 GRENADIERS, 13 JAK RIF and 18 GARH RIF were also awarded Unit Citations. 18 GRENADIERS for Hump, 13 JAK RIF for Point 5140 and 18 GARH RIF for Point 4700.

Whilst 18 GRENADIERS, 2 RAJ RIF, 13 JAK RIF and 18 GARH RIF played the major role in the battles of the Tololing complex, other infantry units like 1 NAGA also contributed to the overall success. Not to forget the artillery units—particularly 108 Medium Regiment (CO Col. Prabhat Ranjen, SM) and 197 Field Regiment (CO Col. Alok Deb, SM)—which closely supported the attacking troops, and many other supporting arms and services units which acted in unison to bring about this first success of the Kargil war. The battle for the Tololing complex was the turning point in Operation Vijay and much credit must go to Brig. A.N. Aul, who led 56 Mountain Brigade with determination and skill against heavy odds, for which he was awarded the Uttam Yudh Seva Medal.

Battle of Tiger Hill

Tiger Hill is the most dominating feature in the Dras sector. It is conical in shape with few spurs and ridges. It proved lethal for the Indian Army. From here the well-entrenched intruders had directed precise artillery fire for over a month on the Srinagar–Leh highway located about 8 km to the south. This had restricted the movement of Army convoys carrying troops, ammunition and supplies. See maps on pages 94 and 117.

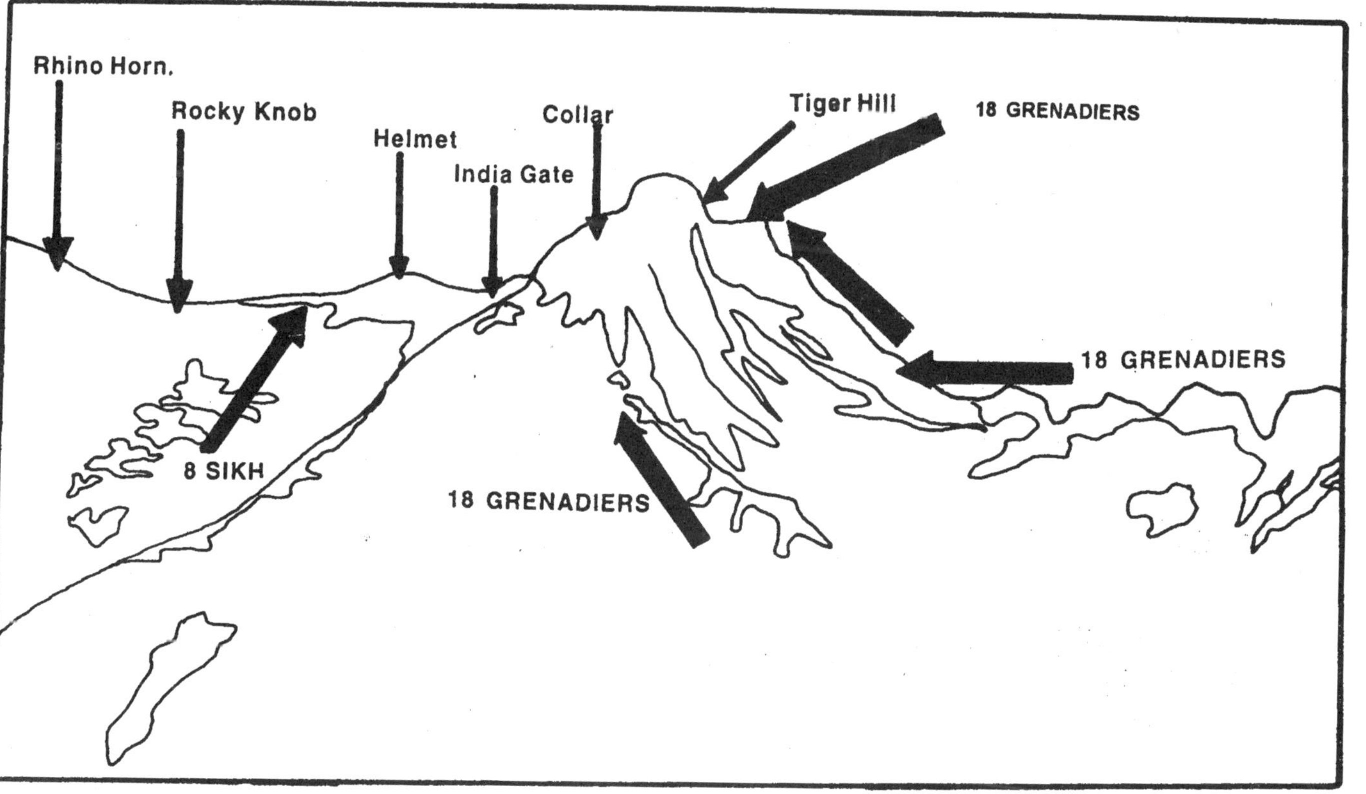

MAP 16: TIGER HILL.

The Tiger Hill complex comprises Top, Eastern Spur and Western Spur. The important landmarks on W :stern Spur going from east to west are India Gate, Helmet and Rocky Knob. Tiger Hill complex was held in strength by approximately one battalion. In times of clear visibility, the enemy could see and fire at Indian troops the moment they raised their heads from behind a boulder. Icy winds and sub-zero temperatures added to their difficulties. It was in these conditions that 8 SIKH (CO Col. S.P. Singh) closed-in on Tiger Hill complex in late May from the east and south and dug in. However, the feature could not be approached from the west as the enemy had occupied the complete ridge in strength. They held firmly on to the ground they had occupied, till the complex was captured more than a month later in the first week of July.

After the recapture of the Tololing complex by end June, 18 GRENADIERS (which had fought in that battle) was tasked to capture Tiger Hill from the east, and 8 SIKH was directed to provide the firm base. Additionally, 8 SIKH was to simulate attacks from the south and north, and also cut off Tiger Hill from the west. The IAF pounded the feature around the clock whilst helicopters carried out reconnaissance flights.

Col. K.S. Thakur, the CO of 18 GRENADIERS, knew that the assault on Tiger Hill was a daunting task. Thakur, who had already lost 25 men at Tololing, had to find a way to minimize his casualties. After studying maps and aerial photographs and making a thorough reconnaissance of the objective, he decided on the most difficult route, that is via the Eastern Spur. It was a sheer cliff that the intruders would have least expected the attackers to climb.

For three days beginning 1 July, the battalion lugged arms and ammunition up the slopes. To give an idea of the difficulties of this task, it needed 270 men to carry 540 mortar bombs of the 81 mm variety. By the evening of 3 July, it was time for action. Soon after sundown, heavy pre-ponderance of guns started a 30-minute pounding of enemy positions so as to stun the intruders and force them to lie low. The attack on Tiger Hill commenced on 3 July at 20.30 p.m. Three companies of 18 GRENADIERS began their climb, two from the eastern slope and one from the south-eastern side. The relatively easy gradient on the south-eastern side brought the troops in front of an enemy bunker at a point called 'Tongue'. The bunker was neutralized with rocket launchers, but the exchange left one soldier dead and four injured. The time was 01.30 a.m. on 4 July.

The other two companies had to slowly inch their way up Eastern Spur in pitch darkness. Subsequently, a company of 8 SIKH moved towards Western Spur and captured the areas India Gate and Helmet by 04.00 a.m. on 04 July. With the capture of these areas, the Pakistanis were completely isolated on Tiger Hill.

The three companies of 18 GRENADIERS continued their advance towards their objectives aided by well-directed artillery fire. The battalion captured area Knob and Tooth by the early hours of 4 July. The Ghatak (commando) platoon was the first to reach the north-eastern side of Tiger Top. Despite a fierce counter-attack by the enemy, the troops held on to the areas captured.

It was now about 04.00 a.m. on 4 July and an unusual act of heroism was in the making. Gdr (Grenadier) Yogendra Singh was part of the Ghatak platoon tasked to capture three Bunkers on Tiger Hill Top. The approach was a vertical cliff face, snowbound at 16,500 ft (5,050 m). Yogendra Singh, who was leading the attack, was halfway up fixing the ropes for further assault when an enemy bunker opened up with machine gun and rocket fire. His platoon commander and two others were killed. Realizing the gravity of the situation, he continued to scale the sheer cliff face alone through a volley of fire. He was hit by three bullets on his groin and shoulder, but, displaying incredible resolve, he persisted in climbing the remaining 60 ft (18.28 m) and reached the top. Though critically injured, he crawled up to the bunker and lobbed a grenade, killing four Pak soldiers and neutralizing enemy fire.

This act was directly instrumental in allowing his platoon to climb up the cliff face. Grievously injured but with a reckless regard for his personal safety, he again charged the second bunker with two of his colleagues who had joined him and neutralized it by killing three Pak soldiers in hand-to-hand combat. His indomitable spirit and grit inspired the rest of the platoon to quickly traverse the treacherous terrain through hostile fire and to charge the enemy at Tiger Hill Top, a vital objective. For displaying the most conspicuous courage and spirit of self-sacrifice well beyond the call of duty, Grenadier Yogendra Singh Yadav was awarded the Param Vir Chakra.

On 6 July, the Pakistanis counter-attacked area Helmet and India Gate from the direction of the western ridge, which was in their possession. These counter-attacks were dispersed with heavy casualties and the Sikhs continued to hold on to the objectives they had captured. Of the Pakistan Army, 17 soldiers were killed. Indian casualties were 3 JCOs and 11 OR killed. The bodies of 7 Pakistan Army soldiers were found dumpe in a shallow pit in the area.

On the night of 7/8 July, 18 GRENADIERS launched an attack on the area of Reverse Slope, Cut and Collar. Despite firm resistance from the enemy, the unit overran all that was encountered and captured these objectives by 08.00 a.m.

On 11 July, 'C' Company of 18 GRENADIERS captured area Rocky Knob and Rhino Horn. The battle of Tiger Hill was at last over. It decisively defeated Pakistan's Kargil adventure. It was due to 8 Sikh and 18 GRENADIERS. The COAS awarded Unit Citations to 8 SIKH for operations 'West of Tiger Hill' and 18 GRENADIERS for 'Tiger Hill'.

Battle of Point 4875

Point 4875 is located north-west of Dras. It is a strategically important feature which dominates a 20-5 km stretch of the Srinagar–Leh road, from Dras to Metayin in the west. Further, any move into the Mushkoh valley from the east is dominated by it. Point 4875 also provides depth to Point 4388, where the enemy's administrative base was located and from where all operations in Dras and Mushkoh were being supported. The recapture of Point 4875 was an operational imperative if the enemy was to be evicted from Mushkoh. See maps on pages 94 and 121.

The task of recapturing this strategic feature was given to 79 Mountain Brigade with 17 JAT (CO Col. U.S. Bawa, VrC), 13 JAK RIF, 2 NAGA (CO Col. D.K. Badula), 12 MAHAR (CO Col. A.P.S. Cheema) and one team of 21 PARA Special Force (SF) (CO Col. Ivan Joseph Crasto, KC) under command. The brigade was given 158 Medium Regiment (CO Col. M.A. Kumar) in direct support and 315 Field Regiment (CO Col. M.A. Subramaniam) in indirect support. The enemy was holding area Point 4875 in strength. Based on his dispositions, the area was divided into unit and subunit objectives. The assault was spearheaded by 'A' and 'D' Companies of 17 JAT and was launched on the night of 4/5 July. The battalion successfully captured Pimple 1 and Whale Back by 05.00 a.m. on 5 July.

The capture of Area Flat Top was entrusted to 13 JAK RIF. Rfn. (Rifleman) Sanjay Kumar of this unit had volunteered to be the

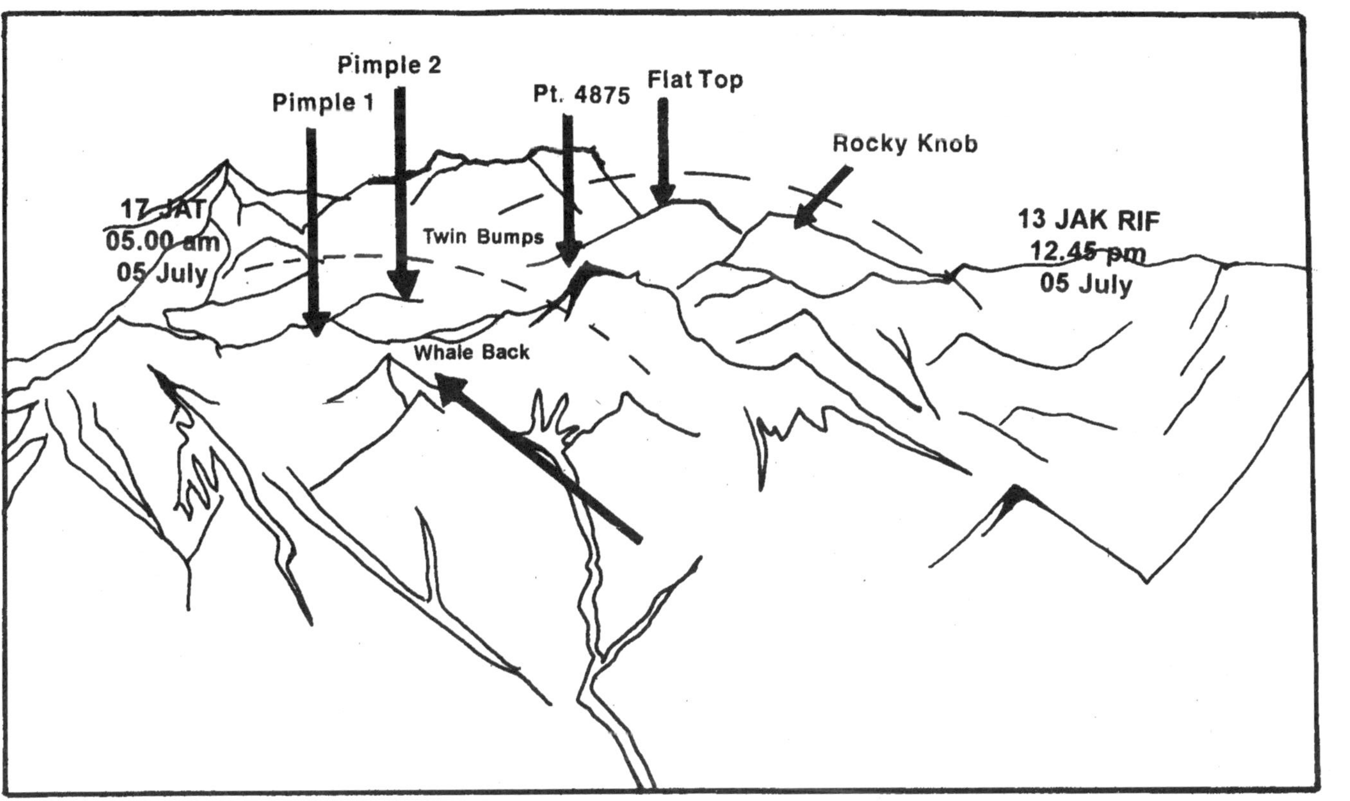

MAP 17: BATTLE OF POINT 4875.

leading scout of the special mission group assigned the responsibility for capturing Area Flat Top. The advance began on 4 July. Having scaled the cliff face, the leading platoon found itself pinned down on a narrow ledge by automatic fire from an enemy machine gun located in a bunker 150 m away. Rfn. Kumar quickly realized the detrimental effect this bunker would have on the success of the mission. With complete disregard for his personal safety, he crawled alone up the ledge along a flank and charged the enemy bunker through a hail of automatic fire. Almost instantly, he took two bullets on his chest and forearm. Bleeding profusely, he continued the charge towards the bunker. Unhesitant, and with complete disregard for his bullet injuries, he then picked up the enemy machine gun and crept towards the second enemy bunker, echeloned in depth. Three enemy soldiers, taken completely by surprise, were killed by this gallant soldier on the spot. Inspired by his daredevil act, the rest of the platoon, emotionally charged, assaulted the feature and captured Area Flat Top.

For this display of the most conspicuous and extraordinary gallantry with complete disregard for personal safety in the face of the enemy, Rifleman Sanjay Kumar was awarded the Param Vir Chakra. The attack then continued in daylight, and 13 JAK RIF captured Point 4875 by 12.45 p.m. on 5 July.

After consolidating these gains, Phase 2 of the brigade attack was launched on the night of 6/7 July. 'B' Company 17 JAT captured Pimple Two, destroying four enemy bunkers; however, due to heavy enemy fire from a nearby ledge, the company was daylighted and could not progress its operations further.

Meanwhile, 2 NAGA, attacking from another direction, made steady progress. Fighting and climbing their way to the top, they captured Twin Bumps by 12.00 noon on 7 July. In these attacks, the Naga Regiment killed 15 Pak Army soldiers including 1 officer, Capt. Imtiaz Malik of 69 Field Regiment. The Nagas lost Capt. Prem Raj, an artillery Forward Observation Officer, and 10 soldiers of their battalion. One company of 13 JAK RIF was then launched to clear enemy positions on the ledge which were pinning down 'B' company of 17 JAT. The Ledge was a feature with sharp cutting edges on either side with well coordinated defences that covered the only approach to the feature. Capt. Vikram Batra who had in June displayed exemplary courage and bravery during the attack on Point 5140 in the Tololing area, led his company once again in a sanguine manner.

In order to speed up the operation, the officer decided to assault the enemy positions along a narrow ridge. Leading the assault, he engaged the enemy in a fierce hand to hand fight and killed five enemy soldiers at point blank range. In this action, he sustained grievous injuries. Despite the serious injuries, Capt. Batra crawled towards the enemy and hurled grenades clearing the position. Leading from the front he rallied his men and pressed on the attack and achieved a near impossible military task in the face of heavy enemy fire with utter disregard to personal safety. In the process he succumbed to his injuries. Inspired by this display of extraordinary junior leadership, the troops fell upon the enemy with vengeance and annihilated them, finally capturing Ledge.

Captain Vikram Batra, thus displayed the most conspicuous personal bravery and junior leadership of the highest order on two occasions—during the attack on Point 5140 and now on Ledge—and made the supreme sacrifice at the latter in the highest traditions of the Indian Army. He was awarded the Param Vir Chakra.

By nightfall, Area Flat Top had been fully captured. In this battle, 51 enemy soldiers were killed (including an officer) and approximately 90 were wounded.

In a last desperate bid to recapture these lost positions, the Pak Army counter-attacked Point 4875 and Twin Bumps on the night of 7/8 July. These counter-attacks were beaten back by 17 JAT and 13 JAK RIF killing 46 Pak Army soldiers. The capture of Point 4875 sealed the fate of Pakistan Army's operations in the Mushkoh Valley and hastened their withdrawal from this sector. Elements of 50 (Independent) Parachute Brigade (Brig. PC Bhardwaj, VrC, KC) were employed for clearing operations in this valley, in the closing stages of the war, and this pressure ensured their eviction.

On 8 July, 2 NAGA executed a daring and well-planned raid on an enemy mortar position, killing 4 Pak Army soldiers and capturing three 120 mm mortars and two 82 mm mortars. Pimple 2 was captured by 17 JAT, which recovered 22 bodies of the enemy. In the Dras sector, following the recovery of several incriminating documents, the presence of personnel of 2, 3, 4, 5, 6 and 7 NLI battalions of the Pakistan Army was confirmed.

Grit, determination and courage against the worst possible odds contributed to the recapture of Point 4875. Having excelled in the battle of Tololing, 13 JAK RIF now added Point 4875 to its laurels, and this feature was also mentioned in their Unit Citation. A Unit Citation was given to 2 NAGA for 'Twin Bumps' and to 17 JAT for

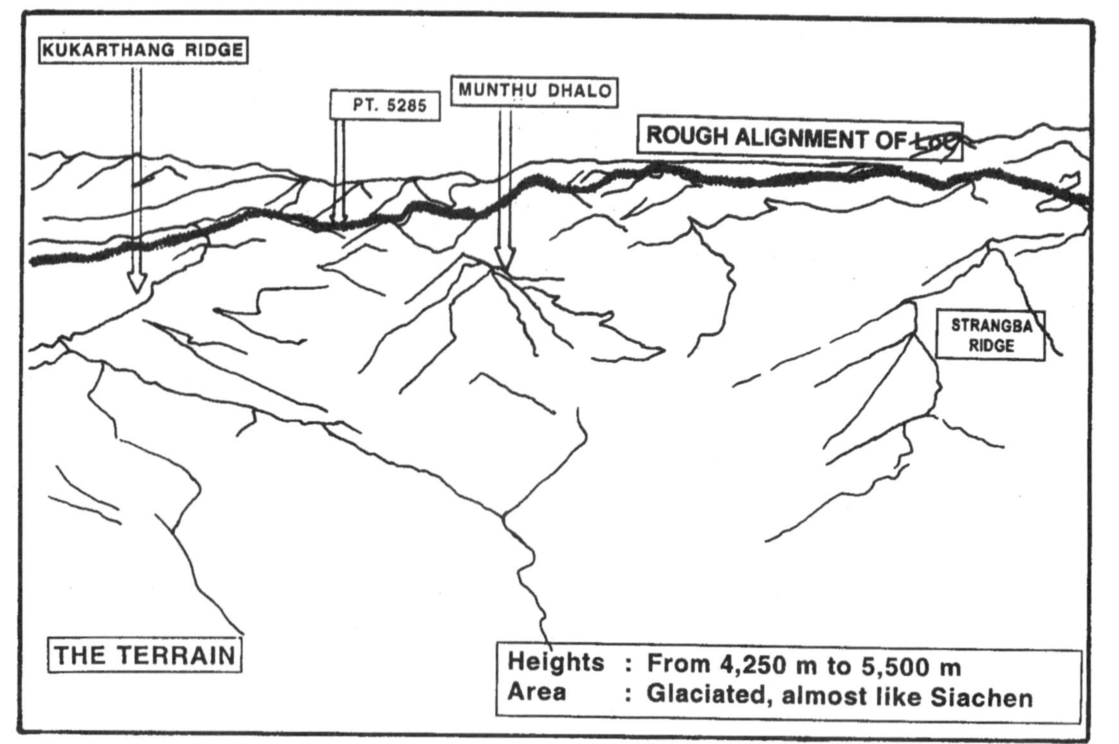

MAP 18: OPERATIONS IN THE BATALIK SECTOR.

'Whale Back and Pimple'. In recognition of the bravery and indomitable resolve of 108 Medium Regiment in providing accurate, relentless and devastating fire resulting in very heavy casualties to the enemy, the COAS awarded them a Unit Citation. The barrage of artillery fire brought down by this regiment facilitated the capture of Tololing Ridge, Point 5140, Tiger Hill and Point 4875.

KAKSAR

In this area Pakistan had occupied the south-western spur of Point 5299 (commonly known as Bajrang Post). This was the only post vacated by Indian troops on March 2, 1999 in the face of extreme snow conditions. The terrain in the Kaksar area is extremely jagged and in winter it becomes highly glaciated. 121 Infantry Brigade (Brig. O.P. Nandrajog, VSM) was responsible for operations in this area. Elements of 4 JAT (CO Col. M.S. Kukshal) and 14 J&K Rifles (CO Col. D.K. Nanda) contained the Pakistani intrusions. Commencing on 5/6 June an attempt was made to evict the intruders, but it did not succeed. Despite hand to hand combat, Pakistan succeeded in holding on to its positions which were spread over an area of approximately 4 km by 4 km.

The elimination of this enemy intrusion was given lower priority than the other sectors as it was not dominating NH 1A. However, 14 J&K RIFLES and 4 JAT with other combat elements including Special Forces were preparing to capture the enemy positions when the Pakistani withdrawal began from here about 9 July.

121 Infantry Brigade also held the LoC in the area north of Kargil, and 3 PUNJAB (CO Col. V. Bakshi) which was part of the brigade supported flank operations in the Batalik sector.

BATTLE OF BATALIK

The Batalik sector came under 70 Infantry Brigade of 3 Infantry Division. In this sector, the Pakistanis had intruded in large numbers and secured three main ridges. The early capture of these ridges was essential to dominate the Batalik–Leh route and prevent any realignment of the LoC. See maps on pages 90 and 124.

In conducting operations, the first step was to carry out aggressive patrolling and probing attacks so as to find out about enemy dispositions and to contain him. 1/11 GR (CO Col. Lalit Rai, VrC) and 12 JAK LI (CO Col. V.S. Bhalothia) succeeded in containing the enemy on the Kukarthang–Tharu ridge and at Point 4812 on the Khalubar ridge. 1 BIHAR (CO Col. O.P. Yadav) launched a battalion attack in the area of Jubar ridge and achieved similar success. [At Chorbat La on the northern flank, a column of the Indus Wing of the LADAKH SCOUTS (CO Col. R.M.B. Baruha) succeeded in containing him there after a hard-fought battle at Rock Fall.] The adversary had been fully repulsed by the first week of June on all the ridges.

The next step was to drive a wedge right up to the LoC through the Junk Lungpa between the two ridges occupied by the enemy. The 12 JAK LI, one company from LADAKH SCOUTS (Karakoram Wing) and one team from 10 PARA (SF) were successfully employed in achieving this task by 3 June. To permit uninterrupted movement along this axis, the eastern flank had to be secured. This entailed the capture of Point 5203 and the north-west spur of Point 5203 (hereafter called 'Western Slopes').

A task force comprising one company of 12 JAK LI, two companies of LADAKH SCOUTS, one company of 5 PARA and one column of 10 PARA (SF) (CO Col. R.S. Bhadauria) were employed to secure the eastern flank by capturing Point 5203 and Western Slopes. Point 5203 was attacked on the night of 7/8 June by columns of 12 JAK LI, which captured Point 5203 Top. The enemy's counter-attack, launched from the west soon thereafter, was effectively repulsed and he was pinned down. Reinforced by 10 PARA (SF), 12 JAK LI held on to the positions captured for twelve long days. In the process, the enemy's defence potential was degraded and his will to fight reduced. On the night of 20/1 June, simultaneous attacks were launched on Western Slopes by a strong column of LADAKH SCOUTS (Indus Wing), 5 PARA (CO Col. A.K. Shrivastava) and LADAKH SCOUTS (Karakoram Wing). The Pakistanis were evicted and the area captured by 07.00 a.m. on 21 June.

The next objective was Point 4812, which offered a foothold on the formidable Khalubar Ridge. In five columns of 30 men each, 12 JAK LI was pressed into the attack on the night of 30 June/ 1 July. The battle was fought with fury on both sides for four days till the jawans of 12 JAK LI captured the position by 04.00 a.m. on 6 July. The Pakistan Army lost 26 soldiers. Lt. Keishing Clifford Nongrum fought gallantly in this battle and was awarded the Maha Vir Chakra (posthumously). On receiving the news of the death of his son, his father responded, saying, 'I am proud of my son and I wish to convey to all ranks of his unit, that they must not feel disheartened on losing their leader. They must continue to put in their best and fight well. I am sure that we will win.'

With the eastern flank secure, it was now opportune to take the Khalubar complex. Khalubar summit is 5,287 m high. The attack was launched by 1/11 GR less two companies, from the direction of Point 4812 on the night of 2/3 July. Although a platoon successfully evicted the enemy from Bunker ridge, the battalion's progress towards Khalubar was halted by a determined enemy firmly entrenched on the commanding heights. The battalion remained pinned down till first light on 4 July. The CO, Col. Lalit Rai, despite being wounded, refused to be evacuated and relentlessly continued to direct the ongoing operations.

Clearing this objective was imperative as the battalion could not continue to remain in an exposed and vulnerable area. Lt. Manoj Kumar Pandey had led his men on 11 June, in the recapture of Jubar Top, a formidable feature of great operational significance. 'But his finest hour', as stated in the citation, 'was approaching in the battle for Khalubar.' Lt. Pandey now stepped forward to take on a dangerous mission. He led his platoon in a daylight attack, on 4 July, through bad weather and poor visibility along a narrow, treacherous ridge towards the enemy positions. While still short of the objective, the enemy responded with a devastating carpet of fire and the attack began to stall.

In a rare display of courage, Lt. Pandey charged the enemy through a hail of bullets. Wounded in the shoulder and leg, he pressed on his solitary charge undeterred. At the first bunker, which he captured, he killed two of the enemy in fierce hand-to-hand combat. Inspired by his valour, his platoon now fell upon the enemy. Unmindful of his wounds, the officer rushed from bunker to bunker urging his men on. Grievously bleeding, he collapsed at the final bunker and succumbed to his injuries, but not before the last of the enemy had been annihilated. This led to the capture of Khalubar.

For this display of the most conspicuous and extraordinary valour and junior leadership of the highest order, in the face of the enemy, Lt. Manoj Kumar Pandey was awarded the Param Vir Chakra (posthumously).

Khalubar was captured by 1/11 GR by 0430 hours on 7 July after clearing 43 enemy-held bunkers. The Pak Army lost 34 soldiers and many more wounded. Maintaining the momentum, the Ghatak platoon of the battalion followed by one company pursued the attack and evicted the enemy from the Garhi feature by 1645 hours.

And on the night of 7/8 July they captured Point 5287. This major gain in the Yaldor sub-sector led to the crumbling of Pakistani defences in this area. The success was well timed with the progress in the Dras sector.

Almost simultaneously, attacks were also launched to capute Point 5000 and Padma Go by the Indus and Karakoram wings of the LADAKH SCOUTS. Point 5000 was successfully captured on 1 July but intense enemy automatic and mortar fire delayed progress towards Padma Go. A gallant attempt on the night of 2/3 July succeeded in scaling Padma Go, but the feature could not be retained due to effective enemy domination. After punishing the objective with heavy artillery and mortar fire over the next few days, the attack was launched afresh on the night of 6/7 July but it had to be called off again due to very stiff resistance. However, a second column fought gallantly against heavy odds and captured Dog Hill (500 m north-west of Padma Go) by first light on 7 July. After gaining this vital foothold attacks were renewed against Padma Go and on 9 July this feature was once again under Indian control. In clearing up operations, on 14th July a wounded and severely dehydrated prisoner of war, Sepoy Hunar Shah of 5 Northern Light. Infantry, was captured. He had been abandoned by his fleeing colleagues. The capture of Point 5000, Dog Hill and Padma Go was a fitting tribute to the fighting qualities of the LADAKH SCOUTS.

At this stage, the Jubar complex was still being held by about one company strength of the enemy. The eviction of the enemy from this complex was important as it would lead to penetration of the enemy's right flank, thereby providing the attacking troops with another axis of advance: this was essential if the entire Batalik sector was to be cleared of the enemy.

Taking of the Jubar complex comprising Point 4268, Jubar OP, Jubar Top and Point 4927 was tasked to 1 BIHAR. They first took Point 4268. Then they proceeded with their attacks towards the well-fortified Jubar OP. After a night-long uphill attack against stiff resistance, this position was captured. The enemy was extremely sensitive to the loss of Jubar OP and launched a quick counter-attack at 09.15 a.m. on 30 June. This was beaten back with heavy casualties. The attempt to capture Jubar Top (4,924 m) was launched after last light, but the assaulting troops could not make much headway against fierce resistance. On the third night, the Pakistanis reinforced Jubar Top. Thereafter, for the next four days this objective was softened with intense air, artillery and mortar fire till the Pakistanis were pulverized.

The attack was resumed on the night of 6/7 July leading to the capture of Jubar Top that night. The unit continued the assault and captured Point 4927 by 10.00 a.m. on 7 July when the entire Jubar complex came under Indian control. This was a major blow to the enemy and led to the complete collapse of the Pakistani defences on the adjoining Kukarthang Ridge. On the night of 8/9 July, 1 BIHAR captured Tharu, 1/11 GR captured Point 4821 and Kukarthang, and 5 PARA took Point 4100 and Muntho Dhalo (Pakistan's principal supply base for the Batalik sector; height 4,065 m). Although Muntho Dhalo had come under sustained air attack, and 105 mm field guns and multi-barrelled Pinaka rocket launchers had been pounding the position from the Silmoo Langpa, the position held out till the end.

When Pakistan announced the withdrawal of its troops on 11 July from areas it was still holding on the Indian side of the LoC, one or two positions in the Batalik sector were still with them. The retreating Pakistan troops had been reinforcing two heights, Peaks 5121 and 5327, over a kilometre inside the Indian side of the LoC. Their pull-out appears to have commenced from these two heights. Reaching these heights would have involved a further assault.

Five units had fought in an outstanding manner in the Battle of Batalik and they were given Unit Citations by the COAS: 1 BIHAR for 'Point 4268, Jubar, Point 4927 and Tharu'; 1/11 GR for 'Khalubar'; the LADAKH SCOUTS for 'Point 5000, Dog Hill and Padma Go'; 12 JAK LI for 'Point 5203 and Point 4812'; and 141 Field Regiment for providing excellent artillery support to the infantry.

Operations in Area Chorbat La

Pakistani intruders had managed to occupy some territory 500 m across the LoC on the Indian side in this sector with a view to expanding their occupation and also to carry out infiltration. On 26 May, Maj. Sonam Wangchuk and his group of 36 soldiers from the Indus Wing of the LADAKH SCOUTS were told to capture a 18,000 ft high ridge (Rockfall) just inside the Indian side of the LoC. The area was glacial and rocky with a gradient of about 80 degrees and with day temperatures warming to just –6 °C. Wangchuk was negotiating an ice wall in the dead of night on 31 May when he heard sounds of picks and hammers on the other side of the ridge facing Pakistan. He quickly radioed a message to his headquarters. His group then moved swiftly towards Ridge Top under heavy fire by Pakistani troops from the flanks. In three hours they neared the top. As Wangchuk led his men towards the enemy-held positions, the mountain ranges echoed with the war cry of the LADAKH SCOUTS, '*Ki Ki So Lhargyalo*' (The Gods Will Triumph).

As morning approached, they spotted a group of intruders trying to scale the ridge from the Pakistani side. Wangchuk told his men to hold on till the enemy came within firing range. Four intruders were killed in the gunbattle that ensued. The soldiers then retrieved the bodies of the intruders, who turned out to be Pakistan Army regulars. Thereafter, Wangchuk led the charge to evict the intruders from the remaining heights which the enemy was in the process of occupying. A major infiltration bid was thus foiled just in time. Wangchuk was awarded the Maha Vir Chakra for his daring and imaginative conduct in uncertain conditions.

Operations in Turtok

India had retained the gains it had made in the Turtok sector in the 1971 war. The residents of Turtok and the villages around it, apart from being co-religionists, are of the same ethnic stock (Balti) as people across the border, and many have families on the other side.

People belonging to three villages—Turtok, Tyakshi and Thang—had been subverted by Pakistan over a period of time with a view to initiating insurgency. A large cache of arms and ammunition was recovered and about 22 personnel taken into custody. Further, it had occupied a ridge on the LoC itself and some armed personnel had come in up to about a kilometre. Timely action taken by the Indian troops pushed back these intrusions and foiled the Pakistani plans. In a gallant operation on 7 June, Capt. Haneef Uddin of the Army Service Corps (ASC) attached to 11 RAJ RIF (CO Col. Anil Bhatia) laid down his life while continually engaging the enemy despite serious injuries. He was awarded the Vir Chakra for his gallantry, and this sector was subsequently named after him. In subsequent stages, Pakistan was to have launched operations to occupy critical areas around Turtok, followed by heliborne and airborne operations in rear areas, and finally to integrate these areas with Pakistan's northern areas. Success would have cut off Siachen and the bases supporting it.

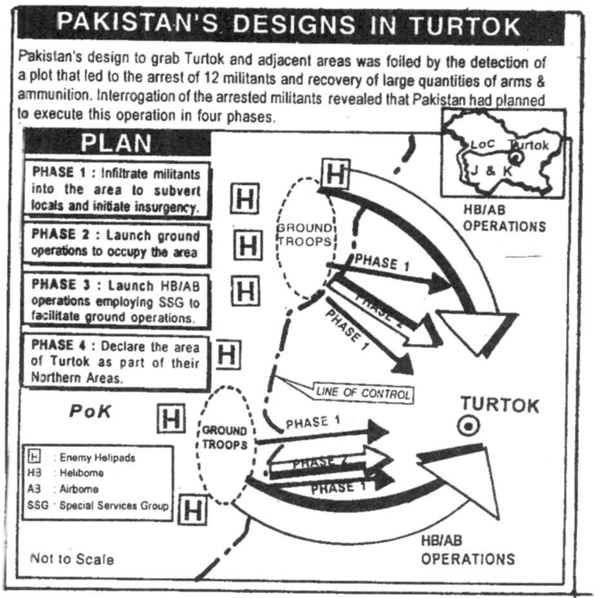

MAP 19: PAKISTAN'S DESIGNS IN TURTOK.

Ground Position as on 11 July

In a face-saving move, Nawaz Sharif met President Clinton on 4 July. The latter had urged him again to withdraw his troops from the Indian side of the LoC. Pakistan then announced the withdrawal of its troops on 11 July 1999. But except from the area of Kaksar, Pakistan did not withdraw its troops from the other sectors, therefore, every inch of territory had to be fought for. It did not pull out its troops from the following three positions, hence, relentless military operations had to be resumed with effect from 16 July and its troops had to be physically evicted. This resulted in casualties on both sides.

1. Mushkoh: a height called 'Zulu'.
2. Dras: a location called 'Saddle'.
3. Batalik: a Ring Contour near the LoC.

These three positions were captured by 25 July and Operation Vijay terminated on this date. However, in the Haneef Uddin sector, the odd localized operation continued even thereafter, till 3 August.

AIR OPERATIONS

The Indian Air Force (IAF) joined the Army in the conduct of Operation Vijay to destroy the Pakistani forces which had surreptitiously infiltrated across the LoC into the Kargil sector. The heavily armed intruders, having well coordinated artillery back-up from across the LoC were well dug in, sufficiently equipped, supplied and intended not only to hold on indefinitely but to spread their tentacles further, thereby jeopardizing the security of Ladakh and of Kashmir Valley. As the Army formations were caught unawares by the turn of events, they needed air support to evict these hard-core elements of the Pakistani Army perched on strongly fortified hill tops, hence the IAF was called in to action to blast the intruders.

The Air Force code-named its part of the offensive 'Operation Safed Sagar'. It had a few unfortunate reverses to begin with. Prior to launching its strikes, the IAF had placed two of its fighter squadrons based at Srinagar and Awantipur on alert. On the first day, 26 May, the IAF launched over 40 strike missions using MiG-21, MiG-23 and Mig-27 aircraft for pounding the intruders while the MiG-29s provided air defence cover. The MiGs were pressed into service to strike at targets at a previously untested altitude because the IAF was confident that they would perform well. The MiG pilots, devoid of sophistication in their machines, had to put in a lot of extra effort compared to the Mirage-2000 multi-role aircraft, which initially provided Electronic Counter-Measure (ECM) support to the strike aircraft. On 27 May, a MiG-27 piloted by Flt. Lt. K. Nachiketa crashed due to engine trouble forcing the officer to bale out. Sqn. Ldr. Ajay Ahuja's MiG-21 that went to its aid was shot down, proving fatal for the daring pilot. The next day, a MI-17 freighter helicopter converted into a gunship was lost to a shoulder-fired Stinger missile, killing its three crew members. Armed helicopters, thereafter, were withdrawn from active combat.

There is no denying that Close Air Support (CAS) to the ground troops is an absolute necessity in order to tilt the scales against the enemy in today's battlefield situation. This, however, becomes a very difficult proposition when the battlefield is situated in high mountains with rocky and snow-covered ridges where the enemy is not only deeply entrenched but has natural camouflage to his advantage. Furthermore, target acquisition in terrain interspersed with mountain tops, valleys, ridge lines, rocky saddles, gorges, rivulets and steep inclines was a most difficult task for an air force pilot flying a combat sortie at near-supersonic speed. He had to spot his minuscule target in the form of a few dug-in intruders and manoeuvre his aircraft for a bombing run. The explicit instructions that the LoC, which ran perilously close to the place of action, was not to be crossed was another drawback. The turning radius of the available aircraft was too great and the lowest speed too high. The IAF found itself severely constrained by the fact that it could not target the infiltrators' supply lines, radars and missile batteries since they were located beyond the LoC, inside the Northern Areas of the POK. The high altitude peaks and anti-aircraft missiles in the possession of the enemy compelled the pilots to fire their weapons at the intruders' bunkers while flying as high as 30,000 ft (9,140 m) above the mean sea level, considerably lessening the impact of the bombs, rockets and missiles. The requisite intelligence inputs, essential for planning the air strikes, were also lacking, specially in the first few days of the aerial combat. The Air Force could overcome these teething troubles only after a week of the commencement of the operations. From then onwards, it went full blast on its devastating missions till the accomplishment of its allotted task in mid-July. In this respect, absence of enemy air opposition was definitely a major advantage for the IAF.

The Air Force utilized an assortment of aircraft for a variety of combat assignments. For intelligence gathering and photo reconnaissance roles, MiG-25R reconnaissance aircraft, procured more than two decades ago from the former Soviet Union and capable of flying at a height of above 80,000 ft (24,400 m) were used. For the same purpose, ancient British-origin Canberras inducted in the mid-1950s were also pressed into service. Even the French-manufactured multi-role Mirage-2000s lent their support for photo reconnaissance. The headquarters-based team of photo interpreters worked overtime in analysing, recognizing and pinpointing the physical locations of numerous enemy bunkers, fortifications, supply lines, ammunition dumps and artillery positions from the dozens of photographs continuously made available by these aircraft flying photo reconnaissance missions throughout the conflict. The likely hostile targets were analysed and reconstructed on the maps with their geographical coordinates, for being passed on to strike squadrons for launching ground attacks.

When the MiG-21 and MiG-27 squadrons initially launched the strike sorties, MiG-29 air superiority aircraft flying overhead provided them with air defence cover. Simultaneously, some of the

Mirage-2000 multi-role aircraft were utilized for Electronic Warfare (EW) missions for guiding and protecting the MiGs during their operational sorties. These EW capabilities enable the Mirage to temporarily blind the enemy command and communication systems by jamming its frequencies.

The IAF, which still happens to be MiG-orientated, used 1960-vintage MiG-21 war-horses for providing ground support to our infantry units. Competent pilots flying these fighter aircraft gave an excellent account of themselves by pounding the enemy positions in the high mountains. MiG-23 and MiG-27 squadrons also participated extensively in strike missions. While MiG-23s acquired in the 1970s comprise attack and interceptor versions, MiG-27s assembled by HAL [Hindustan Aeronautics Ltd] in India and inducted in subsequent years are ground attack aircraft. The technologically sophisticated MiG-29s, which entered squadron service in the late 1980s, are basically interceptor aircraft and they proved their worth in providing air defence cover to the air combat sorties.

The twin-engined deep penetration Jaguar strike aircraft indigenously built under licence from the UK were also intermittently deployed to drop their heavy bomb load to interdict vital Pakistani concentrations. But it was the fly-by-wire multi-role Mirage-2000s that stole the show by their day and night operations. This sophisticated aircraft with its superior navigational attack system released its stand-off weapon load at the enemy fortifications, such as Tiger Hill, Muntho Dhalo feature in the Batalik sector, and the Tololing heights from a height of about 30,000 ft (9,140 m) in order to avoid enemy missiles. Still, the desired accuracy could not be achieved due to highly undulating and rugged mountainous terrain despite the aircraft's sophisticated navigational attack system. During operations, no laser-guided bombs were used. Normal 1,000-pound bombs, modified with a kit to receive laser emissions, were dropped on several occasions. No napalm was used.

During the entire operations, the Air Force flew 550 strike missions, 150 reconnaissance missions and over 500 escort sorties without mishap. It perfected new weapon delivery techniques, which were instrumental in softening enemy targets and enabled the army to launch ground attacks. The IAF's campaign was extremely cost effective, in that it utilized only 25 per cent of the assets under its Western Air Command.

These joint Army-Air Force operations were a fine example of inter-service cooperation and there is a great deal to be imbibed from them for inclusion in our inter-service war manuals. There is, however, always scope for improvement. Certain targets, even though they were located well in depth away from the LoC, could not be interdicted. The main successes of the IAF came against logistics dumps such as the ones at Muntho Dhalo and Point 4388, and targets in the flatter terrain of Mushkoh valley. Further, the priority for the engagement of targets needed better synchronization. For example, the IAF continued on their own with air assaults to isolate Tiger Hill even when it was not an objective in the near future. That too, from the north-east direction, while better dividends were possible from the south-west, as in the south-west was a ledge connecting Tiger Hill to the rest of the ridge. The major lesson which needs to be acknowledged in the context of the tactical battle, was that air power definitely demoralized the enemy and provided the ground troops with a tremendous psychological advantage.

The hard lessons learnt during the action-packed, tense forty-nine days should be of immense value in updating strategy, tactics, doctrines and training pertaining to the deployment of air power independently as well as in support of ground forces in the most effective way. Moreover, combat and support aircraft, and the type of armament and electronic warfare equipment proposed to be acquired from abroad, or to be developed and subsequently manufactured indigenously, must have parameters for effectively operating at very high Himalayan altitudes.

Naval Operations

Once Operation Vijay got under way, the Indian Navy employed its satellites, reconnaissance planes and other modes of intelligence gathering to monitor the movements of the Pakistan Navy. The Indian Navy came to know between 28 and 31 May that Pakistan had alerted its Navy. The Indian Navy was immediately placed on high alert: it moved its Eastern Fleet to join the Western Fleet in the Arabian Sea and deployed its maritime surveillance capabilities. By the first week of June, an exercise was begun off the western coast code-named 'Summerex Phase 1'. These naval manoeuvres ensured that the Indian Navy quickly took a forward position, thus denying Pakistan the initiative. In the absence of the aircraft carrier INS VIRAT which was undergoing refit, the Navy had to improvise and use its ground-based assets such as the Jaguar fighter-bombers.

Pakistan was surprised by the Indian Navy's deterrent deployment

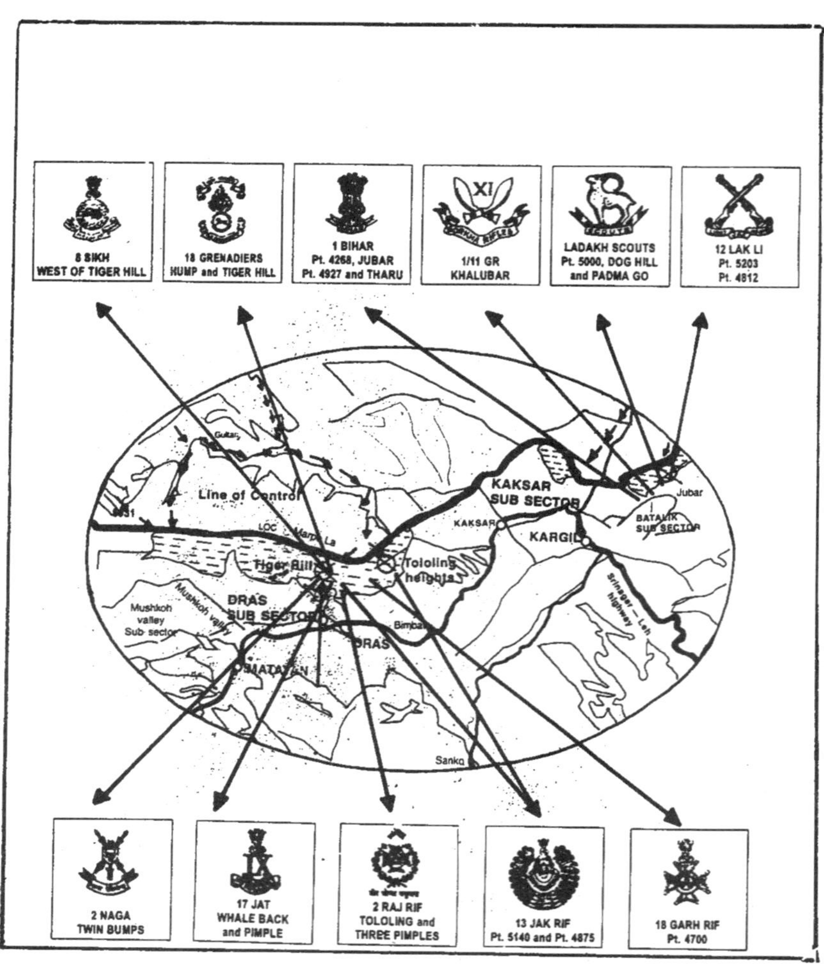

MAP 20: OPERATION VIJAY: UNIT CITATIONS AWARDED BY COAS TO INFANTRY BATTALIONS.

(Operation Talwar) that bottled up the Pakistani fleet in Karachi. This objective was mainly achieved by showing a massive build-up in the Arabian Sea. The Navy's maritime aircraft went on reconnaissance missions over international waters, its versatile Sea Harriers took to the air, and its destroyers fired surface-to-air missiles with a 120-km range, whilst the submarines travelled deep into the sea. It is believed that the naval formations included all Ranjit Class destroyers, some Godavari Class frigates, one Kachin Class destroyer, and Kilo Class submarines. Aware of its vulnerability, Pakistan ordered its ships not to tangle with any Indian vessel.

The Navy was thus ready to impose a naval blockade of Pakistan's coastline in the event of war. Karachi is one of Pakistan's two main ports and contains three of its four refineries. Of Pakistan's trade, 90 per cent is channelized through Karachi, mainly by foreign vessels. Pakistan, for instance, has only one tanker and has to depend on foreign vessels to ferry its oil requirements. If Pakistan were to decide to get its oil requirements via a road which connects an Iranian port with Quetta, it would require 20,000 trucks to transport a tanker full of oil. Pakistan has a maximum oil storage capacity for 7 days. In comparison, India's oil stocks can last for 30 days.

Casualties

The Indian forces suffered the following casualties during Operation Vijay.[11]

TABLE 3.1: INDIAN CASUALTIES

	Army	*Air Force*
Killed	519	5
Wounded	1,365	—
Missing	1	—

There are various estimates of Pakistan Army casualties. Based on published material in Pakistan and Indian calculations, the lowest estimate of Pakistan Army casualties is 737 personnel killed, including 71 officers, 69 of whom have been identified by name. In addition, about 68 SSG and 13 ISI personnel were also killed. The dead bodies of 271 personnel were found, of which 8 were returned and the remaining buried in the battle zone. The Pakistan Army

[11] These figures were given by the Defence Minister, Mr George Fernandes, in a written reply in the Lok Sabha, *The Hindu*, 3 December 1999.

authorities even refused to accept the dead bodies of their fallen soldiers.

Conclusion

Pakistan's plan was brilliant in conception even though it relied heavily on her ability to freeze the situation with international support. Logistically the plan was weak. Had she succeeded in holding on to the areas captured she may have looked further afield. The Dras heights would have enabled Pakistan to send infiltrators towards Pahalgam in the Valley, and from the Batalik complex she would have been able to develop operations between the Indus and Shyok rivers towards Leh. Success in areas east of Turtok would have enabled her to attempt to cut of Siachen.

The Indian Armed Forces responded magnificently to Pakistan's challenge. The Army and Air Force deserve great credit for evicting the well-entrenched Pak Army from Indian territory. The young officers and their troops did a splendid job on the ground. It was they who turned the tables in Kargil. Citations of the recipients of the Param Vir Chakra and the Maha Vir Chakra are at Appendix 7; names of Vir Chakra receipients are also given. Lt. Gen. Krishan Pal and Maj. Gen. Mohinder Puri (commanding 15 Corps and 8 Mountain Division respectively) emerged as very capable field commanders and both were awarded the Uttam Yudh Seva Medal.

4

Lessons, Precepts and Perspectives

Maj. Gen. Ashok Krishna

Introduction

Each battle and each campaign leaves for posterity certain lessons, precepts and perspectives for future guidance. The Kargil war was no exception. This chapter dealing with these aspects has broadly been divided into three parts: the first part pertaining to the main lessons learnt, the second to the imponderables of Indo-Pak confrontation, and the third part to military perspectives.

Main Lessons

INTELLIGENCE

The failure of intelligence needs to be discussed at some length. Pakistan had planned the Kargil venture with meticulous care, right from the training of its Army regulars and some Frontier Corps troops to the logistic back-up required. Pak Army garrisons at Skardu and Astor had received massive stocks of ammunition, equipment and supplies since the beginning of 1998, before these were dispatched to camps close to the LoC. Information now available quite clearly reveals that none of the Indian intelligence agencies had any inkling about Pakistan's war plans in Kargil. Besides, they remained in the dark about the magnitude of the enemy intrusion for as long as three weeks, before a satellite picture showed a colony of enemy supply tents in Muntho Dhalo.

One of the major intelligence failures in the initial stages was the inability to establish the invaders' real identity. The Research and Analysis Wing (RAW) and the Intelligence Bureau (IB) kept insisting during all high-level briefings, that the 'infiltrators' were Taliban militants backed by the Pakistan Army. This they assessed on the basis of signal intercepts which showed that the intruders communicated in Pushto, a language spoken in Afghanistan. It took these agencies nearly a month to realize that the intruders were, in fact, Northern Light Infantry (NLI) soldiers. The NLI troops, locals from Gilgit and Skardu region, talk in Pushto. The intelligence blind spot was so enormous that as late as 17 May the top Intelligence and Army officials were informing during a high-level briefing attended by Prime Minister Atal Behari Vajpayee, Finance Minister Yashwant Sinha and Defence Minister George Fernandes that the intrusions would be cleared 'shortly'.

In the context of intelligence, two major issues need to be emphasized. First, the failure to detect the large numbers of regular Pakistani troops, and some militants employed as porters, who intruded and entrenched themselves in Indian territory. This intelligence lapse has both strategic and tactical dimensions, subsumed within a general failure of national security management. India's strategic intelligence failed because Pakistan's warlike activities in Skardu and Astor comprising the training of militants, building up of stocks of ammunition and food supplies, constructing tracks up to and later beyond the LoC, and transportation of stores to the heights occupied, either went undetected or the correct conclusions were not drawn. For this lapse, RAW is primarily responsible, but the IB, military intelligence and BSF also collect some cross-border information. An enormous amount of information on Pakistan's activities in Kashmir is collected by RAW through its Aviation Research Centre (ARC), with its base in Sarsawa (UP), which flies special electronic intelligence and photo reconnaissance missions. Besides, it has an extensive network of field agents, some of them operating in Pakistan and POK. Although RAW headquarters had information as far back as September 1998 of Pakistan's sinister design, it failed to react appropriately.

The IB with over 400 intelligence personnel has an even stronger presence in the Ladakh region than RAW. In October 1998, according to informed sources, an IB report from Leh spoke of Pakistan's preparations for special operations in the Kargil sector. It has been revealed that the IB officers passed the information not only to their headquarters but also to 121 Brigade Headquarters situated in Kargil. Yet, the information was not followed up with any sense of urgency to assess its authenticity. In June 1998, the IB's Leh office had reported increased activities and build-up on the Pak side of the LoC, but none of the other agencies involved took cognizance of it.

The Armed Forces eventually did a splendid job in evicting the Pakistanis. The battles fought must rank amongst the most magnificent combat actions in the annals of war. But tactical and operational intelligence left much to be desired. Its failure began from the time Pakistan sent reconnaissance parties in November-December 1998, and in late January/early February 1999 these parties started crossing the LoC. They established a first line of administrative bases within a limited distance across the LoC in February. Heavy snowfall in March impeded onward movement, but this was resumed in April when the bulk of the intruders entered Indian territory and moved 2-3 km deeper. These activities went unnoticed because the intruders came across the ridges and Indian troops and sources were not geared to detect movement from this direction. The decades old mindset that this area was fit only for infiltration along the valleys, held sway in operational discussions and exercises. India had been surprised in 1947, 1962, 1965 and 1988 when Pakistan started exporting insurgency and terrorism to J&K for which the country should have been fully prepared in the aftermath of Punjab. In the light of this background and Pakistan's constant attempts at mischief, there was little place for such a mindset. Alertness had enabled India to forestall similar Pakistani intentions in Siachen in April 1984.

Patrolling is feasible in the Kargil heights, in glacial winter conditions, only along nullahs; horizontal patrolling is not possible. Thus, if the LoC has to be approached it has to be along a nullah: for this purpose the troops have to be suitably equipped and trained and some casualties have to be accepted as a consequence. Notwithstanding these constraints and the prevailing mindset, it needs to be emphasized that wherever troops are located, they must be provided with all the wherewithal, right from the outset, to enable them to patrol their area of responsibility in all types of climatic conditions. Brian Cloughley in his book *History of the Pakistan Army: Wars and Insurrections* observes on page 377:

> No commander requires permission to send out patrols unless this caveat has been included in formation Standing Orders or a specific directive to him. The converse is that if no patrolling has been done then the commander and staff at higher HQ (3 Division, Maj. Gen. V.S. Budhwar) should have been uneasy that there was no information coming in about an important sector. It would be standard operating procedure to report on snow-melt,

for example, if for no other reason than to give adequate notice to units about when they would be expected to re-occupy summer positions. Commanders are (or ought to be) unhappy if there is no regular flow of information about terrain and movement conditions, for they never know when they might be required to commit troops to battle. The LoC has never been a holiday camp, and patrols from both sides have tended to stretch the envelope and even trail their coats by what General Pervez Musharraf called 'aggressive patrolling'—in other words, moving across the Line.

The traditional sources of human intelligence (HUMINT) here are local herders who graze their animals on both sides of the LoC, apart from a limited number of sources in POK. They would have reported heightened Pakistani activities in Skardu and areas to the east and south of it. Besides, a fortnightly helicopter patrol carries out surveillance flights of the glaciated and remote areas in the Kargil sector. This patrol, called Winter Air Surveillance Operations, was aimed at giving senior army officers such as battalion, brigade and divisional commanders real time information about activity in the area. This was reinforced by artillery reconnaissance carried out by separate helicopter-borne observation officers. This survey by helicopters, even though of limited value, does not seem to have revealed anything.

Interaction with some of the refugees from Kargil, Leh and Dras has revealed that the intelligence personnel were given adequate information on the military build-up near the LoC by the locals, but for reasons unknown, they did not believe or cross-check these reports. There are laid-down procedures on all these matters which were apparently not complied with, or supervised by higher commanders.

There are no checks and balances in the Indian intelligence system to ensure that the user gets all the available intelligence that is his due. There is no system of regular, periodic and comprehensive intelligence briefings at the political level and to the Committee of Secretaries. In the absence of an overall operational national security framework and objectives, each intelligence agency tends to preserve its own turf and departmental prerogatives. Furthermore, the intelligence agencies need to review their roles consequent upon India becoming a nuclear weapon state, and also in the context of the increasing problems posed by insurgencies and ethno-nationalist movements.

Given the global, regional and internal security environment, India needs a strong intelligence capability to support the defence services and to assist policy makers to formulate and implement policy in non-military realms that affect national security. The main problem is lack of an appropriate organization for acquiring, analysing and disseminating intelligence of value. For external intelligence RAW is responsible, whereas the IB provides internal intelligence. The defence services are responsible for operational intelligence. There is no independent and effective agency, however, to coordinate all these intelligence agencies. The Indian intelligence community lacks overall guidance on what it is expected to do, and in the context of establishing priorities for intelligence collection and analysis to meet the ongoing needs of the government and assessing periodically the performance of intelligence agencies in meeting these needs. There is a requirement, therefore, to restructure the intelligence apparatus to include policy guidance and supervision at the highest level. This would involve:

1. The setting up of a National Intelligence Committee at the level of the National Security Council to provide policy and guidance functions, and the creation of a National Intelligence Board to coordinate the functioning of intelligence agencies.
2. The creation of a Defence Intelligence Agency.
3. The bringing of Technological Intelligence and Space Reconnaissance which include Signal Intelligence, Communication Intelligence, Electronic Intelligence, Imagery Intelligence (aerial and satellite) under a nodal agency for providing inputs to intelligence agencies.
4. Developing a pool of specialists for encryption and decryption of information as well as language skills.

PATROLLING AND CONNECTED ISSUES

Let us examine the capability of a brigade in this type of hazardous terrain. Assume that a brigade has three battalions and each battalion has approximately 500 to 600 men present, the remaining being away on annual leave and courses. Out of this strength, communication and fire support elements, and transport, medical and administrative personnel (like cooks, washermen and safaiwalas) account for nearly 150 men. The four rifle companies thus have about 350 men available for duties within and outside the posts. Of this number, about one-half are deployed on a holding role at various posts and in headquarters. A few men could be away on temporary duty, casual leave, in hospital or other duties. That leaves just about 100 personnel or less in each battalion for long range patrolling to physically traverse their sector of the 160 km over which the intrusions occurred. Each long-range patrol has to carry its ammunition, rations, medicines, snow tents and other equipment to accomplish its task with a modicum of efficiency.

Traversing high altitude areas in winter requires very strenuous effort as the ground is covered with up to 20 ft of snow. Movement is possible only along nullahs. Therefore, a heavily loaded patrol can at best traverse no more than a few kilometres in a day. By the time they accomplish their mission and arrive back at the place from where they set out, about a week or more would have elapsed. These men will thereafter need a week to ten days to recuperate before they can be sent on a patrol again. A few personnel may even suffer high altitude sickness or injury. These patrols are like mountaineering expeditions, the difference being that they are ill-equipped, heavily loaded and get no publicity. Therefore, 121 Infantry Brigade at Kargil with an area of responsibility of 160 km could not have adequately covered its given span even with the most energetic commanders. The 56 Infantry Brigade was raised to take over half this responsibility, but the formation could not be deployed as it was employed on counter-insurgency tasks in the Valley.

Another problem is the availability of officers. Presently, an infantry battalion is woefully understaffed. Against an authorization of 20 officers, the battalions have about 10 to 12 officers. Of these the Commanding Officer, Second-in-Command, Adjutant and Quartermaster cannot be away for long periods like the other officers. Of the remaining, some may be on leave, courses and other duties. That leaves just about 4 to 5 officers for long-range patrols. When these officers get sick or are injured there is no one to replace them. Notwithstanding a host of difficulties, which generally are common to both sides, 121 Infantry Brigade did have the capability to patrol important areas along the nullahs particularly those dominating NH 1A, such as the Tololing feature and other features located in the middle belt between the LoC and NH 1A.

At this stage, it is necessary to take stock of some other connected issues. Due to constant deployment of the infantry in field areas and its employment during its peace tenure on other than training and normal duties, such as aid to civil authority, especially law and order duties, or natural calamities, and for insurgency and counter-terrorism operations, the units are not always fresh, hence, they are prone to battle fatigue. Anything done in excess and under constraints and restraints rebounds. To this condition, we must add erosion of the serviceman's prestige in society, lack of appropriate equipment, paucity of accommodation in peace stations—only 14 per cent married accommodation is authorized for sepoys, problems of children's education, upheaval and uncertainty associated with service life. You thus have a situation wherein the killer instinct is eroded. All this has a bearing on morale. High altitudes bring out the best and worst in men. When the subunits are left to fend for themselves, complacency sets in. Senior commanders should recognize that they have a role to play in inspiring and motivating their troops, so they must go out and visit them and brave their hardships with them for short periods of time. They cannot go everywhere, but physical movement to reach a post and a night's stay there will inspire the men and also in neighbouring posts when they hear about their commanders' concern for them.

There was a rule regarding physical fitness in the British days which was rigorously enforced and which we would do well to follow throughout the Army: a corps commander if he has to successfully command his corps must be as fit as his battalion commanders, and the army commander as fit as the brigade commanders. In this era of indoor briefings and the sand model culture which has crept in the last two decades, physical fitness and personal example have become the main casualty. This eventually manifests itself in creating a chasm in the officer-man relationship. To illustrate, John Masters in his book *The Road Past Mandalay* writes about his posting as General Staff Officer 1 (GSO 1) to HQ 19 Infantry Division during World War II. The Divisional Commander was Maj. Gen Pete Rees, DSO, MC and Bar. When Masters reported for duty at the headquarters and asked about the whereabouts of his boss, he was informed by his GSO 2 that if the General had decided to keep in close touch with his headquarters, he would be with the forward platoon. And if he was in his usual place, he would be with the forward section. Sure enough, Masters found his general watching a platoon-level combat action from near his jeep dressed in his full regalia of red band on his Gorkha hat, red tabs on his collar and a red scarf round his neck. His casual remark to Masters, who wondered if it was really necessary for the general to expose himself, was, 'A dead general is a great morale booster.' Every general does not have to replicate Pete Rees—certainly not in high altitude—but the prevailing ethos of going forward both in peace and war needs to be reinforced for it builds morale, officer-men relations and mutual confidence, which leads to victory.

Furthermore, the recent tendency to have frequent high-level war games in which unit officers are involved, needs to be deprecated. These events at brigade and divisional levels are generally a waste of time for these officers and are often held for the benefit of higher commanders who should, in fact, go to the ground and stand in the cold or heat with their men. Discussions held in the comfortable surroundings of a map or sand model room cannot be a substitute for activity on the ground. During training, the emphasis should be on holding tactical exercises without troops (TEWTs), skeleton or signal exercises, followed by an exercise with troops.

A field tenure should be looked upon as an opportunity to improve the battle efficiency of units and to cement bonds between all ranks: bonding is an essential ingredient of victory. Incidentally, unit and subunit commanders and troops feel insecure when not-too-serious visitors alight from helicopters for a few minutes and think they have done their jobs. The Indian jawan wants little, but he needs to be assured that, under the prevailing circumstances, his commanders in the chain of command are doing their physical and mental best for him. When this realization came about in Kargil, the same young officers and men whose units had been faulted for not patrolling, went hammer and tongs for the enemy showing scant disregard for their lives and accomplished impossible tasks.

Politicians, bureaucrats, journalists and some armchair appointments are quite unaware of these problems, hence, their unrealistic expectations and demands.

CRITICAL SHORTAGES

General

Men and equipment make for a winning combination in war. The high Indian casualties can partly be attributed to the scarcity of critical combat aids. This, many say, is because of the mismanagement of the country's defence spending in the past decade. Vice Adm. (retd) K.K. Nayyar, a member of the 1990 Arun Singh Committee on Defence Expenditure, claims, 'The Kargil crisis is directly attributable to the starvation of funds for the armed forces during the '90s.' Some examples of critical shortages are narrated below.

One of the reasons for such shortages has been the severe defence cuts. From a peak of 3.6 per cent in 1987-8, the share of defence expenditure in India's Gross Domestic Product (GDP) slipped to 2.33 per cent in 1998-9. Though this is a global trend, India spends a much smaller proportion of its GDP on defence than Pakistan and China. Pakistan still spends about 5.3 per cent of its GDP on defence. Experts believe that the shortcoming is not in the *amount* that is spent on defence, but the *manner* in which it is spent. Money is used best when it flows according to plan. The Indian Armed Forces have not had a long-term plan for years. The fault is not really theirs, because the plans made were not approved. In fact, since 1985, defence has been on a virtual plan holiday. The Seventh Five Year Plan (1985-90) was cleared by the cabinet only in 1989, rendering it ineffective. The Eighth Plan (1991-5) was never cleared and even the Ninth Plan (1997-2002) is yet to be approved.

Equipment Shortages

An Army requisition for low-intensity conflict equipment worth less than Rs. 50 crores had been awaiting approval of both the Ministries of Finance and of Home Affairs since 1997. Its clearance would have provided the forces in Kargil with critical aids like night vision devices (cost about Rs. 2 lakh a piece; shortfall about 700), commando equipment (worth Rs. 11 crore), snowmobiles (Rs. 2 crore for 10) and rocket and grenade launchers (requirement: 5,000 and 2,000 costing Rs. 10 crore). Reports from the front suggest that the deficiencies included other mundane items like light-weight rucksacks, snow goggles, all-weather rucksacks and tents, and hand-held thermal imagers. Could the defence budget—now totalling over Rs. 40,000 crore—not provide for these items that are essential for high altitude warfare and living? Why they could not be manufactured and procured within the country needs examination of the working of DRDO and the Ministry of Defence Production.

About 10 per cent of the Bofors FH 77B medium guns were dysfunctional for want of spares. The lack of spares has forced the 'cannibalization' of parts (stripping parts of one gun to use them in another). So grave was the perceived shortage of spares that the Parliament's Standing Committee even suggested 'lifting of ban on Bofors for licensed production' of its spares in India. Less than a month after that warning, India was importing shells for Bofors guns at prices up to $1,000 (Rs. 43,000) a piece. The reason why the Bofors guns is not being licence-manufactured or its ammunition produced in India has to do with politics. It is inexplicable, however, why the desultory inquiry into the malfeasance in this contract could not be separated from taking steps to keep the available guns operational in the interests of national security.

The list of deficiencies could be further extended, but four items are of relevance to Kargil-type conflicts.

First, the Army's lack of battlefield surveillance and gun-locating radars. This would have permitted accurate counter-bombardment of Pakistani artillery positions across the LoC and saved our troops heavy casualties due to shelling.

Second, the Air Force's lack of suitable aircraft to attack targets in mountainous terrain. The Advanced Jet Trainer (AJT) is designed to perform, apart from its primary training functions, an operational role in mountainous areas, deriving from its manoeuvreability and useful bomb load. Its procurement case has been lingering in the Ministry of Defence for over sixteen years.

Third, the Air Force was unable to use its MI-17 helicopters in the Kargil operations after one of them was brought down by Stinger missiles. It is unclear why the Defence Research and Development Organisation (DRDO), which is aware of the Stinger missile threat to our aircraft for over a decade, has not been able to provide the countermeasures to ensure their protection.

Last, inducting surveillance equipment needs greater attention. Apart from surveillance by satellites and remotely piloted aircraft, such equipment comprises sensors of various types. Thermal imaging sensors would enable remotely piloted aircraft to operate by night. This technology has been around since the Vietnam war, and it is disconcerting that the DRDO has not refined them to suit our particular counter-insurgency and counter-terrorism requirements. The need for a 'national surveillance command' for handling satellite surveillance has been highlighted in the Subrahmanyam Committee Report.[1]

A realistic evaluation of the deficiencies highlighted by the Kargil conflict would discover the military equipment essentially required by the Armed Forces. These include special clothing for extreme cold conditions and the new light rifles (5.56 mm Insa) and other equipment needed to lighten the load on the infantry soldier deployed at high altitudes. Fulfilling these requirements would add marginally to the defence budget, but remain relevant to meeting the threat of 'many Kargils' held out by irresponsible Pakistani leaders.

[1] 'National Security to be Reviewed', *The Hindu*, 25 February 2000, p. 1.

If some of this equipment and spares had been available, they would not only have reduced casualties, but deterred the adversary and prevented the very occurrence of the intrusions. Kargil represents a failure of India's conventional military deterrence.

Though not relevant to the Kargil war, it would, however, be pertinent to note that in May 1999, the Army was short of at least 300 T-90 and T-72 battle tanks and about a thousand 155 mm artillery guns to sharpen its edge in a full-scale conventional war. Besides, the other two services were also severely impacted by budget cuts. For the Indian Air Force to score a decisive victory over Pakistan, it should have at least 44 squadrons. It had only 39 and a half squadrons. Naval preparedness was no better. Between 1990 and 1999, the number of principal naval combat vessels like submarines and destroyers fell from 44 to 36.

Manning of our Borders

Taking a cue from the Army Chief's assessment that all heights and borders cannot be physically manned, particularly when part of our one-million Army is also committed to the Chinese front, the insurgency-prone states of the North-East and other internal security duties, it will be necessary to do some rethinking to revamp the monitoring and surveillance systems so that we are not surprised again. Hence, manpower resources would have to be augmented with the induction of thermal imaging and other sensors.

Despite this modernization of armament and equipment, most areas in the mountains will have to be physically manned by manpower considered tactically optimum by the Army. The LADAKH SCOUTS, which demonstrated exceptional valour and skill in fighting in Kargil's inhospitable terrain, reinforced the concept that the locals have an edge over their brethren in terms of knowledge of terrain, expertise in negotiating steep cliffs, and dealing with the vagaries of special climatic conditions that affect warfare. Hence, there is a case for giving serious consideration to enhanced deployment of units with a recruitment base in the Ladakh region, e.g. Ladakhis and Kargil Shias who could man the borders in areas where the conflict occurred. Even landless ex-servicemen volunteers from the Punjab and Himachal Pradesh could be considered for induction and organized into communes sustained on farming, poultry and other cottage industries.

However, it needs to be reiterated that Siachenization of our border areas is not recommended. Such a policy would be wasteful in manpower and resources. Inst ad, a firm declaratory policy pertaining to the consequences should be made known to Pakistan, so that it does not venture in to 'more Kargils'.

Whilst on the issue of our border areas, there is a need to appreciate the constant harassment the civil population suffers in these locations as a result of regular Pakistani firing and Indo-Pak wars. Measures must be taken to make their lives secure and compensate them for their losses. They could even be moved to safe areas at Government expense. It is the Government's responsibility to win the hearts and minds of the border population, and to make them feel that they are a vital component of the country.

Leadership

That there is a dearth of leadership in the country as a whole needs no emphasis. Politicians and bureaucrats hesitate to take timely decisions, they have been unable to streamline tardy procedures, cut through red tape and make for efficient functioning. This inadequacy, which has increased over the years, shows up in a crisis. At the military level, deficiencies were noticed in leadership training. Three points stand out. First, there is too much micro-management by higher-level commanders. Second, while leaders need to think one level up, it is more important to be able to clearly visualize the battle two levels down. And third, whilst tact is important, cringing and subservience have no place in the Armed Forces—a yes man does no good to the organization.

The decisive factor in the outcome of a war is the human element. Defence manpower is the most important of resource elements. But adequate attention has not being given to it. This resource has to be enriched through integrated manpower management, which should include proper education and training, inculcating professionalism, motivation and the right quality of leadership. In this regard, the problems of securing quality manpower for the Services, due to relatively inferior career prospects, has to be clearly recognized by the policy makers. For instance, the Army continues to be deficient of about 13,000 officers, and this deficiency is only in the junior ranks which provide the cutting edge in battle in the units. Higher ranks get filled by promotion, denuding Capts/Lts. This has been the state for some time now. With a population of one billion and so much unemployment, it should not be difficult to remedy this state of affairs. This is, however, not possible till we have a clearly enunciated National Manpower Policy which is approved by Parliament for statutory implementation.

Nature of Indo-Pak Confrontation

THE NATURE OF PROXY WAR AND LOW INTENSITY CONFLICT

Proxy war and pure low-intensity conflict each have a momentum of their own. While in a low-intensity conflict the focus has to be on the militant, proxy war necessitates attention being concentrated on two enemies at least: the militant group(s) within its/their boundaries, and the state sponsoring them (in this case Pakistan). If the will to interact and support each other is successfully destroyed, the cohesion between the two would be shattered and the militant campaign would lose momentum. Prior to the Kargil war, the attention of higher commanders was almost exclusively directed at the militant, even though in all our teaching 'nibbling actions on mountain ranges overlooking the Kashmir Valley' were always regarded as a possibility. It had been correctly assessed by the Indian Army that Pakistan would maintain a balanced defensive posture all along the LoC to ensure that no territory of strategic or tactical significance was lost. Further, defences would be held with adequate strength to enable the capture of maximum territory across the LoC in areas where Pakistan was capable of launching a limited offensive with one or two infantry brigades to improve its defensive posture and capture maximum territory, based on the premise that areas captured along the LoC would be retained by either side. The deployment across the LoC would aim at holding heights and ridge lines and stretching forward to gain direct observation and domination over the lines of communication. Despite a clear perception of these possibilities, the higher Indian leadership did not take adequate ground and aerial measures to deter or detect Pakistani incursions.

It is relevant to note that our response to regular Pakistani infiltration into J&K was to fire equally regularly into the Neelam valley (in Tithwal) so as to block the direct road running along the Kishen Ganga river (the Pakistanis call it the 'Neelam river') to northern POK, forcing them to use more difficult and less developed detours. It, therefore, should have been anticipated that Pakistan would look for an opportunity to also block our lines of communication, and what better area could there be than Kargil? Indeed, Pakistan had pursued this strategy over the past two years by shelling the Kargil–Leh road in summer to disrupt stocking operations for the troops of 3 Infantry Division in Leh. Unfortunately, there was a two-decade-old mindset that Kargil was unsuitable for cross-LoC military action.

PAKISTAN'S IRRATIONALITY

Pakistani actions have invariably belied Indian assessments. Its actions, even though perceived by India to be irrational, are backed by proactive action, indicating both boldness and resolve, and a confidence in the ability of the Western nations and China to bail it out in the event of an adverse situation. On the other hand, rational Indian assessments are premised on reactive action. This constant holding back of the Indian Army will inevitably lead to reaction fatigue.

In the context of irrationality, some Western defence analysts had predicted that if India crossed the LoC with a view to opening a new front, it would pressurize Islamabad to contemplate using the nuclear option, because a weaker nation is forced into taking an earlier decision to use the deterrent for fear of being put in a 'use it or lose it' situation. In an eventuality like this, great care has to be taken not to play into the hands of Pakistan's hawks. In the process, both countries would be provoking the intervention of the international community, since the repercussions of even a limited nuclear exchange could be catastrophic. The UN Security Council would meet within six hours, and a host of sanctions could follow, far more stringent than what followed Pokhran II—a ban on private investments, trade sanctions under the WTO, and oil sanctions. This may seem an extreme view as during the Kargil war no concrete nuclear threat seems to have been held out by either country, though some threatening noises were reported in the media.

Nevertheless, India cannot indefinitely countenance Pakistani belligerence, hence, it must indicate firm thresholds which it will not accept being violated. One such threshold indicated by India in the context of starting talks between the two countries, is that Pakistan must first stop trans-border terrorism. The continuance of proxy war by Pakistan should invite firmer measures—both legal and military—against the intruders inside J&K. Pak army personnel and militants operating on the Indian side of the LoC who kill civilians should be treated as war criminals and tried accordingly; this should be made clear. In the event of incursions not ceasing, measures would have to be considered across the LoC. In the context of possible actions across the LoC, secrecy is mandatory, hence, these do not have to be specified here.

Kargil has to be seen in relation to India's shrinking borders since Independence. India now controls just 45 per cent of the erstwhile state of J&K. It remains under constant pressure on Kashmir. The future will see a rise in militancy in the whole of J&K and the next Kargil is bound to occur unless we are on guard. There is a limit beyond which India cannot tolerate Pakistan's antics. This is the time to display strategic vision. The world must be clearly told that we cannot allow Pakistan to carry out its proxy war unhindered and in this context, it will become necessary to cross the LoC at some stage. Offence remains the best form of defence.

Then there are responses short of war which emphasize the military dimension varying from stoicism, passive defence measures (both already in operation) to proactive responses. These proactive responses comprise reprisal, pre-emption, and retribution. All three can be viewed as coercive measures short of war, although each is also applicable in the context of general warfare. All three forms of responses have legal justification under Article 51 of the UN Charter, which reserves to nations the inherent right of self-defence. Insurgency and terrorism sponsored and supported by a foreign government are forms of aggression which invite a response commensurate with the levels of perceived, projected or actual threat. Governments thus threatened should not be afraid to apply force in protecting their interests, citizens and property, whilst still attempting to find peaceful, long-term solutions to the problems. It is outside the scope of this paper to go into details; the reader is, however, referred to the article, 'Insurgency and Terrorism: Proactive Responses', in *Strategic Analysis* of August 1995.

The international insurgent or terrorist has added substantially to the existing atmosphere of instability that endangers the progress of peaceful international relations. Under these circumstances, to maintain a posture of injured innocence and vacillation in the face of militant activity is to substantiate its validity as a political stratagem. The main weapons of the insurgent and terrorist of today are fear, murder and laws which flow out of the barrel of a gun. These proactive responses to insurgency and terrorism must be judged in the context of the circumstances in which they are employed, the limitations imposed on the use of force and the ends designed to be achieved. No response can ever be completely clean or pure. The temptation to compromise by adopting a reactive course must be resisted, notwithstanding the failure to define rightful responses to proxy war, to international satisfaction. The outcome of proxy war will not only depend on the development of militant strength, but, more important, on the vigour, determination and dexterity with which the victim state puts its act together, both politically and militarily. Some gesture of political accommodation to the local Kashmiris must also be made by India.

Failure to indicate a threshold in the past has resulted in the J&K conflict remaining as a festering sore between the two countries. Except on the basis of its boldness, Pakistan can lay no claim to anything in J&K on legal, constitutional or any other grounds, yet it dictates events. Here, the international community and particularly China and the Western nations cannot be absolved of the blame for encouraging Pakistani actions and even pressuring India to restore the status quo ante as in 1965 and 1971.

Pakistan's irrationality has to be addressed through political and military preparations, by never lowering our guard, and by firm action and not mere words. Further, we must apprise regional and global powers of Pakistan's irrational activities and behaviour, which, now with the nuclear trigger in the hands of its military, could increase further.

RESPONSE TIMING AND FORCE LEVELS

One of the main lessons of this conflict is the need for maintaining a balanced force level, one commensurate with the anticipated threat, and so positioned as to be able to counter rapidly any hostile attempt to seize the initiative in any sector. The assessment of hostile objectives and the placement of hostile forces would be the main consideration in the location of one's own resources and the development of allied facilities for logistics and communications. The cushion afforded by territorial space can no longer be relied upon without serious jeopardy to the eventual recovery of territorial losses suffered in the initial exchange. The main strike components should be so located as to be within easy access of their likely deployment areas. Other less important elements could be moved to peripheral areas.

As a corollary to the strategy of 'response timing', the side with the briefest time lag in committing its forces to battle would achieve 'strategic surprise' over its adversary. The Pakistanis were able to achieve total 'strategic surprise' over the Indians by the rapidity with which the Pakistani forces were deployed initially. It would, therefore, appear inadvisable to base contingency plans on the accepted norms of a well-defined warning period. Prudence would dictate that reaction capability be so developed as to position combat formations to thwart a major offensive within 72 to 96 hours of the receipt of warning of an impending attack or a sharply deteriorating political situation.

MILITARY PERSPECTIVES

INFANTRY

All arms and services contributed to India's victory in Kargil. But, in the ultimate analysis, it was the infantrymen who faced the murderous fusillade of the enemy's infantry and artillery fire, and the icy winds that lashed their faces for days together. They stood up to adversity cheerfully, absorbed heavy casualties, attacked along unexpected approaches and cliff faces, continued fighting, and triumphed in the end. Capturing heights in high altitude requires a six-to-one superiority at least, but boldness, courage and audacity enabled the infantry to capture objectives by employing much lesser strength. Units like 2 RAJ RIF and 18 GRENADIERS fought in the Tololing sector and then in the Tiger Hill sector, displaying great resilience over an extended period of time. Of those killed and wounded, 95 per cent were from the infantry.

Two important tactical lessons emerged.

1. *Momentum in the Offensive.* All offensive operations must ensure that the momentum is maintained and the initiative retained throughout by judicious use of reserves. Once Tololing was captured, nothing could stop the Indian infantry.
2. *Boldness.* On account of the operational restriction placed by the political executive that the LoC not be crossed, offensive options were considerably reduced. This factor, as also shortages in men and material, were overcome by boldness in planning with an element of acceptable risk, and executed with alacrity and resolution. Consequently, operations after the capture of Tololing proceeded apace, and within one month the enemy was evicted from the entire area—a most creditable feat of arms.

India has a 1,094 km mountainous frontier with Pakistan and 4,576 km with China. In this type of terrain, the infantry is the predominant arm, hence, it must be ensured that infantry battalions are appropriately equipped and trained and there are no deficiencies of officers and men in the units. India is a manpower-intensive nation and every endeavour should be made to make up shortfalls, particularly in the officer cadre. The infantry's needs with regard to the provisioning of radars, lighter weapons and more firepower must also be met with dispatch, as also its requirements in the context of better communications, vehicles and combat gear. Night attacks will be the rule rather than the exception, hence, night vision and night fighting devices must be provided. Intensified training and procurement of state of the art equipment for high altitude warfare is the need of the hour. Due to the varied roles and tasks that it has to perform within the existing availability of battalions, it will be necessary for units to be adequately trained to switch roles. Being a developing country, we have to be content with a combination of state of the art equipment and some obsolescent equipment, with a higher proportion of the former.

It is conceded that industrial strength combined with technical sophistication is a powerful formula. Given the will, plus space, geography and time, whatever the state of their material equipment, human beings on foot will remain a premier segment in any conflict scenario. The victory at Kargil will remain an enduring edifice to the infantryman's hardihood, courage and endurance to be emulated in future.

ARTILLERY

Between 8 May when Operation Vijay began and 11 May, more than 20 infantry soldiers were killed in hand-to-hand combat. This made it obvious that it was first necessary to hit the enemy from the air and by artillery fire. But after the loss of three aircraft, the Air Force flew well above the targets to avoid being hit by Stinger missiles. Thus, a heavy burden fell on the artillery and within days, about 90 Bofors guns (and later 30 more) were moved to Dras, Kaksar and Batalik sectors. Since most of the strategic positions had been lost, it was difficult for the observation officers to direct fire. However, after some hard work and effective ground reconnaissance, the guns began to deliver.

Yet, the casualty rate did not come down. It became obvious that the covering fire was not sufficient. The prescribed rule is that for every infantry unit, there are 6 guns in direct support. In Operation Vijay, this was enhanced to 18 guns. This provided much-needed insurance for the troops. To ensure sustained and effective fire on the enemy, Indian gunners fired 5,000 to 6,000 shells on an average each day. Much of the ammunition could have been saved if India had a few more vantage-points to observe from and direct fire. Pakistan had this advantage, and, therefore, fired only 500 to 600 shells each day. While the Bofors alone fired 1,000 to 1,200 shells per day, this figure increased on the day of the assault. For instance, 9,000 shells were fired on the day Tiger Hill was regained. As the assault began on Tiger Hill, over 1,200 rounds of high explosive (HE) rained down on the feature in the space of five minutes. During the war, about 42 fire units were deployed to support the fighting formations on the Indian side; of these, 20 were of the medium and heavy variety. Thus, there were over 250 guns in the area of operations. If this were a full-scale war, the maximum threat to Indian gun areas would have come from the enemy air force. The absence of enemy air attacks helped the quicker deployment of guns. Most of the gun emplacements were in the open, on either side of the National Highway (NH 1A).

All infantry attacks were preceded by sustained fire assaults from over 100 artillery guns, mortars and rocket launchers. Thousands of shells, bombs and rocket warheads caused havoc on the targets and prevented the enemy from interfering with the assault till the fire was lifted for safety reasons. Despite the controversy over its induction into service, the 155 mm Bofors FH 77B medium gun performed extremely well, and was the mainstay of artillery fire power. Its range of 30 km enabled it to be used for deep strikes against enemy gun positions, administrative installations, ammunition dumps and headquarters. It was even used in the direct firing role. The 130 mm medium gun with a maximum range of 27 km also achieved good success against enemy targets. This gun fires only in low angle, that is, below an angle of departure of 45 degrees. The 105 mm Indian Field Gun (IFG) with a range of 17,500 m provided close support to infantry battalions by destroying targets in close proximity of the attacking troops. This gun, and the Bofors firing in a direct firing mode, destroyed visible enemy *sangars*. The 122 mm GRAD multi-barrelled rocket launchers (MBRLs) were employed to destroy soft area targets in the open like camps, installations and headquarters with its high volume of fire delivered in a compressed time frame. A battery of six 122 mm MBRL can fire a salvo of 240 rockets in 20 seconds.

The availability of longer range MBRLs like the 300 mm BM 9A52 SMERCH Multiple Rocket System (in service with countries of the Russian Federation) with a range of 70 km would have enabled the engagement of Skardu and deeper targets from Kargil. This system had been ordered by India to equip regiments within the newly formed artillery divisions, but the order had yet to materialize. India's own multi-barrel rocket system, the Pinaka, proved very successful during field testing in the Kargil war. Having a range of 39 km, Pinaka can fire a salvo of 12 rockets within 44 seconds. One salvo each (12 rockets) fired from a battery of six launchers can neutralize a target of 3.9 sq. km. It has the capability of being fitted with different types of warheads. The blast-cum-pre-fragmented high explosives (HE), anti-personnel (AP) minelets for targeting troops, and anti-tank (AT) minelets, are a few of its special features. The Bofors medium gun requires upgradation. There is a need for enhancing firepower with guns of higher calibre, capable of firing larger shells for rapid destruction of the enemy's war-sustaining capability on the battlefield. The country having achieved a reasonable degree of self-reliance in design and development of most missile systems and other field guns and weapon systems, would be able to give stronger support to the Indian Army in future.

The artillery played a crucial role in aiding the advance of the infantry. As a result, at places the infantry faced less resistance. Point 4875, a post south-west of Tiger Hill, was captured with minimal casualties to the infantry. The post was renamed 'Gun Hill'. The destruction of a fuel and ammunition dump north of Kukarthang in Batalik by the devastating fire of 105 mm guns aided the capture of Jubar in that sector. Three artillery units received the COAS' Unit Citation: 141 Field Regiment, 197 Field Regiment (CO Col. Allok Deb, SM) and 108 Medium Regiment.

In this war, the Indian artillery fired more than 1,50,000 shells in about a month: it was most successful when it was used in an unconventional manner. Likewise, the use of air defence guns in a direct fire role paid useful dividends against enemy positions. Enemy artillery fire, caused 80 per cent of our own casualties, a clear indication that in the absence of gun locating radars, the Indian artillery could not silence Pakistani guns, which fired about 1,00,000 rounds in the conflict. Pakistani troops also suffered a high percentage of their casualties as a result of Indian artillery fire. On the Indian side, Brig Lakhwinder Singh commanded 8 Mountain Artillery Brigade with distinction.

ARMY AVIATION

The versatility of the helicopter for combat assault, for command and control missions for observation, movement of troops, logistics and casualty evacuation, was more than amply demonstrated by the Kargil war. The Indian Army Aviation Corps must get an agile medium transport helicopter like the Puma if it is to perform efficiently in high altitude terrain. 663 and 666 Reconnaissance and Observation Squadrons were awarded the COAS' Unit Citation in the Kargil war.

USE OF AIR POWER

The employment of air power was seen in the Air Force and at the Governmental level as a step that could lead to the escalation of the conflict to a higher level of war. Therefore, the Cabinet Committee on Security (CCS) could not clear the Army's request for air support till the concerned Air Commands had been alerted and the magnitude of the intrusion had been more or less fully assessed. This is a conservative approach that needs to be jettisoned. Air power today is central to any military endeavour, be it counter-insurgency, limited war, conventional war, or general war involving nuclear weapons. It is an integral component of a nation's military capability both in peace and war.

The Air Force had a tremendous psychological impact during the Kargil war; its use was also an indication of national resolve. In the absence of enemy air, worthwhile lessons in the context of aerial combat could not emerge. The photo reconnaissance capabilities of the Air Force based on MiG-25 aircraft were found to be deficient and need to be upgraded. The need for a more manoeuvrable aircraft like the Advanced Jet Trainer (AJT) has already been highlighted.

THE NAVY

The Navy played a stellar role by moving fast to take a forward position and deny Pakistan the initiative, thus making naval deterrence a success in the conflict. The Navy must not be neglected if we are to successfully dominate the Arabian Sea and the Bay of

Bengal. Its strength and modernization are issues that need immediate attention. Unfortunately, our nuclear submarine project (Advanced Technology Vehicle) has been stumbling along for the last thirty years, and after spending more than Rs. 2,000 crore on the project, the fear is that even when a prototype is launched, it may be a case of too little too late. For a submarine to play the role of a nuclear deterrent, it has to have nuclear propulsion. But that is just one small part of the true submarine. In the light of the military psychology of Pakistan, evident in their Kargil operation, India could be forced to fight a full-fledged war with Pakistan sooner or later. In our interest, therefore, we should have a submarine capable of performing its strategic role of providing a second strike capability, at the very earliest. Its specifications have to be such that it has a clear speed advantage on surface ships to maintain locational secrecy. This can be achieved only if the submarine has sufficient power and an optimally designed hull and propulsion system to impart a speed–distinctly higher than the speed of surface ships.

STRATEGIC TECHNOLOGICAL RESEARCH

Even at the end of the millennium, India fought a war that was no different from the Indo-Pak wars of 1948, 1965 and 1971, and ridges and cliffs that should have been cleared with laser- and TV-guided bombs were drenched with human blood. It is essential that a programme of continuous development, specially in the electronic field, be implemented so as to acquire and deal effectively with the broad spectrum of various electronic systems, heat seeking weapons, laser, electronic snooping, rocketry and hostile communication links. For example, a Sideways Looking Airborne Radar (SLAR) would have been extremely useful in the Kargil imbroglio. The technology is so sophisticated that the US does not share it even with its NATO allies. The advantage of SLAR is that the reconnaissance aircraft can fly at a stand off distance and not expose itself to hostile enemy air defences. This technology was developed by Indian Space Research Organisation (ISRO) more than ten years ago. In 1989, it was fitted on an AN-32 aircraft and trials carried out in the deserts of Rajasthan. But an influential body within the Cabinet Secretariat favoured the import of SLAR. The DRDO then wanted to develop its own SLAR: there was no point in wanting to start all over again, when we already had a flightworthy ISRO system in 1989. Had the SLAR been accepted in 1990 by the IAF, it would have been in operational use long ago. The SLAR is a powerful reconnaissance radar equally effective by day or night. It does not require the aircraft to fly over the target. Its use in the Kargil sector would have revealed the build up across the LoC.[2]

THE NUCLEAR FACTOR

Pakistan has had the bomb since 1987 and India from 1990. Both countries were developing their weapons. Pakistan was getting assistance from China and the US was looking the other way. The US knew all about Pakistan's programme, but it took no notice because it needed Pakistan's support for the Afghan war. Only after the Soviets withdrew from Afghanistan did the US come down on Pakistan with the Pressler Amendment, and that too when Gen. Aslam Beg openly started siding with Saddam Hussein. Both India and Pakistan are now nuclear and the Pakistanis are in a position to deliver a first-generation nuclear weapon on India by aircraft as well as missiles which Pakistan has obtained from China and North Korea. India also is in a position to deliver nuclear weapons on Pakistan with its aircraft and Prithvi missiles. This is a reality which cannot be overlooked. However, that does not necessarily mean that the subcontinent has become a nuclear flashpoint. Many people think that as soon as nuclear weapons are produced, they would be distributed to forward areas. That is not so. We can be reasonably certain that all Pakistani nuclear weapons are safely kept under the direct control of their Chief of the Army Staff.[3] He is not going to hand over these weapons to any of his corps commanders because it might provide them with an opportunity to challenge him. In the Cold War era, the nuclear powers had battlefield or tactical nuclear weapons, hence, one could fire that kind of warhead with the 155 mm gun like the Bofors with India or the M-9 gun which the Pakistanis have. Battlefield, i.e. tactical nuclear weapons do not exist with either Pakistan or India, and that kind of confrontation is not being anticipated by either country.

A nuclear weapon will invoke a nuclear response. In that respect

[2] Wg. Cdr. Joseph Thomas, 'IAF Ignored Reconnaissance Radar', *International Defence Review*, July-September 1999.

[3] K. Subrahmanyam, 'Nuclearization of the Sub-Continent and the Changing Defence Scenario', in *Kargil: The Crisis and its Implication* (Nehru Memorial Museum & Library, Delhi, 1999), pp. 50-1.

Pakistan is extremely vulnerable. Most Pakistani cities are very close to the Indian border. They are all within the range of Indian aircraft and the Pakistani population is concentrated in their eastern border areas. The Pakistani high dams are all within the range of Indian aircraft and some 10-12 nuclear weapons will totally devastate them. Hence, the Pakistanis are unlikely to use the nuclear weapons they possess because they had a setback in Kargil. They are not going to use nuclear weapons even if there is large-scale fighting on the LoC: if one uses nuclear weapons, he does not know what the adversary may do.

Therefore, one should not expect Pakistan to take any such risk. Further, India has offered a no-first-use agreement. Under these circumstances, the risks of a nuclear war starting between India and Pakistan are negligible. At the same time, nuclear weapons do have an impact on the military relationship between two countries. That impact will be that a nuclear weapon country cannot be threatened beyond a particular point. There are some tolerance limits beyond which one country cannot push the other.[4] For instance, India cannot launch a piercing thrust into Pakistan. That would be seen as an attempt to destroy Pakistan and could invite a nuclear response. But India has never sought to dismember Pakistan. In 1965 when Pakistan started the war, the Indian objectives were limited to the Ichhogil Canal, and in 1971, the Indian 1 Corps held itself in check on the western front and penetrated only a few kilometres inside Pakistan. Further, it is not in India's interests to cause the disintegration of Pakistan. If a country threatens to punish the other, then it could be driven to a point where it may have to think about resorting to nuclear weapons. Therefore, care has to be exercised in using language. Hence, there is a limit beyond which one should not risk testing the tolerance of a nuclear adversary. Both India and Pakistan will have to bear this in mind, and they do bear it in mind.

There is yet another dimension which one has to think of in the nuclear context. Some people are talking about the US and its influence on the subcontinent. Americans are not going to permit any other country in the world to use a nuclear weapon. It has got nothing to do with whether they like you or not. It is not in their security interests to permit any nation in the world to use a nuclear weapon and get away with it. The Americans will consider that development as a threat to their national security, and they have the

[4] Ibid.

means of finding out what India or Pakistan are doing. 'If the Pakistanis start even fitting their aircraft with nuclear weapons or getting their missiles out and start fitting them with nuclear warheads, the American satellites will pick them up and in real time the information will be available to the US. The Americans have got the necessary means of disarming Pakistan.' The question does not arise in the case of India because we are not thinking of using nuclear weapons first at any time. But if Pakistan were to think of using a nuclear weapon, if they start making any preparations, we will retaliate if they hit us. But much before that happens, it is most likely that the Americans will disarm them. When the Americans hit Osama Bin Laden, one message was directed at Pakistan, saying, 'We watch over you and we will know what you are doing and therefore we can do what we did to Bin Laden.' In 1990, the Pakistanis did try nuclear blackmail by giving the message that in Kashmir they had got the upper hand. But the Americans intervened, though they did not convey the same to India. They wrote about it much later. When Robert Gates came to Delhi, he did not speak to V.P. Singh or Raja Ramanna or to the Chief of the Army Staff or the Defence Secretary about the nuclear issue, but the Americans did lecture Ghulam Ishaq Khan and Aslam Beg and warned them not to try nuclear blackmail.[5]

They told them that the Indian retaliatory capability itself would take care of them. The Pakistanis are not likely to forget that lesson. Therefore, we should look at the nuclear issue in proper perspective. Some people wrote articles about the nuclear issue during the Kargil crisis, but in all the official pronouncements of the US, there was no mention of the nuclear issue. They are focused on it and know that the Indian nuclear capability does not create any problem.

There is, however, one point which we must remember, and it is regarding the situation of asymmetry which developed in 1987 when Pakistan acquired nuclear weapons and India did not have them. If India had permitted that situation of asymmetry to continue, it would have been in a far worse situation at the time when Pakistan launched a military operation in Kargil. The morale of the soldier counts, and he must have the confidence that his country possesses retaliatory capability. Possession of nuclear weapons does not involve their being used. They are necessary because only then will our soldiers be able to fight with confidence against a nuclear armed adversary. In 1990, when India acquired nuclear weapons, due to

[5] Ibid.

our system of functioning at the Prime Minister's level, the Indian Army was in the dark about India's nuclear capability while its Pakistani counterpart as the custodian of Pakistani nuclear weaponry was fully aware of its own capability.

Therefore, we should have a balanced and sober view about the nuclearization of the subcontinent. It was inevitable under the circumstances and India did not trigger Pakistan's nuclear weapons programme. Zulfikar Ali Bhutto was quite capable of doing it without India having done anything. Our nuclear weapons have restored balance, they have imposed certain ceilings on the kind of violence that can take place between the two countries, and that has not hurt anybody.

As indicated in an earlier chapter, the Kargil aggression could have been planned in 1997 and preliminary reconnaissance and training of personnel may have commenced that year. In that case, while Pakistan's reliance on its nuclear deterrence to prevent India from escalating the crisis would still be important, the nuclear tests conducted in May 1998 would not in themselves be all that significant, as nuclear deterrence between the two countries was in place since 1990.

THE HIGHER DIRECTION OF WAR

PAKISTAN

War is an extension of a nation's foreign policy by the use of force. A nation's strategic compulsions may stem from political, economic or social considerations. In this case, the only political compulsion on the Pakistani side was to internationalize the 'no war, no peace' stalemate with India which commenced in 1972 to stir world opinion into action. On the social plane, the J&K dispute was being projected in the Islamic world as jihad to free the so-called 'oppressed' population. There were no economic compulsions for the conflict.

In the direction of a nation's war aim, it is fundamental that a clear channel of authority, decision making and responsibility be evolved to implement political or strategic decisions with alacrity and dispatch at the military level. With the benefit of hindsight, it is clear that there was suspicion on the Pakistani side between the political and military centres of power, which eventually led to one blaming the other for the fiasco, and subsequently to Nawaz Sharif dismissing Gen. Pervez Musharaff, and the latter seizing power in Pakistan.

Political directions to the Armed Forces have perforce to be related to the latter's capabilities and the degree of national involvement and capacity to implement such directions. In the tactical execution of the military aim, the Pak GHQ chose an extended area for its intrusion, thereby failing to ensure a realistic selection of limited trans-LoC objectives to attain the military aim. They relied too greatly on Western and Chinese support to freeze the situation soon after the intrusions were discovered. The secrecy surrounding this operation led to confusion on the Pakistani side when the Indian response got under way, and international opinion based on full knowledge of what was actually happening on the ground (due to precise satellite imagery and accurate media coverage) did not side with them.

The initial surprise and deception achieved by the Pakistanis caught the Indian Army off balance to the extent that a clear picture of these happenings only emerged a fortnight later. This has highlighted the limitations of intelligence organizations to detect and assess well-conceived and meticulously planned preparations. Equally important is the fact that notwithstanding its access to certain hard facts indicative of warlike preparations by the Pakistanis, India drew the wrong conclusions due to a conditioned mentality of complacency and inability to understand the Pakistani psyche.

Deception on the part of Pakistan was not only given effect to in the military sphere, but also by the Lahore Declaration of February 1999 which was a well-contrived diplomatic and international subterfuge. The Indian side failed to read the situation due to its inability to synthesize and assess the intelligence that had been acquired and collated.

The Pakistan Army seems to have forgotten Clausewitz's maxim that war is ultimately an extension of diplomacy. The G-8 countries reiterated that Pakistan had launched military aggression into Indian territory, and that it was not an act of militancy by Kashmiri crusaders fighting their jihad. The US Senator Republican Benjamin Gilman (Chairman of the Foreign Relations Committee of the House) and his colleague Democrat Sam Gejdensin squarely blamed Pakistan for armed aggression and supported the actions of the Indian Army. The Kargil conflict demonstrated to the world what India was telling it about Pakistan, that it was a dangerously irresponsible and volatile country, and a rogue nation that did not believe in the sanctity of its treaty obligations and assurances, and could not, therefore, be trusted. Further, that it was a revisionist country that did not mind unleashing war, perhaps even nuclear war, to change the status quo in South Asia.

INDIA

All political aims when translated into actualities require impulsion essentially in three spheres, namely, national psychology, military direction, and political alliances or support. In this regard, because of the limited overall political aim (to evict the aggressors from Indian territory without crossing the LoC) all these impulsions were generated in good measure on the Indian side. World opinion was in India's favour.

The political direction of war was firm and clear. Prime Minister Vajpayee left no doubt that the intrusions had to be vacated. While urgency in this regard was natural, once it was realized that eviction would involve the launching of deliberate operations, the Armed Forces were left to work out their own time frame, and there was no political interference. Except for crossing the LoC—which was not permitted to keep the war limited in nature—full support was given to the Armed Forces by the Prime Minister and the Defence Minister. The country rallied behind the Armed Forces and this enabled them to fight in the full knowledge that the entire country was with them: this national psychological support elicited valour in adversity.

The inhibiting factors on the Indian side were the psychological neglect of the Armed Forces for over a decade—both generally and in the context of fighting a proxy war—which cost them dearly and emboldened Pakistan to embark on its misadventure. This neglect also conveyed the impression to the adversary that it was dealing with a soft and forbearing state. Notwithstanding the access to intelligence 'facts' indicating war preparations, the Indian leadership misjudged the intentions of the opponents. None the less, India overcame its initial reverses by dint of sheer sacrifice and competence of its Armed Forces, which is a tribute to the country's maturity and integrity.

Military Direction

It has been advocated that limited wars are likely to be of relatively short duration but high intensity, wherein the initial success or reverses assume a degree of permanency. In this case, India fought a war of fairly long duration—two months—necessitated by the need to prepare thoroughly for battles in high altitude terrain. The adversary was fully evicted by the Indian Army. American pressure on Pakistan came towards the end when 95 per cent or more of the area had already been regained.

The COAS along with the Chief of Air Staff (CAS) exercised firm control over their field commanders by frequent visits to the front. A limited war requires that the political leadership be kept frequently apprised about the progress of the battle on a continuous basis, hence the COAS was directly involved in the war effort in addition to the Army Commander who concentrated on logistics support and counter-insurgency operations. This resulted in quicker reaction and faster availability of resources, which had to be moved from outside the theatre. In the absence of any friction in this arrangement, the 15 Corps Commander, Lt. Gen. Krishan Pal and GOC 8 Mountain Division, Maj. Gen. Mohinder Puri, were able to generate faster responses. The other option, wherein the Army Commander moved his tactical headquarters to Srinagar whilst the Corps Commander moved to the Kargil sector, was a possibility but one which could have caused disruption in the smooth functioning of these headquarters and also affected the counter-insurgency effort in the corps zone and army theatre. Further, the threat of many more Kargils was best insured against from existing locations. The helicopter made it possible for these commanders to visit forward areas without inhibition. Under the circumstances, the arrangements made served the national purpose in a most effective way. Gen. V.P. Malik, Air Chief Marshal A.Y. Tipnis, Lt. Gen. H.M. Khanna and Air Marshal Vinod Patney (commanding Western Air Command who led the IAF in the Kargil war) deserve credit for their part in the operations.

Soon after the intrusions were discovered, there was a flurry of irresponsible political utterances on the war in Kargil. First, George Fernandes, the Defence Minister, confounded the most stubborn Islamabad watcher by insisting that the recent invasion was an autonomous operation of the Pakistan Army. Having absolved Prime Minister Nawaz Sharif as well as the infamous Inter-Services Intelligence (ISI) of all blame, Fernandes then came up with a suggestion of 'safe passage' to the infiltrators. Sharif was arguably the most powerful ruler since M.A. Jinnah, having only a few months ago replaced the Army Chief with a personal favourite. He obviously knew what his military brass was doing.

Military and Economic Strength

Even today there is no substitute for military power. In this context, let us see how the Chinese view national defence. In his report to the Eighth National People's Congress, Premier Li Peng had stated: '. . . strengthening national defence modernisation is an important guarantee for economic construction and our country's long lasting stability and tranquility'. The present allocation for defence is 2.3-2.4 per cent of GDP. Even the most conservative analysts would say that this is grossly inadequate and should be raised to more than 3 per cent. Defence expenditure does not mean using force. Considering our extensive modernization requirements, the need for information technology, and taking into account the existing shortfalls of equipment and accommodation (approximately Rs. 12,000 crore of each), the country needs a defence budget of 4 per cent of GDP for some time to come. It must be made available and there is no point in squabbling over it: the slide in the capacity and capability of the Armed Forces has to be arrested.

The Government must ensure adequate generation of resources by better revenue collection, reduction in other non-developmental expenditure and far better governance together with meticulous financial management. We should learn from China how to become an economic superpower, which automatically ensures the sustenance of a superior degree of military strength. A better and healthier economy will enable us to improve the lot of our people in our borderlands and solve the ongoing disputes.

LACK OF INTEGRATION IN THE NATIONAL SECURITY APPARATUS

The National Security Council (NSC) was formally constituted by the Government in November 1998. It had long argued that an NSC was necessary to streamline the higher security management. When it came to implementation of the K.C. Pant Committee's recommendations for structuring the NSC, they were not implemented in their entirety.

The NSC, as distinct from the Cabinet Committee on Security Affairs (which is involved in day-to-day matters relating to security), is supposed to look into the strategy for the future, and evolve solutions for the various challenges that may arise. It ought to be provided with a host of options by specialists who integrate inputs from intelligence agencies, the Armed Forces, the Foreign Ministry and the Ministry of Finance. Unfortunately, the instrument the NSC gave itself was not satisfactory. The Joint Intelligence Committee, which is supposed to collate information from various agencies and provide assessments to the Cabinet has been dormant for quite some time, and is now functioning as a secretariat to the NSC. Therefore, it cannot process minute-by-minute information which is so necessary in today's information age. It is headed by Satish Chandra, a former diplomat, who lacks any formal training or experience in intelligence work.

At the apex of the NSC is a ministerial group comprising the Prime Minister, and Defence, Foreign, Home and Finance Ministers. Since a more participatory role for the Armed Forces was envisaged by the NSC, direct contact between the Services Chiefs and this Core Group of the Cabinet was called for. Here again, bureaucratic skulduggery played its part. The three Service Chiefs and the Heads of RAW and IB were instead clubbed together with the Cabinet, Defence, Home and Finance Secretaries to form the Strategic Policy Group (SPG).

The NSC's key official is the National Security Adviser (NSA) who is the Coordinator between these bodies. Here again, Brijesh Mishra, Principal Secretary in the PMO, was appointed to the job. This demoted Mishra to a part-time NSA. The JIC/NSC Secretariat has been unable to carry out the dual functions of coordinating the work of intelligence agencies and setting them specific tasks to generate quality analyses. In addition, the National Security Advisory Board (NSAB) was created to provide inputs from a combination of retired service and civilian officers and journalists. In recent months, this body has met a few times to discuss the nuclear doctrine and strategic defence review. It is obvious that adequate inputs were available, but proper processing and assessment of intelligence was not done.

HIGHER DEFENCE ORGANIZATION

As in previous wars, the Kargil war emphasized the need for a proper higher level defence security set-up and an integrated higher defence organization. The present structure has often been faulted in the past, but little has been done to streamline it. The existing organization of three separate service headquarters prevents integration and leads to inter-service parochialism. In the absence of a Chief of Defence Staff, the political leadership does not get single-point advice. Furthermore, unless there is close integration between service headquarters and the Ministry of Defence and a joint defence staff concept introduced, the Indian military effort will remain unfocused, wasteful and underutilized due to service rivalries and resource limitations.

The above aspects need some elaboration. The threat to the country is not limited to acts of external aggression but extends to a multitude of external and internal sources in the political, demographic, economic and military spheres. The threat to India in the twenty-first century is exceptionally complex, and if not defined correctly, would invalidate policies. It is necessary to define the nation's vital interests and national policy objectives dictated by these interests. The Government must evolve national strategy based on global and regional perceptions and their linkage to national interests, followed by an analysis of the areas where these interests may clash with other global and regional powers. This would provide the basis for a pragmatic national security strategy to deal with the threats and impediments to achieving national objectives. The strategy would encompass all political, economic, diplomatic and security issues.

The ensuing national strategy must identify the objectives that would be laid down for individual ministries and the Ministry of Defence (MOD). Therefore, the defence objectives would flow on the basis of political and socio-economic considerations, thus taking into account the availability of resources. Such a wide-ranging exercise must emanate under the authority of the highest echelons of the Government. The National Security Council can advise, but for obvious reasons cannot carry out this function. In our case, the task should be done by the Cabinet Committee for Political Affairs (CCPA). This complex and time-consuming endeavour requires detailed and continuous examination, and it must be undertaken on an institutionalized basis. In this regard, the CCPA needs to be supported by a National Security Secretariat of multidisciplinary experts, independent of main-line ministries. The secretariat would perform the following.

1. Providing the CCPA with a strategic, technological and economic assessment of the regional and global environment.
2. Work out comprehensive policy options extending into the next 5-15 years.
3. Make viable contingency plans.
4. Issue political directives to all ministries, laying down core inputs, fixing objectives and suggesting the means to institute security policies.

5. Monitor decisions—a very important function.

When this organization is in place, the CCPA would be able to evolve and implement national security strategy and evolve structures, systems and procedures for cost-effective use of all resources and to oversee their functioning.

Having been given clear-cut defence objectives, the MOD would be required to formulate a defence plan, identify the military objectives which would provide the basis for creation of force levels and execution of missions. To achieve this, the structural and functional systems within the MOD require considerable streamlining in the context of:

(a) organizational mismatches leading to loss of efficiency;
(b) lack of expertise in specialist fields within the bureaucracy; and
(c) lack of compatibility in authority, responsibility and accountability at different stages of the planning and implementation processes.

Notwithstanding the existence of a Chiefs of Staff Committee (COSC), the Defence Minister does not get the much-needed single-point advice. The solution would be the acceptance of the concept of a Chief of Defence Staff (CDS) who would be provided by the three Services in rotation. But the Navy, and particularly the Air Force, have their reservations regarding this concept because they fear that being smaller Services their requirements may get diluted, and that the present system is working satisfactorily as they have equal say in matters military. Since this concept has not been accepted, we must have a strong and functional Joint Chiefs of Staff organization. This organization should be headed by each Service Chief on a rotational basis and consist of an integrated tri-service staff. This integrated staff should be under a very high-calibre officer of the rank of lieutenant general or equivalent, who would serve up to the age of 60 years like the Service Chiefs. Such an officer should be given a tenure of three years. He should be the best available officer for the appointment in the three Services. Headquarters Joint Chiefs of Staff would have the following main functions.

1. To render single-point advice to the Raksha Mantri (Minister of Defence) on all matters pertaining to operations, operational intelligence, operational logistics, technology, management of forces, and communications.

2. Processing of all directives received.
3. Implementing decisions.

This synthesized military command structure should report directly to, and be under the control of, the Defence Minister. In this event, the role of the MOD would be confined to looking after non-operational and non-intelligence issues, such as management and budgeting, procurement, coordination with other ministries; parliamentary affairs, and any other matters.

Once we have a functional national security set-up and an integrated higher defence organization, it will be possible to carry out long-term perspective planning in a meaningful manner. Military plans must be based on a perspective of 20-5 years. Of this, the first five years must be supported by confirmed budgetary allocations. The next five years would entail iteration of ongoing projects in their broader perspective and would, therefore, be supported by a clear indication of the likely availability of resources. The next decade falls in the category of over-the-horizon policies, for which planning and initial research needs to be started at present, with the final decision on resource allotment being dependent on defence plan reviews.

THE MASS MEDIA

The silver lining in an otherwise gruesome and barbaric war was that it was able to evoke tremendous unity, patriotism and nationalism amongst the people of India. Men, women and children in villages, decrepit towns and teeming cities came together in a moment of remembrance for the fallen soldier who came home in a coffin, very often made of wood from ammunition boxes. For the first time the battle reached into Indian homes. This was largely on account of the visual and print media. Perhaps Kargil has done to the Indian public what Vietnam did to the American people. There is no doubt ample scope for further improvement in media coverage by conveying the latest battle situation in an accurate and timely manner.

It is imperative for India to win the public relations battle and to convince the world that Pakistan is not interested in the welfare of the Kashmiri people, that it is a terrorist state which has planned the ethnic cleansing of Buddhists and Hindus from J&K. Its suppression of human rights in POK and its nexus with fundamentalist and terrorist organizations is easy to corroborate. Neither the Government nor the media were able to transcend the borders of India and reach out with the facts to the regional and international audiences. This would have helped build a consensus in India's favour much earlier. It is in this field that there is need for considerable forward movement. Some sections of the media played a negative role when they fell prey to the machinations of certain utterances aimed at politicization of the war to gain political mileage from the country's predicament. There was no justification to highlight Brig Surinder Singh's transfer from 121 Infantry Brigade, which would have occurred for good reason, except that this was done in an endeavour to embarrass the Army and the Government. Such actions only reveal how immature and unpatriotic political parties can be to further their narrow ends. The media must give such negative trends the treatment they deserve. At best a public examination of the issue could have been called for to rule out the possibility of his having been removed to cover up any lapses of higher headquarters. In the last decade, the media could have with advantage forcefully highlighted the neglect that the Armed Forces were being subjected to due to inept political and bureaucratic handling, despite warnings from the three Services, regarding their budgetary and equipment profiles, which were the real causes which emboldened Pakistan. The country has not got its act together, and there is too much internecine warfare within our political parties, structures and organizations which causes the nation to *react* rather than *act* with vision and foresight.

The function of briefing during the Kargil crisis was taken over by a triad of senior military and civil spokesmen. Army Headquarters set up an Information and Psychological Warfare Cell under an officer of the rank of major general with direct access to the Army Chief. This enabled Army Headquarters to monitor and disseminate information in an effective manner. (Normal peacetime activity is handled by the regular Information Service cadres of the Ministry of Defence, an establishment that is not equipped to handle media relations during war.)

The Kargil war, however, brought to the fore the need to review information handling procedures within the Armed Forces and their public dissemination. The Army needs a much improved public relations capability not only during war but equally, when it is deployed for counter-insurgency, terrorist, proxy war and other Internal Security duties.

The immediate necessity is to have a Central Communications Unit at Corps Headquarters for Corps level editing comprising selected service officers and men, and an element from the DPR. This unit should collect and disseminate information as also co-ordinate with media persons and organizations, such as visiting journalists, TV teams and film producers. There is also a need to have media teams at division, brigade and even battalion level. At the lowest level—battalion—it could be an officer who can write well and another person who can operate a hand held camera. The size and composition of media teams would be dictated by the size of the headquarters and its requirements. These media teams would be of great help in projecting the activities of the armed forces through films and other processes.

There is also a need to train selected service officers and men in media work by running suitable cadres for them on a regular basis. Likewise, media personnel need to understand the organization, role, ethos and fighting capabilities of the armed forces and the characteristics of its various units. There is need to train them too. A media-military interface in this context would be most beneficial. Perhaps, an Institute of Journalism needs to be established for this purpose.

The procedure evolved should also provide for regular operational briefings being given by the operations/intelligence staff at corps/divisional HQ or by the corps/divisional commanders.

RAILWAYS

War entails considerable movement of troops. As in previous wars, the Indian Railways once again rose to the occasion and provisioned rolling stock in time and moved it on top priority from one place or sector to another. This organization deserves considerable credit for its dedication to the nation in time of war. The development of railway communications to border areas as envisaged in future plans must proceed apace so that the Armed Forces can reach their assigned areas on time and in a reasonably rested state.

INDIA'S FUTURE STRATEGY

Following the Kargil war, Pakistan now knows India's threshold in a proxy war. On India's part, it must devise a strategy to raise the cost of Pakistani misadventures. The quickest way to liquidate intrusions and vacate territory is by cutting off the supply lines across the LoC. For instance, there are about seventy supply routes which radiate from Skardu, of which only about a dozen were effectively neutralized in the Kargil war. The political leadership will be confronted with such hard decisions, and a balancing act will have to be done by the strategists. In the event of the conflict escalating into a full-scale conventional war, the possibilities of a nuclear first strike by Pakistan against India, no matter how remote the contingency, will have to be taken into account.

In the immediate future, Pakistan is likely to escalate insurgency and terrorism in Kashmir Valley, Rajouri, Poonch, Doda, Uri, Naushera and other sensitive areas of J&K. In urban Jammu, they may resort to bomb blasts and other methods to disturb normal life. The advent of regular military units in Ladakh constitutes open aggression and can have far-reaching effects on Indo-Pak relations. Pakistani plans to carry out a Taliban type of operation could lead to an Indo-Pak war. Their threat of 'many more Kargils' has to be taken seriously by India, and it must ensure readiness for a war in Ladakh and other parts of J&K.

In mountain and high altitude warfare, whoever takes the initiative gains the advantage. Apart from 14 Corps, which has been raised to control the area in which the Kargil war occurred and Ladakh, India should have a strike corps suitably trained and located for swift offensive operations across the LoC in J&K. The endeavour should be to achieve decisive results. A convincing defeat will affect the morale of the Pak Army and lead to peace.

An analysis of ninety-seven armed conflicts in the period 1919-86 reveals that these conflicts were resolved through one of the following methods:[6]

(a) Conquest	32 %	
(b) Compromise	20 %	
(c) Successful deterrence	19 %	
(d) An award	12 %	
(e) Avoidance/withdrawal of demands, claims or positions	11 %	
(f) Passive	4 %	
(g) Ongoing at the time of survey	2 %	(Iran-Iraq war)

[6] K.J. Holsti, 'Paths to Peace? Theories of Conflict Resolution and Realities of International Politics', *International Conflict Resolution*, ed. Ramesh Thakur (University of Otago Press, Dunedin, 1988), pp. 115-16.

Thus, there are really at least six theoretical outcomes of international conflicts: (1) conquest; (2) avoidance, where 'A' withdraws demands, claims, or actions against 'B'; (3) deterrence, where the initiator is forced by retaliatory threats to withdraw his demands, claims, and actions; (4) compromise; (5) awards, where the adversaries agree to allow a third party to fashion a settlement through non-bargaining procedures such as court decisions, plebiscites, and arbitration awards; and (6) passive settlement, where there is no formal outcome negotiated by the adversaries or third parties as was the case in J&K prior to the outbreak of hostilities in 1947. One party creates a new situation (alters the status quo) as Pakistan did in 1947 and eventually both parties learn to live with the situation to the point where no one is willing to seek modification through resort to arms. The conflict is resolved through obsolescence, although in some instances a formal settlement through treaty arrangements may legitimize that outcome. The Kashmir problem, and possibly the India-China frontier, may have reached that stage in international perceptions, but Pakistan has periodically tried to revive the dispute. This could have been resolved in 1947-8 by conquest or compromise; thereafter, its resolution in the true sense was not possible due to great power rivalry and the induction of US arms into Pakistan.

Assaults on the status quo as in the case of the Kargil war can rarely be settled by third-party intervention. The conflict can continue short of war, but if there is to be a resolution, it would seem to result from conquest, successful deterrence, and exhaustion after a lengthy test of arms. India must prepare for these contingencies.

The proxy war in the Valley is a more difficult proposition as the enemy is using civilians as a shield. Collateral damage to the locals cannot be avoided. The nature of this type of warfare is such that it can turn military success into political disaster. A fresh attempt should be made to totally defeat Pakistan's proxy war in J&K. Then and only then will that country realize that it has no other option but to live at peace with India. A few steps in this context are outlined below.

1. Combating fundamentalist propaganda through sociocultural drives.
2. Inroads must be made into terrorist outfits operating in J&K. Unless we have moles in terrorist organizations, we will not get timely warning. The inability to penetrate Pakistan-inspired

militant outfits has been the most singular weakness of Indian intelligence agencies. Hence, the need for a far more aggressive intelligence set-up.

3. Armed volunteer groups must be raised to provide protection to village and population centres, as also information about the militants.
4. An effective programme of psychological warfare must be launched to mobilize the local population.
5. Even though we are a true democracy, in view of the peculiar circumstances obtaining in J&K, effective media control, including the local vernacular press and madrassas which are spreading communalism, will have to be firmly exercised.
6. There is also a need to send suitable young IAS officers to these troubled areas. They should be able to establish effective administration, dispense justice and give on-the-spot decisions.
7. There is a case for the police forces to replace the Army in urban centres and long term in the interior areas. This must, of course, be done after suitably training and equipping them.

In elaboration of the last point, it needs to be stated that British counter-insurgency doctrine tends to favour the primacy of the armed police in fighting insurgents and a more restricted role for the army. There were several reasons for this. The police were more effective in gathering intelligence, more likely to be sensitive to local opinion, and, therefore, more effective at winning hearts and minds. The police help to create an image of normality, they are cheaper to use than the army, and better suited for a peace-keeping role.

The police would operate in an area on a long-term and would attempt to build relations with the locals. They would also be more familiar with the terrain, culture and population than the army. They would be more skilled at gathering intelligence. On the other hand, there are drawbacks with a policy of police primacy. It could exacerbate ethnic antagonisms. The use of the police in a para-military role could inhibit normal policing activities. The police, if they are drawn predominantly from one ethnic community and have to police another community, could be perceived as partial and sectarian by the latter. The ethnic group from which the police are drawn may also see an attack on the police as a sectarian assault on their community. The locally recruited police forces, though they may not be totally impartial or unsympathetic to the interests of their own ethnic group, can be made to act in a balanced manner. It can be ensured that they are not brought into conflict with their own community. Further, they would act as a buffer if the army is forced into the breach.

The sorry state of affairs in J&K over the last few years has brought out the need for close coordination between the politicians, the administration, the police, the intelligence agencies and the Army. The Army is peculiarly placed in J&K. Its task along the line of control is exceptional and cannot be performed by another force till there is peace along the LoC. It is best to eliminate a militant on or near the LoC. Once he merges with the population, it is difficult to eliminate him. Therefore, the Army must counter infiltration more effectively along the LoC by increasing its strength or the timely movement of reserves, as also a combination of both methods. The option of a proactive response must not be eschewed: after all, Pakistan is engaging in activities that are directed at severing J&K from India.

In areas in the interior, the Army has hitherto been playing the leading role in combating the proxy war. This has resulted in its excessive involvement at the expense of its conventional capability and role. This commitment must be reduced at the earliest. But proxy war cannot be fought by the police forces. Hence, the need for a structured force of the Army for this purpose. Such a force exists in the form of the Rashtriya Rifles (RR) but its strength will have to be increased considerably if it is to adequately relieve the Army in J&K for its conventional role. Many more battalions of the RR must be raised to fight the proxy war which, on present indications, is expected to last for up to a decade or so. Eventually, as the situation improves, the RR should act in support of the civil armed police, as was done in Punjab. The endeavour should be to strengthen and to give confidence to the J&K State Police and the Centre's paramilitary forces—the BSF and the CRPF. The state must build a high-quality police force, and Delhi should take measures to make the BSF and CRPF far more effective than they are at present. These measures will, however, take a long time to fructify due to years of neglect.

The Kashmir dispute is sought to be given the complexion of a jihad by Pakistan to obtain the benefits of support from fundamentalist organizations in Islamic countries. Though this is a misuse of religion, it does attract recruits and money for fighting in J&K. Radicalization of various Muslim states like Bangladesh is a part of the Pakistani agenda. The Muslims in India are also their targets. These designs must be exposed firmly and contested by the Indian state on a war footing.

Conclusion

The Kargil war proved that Indian governments in the last ten years had valued budgets more than territorial integrity and the lives of its soldiers. In future, the country will have to be prepared for insurgency and terrorism, proxy war, limited war, conventional war as also nuclear (or general) war. This preparation can no longer be based on military defence alone. A host of non-military threats to national security have steadily gained ascendancy over the years. The Kashmir issue, for instance, displays elements of ethnic, communal and political strife. These new circumstances demand a fresh outlook on security: a nation's strategic policy is a blend of aims and capabilities each reacting with the other. Hence, this policy will have to blend together the external and internal dimensions of defence as also the political and economic constituents of security. Therefore, budgeting, military capabilities, induction of new technology, human resources development and the like will have to be taken in hand with a new perception. Within it, the Armed Forces will be able to develop their full potential and will be better able to deal with external threats and internal strife when other means fail.

5

India's Political and Diplomatic Responses to the Kargil Crisis

Arpit Rajain

Conflicts, like chess matches, have both structured and unstructured features. Given reliable information, the respective intelligence services of two warring states are aware of each other's capabilities, men, material and weapons. But the elements of determinism are nowhere more confounded than in efforts to end wars; this becomes a far more difficult process when they involve regular and irregular forces. In other words, terminating a war is difficult, although they must end sooner or later, if only due to the mutual exhaustion of the warring states.[1] A policy maker who is determined to terminate a war according to calculations arising from concrete policy objectives must impose a war termination plan on a fluid military and diplomatic situation. But this is easier done in operation rooms and on sand models. Ending a conflict with the constraints of actual combat and the pressures of the international community is a difficult job. It is possible there may no final solution of a political dispute by using military force, or, perhaps, new issues will arise during hostilities that plant the seeds for subsequent wars.[2] Based on the strategic-rational model, one realizes that military strategists assume that decision makers on both sides will act rationally. This assumption is important as it helps them in calculating moves and predicting outcomes. In its ideal form, rationality is taken to mean the following:

[1] A typology of how wars end is constructed by Paul Pillar in *Negotiating Peace: War Termination as a Bargaining Process* (Princeton University Press, Princeton, 1983).

[2] One may recall the Pakistani promise of 'many more Kargils'.

1. One or both sides have a single centre of decision making.[3]
2. One or both sides can identify and compare the anticipated costs available for various courses of action.[4]
3. Both sides have all the necessary information to evaluate the course of action of the adversary.[5]

This approach does have its shortcomings as complete knowledge of the adversary is difficult to obtain. Second, predicting courses of action and outcomes is difficult. Third, critics of this approach are sceptical regarding the ability of decision makers to compare the costs and benefits of alternate courses of action in any authoritative way.[6]

Determining the course of action in a scenario where the risk taking capability of one adversary is much more is very difficult. In fact, complete understanding of the intentions of an adversary is difficult. Under these circumstances, formulating the political and diplomatic response of one of the adversaries is not an easy task.

The 1999 Indo-Pak border war in the Kargil heights—'Operation Vijay'—was a military response following an intelligence failure. It also represented the will of the Indian Government that had failed to respond in time to the various warning signals that were filtering in. The intelligence agencies failed to anticipate the threat along the LoC (Line of Control); this was a colossal blunder. As bits of information began to pour in, it seemed apparent that the Government had failed to act until the last week of May 1999. What occurred over the next two months was the transformation of an intelligence failure into a military and diplomatic victory.

Militarily and diplomatically, Prime Minister Atal Behari Vajpayee handled the situation with great competence. Considered from Pakistan's viewpoint, it was a win-win situation: the intruders were inside India and had occupied the strategic heights along the NH 1A highway between Srinagar and Leh. If they had continued to remain, they could have cut off the supply route to Leh; this would lead the Indian Army to lose its flexibility to move, redeploy or augment troops from one theatre to another besides choking one of the supply

[3] William O. Staudenmaier, 'Conflict Termination in the Nuclear Era', in Stephen J. Cimbala and Keith A. Dunn (eds.), *Conflict Termination and Military Strategy* (Boulder: Westview Press, 1987), p. 18.

[4] Ibid.

[5] Ibid.

[6] Michael I. Handel, *War Termination: A Critical Survey* (The Hebrew University of Jerusalem Press, Jerusalem), p. 29, as cited in Staudenmaier (1987).

routes to Siachen. Pakistan could then launch operations in Turtok close to the southern Siachen glacier and redraw the LoC.[7] If these intruders engaged in battle with the Indian Army (which they did), they would have been in a position to draw the attention of the world. One possibility the intruders failed to take into account was a hard military response by India. Diplomatically, what they did not calculate was the restrained approach by India at a time when military logic dictated that India cross the LoC.

The conflict was significant since both states involved in the conflict had nuclear weapons, which attracted the attention of the world. It was vital for India to inform the world of the situation and persuade it to take an objective view. Diplomacy has its limitations: it is not an alternative to action but supplements it. India was dealing with deliberate and blatant aggression; therefore, a strong display of its commitment to use all necessary military means became imperative. With the signing of the Washington Agreement, in agreeing to restore the LoC's sanctity, Sharif conceded that there was an LoC which had been breached, and his appeal to the intruders to withdraw did work in effect to reaffirm the position India had been taking all along, even as Aziz was made to eat his words that there was no LoC. By signing the pull-out agreements Sharif too in effect acknowledged that an intrusion had taken place and that he had authority over the 'infiltrators'. The other myth that was shattered was that of the autonomy of the intruders. In fact, this myth was shattered later again when Pakistan awarded medals to personnel of the 12 Northern Light Infantry, which amounted to acceptance of the fact its Army regulars were involved in the intrusion.

This chapter seeks to examine India's diplomatic response against the following background:

1. The shadow of nuclear weapons, the issue of safe passage and confidentiality of communications.
2. The diplomatic response of the international community, official initiatives, back-channel parleys, military and diplomatic costs.
3. The institutions that have a potential to play a more positive role in crisis situations.
4. An assessment of the response.

[7] One may recall that India has a history of losing territory through infiltration between 7 November 1959 and 8 September 1962 when there was gradual intrusion by China into Indian territory resulting in Chinese occupation of about 2,500 sq. miles in Arunachal Pradesh.

The Overview

THE NUCLEAR SHADOW

With India and Pakistan having gone nuclear in May 1998, a nuclear shadow was bound to appear over any armed conflict between the two neighbouring states. They continued to insist after the May 1998 nuclear tests that they were responsible nuclear states. India went to the extent of offering an unconditional NFU (No First Use) declaration. But with war being declared in Kargil the Western countries sounded an alert over a possible nuclear flare up between the two countries. Pakistani generals also believed they had an advantage over India as they claimed to have deployed nuclear missiles like Ghauri, while India was still working on a medium range missile. They would have been prepared to gamble on a blind nuclear strike and expecting people in Kashmir Valley to rise in support of independence.[8]

One of the key elements that altered the perceptions of the international community in India's favour was that India responded to the Kargil crisis with a conventional military response. The Indian diplomatic response indicated that it was prepared to discuss any non-military approach for restoring status quo ante with Pakistan, but would first flush the militants out of Kargil. The fact that India decided to use its Air Force (the first time in an operation after 1971) must have weighed heavily on decision makers in South Block. The Indian crisis management principles were premised on firmness on the battlefront, a political will to bear its costs and sophistication in handling the diplomatic fall-out.

For the last twenty years or so, Islamabad has sought to link its nuclear capability with the Kashmir issue. It has felt its nuclear capabilities could balance the Indian conventional force advantage. Thus, some strategists have said that a bold Pakistani strike to liberate Kashmir might go unchallenged if there was a weak central Government in India, or so ran the Pakistani logic. The fact that India had a coalition caretaker government in May 1999 explains the timing of Pakistan's operation. Pakistan did cry nuclear wolf in

[8] A PTI report quoting *The Times* (London) in 'West Pensive over "Blind" N-Strike', in *Pioneer* 30 May 1999.

the crisis at least once.[9] The statement of Pakistan Foreign Secretary Tariq Aziz that 'we will not hesitate to use any weapon in our arsenal to defend our territorial integrity' was interpreted by many as an overt nuclear threat. The very next day there were denials by Islamabad, and the Indian National Security Adviser, Brajesh Mishra, described the pronouncement as utterly irresponsible. This can be viewed as psychological warfare. Subtle nuclear blackmail can also be discussed in Pakistan's strategy to call for US or UN intervention in the region by projecting the Kashmir issue as a potential nuclear flashpoint.

It was on this premise that Pakistan could elicit a quick American intervention as Pakistani officials started discussing the possibility of the use of nuclear weapons. But it boomeranged seriously. The US held the position all along that their Kargil aggression undermined the Lahore process and it must be quickly resolved. 'The Clinton administration believes that the rules of engagement in the sub-continent have fundamentally changed with the advent of nuclear weapons.'[10] What was reassuring in this context was India's offer of a no-first-use policy. So the responsibility for any confrontation would rest solely with Pakistan. Pakistan's appeal effectively was, 'We are fighting over Kashmir, the conflict can widen, this is a likely nuclear flash-point, so please intervene.'[11]

SAFE PASSAGE

As diplomatic efforts to de-escalate the Indo-Pak tensions continued, Indian Defence Minister George Fernandes said that India was prepared to consider 'safe passage' for the armed intruders to go back into Pakistan.[12] Fernandes exhorted, '. . . all those who have been pushed into our territory by Pakistan including their troops to go back, dead or alive'. This move to permit 'safe passage' drew flak in the country and was denied the very next day, although it did have its merits. First, India would have convincingly proven to the

[9] According to noted analysts Achin Vanaik and Praful Bidwai, the nuclear threat was exchanged thirteen times during the Kargil crisis: Achin Vanaik and Praful Bidwai, *South Asia on a Short Fuse* (Oxford University Press, New Delhi, 1999), p. vi.

[10] C. Raja Mohan, 'The US and Kargil', *The Hindu*, 10 June 1999.

[11] Shekhar Gupta, 'Winning without a War', *Indian Express*, 2 June 1999.

[12] C. Raja Mohan, 'Non-Military Option "open" ', *The Hindu*, 2 June 1999.

West that an intrusion had taken place.[13] Second, more Indian lives would not have been lost, and finally, a war would have been averted with less economic cost. Various political parties questioned this offer as compromising Indian sovereignty. Even the Armed Forces, which were already perturbed by an earlier statement of George Fernandes, giving a clean chit to Nawaz Sharif, did not take kindly to this offer.[14] According to analyst Lt. Gen. V.R. Raghavan, 'It will mean withdrawal and why should we give safe passage to the enemy which opted for naked aggression on Indian soil. The enemy has to pay a price through military action.'[15] Former Air Chief Marshal S.K. Mehra also noted, 'We have paid a heavy price of lives and limbs. The infiltrators should either surrender or get killed because we cannot afford to fritter away the gains made by our men over . . . dinner diplomacy.'[16]

Confidentiality of Communications and Diplomatic Turnaround

On 11 June 1999, India released the taped conversations of Chief of Staff Lt. Gen. Mohammed Aziz and Pakistan's Chief of the Army Staff Gen. Pervez Musharraf. From the tapes it was revealed that:[17]

1. The Pakistan Army was virtually a state within a state and continued to play a dominating role in the governance of the country.
2. Prime Minister Nawaz Sharif was not kept informed of the precise nature of the intrusions and had learnt of these developments much later.
3. The two generals discussed and decided on the agenda for Pakistan Foreign Minister Sartaj Aziz's forthcoming talks with his Indian counterpart, Jaswant Singh.
4. The Pakistan army was planning on altering the Line of Control which confirms Pakistan had masterminded the whole operation.[18]

[13] Also to Japan which even raised suspicion over India's claims on the intrusion in Kargil. This mutual suspicion started soon after the nuclear tests, and, therefore, did not come as a surprise.

[14] 'Government under attack for "safe passage" idea', *The Hindu*, 3 June 1999.

[15] Ibid.

[16] Ibid.

[17] The transcript of the conversation appeared in *Hindustan Times*, 12 June 1999.

[18] 'Tapes Confirm Pak Backing Infiltrators', *Times of India*, 12 June 1999.

Just before Mr Sartaj Aziz's visit to New Delhi, Pakistan's Inter Services Public Relations Directorate acknowledged—quite surprisingly—the presence of Pakistani troops in the Kargil and Dras sectors. This assertion lends credibility to reports that Pakistan was sending reinforcements to the Kargil region.[19] This was exactly what India had been saying all along, but the Pakistani admission certainly helped India diplomatically. The Indian response continued to be tough. As Jaswant Singh said, 'The aggression has to be undone, militarily or diplomatically, whichever is done first.'[20]

Pakistan's diplomatic game plan was intricately designed. First they pushed intruders into a place where the LoC was not marked on the ground but has been delineated on mosaics following the 1972 Simla Agreement. Pakistan thought it could alter the Line of Control to its advantage. Second, it showed to the world that by sending Aziz (even though he came via Beijing), Pakistan wanted to de-escalate the situation: it went on to offer India a three-point programme and floated the idea that it was the aggrieved party. Pakistan also projected the 'don't blame us later' attitude as Aziz stated on going back to Pakistan after the talks had failed, 'In sum we want peace, but if war is imposed on us, we have the capability to defend ourselves and our vital national interests.'[21] In the meantime India declared that it was putting its 'composite dialogue' with Pakistan on hold, and repeated its demand that Islamabad vacate its intrusion in Kargil as soon as possible.[22] The Foreign Ministers' dialogue failed, quite predictably.

Following the Aziz visit, Sharif called up Indian Prime Minister Atal Behari Vajpayee and said, 'It is incumbent on the leadership to avert any further aggravation which will be detrimental to the economic development efforts of both countries.' Vajpayee, in turn, stressed the need to promote durable peace and security through the process of dialogue and peaceful negotiations in pursuance of the Lahore Declaration.[23]

19 'Pak Admits Troops Presence in Kargil', *Indian Express* 12 June 1999.

20 'Talks with Aziz in Deadlock', *Indian Express*, 13 June 1999.

21 'We've Made Proposals to Reduce Tension: Aziz', *Hindustan Times*, 13 June 1999.

22 'Composite Dialogue Put on Hold', *The Hindu*, 13 June 1999.

23 A press release quoted, 'Sharif Calls up Vajpayee', *Hindustan Times*, 14 June 1999.

The Diplomatic Process during Kargil

THE SECURITY COUNCIL

There was no initial indication from the United Nations that it would take up the Kargil issue. The US, Russia, France and UK assured India that they would not raise the issue in the United Nations Security Council.[24] Fernandes cleared the position on third-party role in Kargil: 'All of them [members of the Security Council] made it clear that they would not take up the matter in the United Nations Security Council.' He added that India too was not planning to take up the matter in the United Nations.[25] Kofi Annan also called up Vajpayee when he became convinced that Pakistan had crossed the LoC and '. . . volunteered to send its [UN] observers to the two countries . . .'.[26]

These countries had assured India that they would not raise the Kargil issue in the Council.[27] The UN remained unwilling to play a role in defusing tensions and would have intervened only if India and Pakistan agreed.[28] Pakistan Prime Minister Nawaz Sharif wrote a letter to Secretary Gen. Kofi Annan, just as the situation was escalating, stating that 'India's reckless actions along the LoC have created a dangerous situation in the region', whilst adding that the United Nations should immediately send observers to monitor the area and strengthen the United Nations Military Observer Group in India and Pakistan (UNMOGIP). This was unacceptable to India. Kofi Annan called Gujral and expressed concern over the Kargil situation, whilst pleading for restraint. Gujral is believed to have informed him of the sanctity of the LoC.[29]

Kofi Annan admitted that Pakistan had crossed the LoC and volunteered to send observers. This was in keeping with the overall game plan of Pakistan to talk from a position of strength. Kofi Annan also spoke to Vajpayee, whose response was, 'We are the aggrieved party as our land is being occupied. We have not started the war.'[30]

24 'Security Council Hands off on Kargil', *Statesman*, 30 May 1999.
25 Ibid.
26 'Pakistan Crossed LoC Says UN Chief', *The Hindu*, 30 May 1999.
27 Ibid.
28 'UN Still Willing to Mediate', *The Hindu* (Reuters), 1 June 1999.
29 'Pak Must Take First Step: PM', *The Hindu*, 29 May 1999.
30 *The Hindu*, op. cit., n. 26.

RUSSIAN RESPONSE

Russia was the first country to come out openly in support of India by a categorical declaration that it would foil Pakistan's bid to internationalize the Kashmir issue, whilst reiterating its support for New Delhi's action against the infiltrators in Kargil.[31] India has always found Russia to be a time-tested ally. Russian support has been consistent on the Kashmir issue and this has saved India from embarrassing situations in many international forums. There were some apprehensions about the future of Indo-Russian relations after the break-up of the Soviet Union. Russia had in recent times moved towards the US due to its financial crisis and Indo-Russian ties had a temporary cooling off phase, but the two countries have since been coming closer, and hoping to raise Indo-Russian ties to the level of a 'strategic partnership'. There has been increased support on military hardware. During Premier Yevgeny Primakov's visit in 1998 there were proposals for a Russia–China–India 'strategic alliance'. One reason for it could be the NATO action in Yugoslavia, which may bring Russia and India closer as they come to terms with a unipolar world order.

CHINESE RESPONSE

China invariably figures in the security calculations of India and Pakistan. The fact that Aziz and Singh visited Beijing substantiates this viewpoint. But what is of particular interest is that just a day before Aziz was to visit India, he sought to visit China. China has been Pakistan's time-tested ally, and following its diplomatic isolation Pakistan sought help from Beijing. But the visits of Singh and Aziz were qualitatively different. The Singh visit was scheduled after the meeting of the Joint Working Group between India and China in April 1999. The agenda for this meeting was a broad one to reduce tensions between the two countries following the nuclear tests in May 1998 and Vajpayee's letter to Clinton following them. Singh's visit was the culmination of the process of engagement that had begun many months prior to the visit. As against this the Aziz visit was a rushed affair. Strictly speaking, though he was invited by his Chinese counterpart, actually Pakistan invited itself.[32]

China's stand on Kargil had been clear: it called for a resumption

[31] 'Assurance from Russia', *Hindustan Times* (editorial), 30 May 1999.

[32] K.K. Katyal, 'Pak Wooing China', *The Hindu*, 10 June 1999.

of dialogue, restraint, and the settlement of all disputes between India and Pakistan in the spirit of the Lahore process. Over the last three decades there have been marked changes in China's position on Kashmir. During the 1960s through to the mid-1970s China supported the 'just struggle of the Kashmiri people for self-determination'. This could be attributed to Indian support for Tibetan nationalism. Through the 1980s China gradually dropped all talk of self-determination. After Rajiv Gandhi's visit to Beijing in 1988 even the references to United Nations' resolutions decreased. During Jiang Zemin's visit to the subcontinent in 1996 he called upon India and Pakistan to build a cooperative relationship and put aside difficult issues.[33]

FRENCH RESPONSE

France firmly rejected the idea of foreign intervention and an external solution to resolve the flare-up in Kashmir. A French External Affairs Official said, 'There can be absolutely no comparisons between the crisis in Kosovo, which involves over one million refugees . . . to the situation in Kashmir, which is a bilateral issue between India and Pakistan. We cannot superimpose the solutions that we have for Kosovo in Kashmir.'[34] This statement can be evaluated in the light of the three-day visit of Foreign Minister Jaswant Singh to Paris in May 1999.

INTERNATIONAL ORGANIZATIONS

India and Pakistan raised the Kargil issue at the Disarmament Conference in Geneva in early June 1999. The Indian Ambassador, Savitri Kunadi, said, 'This was yet another instance of Pakistan's persistent efforts to infiltrate terrorists across the LoC in pursuit of its designs on Jammu and Kashmir which is an integral part of India.'[35] She was responding to a question raised by Munir Akram, the Pakistan Ambassador who took the floor to claim that Pakistan had raised the Kargil issue as it directly affected international peace and security. He claimed that Jammu and Kashmir was not Indian territory but disputed territory as any official UN map portrayed.[36]

[33] C. Raja Mohan, 'China Unlikely to Adopt Anti-India Posture', *The Hindu*, 11 June 1999.

[34] 'Kashmir is Not Kosovo : France', *Pioneer*, 30 May 1999.

[35] 'Indo-Pak Duel at UN over Kargil', *Pioneer*, 6 June 1999.

[36] Ibid.

What was evident was that both India and Pakistan had been keen on using 'back channels' to work out some face-saving formula. India, however, continued to insist that Pakistan would have to undo what it had done, i.e. Pakistan had to withdraw its forces since the LoC was sacrosanct.

AZIZ'S NEW DELHI VISIT

Any form of dialogue to de-escalate tensions has importance. A dialogue helps clear misperceptions, avert miscalculations and avoids escalation in the conflict.

The visit of Foreign Minister Sartaj Aziz at the height of the conflict to New Delhi can be termed as a crisis management venture. Nawaz Sharif suggested that air strikes be stopped as a precondition for talks, which was not accepted by India. The importance of it lay in the fact that this dialogue was at the highest levels between the two Governments. Sharif and Vajpayee were in touch over the phone and the Indian Premier made it clear that Pakistan would have to take the first step to de-escalate the situation Sharif offered to send his Foreign Minister to New Delhi at the earliest available opportunity to de-escalate the ongoing conflict.

Aziz's statement that the LoC was not delineated was a part of a larger Pakistani game plan to first claim that the LoC was not delineated and then alter it to suit its strategic interests: getting closer to the Srinagar–Leh highway and then disrupting India's military supplies to Leh. This was largely caused by the reaction of the international community, which refused to accept the Pakistani line that 'Kashmir is a nuclear flashpoint'. This was for the first time that the international community's reactions favoured the long-held Indian position on Kashmir. Indian analysts were quick to point to a new sophistication in the Indian response to the Pakistani aggression that sought to appreciate the difference between Sharif who wanted to normalize relations with India, and the Pakistan Army which wanted to heighten the tension between the two nations.[37]

This can also be seen against the backdrop of the 'clean chit' given to Sharif by Fernandes. Early into the crisis, Fernandes said that Sharif was not fully aware of the Kargil adventure planned by the Army. There is speculation that George Fernandes' statement was a carefully calculated move to sharpen the differences between the civilian and military establishments in Pakistan.

[37] C. Raja Mohan, 'Onus on Islamabad', *The Hindu*, 29 May 1999.

India made it clear that Aziz was welcome to come and talk, but the air strikes in Kargil would not stop. The Indian negotiating position on Kashmir changed slightly when the Prime Ministers of the two neighbours met in New York on 23 September 1998. In a joint statement they reaffirmed their common belief that an environment of durable peace and security was in the supreme interest of both India and Pakistan and the region as a whole. They also expressed their determination to renew and reinvigorate efforts to secure such an environment. They agreed that the peaceful settlement of all outstanding disputes, including Jammu and Kashmir, was essential for the purpose. India never wanted to link the issue of Kashmir to the issues of peace and security. With this joint statement, however, India conceded that a resolution of the Kashmir issue was essential for creating a durable environment of peace.

The one window of opportunity that appeared was lost quite predictably when both sides adopted non-negotiable positions. During Aziz's visit both sides adopted '. . . a high pitch in projecting their rationale of the Kargil situation, with Pakistan terming it a part of the Kashmiri freedom struggle and India asserting that it was nothing more than armed intrusion amounting to aggression, sponsored, planned and engineered by Pakistan, without any involvement of Kashmiri militants'.[38]

The position taken by Pakistan was to absolve itself of any involvement in the intrusions and to question the authenticity of the taped conversations. Mr Aziz said that the jihad for Kashmir had been going on for ten years and that these things 'keep happening'.[39] He added, 'It is a local problem and should be locally handled'.[40] The question that ought to have been asked of Aziz was whether he had come as a representative of the intruders, since he had asked India to stop its air strikes. Pakistan had earlier questioned the validity of the LoC which shook the very foundations of Indo-Pak relations that have hinged on the 1972 Simla accord.

Aziz gave a three-point formula which India promptly rejected. The Aziz formula envisaged (1) a cease-fire, (2) a joint working group to review the LoC and demarcate it on the ground, and (3) an invitation to Jaswant Singh the following week for further talks.

India turned down all these offers quite predictably. If India had

[38] 'India Rejects Pak Proposal, Refuses to Halt Strikes', *Statesman,* 13 June 1999.
[39] Ibid.
[40] Ibid.

agreed to the cease-fire, then it would have meant altering the LoC to Pakistan's advantage. India rejected the setting up of a Joint Working Group to review the LoC as it would have entailed altering the existing LoC to Pakistan's advantage, besides questioning the Simla Agreement which is one of the foundation pillars of Indo-Pak relations. India also made it clear that further talks would resume only after Pakistan had withdrawn its mercenaries.

THE NIAZ NAIK VISIT

Just as the conflict was winding down, a low-profile visit was made by the former Foreign Secretary of Pakistan to New Delhi. This visit was bereft of any hopes. His visit falls in the category of diplomatic back channels which, even when critically examined, work well in most crisis situations. Not much is known about his stay in Delhi. He reiterated that his visit was 'private', although one wonders how on a 'private' visit one would reach the office of the PM, have a meeting with the National Security Adviser, and other important figures in New Delhi. He said '. . . I think the situation will be resolved. I can't say that a deal is in the offing but efforts are being made in that direction.'[41] On his return to Islamabad he claimed that the Kargil situation could be resolved. In the BBC programme 'World Today' on 29 June 1999, Mr Naik claimed,

> Well, we are trying to arrange the first meeting of DGMO's (Director General Military Operations) who are on the Line of Control on both sides. And if necessary the senior military officers and others can meet but so far we have not been able to agree as to when, where and how, and with what mandate the senior military officers will meet.

I.K. GUJRAL'S ROLE

As a propounder of the Gujral Doctrine which called for improvement of bilateral relations between India and its neighbours, Mr Inder Kumar Gujral, former Prime Minister of India, played a quiet role in the Kargil crisis. He stated that the UN Secretary General Kofi Annan had been in touch with the two Prime Ministers. There was no indication whatsoever that Annan was going to take up the issue in the UN. Gujral spoke to Sharif about the need to preserve the atmosphere of friendship between India and Pakistan.

[41] 'Efforts on to End Kargil Conflict: Naik', *The Hindu*, 1 July 1999.

I told him that a lot of effort had gone into building an atmosphere which led to the Lahore Declaration and it should not be frittered away. I told Mr. Annan that for more than three decades India and Pakistan have maintained peace despite the problem of militancy because the LoC has not been violated by either side. India cannot accept the violation of the LoC. India is willing to discuss all the issues, including Kashmir, but not when there are intruders from across the border.[42]

But as the war in the mountains continued, India rejected the offer by the UN to send a special envoy to defuse Indo-Pak tensions and reaffirmed its determination to vacate the aggression in Kashmir.[43] India confronted Aziz with well-documented evidence of the Pakistan Army involvement in the operations (tapes of the conversation between two Pakistani generals), the savagery of the Pakistan Army (mutilated bodies of Indian soldiers), but the only response from Aziz was that of plain denials. Aziz did not appreciate the gravity of the situation. This was evident by the conspicuous absence of any senior civil or military officer in his team. Aziz came with an inflexible position in mind and stuck to it. In a crisis de-escalation scenario the negotiating dynamics call for gradual shift in position. A stalemate resulted after the failure of the talks, it was a facade constructed by Pakistan to publicize its noble intentions.

DIPLOMATIC SUPPORT & COSTS

Commentators have been quick to point to the paradigm shift in India's relations with the Western world by referring to the 'restraint' statements issued by various countries. The support of these nations may not have come without costs. Initially, some countries like Japan even went to the extent of questioning India's claims of any infiltration having even taken place. It took time for India to alter world opinion in its favour. Pakistan had clearly blundered and was caught on the wrong foot. The Aziz visit did not yield any desired results. What won international support for India was its decision not to cross the LoC. Kashmir was considered by them to be an issue over which a potential nuclear war could be fought. The Indian diplomatic community was unable to mitigate this belief in the same way as India has been unable to withstand the internationalization

[42] 'Gujral: Annan will Convince Sharif to Withdraw Intruders', *The Asian Age*, 30 May 1999.

[43] C. Raja Mohan, 'PM Rejects UN Offer', *The Hindu*, 31 May 1999.

of the Kashmir issue. This could result in the US and other countries demanding an early settlement of the issue. Former Pakistan Prime Minister Benazir Bhutto suggested that Kashmir be resolved on the lines of a Camp David Accord. There may be some takers for this.

There is also the possibility of renewed US involvement in particular and the P-5 in general in persuading India to sign the CTBT. With Kosovo behind him, the then US President Bill Clinton would have wanted another achievement to show for his presidency. It could be seen as a sort of quid pro quo in the negotiating dynamics fall-out of the Kargil conflict with the US increasing pressure on India to sign the CTBT, and also towards a settlement of the Kashmir issue.

Euphoria apart, Western support may not have been the result of a diplomatic effort but the consequence of Indian military restraint, which the world noticed. Moreover, the Western backing was event-specific and cannot be taken for granted. This was proven when the world responded critically to India's shooting down of the intruding Breguet Atlantique Pakistan plane. On 10 August 1999, an Indian Air Force MiG-21 shot down a Pakistani maritime surveillance aircraft, killing all sixteen personnel on board, for intruding into Indian territory in the Sir Creek area of Gujarat. According to the Indian version, the MiG 21s tried to force the Atlantique to land in India, but the 'intruder aircraft turned in towards the MiG 21 in an attack position'. The Pakistani official version, however, was that the Atlantique was unarmed and on routine training within its territorial limits when it was shot, without any warning. It was precisely for avoiding such incidents that both countries had entered (in 1991) into an Agreement on Prevention of Air Space Violation. The fact is that this agreement does provide for avoiding incidents like this, and yet it occurred.[44] India did not benefit diplomatically from the shooting of the plane.

One cannot expect the world, specially the Western countries, to support India all the time. They have their domestic political constituencies and their foreign policy agenda. Issues and concerns apart, Kashmir is firmly placed high on their list of concerns. After

[44] Article 2 of the 1991 Agreement Between Pakistan and India on Prevention of Air Space Violation states: '. . . the following restrictions are to be observed by military aircraft of both the forces: (a) Combat aircraft (to include fighter, bomber, reconnaissance, jet military trainer and armed helicopter aircraft) will not fly within 10 kms of each other's air space. No aircraft of any side will enter the airspace over the territorial waters of the other country, except by prior permission.'

the talks failed, Pakistan launched a war of words as well. It had to publicize that it wanted a peaceful settlement through the process of dialogue. As Sharif said 'The Lahore Declaration is intact, we want to defuse tension through dialogue'. Pakistani President Rafiq Tarar blamed India and said, 'India has rejected all offers for talks, and it shows that it wanted to impose war on Pakistan. Our people and our army are ready to defend every inch of the motherland and beat back any aggression.'[45] Yet another account of the failed Foreign Ministers' talks was given by a spokesman who said that while India's approach was that of 'war mongering', Pakistan was interested in 'peace-making'. Islamabad, he said, had not shut the door on dialogue with India. It was New Delhi which had stone-walled the possibility of a dialogue and rejected 'constructive' proposals made by the Pakistani side.[46]

Domestic Institutions and Politics

National elections had been announced on the day Pakistani forces began their retreat from Kargil. The fact that India emerged victorious decisively snuffed out the promise of an election that would not be influenced by extraneous factors. Kargil had to feature in the elections.

PARTY POSITIONS

Congress (I)

The Congress (I) believed that what happened in Kargil was well thought out. The Congress supported the military action, but wanted the Government to explain why Kargil happened. Like other political parties, it wanted the government to call a session of the Rajya Sabha (Upper House). The party maintained that the Government got carried away by the euphoria of the Lahore process and lowered its guard. 'The Cong (I) had welcomed the Lahore Declaration but at the same time recognised that it was nothing but an extension of the Simla Agreement. . . . We all support the military action going on to expel the intruders.'[47]

[45] 'Pak Interested in Peacemaking', *The Hindu*, 15 June 1999.
[46] Ibid.
[47] Interview with K. Natwar Singh (Congress), *Frontline*, 2 July 1999.

Communist Party of India, CPI (M)

The CPI too believed that the Indian leadership got carried away by the Lahore process and the belief that the Pakistan Prime Minister was keen to sort out problems through negotiations thus becoming complacent. The CPI was firmly behind the government on the military response.[48]

ON HOLDING A RAJYA SABHA SESSION

The debate on calling for a Rajya Sabha session for the Kargil crisis was founded on several premises. First, since the 12th Lok Sabha had been dissolved and the Rajya Sabha remained the only legislative forum where the national government could be held accountable (since it is never dissolved). Second, the Opposition, which was in a majority in the Rajya Sabha, wanted to play a larger role in the crisis with an eye on the forthcoming elections.

Atal Behari Vajpayee convened an all party meeting on 28 June. A decision was taken to defer the special session of the Rajya Sabha since the Lok Sabha had been dissolved. This was the culmination of a process initiated by the Opposition which included a complaint to the President K.R. Narayanan that they were kept in the dark about steps taken by the government regarding the developments leading to Kargil. Former Finance Minister Manmohan Singh led a Congress delegation to the President and pointed out that a national consensus was needed to ensure that the caretaker Government's military and diplomatic moves reflected the united will of the nation. The other parties, including the CPI, also submitted a memorandum to the President demanding that a session of the Rajya Sabha be called immediately. Prakash Karat of the CPI (M) echoed his party's stand demanding a Rajya Sabha session as 'an informed and responsible debate on how the Kargil situation developed and the measures taken so far are necessary so that a common understanding develops which will help the national endeavour'.[49] The Prime Minister met the President in this regard and assured him that holding a session of the Rajya Sabha could be considered, while also adding that an all party meeting would be called soon. The BJP and its allies stuck to their stand that there was no need to call this session. The TDP

48 Interview with Harkrishan Singh Surjeet (CPI), *Frontline*, 2 July 1999.

49 V. Venkatesan, 'For a Democratic Debate', *Frontline*, 16 July 1999.

(Telegu Desam Party), the National Conference and the Indian National Lok Dal backed this position. One can understand their apprehensions being in a minority in the Rajya Sabha and the expected criticism from other parties for the Government's failure to anticipate the problem.

The Government of India appointed a committee of four members with the most 'anodyne terms of reference terminating sharply at the intrusion'.[50] The terms of reference for this committee were 'to review the events leading upto the Pakistani aggression in the Kargil district . . . and to recommend such measures as are considered necessary to safeguard national security'. The four members of this committee were K. Subrahmanyam, B.G. Vergese, Lt. Gen. K.K. Hazari and Satish Chandra. However, the committee did not have any statutory authority. It has since submitted its report in January 2000 blaming the intelligence agencies for their failure to anticipate the intrusion.

INSTITUTIONAL DILEMMA

Prime Minister Vajpayee was in a dilemma on whether to permit troops to cross the LoC, in the process lose all goodwill earned through restraint, or continue to lose brave young men as the intruders continued to fire from strategic heights with their supply lines remaining intact. Any such escalation from India's side would have had two losses. (1) The loss of the little respect that the Indian diplomacy earned after the nuclear tests projecting India as a responsible nuclear weapons state. Any violation of the LoC would make Pakistan feel insecure, thereby resulting in a possible nuclear exchange. Most Indians believe Pakistan, if pushed to a corner could respond with a nuclear strike. The international community would respond quickly. (2) The public relations battle over Kashmir, which India has always been losing, would have been lost forever. Already people around the world have asked the uneasy question: If East Timor why not Kashmir? The Government of India acted responsibly in managing a response which would not bring any disrepute to India and undo the efforts put in by Indian diplomats in extracting a pro-India response to the Kargil crisis.

[50] A.G. Noorani, 'A Dubious Exercise', *Frontline*, 27 August 1999.

ROLE OF THE NATIONAL SECURITY COUNCIL

The National Security Council is meant to assess the threat perception a state faces. The concept of the National Security Council—on the lines of what the United States has—was first mooted by Arun Singh, the Minister of State for Defence in the late Rajiv Gandhi's Government. The V.P. Singh Government set up the nucleus in 1990, but it did not go beyond the appointment of a middle-ranking police official who was allotted a one-room office and little staff. Amid clamour from retired civil and military officers, the Narasimha Rao Government shot down the idea, broadly on the ground that the NSC's role could only be limited in a cabinet form of government.

A six-member National Security Council (NSC) headed by Prime Minister Atal Behari Vajpayee was announced in November 1998. It got formed nearly five months after the Task Force submitted its report recommending the formation of an NSC. The NSC is headed by the Prime Minister. The other members are the Home Minister (L.K. Advani), the Defence Minister (George Fernandes), the External Affairs Minister (Jaswant Singh), the Finance Minister (Yashwant Sinha) and the Deputy Chairman of the Planning Commission (K.C. Pant). The Principal Secretary to the Prime Minister becomes the National Security Adviser. The NSC is a three-tiered body, comprising the Strategic Policy Group, the National Security Advisory Board and a Secretariat represented by the Joint Intelligence Committee (JIC). The Strategic Policy Group is supposed to undertake a Strategic Defence Review, a blueprint of short- and long-term security threats as well as possible policy options on a priority basis. The National Security Advisory Board (NSAB) consists of persons of eminence outside of the government with expertise in external security, strategic analysis, foreign affairs, defence, the Armed Forces, internal security, science and technology, and economics.

There was criticism even when the NSC was constituted in November 1998. The most important came from K. Subrahmanyam, who said, '. . . by making the JIC the Secretariat, the long-term intelligence is bound to be neglected and strategic defence review will not have any solid foundation on long-term assessments but will be a collection of ad hoc views of individuals'.[51]

[51] K. Subrahmanyam, 'New Set-Up Leaves Much to be Desired', *Times of India*, 20 November 1999.

There has been one meeting of the NSC (at least one about which there is public information). This was convened during the Kargil conflict where members were told to confine their observations to less than three minutes and voice only constructive suggestions and not criticize past handling. There has been lack in transparency about the working of the NSC—about its functions and about its agenda. The NSAB has also received flak for having a Delhi-centred approach 'with very little inputs from, and interactions with, the security bureaucracies of the State Government which have to confront the non-nuclear, covert threats to security in their territory and with non-governmental experts located in different parts of the country'.[52] India's National Security Council, which is supposed to assess threat perceptions and should have been among the first ones to bring affairs to the notice of the country, did precious little during this conflict. The one and only meeting that the NSC had was on 8 June 1999 when the NSC met the PM in Hyderabad House to deliberate on 'the situation in Kargil' and 'the broader question of India-Pakistan relations'. In the three hours it met, this agenda is supposed to have been accomplished. As a press release the following day claimed, 'The meeting undertook an in-depth and wide ranging analysis of the motivations and politico-strategic objectives of the current Pakistani intrusion, in both the short-term and long-term perspective. A clear understanding of Pakistan's aims emerged from the discussions.'[53] But this was not to be. Large number of intruders were well and truly entrenched in bunkers within Indian territory, and even after the air raids began, the NSC met after fifteen days. The NSC is supposed to undertake an assessment of the threat perceptions based on inputs from agencies like RAW to conclude definitively on where the threat lies.[54] The NSC's work ends well before an intrusion takes place.

CONSTITUTIONAL PROVISIONS FOR TACKLING SUCH CRISES

The semantic jugglery necessitated by the term 'war' leaves space for its various synonyms to be accommodated in a military crisis, be it encounter, insurrection, armed conflict, armed rebellion or internal disturbance. Lack of declaration of war by Pakistan does not absolve

[52] B. Raman, 'NSC: A Take-Off in Wrong Direction', *Business Line*, 7 December 1999.

[53] A.G. Noorani, 'End this Sham', *Statesman*, 16 June 1999.

[54] Ibid.

it of endangering what in the United Nations Charter is termed 'international peace and security'. Under Article 352 of the Indian Constitution, a provision exists for an emergency due to war, external aggression or armed rebellion.[55] 'A 'Proclamation of Emergency' may be issued by the President at any time he is satisfied that the security of India or any part thereof has been threatened by war, external aggression or armed rebellion' (Art 352). It may be made even before the actual occurrence of any such disturbance, e.g. when external aggression is apprehended.[56] The President of India holds the authority for the 'Proclamation of Emergency'. Sub-clause (3) of Article 352 reads: 'No such Proclamation can be made by the President unless the Union Cabinet, headed by the Prime Minister recommend to him, in writing that such a Proclamation should be issued.'[57] Article 352 clearly mentions: '. . . whole of India or only a part thereof . . .'. This may be read with Article 355 which stipulates the 'duty of the Union to protect States against external aggression and internal disturbance'. One can conclude that a situation did arise when constitutionally the PM was empowered to make use of the emergency provisions.

He chose not to do so perhaps due to the following factors:

1. The previous experience on one such occasion—the emergency of 1976.
2. That there was a caretaker government at the centre.
3. That the conflict did not warrant such a drastic measure as it was too localized a conflict.

Elections were not postponed. This revealed the strength of the Indian democracy although it was headed by a caretaker government. India, at some stage in the conflict, did consider moving the International Court of Justice to expose those responsible for the current crisis. Union Law Minister Mr. Ram Jethmalani said that 'The government would move the International Court of Justice

[55] Article 352. 'Proclamation of Emergency.'

(1) If the President is satisfied that a grave emergency exists whereby the security of India or of any part of the territory thereof is threatened, whether by war or external aggression or [armed rebellion], he may, by proclamation, make a declaration to that effect [in respect of the whole of India or of such part of the territory thereof as may be specified in the proclamation].' D.D. Basu, *Introduction to the Constitution of India* (Prentice-Hall, New Delhi, 17th edition, 1995).

[56] Ibid., p. 337.

[57] Ibid.

against those responsible for the recent conflict', he further added, '. . . those responsible for the intrusion should be tried and a lesson not to cross the defined Line of Control needs to be taught, those responsible should be treated like Nazis after the World War II'.[58]

The Indian response has been what Jaswant Singh summed up as '. . . the right of self-defence being inherent, and since all the fighting is taking place on our side of the LoC, no solution is possible until Pakistan first agrees to restore the status quo ante'.[59]

An Assessment

India exercised a high degree of restraint. It chose to clear the Kargil peaks in a protracted struggle but decided not to cross the LoC to cut off the intruders' supply lines. Militarily, the Indian Army gave a befitting reply to the enemy at the individual, company, battalion and brigade levels.[60]

The national response too was laudable. The country stood together as one unit. It made generous contributions to the Army Welfare Fund. There were no communal flare-ups. Even the various insurgent groups all over the country chose not to take the sheen away from an emphatic Indian victory.

Politically, the senior leaders kept their cool. Barring a few rhetorical statements, public pronouncements were measured and structured. The government aimed at clearing the intruders whilst declaring that its stand on this issue was non-negotiable. The Indian diplomatic approach was calibrated and the world was informed that there was an LoC and that Pakistan had breached it by backing the infiltrators. Pakistan made its case worse by knocking at the doors of various capitals to garner support for a lost cause. It found disapproval everywhere, be it China or the G-8[61] or the US. Pakistan's nuclear blackmail did not find any takers. The Indian restraint was well thought out, diplomatically as well as militarily. Most important, Pakistan tested the limits of Indian restraint while playing the brinkmanship game.[62]

India learnt a few lessons in statecraft. If you are dealing with an unreliable neighbour, who has lured you into war, then one's vision

[58] 'India Planning to Move ICJ' (UNI), *The Hindu*, 4 July 1999.

[59] 'Onus on Pak to Make Talks Click: Jaswant', *Times of India*, 2 June 1999.

[60] For the operational details, refer Ch. 3 by Maj. Gen. Ashok Krishna.

[61] For the G-8 statement, refer Appendix 8.

[62] Kanti Bajpai, 'Testing the Limits', *Times of India*, 6 July 1999.

has to be coherent and clear. Diplomacy can only *supplement* the gains on the ground, it cannot be a *substitute*. Without a clear definition of the goals there can be no effective gain, neither militarily nor diplomatically. Democracy and transparency go hand in hand; intelligence lapses cannot be covered up. There has to be an institutionalized mechanism for threat assessment and formulation of an adequate state response.

6

Role of the United States: Mediator or Mere Facilitator?

D. Suba Chandran

The role played by the United States in de-escalating the Kargil crisis was significant. Though hesitant initially to get involved, the US, at a later stage, sent Gen. Anthony Zinni, Commander-in-Chief of the US Central Command and Gibson Lanpher, the Deputy Secretary of State, to Pakistan. Lanpher also visited New Delhi after Islamabad. But the breakthrough came when the President Clinton met Pakistan Prime Minister Nawaz Sharif on 4 July.

What role did the US play during the crisis? Why was the US hesitant to get involved initially? What prompted the US to send Anthony Zinni and Lanpher to Pakistan, and later Lanpher to India? Does the Sharif–Clinton meeting amount to mediation by the US, or was it only an effort to make India and Pakistan come together and negotiate? Finally, how much did the US involvement help in resolving the crisis?

Initial Reaction of the United States to Kargil

The initial reaction of the US at the beginning of the crisis was that 'the Pakistanis are plainly to blame for having started the fighting. If it was not the elected government of the country that was responsible, then perhaps worse it may have been a sort of a Pakistani military-fundamentalist axis that the government is not in a position to know fully about, let alone to subordinate.'[1] By the end of May, the US made it clear that the militants should leave the area if peace was to return. Karl Inderfurth, Assistant Secretary of State for South Asian Affairs, in an interview on 30 May, said 'Clearly, the Indians

[1] *Washington Post*, 28 June 1999.

are not going to cede this territory that militants have taken . . . . They have to depart and they will depart, either voluntarily or because the Indians take them out.'[2] Elsewhere, Inderfurth also said, 'There is always the possibility of events spinning out of control. Clearly the ingredients are there for miscalculation. Our hope is that both sides will take steps to move this in a peaceful direction.'[3]

These statements implied the following. First, the US considered those who had infiltrated as 'militants' and not 'freedom fighters', as Pakistan preferred to call them. Second, removal of the militants from the Indian side of the LoC was essential to bring back peace. Third, the US recognized the nature of the conflict and hoped that both India and Pakistan would engage themselves in finding a peaceful solution to the conflict, instead of escalating it further. Thus, the initial reaction of the US was to keep the situation under control.

The US, however, did not want to mediate between India and Pakistan initially; it expected them to negotiate and find a solution. This was reflected in the statement made by James Rubin, the spokesman of the State Department. He said:

> We strongly support talks between India and Pakistan to resolve this latest dispute and believe these talks should take place as soon as possible. Ending the fighting in the Kargil area can only be accomplished through direct engagement by India and Pakistan. We remain in touch with the Indian and Pakistani Governments to express our strong concern, to urge them to show restraint and to prevent the fighting from spreading and to urge both countries to work together to reduce tensions. . . . We certainly would want them to talk to each other to work out an arrangement to stand down from the conflict. We certainly would want them to talk to not take steps to expand the conflict beyond the current Kargil area.[4]

Richard Celeste, the US ambassador to India, also elsewhere echoed the same policy of the US. 'The US will never interfere (in Kashmir). Never . . . . Kashmir is an issue, which can be only settled by peaceful talks between the two countries, without any intervention. The US realises this.'[5]

Thus, the US did not have any plans initially to mediate between the

[2] Quoted in N.C. Menon, 'Ultras Will Have to Go: Inderfurth', *Hindustan Times*, 31 May 1999.

[3] Quoted in Sridhar Krishnaswami, 'Kargil Situation Unpredictable: US', *The Hindu*, 31 May 1999.

[4] Sridhar Krishnaswami, 'US Extends Support to Indo-Pak Talks', *The Hindu*, 6 June 1999.

[5] Quoted in 'No Interference in Kashmir: Celeste', *Asian Age*, 6 June 1999.

two countries nor were there any ideas to send an envoy to de-escalate the tensions between both countries. James Rubin, the State Department spokesman, in response to a question whether the US was sending an envoy replied, '. . . our position regarding Kashmir is well known. At this time there are no plans to send a US envoy to the region'.[6]

Why did the US hesitate to involve itself in the conflict situation in the initial stages? According to an editorial, '. . . the refusal to get involved in the situation may have something to do with Kosovo-induced fatigue'.[7] However, the real reason seemed to be that the US did not want to take sides, but remain neutral. Joe Lockhart, White House spokesman, said, 'The President has written to both leaders urging restraint. . . . This is an issue of getting the two sides to talk and resolve their differences rather than taking sides.'[8] The other reason could be that the US was not aware of the extent of infiltration initially, in terms of numbers of the infiltrators and the area that they held on the Indian side of the LoC. Besides, the US wanted the issue to be sorted out between the two countries based on the Lahore Declaration.

The first major change in the US position on Kargil came when the US decided to send Gen. Anthony Zinni to Pakistan.

The Zinni and Lanpher Mission

The Zinni and Lanpher mission marked the beginning of serious efforts by the US to defuse the crisis in Kargil. Why did the US decide to send this team to Pakistan, specially after denying that the US had no plans to send an envoy to defuse the situation? What were the objectives of this mission? Were they able to succeed in achieving their objectives?

Certain events in the first two weeks of June forced the US to realize the grave nature of the situation in the South Asian region. Consider the following events in the first fortnight of June.

On 31 May 1999, the Pakistan Foreign Secretary, Mr Shamshad Ahmad, warned, 'We will not hesitate to use any weapon in our arsenal to defend our territorial integrity.'[9]

6 Aziz Haniffa, 'US Sending no Trouble-Shooter', *Pioneer*, 30 May 1999.

7 *Indian Express*, 7 June 1999.

8 'No Questions on the Sanctity of LoC: US', *Times of India*, 10 June 1999.

9 Amit Baruah, 'Any Weapon Will be Used, Threatens Pak', *The Hindu*, 1 June 1999.

On 5 June 1999, the Indian Army released documents recovered from three Pakistani soldiers killed in the Batalik subsector to substantiate its claim that Pakistan regulars were involved in the Kargil conflict.[10] On the same day, India refused a visit by the Pakistan Foreign Minister, Mr Sartaj Aziz, to New Delhi. A Foreign Office spokesman said, '. . . the date is not convenient and we will revert shortly to the Government of Pakistan with alternative dates'.[11]

Again, on the same day, Pakistan Prime Minister Nawaz Sharif accused India of being '. . . not serious about holding peace talks', and warned, 'Chances of a war between Pakistan and India cannot be ruled out.'[12]

On 8 June 1999, Hafiz Muhammad Sayeed, chief of the Lashkar-e-Toiba, one of the 'jihadi' group that infiltrated in the Kargil–Dras sector, said, 'We are not going to withdraw even an inch from Kargil and Drass at the request of [the] United States or Pakistan.'[13]

On 11 June 1999, India released the tapes of a conversation between the Pakistani Chief of General Staff, Lt. Gen. Mohammad Aziz, and the Pakistan Army Chief, Gen. Pervez Musharraf, on 26 May and 29 May to prove the involvement of Pakistan.

On 12 June 1999, a two-hour meeting between Jaswant Singh and Sartaj Aziz failed to find a solution to the conflict situation.[14]

On 13 June 1999, the Indian Prime Minister, Mr Vajpayee, said, 'We will give a befitting reply. We will not rest till all the intruders are driven out (from our territory).'

On 14 June 1999, Mr K.N. Govindacharya, the BJP General Secretary and spokesperson said, 'We intend to keep on our side of the LoC; we do not want escalation, but we are determined to push the intruders out from our territory.' He also warned Pakistan that India 'may eventually end up with changing the LoC all along the Kashmir border . . . pushing Pakistan beyond Pakistan Occupied Kashmir.'[15]

These events produced a strong public reaction inside India against Pakistan. The fact that the infiltrators had occupied Indian territory, the flow of body bags and return of the mutilated bodies of six

[10] 'Clear Proof of Pak Role, *The Hindu*, 6 June 1999.

[11] 'June 7 "Not Convenient" for Talks', *The Hindu*, 6 June 1999.

[12] 'Indo-Pak War is a Possibility, says Sharif', *Hindustan Times*, 6 June 1999.

[13] 'No Retreat from Dras or Kargil: Militants', *Asian Age*, 8 June 1999.

[14] K.K. Katyal, 'Stalemate in Indo-Pak Talks', *The Hindu*, 13 June 1999.

[15] 'If Pushed, India will Take Back PoK: BJP', *The Hindu*, 15 June 1999.

Indian soldiers greatly inflamed the sentiments of people in India. The print and electronic media gave wide coverage to events like the relatives of soldiers receiving the bodies of their dead, and airing the interviews of war widows. The entire Indian nation was incensed and expected the Indian Government to give a fitting reply. Consider the following reaction from a journalist:

> Six of our soldiers were brutally hacked by the enemy troops. They were not killed in firing. They were chained, burnt by cigarette butts; their eyes were gouged out, their ears, noses and genitals chopped while they were alive. There could only be few parallels of such barbarism between two nations who are otherwise talking of friendship. . . . And it is all Pakistan's creation. Not ours. Not at all. Now tell Sartaj Aziz to go back. Tell him, we will talk to him when we throw his troops out of our home. Don't give them any safe passage. Catch them alive or dead. Rub it into Aziz. What are we going to talk anyway? The line of control is debatable? That the death of our men is merely statistics? That the areas captured by Pak brigands can be negotiable? That there is no war? . . . Our soldiers are not fodder for Pak cannons. Let them fight the enemy as an enemy. We cannot let the sacrifices go. *For every drop of blood shed by our men, [a] thousand drops should be extracted from across the border. The bus can wait. It is a question of a nation's self-esteem. A nation without self-esteem is not worth dying for.*[16] (Emphasis added.)

The US must have realized that with the entire Indian nation being charged and with elections forthcoming, the BJP would take firm military action against Pakistan. Besides, Indian Prime Minister Vajpayee would have informed the US President during their telephonic conversations about the grave situation inside India and along the border. A letter from the Indian Prime Minister sent to President Clinton in July, which was sent through Samuel Berger, the US National Security Adviser, could also have acted as the catalyst. According to a *Washington Post* report, 'Vajpayee's message was that India might have to attack inside Pakistan, if Pakistan did not pull back troops who had seized Indian outposts in the disputed territory of India. It stoked already high US fears that India . . . would storm across the cease-fire line that divides Kashmir or open a second front elsewhere.'[17] The US, having realized the grave nature of the crisis, specially after Vajpayee's letter, decided to take steps to defuse the situation. Hence, the US decided to send an envoy to the region.

[16] Wilson John, 'Enough. Now Teach Them a Lesson', *Pioneer*, 11 June 1999.
[17] Thomas W. Lippman, 'India Hinted at Attack in Pakistan', *Washington Post*, 27 June 1999.

What were the objectives of the Zinni-and-Lanpher mission? The main objective of the visit was to ask Pakistan to withdraw the infiltrators from the Indian side of the LoC. While Zinni and Lanpher were in Pakistan, James Rubin said, 'We want to see withdrawal of forces supported by Pakistan from the Indian side of the Line of Control.'[18] At a later date, P.J. Crawley, spokesman for the National Security Council, confirmed, 'His [Zinni's] trip to Islamabad was focussed, specifically on the current situation. We want the fighting to stop and both countries to respect the Line of Control. The cause of the war is Pakistan-supported militants which we want to see out of those areas.'[19]

How did Pakistan react to Anthony Zinni's visit? Though Pakistan considered the visit of Gen. Anthony Zinni to be 'within the process between Washington and Islamabad',[20] there appeared to be 'little enthusiasm' in Pakistan to receive Gen. Zinni and Lanpher.[21] They met the Chief of the Army Staff, Gen. Pervez Musharraf, on 24 June at the Joint Staff Headquarters, in which the latter briefed the US general about the situation prevailing on the LoC and international borders, claiming that India was increasing tensions as its forces were posing an offensive threat to Pakistan.[22] Though the content of the talks was not made public, it is believed that Zinni conveyed the US concerns. He also met Pakistani Prime Minister Nawaz Sharif on 25 June. Zinni said, 'Pakistan should withdraw the Kashmiri freedom fighters from the peaks they have occupied across the Line of Control.'[23] Zinni's meeting with the Prime Minister, which lasted about 45 minutes, also 'ended inconclusively as both sides remained stuck to their known and stated positions on the Kargil crisis'.[24] A press statement released after Sharif's meeting with Zinni stated, '. . . the Prime Minister apprised the US General of Pakistan's viewpoint on the current crisis, which required a balanced and

18 'State Department Asks Pakistan to Withdraw "insurgents"', *News*, 25 June 1999.

19 'Azim M. Mian, 'Withdrawal of Pakistan-Supported "Militants" Goal of Zinni's Visit: White House', *News*, 28 June 1999.

20 Hasan Akhtar, 'Pakistan Tells Zinni "Narrow" View can Escalate Conflict: US Asked to Adopt Fair, Balanced Approach', *Dawn*, 25 June 1999.

21 Nasim Zehra, 'Zinni's Islamabad Mission', *News*, 25 June 1999.

22 Shakil Shaikh, 'US Asked to Force India to Reduce Tension', *News*, 25 June 1999.

23 'A One-Sided Approach will Not Work', *Dawn*, 26 June 1999.

24 'Nawaz-Zinni Talks Remain Inconclusive', *News*, 26 June 1999.

constructive US approach, if durable peace was to prevail in the region.'[25]

Chief of the Army Staff Gen. Musharraf commented later that 'We held negotiations in a very congenial environment for about two hours. . . . They had their own opinion and they forwarded it, while we gave our point of view.'[26] Later, commenting on Zinni's visit, Musharraf said, 'They gave us their opinion and we gave our opinion. We are trying to find a solution which is agreeable to us, to the United States and to the Indians also.'[27] However, Pakistan was not happy with whatever Zinni conveyed in his meetings with the Chief of the Army Staff and the Prime Minister. In a statement made after Zinni's meeting with Musharraf, Pakistan wanted the US to adopt a balanced approach to the tension along the LoC. It expected the US not to focus only on Kargil. 'To focus on one incident, which can be repeated here and there again, is wrong. It is a focus not evenly spread. You can never have a fair solution to a dispute unless you have a fair and balanced approach. You cannot forget India's continuous violations of the Line of Control.' [28] By designating those fighting the Indian troops along the LoC as 'militants', Pakistan felt that the US had encouraged India to talk about war. Tariq Altaf, Foreign Office spokesman, said, 'This (considering the mujahideens as militants) is their (US) point of view. They could have taken a more balanced view. By focussing on the withdrawal of Mujahideens from Kargil, the United States will encourage India to talk of war. It would encourage India to talk of war and wider conflict.'[29]

What was the outcome of Zinni's visit to Pakistan? State Department spokesman James Rubin declared Anthony Zinni's visit as 'productive'.[30] Two significant developments took place after the visit. First, the announcement by Musharraf of a meeting between Nawaz Sharif and President Clinton.[31] Second, the sending of the

[25] Ibid.

[26] 'COAS Says Pakistan, US Leaders may Meet on Kashmir', *Dawn*, 27 June 1999.

[27] Mukhtar Alam, 'Nawaz-Clinton Meeting Soon, says COAS', *News*, 27 June 1999.

[28] Foreign Office spokesman Tariq Altaf, quoted in 'Pakistan Urges US to Adopt Balanced Approach', *News*, 25 June 1999.

[29] Ibid.

[30] 'US Clarifies', *Pioneer*, 29 July 1999.

[31] Mukhtar Alam, 'Nawaz-Clinton Meeting Likely Soon, says COAS', *News*, 27 June 1999.

former Foreign Secretary of Pakistan, Niaz A. Naik as a special envoy to India on a secret visit.

Lanpher's Visit to India

Lanpher came to India immediately after visiting Pakistan. His objective was to brief the Indian Government on what had transpired in Islamabad between the American delegation and the Pakistan government.[32] During his visit, Lanpher told India that he did not bring any proposal of 'safe exit' of the militants from the Indian side of the Line of Control.[33] It is possible, besides each other reiterating their own positions on the crisis, Lanpher would have persuaded India to receive a special envoy from Pakistan on a secret mission to defuse the situation. It should have been more than a coincidence that Niaz Naik visiting India on a secret mission followed up Lanpher's visit. The US, however, insisted that Zinni and Lanpher's visit to the subcontinent was not an attempt to mediate between India and Pakistan. State Department spokesman James Rubin said the issue must be settled 'directly between India and Pakistan. The US is not a mediator nor have we offered any specific solution for resolving this dispute. . . . We are urging the two sides to talk and resolve the dispute.'[34]

The next major step that involved the US in defusing the conflict was the Clinton-Sharif meeting on 4 July.

The Clinton–Sharif Meeting

This meeting had a positive impact on containing the conflict situation in Kargil. Both the leaders met at Blair House on 4 July in the US. The Foreign Minister Sartaj Aziz, Foreign Secretary Shamsad Ahmed, Principal Secretary Saeed Mehdi, Additional Secretary Tariq Altaf and others accompanied Nawaz Sharif.[35] Why did Sharif suddenly decide to meet Clinton? Did he go to the US at the invitation of Clinton, or did he ask for a meeting with Clinton? What

[32] Sukumar Muralidharan, 'Missions and Concerns', *Frontline*, 16 July, 1999, p. 8.

[33] 'Safe Exit Not Part of Talks with US: India', *Hindustan Times*, 28 June 1999.

[34] 'US Clarifies', *Pioneer*, 29 July 1999.

[35] Shakil Shaikh, 'Nawaz Rushes to US for Talks with Clinton', *News*, 4 July 1999.

did both the leaders discuss? What was the outcome of the meeting? How did India react to this meeting?

According to a Pakistan Foreign Office release, the meeting was not a sudden development. It was 'the result of the recent contacts between the two leaders on the deteriorating situation and the need for a settlement of the Kashmir dispute which holds the key to durable peace and security in South Asia'.[36] The meeting between the two leaders could have been discussed during Zinni's visit. The fact that Pervez Musharraf, Chief of the Army Staff in Pakistan said that a Sharif-Clinton meeting would take place soon corroborates this.[37]

The meeting seems to have been arranged at the request of Sharif, though a section in Pakistan claimed that it was Clinton who had invited Sharif. According to a White House release the meeting was arranged 'at Prime Minister Nawaz Sharif's request . . . to discuss how to resolve the immediate situation'.[38] In the press briefing held on 4 July after the Clinton-Sharif meeting, a senior Administration officer, responding to a question said,

> On Saturday (July 3, 1999) morning, Prime Minister Sharif asked to call the President. . . . They spoke for a while. The Prime Minister asked the President if he could come to Washington on an urgent basis. The President proposed this afternoon. I think many of you know the President is leaving on a domestic trip tomorrow, so he said, come this afternoon. The Prime Minister agreed.[39]

The following factors would have contributed to Sharif's sudden visit to the US.

First, the increasing military pressure from the Indian side. By 23 June, Pakistan admitted that 76 soldiers had been killed and 80 wounded in the fighting with India.[40] By the end of June, the Indian Army had recaptured Point 5140,[41] Point 5203,[42] 6 more heights, including the strategic Point 5203,[43] 2 more major peaks

[36] Ibid.
[37] *Dawn*, 27 June 1999.
[38] 'Meeting Arranged on Nawaz's Request: White House', *News*, 4 July 1999.
[39] Official text, United States Information Service, 7 July 1999, p. 3.
[40] Amit Baruah, 'Pak Admits Loss of 76 Soldiers', *The Hindu*, 24 June 1999.
[41] 'Army Recaptures Point 5140', *Pioneer*, 21 June 1999.
[42] 'Another Key point in Batalik Regained', *Hindustan Times*, 22 June 1999.
[43] 'Troops Capture 6 More Heights', *Pioneer*, 24 June 1999.

including Point 4070[44] and 2 peaks on Jubar hills—Point 4700 and Black Rock.[45]

Second, the failure of Pakistan on the political front. India rejected all the 'peace' moves by Pakistan, insisting on withdrawal of the Pakistan backed forces from the Indian side of the LoC as the first condition before any talks could be held between the two countries. During the Lanpher visit and Naik's visit, India made its position very clear. On 1 July, India rejected Pakistan's proposal for talks between the Directors General of Military Operations (DGMOs).[46] On 2 July, Brajesh Mishra, Indian National Security Adviser, said that the possibility of Indian forces crossing the LoC to flush out the militants was not ruled out.[47] On the same day, the Defence Committee of the Pakistan Cabinet, which included members from the military declared that Pakistan wanted to resolve the 'current crisis' through 'negotiations in the spirit of the Lahore declaration'.[48] Besides, according to *The Times* report, Pakistan had prepared a blueprint to withdraw from the LoC by 2 July. According to the report, 'The politicians were ready to give in first, only the army was adamant. But now the army too looks like giving in. . . . All Pakistan needs now is a way of saving face.' [49] With India firm on its position, Nawaz Sharif had no option other than asking Clinton to arrange for the withdrawal.

Third, the increasing economic pressure on Pakistan. By the end of June, according to a *Washington Post* report, the US had plans to withhold the $100 million disbursement that the IMF was planning to release in the next few days if Pakistan failed to make serious efforts for pulling out its troops.[50] With Pakistan's economy already in bad shape, such an event would have totally crippled it.

Fourth, the international isolation of Pakistan on Kargil. With Zinni's visit, the US had already made its position clear. The G-8 communique did not condemn Pakistan. However, it made it very clear that it was 'deeply concerned about the continuing military

[44] 'Two Major Peaks Recaptured', *The Hindu*, 30 June 1999.

[45] 'Two Peaks on Jubar Hills Recaptured', *Hindustan Times*, 1 July 1999.

[46] Amit Baruah, 'Pak Keen on Talks Between DGMOs', *The Hindu*, 2 July 1999.

[47] 'Mishra does Not Rule out Crossing LoC', *The Hindu*, 3 July 1999.

[48] Amit Baruah, 'Pak Calls for Talks', *The Hindu*, 3 July 1999.

[49] 'Pakistan Prepares a Blueprint for Pullout: Report', *Hindustan Times*, 4 July 1999.

[50] Quoted in 'USA may Block $100-m IMF Loan to Islamabad', *Statesman*, 28 June 1999.

confrontation in Kashmir following the infiltration of armed forces which violated the line of control' and regarded 'any military action to change the status quo as irresponsible'.[51]

The only possible sympathizer with Pakistan at this juncture was China and Sharif's visit to Beijing was designed to secure its support. With Chinese Premier Zhu Rongji telling Sharif that 'this is an issue left over from history concerning territory, ethnic nationalities and religion and can be only resolved through peaceful methods',[52] Pakistan felt totally isolated on the issue. It should be remembered that there was not even a joint statement made at the end of Sharif's visit to China, and he had to cut short his trip and return.

Faced with a serious military challenge from India, its economy in bad shape and isolated internationally, Pakistan needed a face-saving formula to withdraw from Kargil. Why did the US agree to such a meeting? The major objective of the US in agreeing to the meeting was to reduce tensions rather than mediate. Jake Siewert, White House spokesman, said, 'The purpose of the meeting is to review the situation in Kashmir and see what if anything, we can do to lessen the tensions there.'[53] The immediate reason was recognition by Clinton 'that this was a very serious situation and one that had danger for wider escalation'.[54] Even at this juncture, P.J. Crowley said that the United States did 'not plan to mediate. . . . This is a situation that has to be resolved by these two countries and these two governments directly.'[55]

The Clinton-Sharif meeting lasted for almost three hours, and ended with a joint statement.[56] According to it:

1. The President and the Prime Minister agreed that respecting the Line of Control in Kashmir in accordance with the Simla agreement was vital for the peace of South Asia.
2. 'Concrete steps' to be taken for the restoration of the LoC.
3. Immediate cessation of hostilities.

[51] See the text of the G-8 Communiqué relating to the Kargil crisis, 20 June 1999, www.ipcs.org/documents/99/2-apr-jul.htm#G-8

[52] 'Resume Talks, China Tells Sharif', *The Hindu*, 29 June 1999.

[53] Azim M. Mian, 'Nawaz, Clinton Agree to Take Concrete Steps to Restore LoC', *News*, 5 July 1999.

[54] Official text, United States Information Service, 7 July 1999, p. 2.

[55] Mian, op. cit., n. 53.

[56] The full text of the statement can be accessed at the IPCS web-site http// www.ipcs.org/documents/ 1999.htm

4. The Lahore process was the best forum for resolving all issues dividing India and Pakistan, i cluding Kashmir.
5. The President would take 'personal interest' in resumption of bilateral dialogue.
6. The President would pay an early visit to South Asia.

This agreement was the turning point in the two-month-old crisis. Clinton succeeded in defusing the crisis by making Pakistan agree to the withdrawal of troops from the Indian side of the LoC. Even more significant was the decision to resolve all issues between India and Pakistan (including Kashmir) on the basis of the 'bilateral dialogue begun in Lahore'.

What are the implications of this agreement for India? Critics argue that the Nawaz–Clinton agreement has nothing tangible to offer India, nor did it imply a shift towards India. Second, the phrase 'personal interest' in the agreement is vague, which could mean mediation. If this is true, then it implies that the Kashmir issue has been internationalized. Third, the joint statement between the two leaders refers only to withdrawal of those who were engaged in fighting the Indian troops in and around Kargil, but does not include other terrorist activities carried out on Indian soil. Fourth, even if the recent events were to be considered as a shift in US policy towards India, it would not have any lasting implications for the future of Indo-US relations, since Clinton is on his way out. Fifth, the recent events are Kargil-specific, and will have no impact on other US policies towards India such as the signing of the CTBT and FMCT.

It is not entirely true that the joint statement has nothing to offer to India. The statement clearly says '. . . steps will be taken for the restoration of the Line of Control in accordance with the Shimla agreement.'[57] What does the Simla Agreement say in this regard? It says,

> In Jammu and Kashmir, the Line of Control resulting from the cease-fire of December 17, 1971 shall be respected by both sides without prejudice to the recognised position of either side. Neither side shall seek to alter it unilaterally, irrespective of mutual differences and legal interpretations. Both sides further undertake to refrain from the threat or use of force in violation of the line. (Emphasis added.)

Second, the Sharif–Clinton joint statement also mentions 'that

[57] http//www.ipcs.org/documents/ 1999.htm

the bilateral dialogue begun in Lahore in February provides the best forum for resolving all issues dividing India and Pakistan'.[58] According to the Lahore Declaration, India and Pakistan have agreed to '*intensify their efforts to resolve all issues, including the issue of Jammu and Kashmir*' and '*reaffirm their condemnation of terrorism in all its forms and manifestations and their determination to combat this menace*'.

Third, the question of mediation and internationalization by the US. Throughout the crisis, the US continuously emphasized that the role played by it in the crisis was not that of a mediator. Even after Pakistan announced its decision to pull back, James Foley, State Department spokesman, said, 'Our interest is in encouraging an expeditious resumption and intensification of efforts by India and Pakistan to resolve their outstanding differences, again, including Kashmir. The US is not a mediator, nor did we offer any specific proposal for ending the fighting in Kargil.'[59] The term 'personal interest' of the President has been interpreted by some analysts to mean mediation. In a Press briefing held immediately after the Clinton–Sharif meeting on 4 July, a senior Administration official said, '. . . the President is going to take a personal interest in encouraging an expeditious resumption and intensification of these bilateral efforts'.[60] Hence, the criticism of the US mediating or planning to mediate in future between the two countries is not correct.

How did the Indian Government view the US stand on the Kargil crisis? According to Jaswant Singh, the External Affairs Minister, US support to India on Kargil was 'both a recognition of the correctness of India's case and the folly of Pakistan's misadventure. It is a recognition, too, of the altering geostrategic contours in the region.'[61] On the future of Indo-US relations, he said, 'The legacies of the past continue to occupy space in our thinking, I do believe that, if properly handled, there is a great future for this relationship between two of the largest democracies in the world.'[62]

[58] Ibid.

[59] Chidanand Rajghatta, 'Indo-US Ties Move from Nuclear Winter to Kargil Spring', *Indian Express*, 15 July 1999.

[60] Official text, United States Information Service, 7 July 1999, p. 4.

[61] C. Raja Mohan, 'A Chance to Shed Preoccupations of the Past: Jaswant', *The Hindu*, 24 July 1999.

[62] Ibid.

CONCLUSION

What role did the US play during the crisis? Was there a paradigm shift in its South Asia policy? How much did US efforts contribute to the defusion of the crisis? The role played by the US during the crisis was that of a facilitator and not of a mediator. At no point did the US plan to mediate. The Zinni mission was Pakistan-specific and Lanpher's visit to India was to 'brief the Indian government on what had transpired in Islamabad between the American delegation and the Pakistani government'.[63] Though Clinton invited Vajpayee also to the US, it was not for mediation. Thus, the role played by the US was that of a facilitator, not mediator.

Analysts like Robert Wirsing did not believe that any difference existed between them. According to him, the Kargil crisis 'will be dragged out with a formal additional participant in Washington. You may not call it mediation, but facilitation is mediation.'[64] However, others believe there is a difference between 'mediator' and 'facilitator'. According to Stephen Cohen, the specific role of the US was that of facilitating. He said, 'There is such a thing as a facilitator without being a mediator.'[65] Leo Rose, agreeing with this, added, 'Mediators try to set the lines and terms of a settlement and try to get the parties to agree to these. A facilitator wouldn't set terms.'[66]

Did the US policy on Kargil imply a paradigm shift? It is too early to consider the US support in Kargil as a 'paradigm shift' in US South Asia policy. With the end of the Cold War, Pakistan appears less significant in the geostrategic calculations of the US. The presence of Osama bin Laden in Afghanistan is of prime importance to the US, but the refusal of Pakistan to take any positive steps for handing him over to the US and the continuing Pakistan–Taliban relations besides Pakistan's position on the CTBT work against US–Pak strategic relations. Does a decline in US–Pak strategic relations imply closer Indo–US strategic relations? It need not necessarily be so. The interests of the US in South Asia have always been guided by its strategic interests at the regional and global levels. US strategic interests in India are based at present on nuclear and missile proliferation. The future growth of Indo-US strategic relations will

[63] Sukumar Muralidharan, 'Missions and Concerns', *Frontline*, 16 July 1999, p. 8.

[64] Quoted in 'Us, Them and the US', *Outlook*, 19 July 1999, vol. V, no. 27, p. 28.

[65] Ibid.

[66] Ibid.

depend on India signing the CTBT and FMCT, and its policy towards development of long-range and intercontinental ballistic missiles. Once Pakistan withdraws its troops, the US is bound to apply pressure on India to resume the dialogue with Pakistan. The current support of the US to India should be seen as Kargil-specific.

Last, what was the contribution of the US towards defusing the crisis? Many hawks in India believe the Kargil crisis was overcome mainly due to the military efforts made by India. The pro-BJP hawks hold that the crisis was defused due to the diplomatic and military offensive of the BJP Government. This is not entirely correct. It is true that the Government undertook serious efforts at the international level and the Indian military, after the initial setbacks, responded to the crisis very professionally. However, due regard should be given to efforts by the US in ending the crisis. Had it not been for tough talking on the part of the US regarding the issue of the mujahideen, the violation and the sanctity of the LoC, Pakistan would not have agreed to withdraw its troops by the first week of July itself. Many in India believe that the Indian military operations would have taken another six months to drive out the intruders and led to increasing the casualties already suffered. In fact, some believed that 'considering the nature of tasks involved in the successful culmination of Operation Vijay, it would be hazardous to lay any time frame for the (Indian) military leadership'.[67]

Besides sending Zinni to Pakistan the US made sure that the G-8 also followed the same policy. The Indian military efforts were very effective. Pakistan would have prolonged the struggle, had it not been for these factors. Equal credit should, therefore be given to the efforts made by the US at bilateral and multilateral levels as much as to the efforts of the Indian Army and the Indian Government to bring the crisis to an end.

To conclude, the possibility of a full-scale war between the two nuclear powers (India and Pakistan) induced the US to pressurize Pakistan to avert further escalation. The pressure applied on Pakistan by the US does not represent a 'paradigm shift' in US policy towards India, but only a de-escalation venture.

[67] N.N. Vohra, 'It's Inappropriate to Set any Time Frame', *Hindustan Times*, 11 June 1999.

7

Contextualizing Kargil within China's Security Paradigm

Bhartendu Kumar Singh and Satyajit Mohanty

The recent Kargil conflict between two nuclear powers—India and Pakistan—attracted worldwide attention because of the fear that the crisis could have escalated into a nuclear armageddon. The major powers reacted to the situation with alarm and consternation and indulged in diplomatic coercion to defuse the crisis. China was one of the countries whose views had great significance for both India and Pakistan not only because it is a great power, but also because the 'China Shadow' looms large over the Kashmir terra firma. Pakistan transferred nearly 5,000 sq. km of Kashmir to China in 1963. This area occupied by China is within the geographical vicinity of Kargil.

An analysis of China's Kargil policy shows that it adopted a balanced and neutral stand as contrasted with the earlier Chinese positions in the previous conflicts between India and Pakistan where a pro-Pak approach was discernible.

This chapter seeks to explicate Chinese views on the Kargil conflict and locate it within the broader context of China's Kashmir policy. It seeks to argue that a changed Chinese perspective need not necessarily be interpreted as a more favourable attitude towards India. The shift in China's stand can rather be seen in the context of a general reorientation of Chinese security concerns and strategic calculations in the post-Cold War era.

Kargil Conflict and China's Diplomatic Neutrality

In retrospect, China's stand on Kargil seemed to appease both India and Pakistan. Unlike the G-8 countries (excluding Japan), China has not blamed Pakistan for the infiltration of militants across the Line of Control (LoC). Although Mr Li Peng, Chinese Premier, described Kashmir as a 'complicated affair' during his meeting with Pakistan Foreign Minister Mr Sartaj Aziz, it was meant to keep Pakistan in good humour.[1] But unlike Iran and Libya, China has not offered to play a 'third-party role' to defuse the Kargil crisis. Right from day one of the conflict, China has emphasized that resorting to military confrontation by India and Pakistan would not bring them to any resolution of the crisis. A leading Chinese newspaper's editorial on 7 June 1999 remarked, '. . . history has repeatedly told us that war will do nothing to the settlement of the border disputes but crank up tensions'.[2] Reiterating that continued Indo-Pak hostility would be detrimental to the maintenance of peace and security in South Asia, China pleaded with both India and Pakistan to exercise restraint to prevent the flaring up of the Kargil situation. This was underlined by the Chinese leaders during the visit of the Pakistani and Indian dignitaries to Beijing.

On 11 June 1999, during Pakistan Foreign Minister Sartaj Aziz's visit to Beijng, Li Peng told Pakistan firmly to 'settle its disputes with India peacefully through dialogue and negotiations'.[3] Li Peng urged Sartaj Aziz that 'out of consideration for maintaining peace and stability in the South Asian Region, Pakistan should remain cool-headed and exercise self-control and solve conflicts through peaceful means and avoid worsening the situation'.[4] China's neutral stand was further emphasized by the Chinese leaders during Nawaz Sharif's visit to Beijing. The Chinese Premier, Mr Zhu Rongji, told his Pakistani counterpart on 28 June 1999 that China sincerely hoped that Pakistan and India would alleviate tensions in Kashmir through talks and thereby return stability to the region.

Not only China's neutrality, but its sensitivity to the Indian position was amply demonstrated during External Affairs Minister Jaswant Singh's visit to Beijing. Jaswant Singh's Beijing visit did not come in the context of the Kargil crisis, but was planned much before that. Since the Pokhran II tests, when Sino-Indian relations nose-dived, both sides took positive steps to put the bilateral relationship on the right track. It took a long time for the Indian officials to undo the damage that had been done after India justified the Pokhran II

[1] *The Hindu*, 13 June 1999.
[2] *China Daily*, 7 June 1999.
[3] *China Daily*, 12 June 1999.
[4] Ibid.

tests by espousing the 'China threat' theory. The External Affairs Minister, Jaswant Singh, and his Chinese counterpart Tang Jiaxuan discussed a number of issues which included, inter alia, Confidence Building Measures (CBMs) along the Line of Actual Control (LAC) as part of the normalization package. Only a passing reference was made to the Kargil conflict.[5] China has respected the Indian sentiments of not wanting the Kashmir issue to be internationalized. India has also resisted efforts for third-party mediation like a Camp David summit to resolve the Kargil crisis in particular and the Kashmir crisis in general. Neither had India sought any support from China (or for that matter any other country) on the Kargil issue, nor has China extended its good offices for mediation. Further, instances of Chinese neutrality can be illustrated by citing Beijing's stand on the LoC in Kashmir. In response to a question on the LoC, a Chinese Foreign Ministry spokesman refrained from making any detailed comments. He merely said the question 'may also be discussed' in the (then) forthcoming talks with Pakistan and India and the sanctity of the LoC should be maintained.[6]

Although not supporting Pakistan, China—unlike the Western countries—has never blamed Pakistan for propping up militancy in Kashmir. In an act of diplomatic finesse, China deliberately absented itself from the gathering of military attaches in New Delhi called to witness the seized weapons from the Pakistan-backed infiltrators.

Hence, China's posture during the Kargil crisis was tailor-made so as not to antagonize either India or Pakistan. In general terms, China called upon both the countries to restore the Lahore process and settle their differences through peaceful dialogue in a frank and patient way. China views that economic development and regional integration should figure high on the priority list of both countries.[7] However, China has not changed its firm stance on the Indian and Pakistani nuclear tests. In the light of the recent crisis, Beijing has again asked both the countries to abide by United Nations Security Council Resolution 1172, which calls upon both India and Pakistan to sign the Nuclear Non-Proliferation Treaty (NPT) and the Comprehensive Test Ban Treaty (CTBT) immediately and unconditionally.[8]

[5] *The Hindu*, 15 June 1999.

[6] *The Hindu*, 11 June 1999.

[7] *China Daily*, 5 June 1999.

[8] John Cherian, 'Signals from Beijing', *Frontline*, vol. 16, no. 4, 3-16 July 1999, pp. 26-7.

China's Kashmir Policy

This policy on Kargil has to be located within the broader context of China's Kashmir policy as it has evolved since the 1950s. Right till the 1980s China's policy towards Kashmir had been two-fold: (1) it had always regarded Kashmir as a disputed territory, and (2) it had stood for the principle of self-determination for the people of Kashmir.

Even during the height of Sino-Indian animosities in the early 1960s, China recognized that Kashmir was a disputed territory and not an integral part of Pakistan. The Sino-Pakistan Joint Communiqué of 3 May 1962 and the subsequent Boundary Agreement on 2 March 1963 recognized the disputed nature of Kashmir. The 1963 agreement between China and Pakistan provided for the formal delimitation and demarcation of the boundary between China's Xinjiang and the contiguous areas of Pakistan-Occupied Kashmir (POK). However, Article VI of the agreement stated that after the settlement of the Kashmir dispute between India and Pakistan, the sovereign authority concerned would reopen negotiations with the Government of the People's Republic of China on the boundary as delimited by Article II of the same agreement.[9] Commenting on the Sino-Pakistan boundary agreement the editorial in *People's Daily* on 5 June 1962 noted that 'the Chinese government had always hoped that India and Pakistan should settle this dispute over Kashmir through mutual consultations without (outside) interference'.

Having recognized that Kashmir was a disputed territory, China, till the 1980s, stood for the application of the principle of the right to self-determination for the people of Kashmir. From the early 1960s to the mid-1980s, China strongly supported the 'just struggle of the Kashmir people for self-determination'. A thaw in Sino-Indian ties since the 1980s, particularly after the visit of the Prime Minister Rajiv Gandhi to Beijing in 1988, helped in modifying China's stand towards Kashmir. China dropped the mention of the term 'self-determination' and the references to the UN resolutions on Kashmir because India had all along disliked them. Chinese President Jiang Zemin, during his visit to the Indian subcontinent in November-December 1996, surprised the Pakistani Senate by calling on both India and Pakistan to build a cooperative relationship and put aside

[9] For details, see the Sino-Pak Boundary Agreement of 2 March 1963.

'difficult issues'. Although he did not mention Kashmir, the reference was obvious.[10]

Hence, on the Kashmir issue the Chinese stand has shifted from a distinctly pro-Pakistan to a more or less balanced and neutral stand. Therefore, the Chinese position on Kargil should be interpreted keeping its larger Kashmir policy in the background. Within the immediate context China's Kashmir policy is guided by the twin objectives of improving the relationship with India and maintaining its 'all-weather' partnership with Pakistan. However, moving beyond the surface to the deep structural dynamics would underline the fact that China's policy on Kargil is guided by its own grand strategic calculations and long-term security perspectives.

China's Security Paradigm and Kargil

The Chinese grand strategy is based on a calculation of both its external and internal security dimensions. The Chinese conception of security has undergone a radical reorientation since the Four Modernizations programme announced by Deng Xiaoping in 1979. China's Kargil stand would be situated within its external security considerations and constraints. Thereafter, China's position on Kargil would be located within its domestic and internal security policies and parameters.

CHINA'S EXTERNAL SECURITY CONSIDERATIONS: LOCATING KARGIL

Chinese policy makers and scholars are firmly convinced that after a century of humiliation China has to seek its rightful place in the comity of nations. Its quest for great-power status enables it to a diplomatic culture of entitlement[3] and to have a powerful voice in global affairs. Hence, China is seeking to alter the present international structure which many analysts like Charles Krauthammer have described as the unipolar moment.[12]

[10] C. Raja Mohan, 'China Unlikely to Adopt Anti-India Posture', *The Hindu*, 11 June 1999.

[11] Michael Yahuda, 'How Much has China Learned About Interdependence', *China Rising: Nationalism and Interdependence*, ed. David G. Goodman and Gerald Segal (Routledge, London, 1997), p. 15.

[12] Charles Krauthammer, 'The Unipolar Moment', *Foreign Affairs*, vol. 70, no. 1, 1991, pp. 23-33.

China's quest for diplomatic flexibility and strategic manoeuvrability is seriously constrained by the increasing American presence in the Asian theatre. China's 1998 Defence White Paper views the growing US presence in Asia as a threat to its own security. However, the easy acceptance of 'Pax Americana' to any other conceivable alternative and the apprehensions of the 'China threat', particularly in the Asia-Pacific region, has made China's quest to gain a regional strategic and diplomatic foothold an uphill task.

The initial years of the post-Cold War era witnessed a vacillating American policy towards Asia. The 1990 and the 1992 *East Asia Strategic Initiative* (EASI) hinted at the reduction of US forward deployment in the East Asia Region.[13] The US-Japan trade wars, the closure of Subic Bay and Okinawa bases coupled with domestic pressures to reduce US global commitments convinced Chinese leaders that it would be able to fill up the perceived 'power vacuum' and thereby be able to play an independent role in the Asian continent. Such a view of China in Asian affairs moulded the Chinese leaders' opinion, and thereby they rejected the role of India as an important player in shaping the future of the multipolar world.

But since 1995, the US policy in Asia has undergone a sea change. It has realized the need to maintain a formidable presence in Asia. The 1995 US Security Strategy for the East Asia-Pacific region stated that 'if the American presence in Asia were removed, the security of Asia would be imperilled with consequences for Asia and America alike. Our markets and our interests would be jeopardized.'[14] In keeping with the changed strategy, Clinton, during his second term, renewed the US-Japan Security Alliance in mid-April 1996. The September 1997 Revised Guidelines for US-Japan Defense Cooperation enhanced this security alliance. American bilateral ventures in the region such as the Joint Security Declaration between the US and Australia (the Sydney Statement of 1996), the Joint Military Training Exercises with Thailand, the Team Spirit Exercises with South Korea, and the Visiting Forces Agreement (VFA) with the Philippines (January 1998) are indicative of a revamped American policy towards Asia.[15] The renewed American com-

[13] Stanley Chan, 'The American Military Capability Gap', *Orbis*, vol. 41, no. 3, Summer 1997, pp. 385.7.

[14] Cited in David L. Asher, 'A U.S.-Japan Alliance for the Next Century', *Orbis*, vol. 41, no. 3, Summer 1997, pp. 358-9.

[15] 'The US Security Strategy in the East Asia-Pacific Region 1998' is available on www.defenselink.mil/pubs/easr98

mitment in the Asia-Pacific region coupled with the dispatch of USS *Nimitz* and USS *Independence* without second thoughts during the third Taiwanese Straits crisis has been viewed with alarm in China. Beijing now fears that the US is trying to contain China and form a cordon sanitaire around the Middle Kingdom.

It is within this changed strategic context that China is re-evaluating its policy. China, which never had a well-defined regional policy, now realizes that increased regional acceptability will serve as a stepping stone for a greater say in global affairs. To achieve this goal, China has engaged in diplomatic manoeuvres and skilful engagement with other countries. The PRC (People's Republic of China), drawing upon its deep diplomatic traditions, has developed a set of sophisticated strategies. The first is freedom of action. The PRC leaders believe that an independent diplomatic posture enables China to exploit every possible opportunity in international relations, and this maximizes its leverage in the international system. The second approach, which is deeply rooted in China's strategic tradition, is to create or maintain a favourable balance of power in the world arena. Currently, the PRC leaders believe that the US, as the only remaining superpower, constitutes the primary constraint on China's international manoeuvring. A final approach is to pursue omnidirectional diplomacy. To create a favourable international environment, the PRC leadership manages its foreign relations pragmatically.[16] This is more so since the late 1980s. As Deng Xiaoping emphasized in the wake of the Tienanmen Square incident:

> In spite of troubles in East Europe and [the] Soviet Union, inspite of the G-7 sanctions against us, we stick to one principle; to continue to deal with the Soviet Union and manage well relations with it, to continue to deal with the US and manage well relations with it, to continue to deal with Japan and Europe and manage well relations with them.[17]

Thus, China's diplomacy of neutrality in the Kargil crisis can be situated, within the broad contours of a modified diplomatic approach, and more so its 'omnidirectional diplomatic strategies'. This, in turn, is linked to the broader and long-term strategic calculations that the Chinese leadership has ostensibly made.

With countries along the Pacific Rim more or less favourably

[16] Wu Xinbo, 'China: Security Practice of a Modernizing and Ascending Power', *Asian Security Practice: Material and Ideational Influences*, ed. Muthiah Algappa, (Stanford University Press, Stanford, 1998), pp. 148-9.

[17] Ibid., p. 149.

disposed towards the US, India can play a vital role in the emerging balance of power within the Asian security system. China has all along feared an encirclement, and this fear, rooted in its strategic culture, has been one of the driving forces for China's wars with India (1962) and Vietnam (1968). In spite of India's faux pas after Pokhran II, China did not take an anti-India posture as it feared that this would result in an 'arc of potential hostile countries' from Seoul to New Delhi. China has not forgotten that during the 1965 war, it issued two ultimatums against India forcing Delhi into signing an accord with the erstwhile Soviet Union in 1971 before the Bangladesh war.[18] China fears that an anti-India stand would tilt India in favour of the US. Further, the American influence in Pakistan, could enhance its ability to encircle China. This concern was clearly articulated by the Chinese military analyst Ding Zengyi, who wrote in a Chinese newspaper that 'where the United States is concerned, the present South Asian strategy is to control India and Pakistan, maintain the balance of power in South Asia and use India to contain China'. He went on to observe that such a confrontation would 'result in a weakened Pakistan and a limited India for the US and such a scenario would benefit the United States' South Asia strategic scheme'.[19] Hence, to avoid a US gain from the Kargil crisis, China urged upon both the countries of the subcontinent to restore peace and stability. Further, to pre-empt any third-party intervention or a Camp David type of solution (which would naturally involve the US) to the Kargil conundrum, China has insisted upon a bilateral resolution of the Kashmir dispute. For that matter, China has all along insisted upon a bilateral resolution of disputes involving any two of its neighbours, be it Japan and Russia, or Japan and South Korea, etc. The tacit acceptance of the Indian logic of a minimum nuclear deterrence and the strong backing of India's Kargil stand by the US has not gone unnoticed in Beijing.[20] Hence, China cannot afford to antagonize India and thereby nudge it towards a pro-US stand in future. While in the early 1990s China had rejected a role for India in global affairs, now it is willing to accept India as a major player in shaping a multipolar world with a view to help check the wave of US unipolarism and hegemony.

[18] Rajesh Ramchandran, 'The China Syndrome', *Hindustan Times*, 20 June 1999.

[19] Cited in Rifaat Hussain, 'China's Kargil Stance in Perspective', *News*, 27 June 1999.

[20] C. Raja Mohan, 'Third Parties in Sino-Indian Ties', *The Hindu*, 15 June 1999.

Thus, China's security strategy is slowly gearing towards facing an 'incipient bipolarity', hence it cannot take any stand which would provide the remotest chance of bringing the US right into its Himalayan back door.

DOMESTIC COMPULSIONS AND CHINA'S KARGIL STAND

China is itself in the thick of a transitional phase battling out the problems of regime survival and secessionism. Along the north-west front, China faces the problem of ethnic disturbance in the Xinjiang Uyghur Autonomous Region (XUAR). Along the southern front, the Tibetans are leading a strong resistance movement, and in Inner Mongolia the signs of ethnic disturbances are increasingly visible.

The Chinese leadership is totally averse to the idea of self-determination. China now fears that the West would raise the human rights issue and press for the application of the principle of self-determination for Tibet or Taiwan. China's disapproval of the principle of self-determination was vindicated in the recent Kosovo crisis. It has also rejected third-party interference in the domestic or bilateral disputes of countries. China is apprehensive that in case of an escalation of either the Taiwan crisis or the South China Sea disputes, outside powers, particularly the Western countries led by the US, might seek solutions within a framework (including the UN) where they would have a dominant say. India's stand on Pakistan-Occupied Kashmir (POK) and China's stand on Taiwan are more or less similar. Hence, China feels that in case it advocates third-party mediation in Kashmir, it could be setting a trap for itself by offering the West an analogical case to apply the same principles in Taiwan and Tibet.

Thus, China's own emphasis on bilateral resolution of disputes has moulded its views on Kargil. Beijing dislikes and even lacks confidence in its ability to manage complex multilateral relations, preferring the simplicity of bilateral interactions.[21] A classic instance where China prefers bilateralism over multilateralism is the South China Sea dispute, particularly the Spratly Islands dispute. The Spratly Islands are claimed fully or partly by the PRC, Taiwan, Vietnam, the Philippines, Malaysia and Brunei. In spite of the

[21] Xinbo, op. cit., n. 16, p. 149. Another important reason for which China prefers bilateralism is because it allows China to exploit its relative superiority over a weaker adversary.

multinational nature of the disputes, China is reluctant to discuss the contesting claims of sovereignty over the islands in intergovernmental fora like the ASEAN Regional Forum (ARF). Having shown its preference for bilateral negotiations, to deny the same privilege to India would be an act of hypocrisy and doublespeak.

China is also apprehensive of a 'Green Crescent' being formed along its north-western frontiers. Xinjiang has been an area of concern for Chinese leaders. The ethnically dominant Hans in China have nothing in common with the Uyghurs. Rather, any lay observer would easily pass off the Uyghurs as one of the Central Asian tribes. The Uyghurs are intensely aware of their cultural distinctiveness and have been striving for independence for some decades. At the Almaty Summit of the Shanghai Five in 1998 (China, Russia, Kazakhstan, Kyrgyzstan and Tajikistan), China took an initiative to secure a vital pledge from its partners to reject 'all manifestations of national separatism and religious extremism and to ban on their territories activities harmful to the state, sovereignty and security . . .'. This highlights the importance Chinese leaders have given to the Muslim extremist factor in their internal security calculations.[22]

Reports of Uyghur Muslim terrorist training camps in Pakistan and the movement of militants along the porous borders of the Central Asian Republics (CARs) have threatened China's territorial integrity. China had lodged a formal protest with Pakistan in February 1999 over alleged support provided by Pakistan to the Uyghur separatists. The fears of increased narco-terrorism and fundamentalism along the Chinese borders has also not been undermined in the long-term Chinese internal security considerations.[23] Some sections of the press reported that a section of the Pakistan-backed infiltrators, on their way towards Kargil had even entered Xinjiang. Hence, with the negative consequences of a resurgent Muslim backlash not ruled out within Chinese territory, China could not have possibly extended support to the Pakistan-backed 'muslim militants' (as the Chinese media calls the infiltrators). China, finding itself in a delicate situation, did not want to antagonize its trusted ally (Pakistan) and thereby maintained a diplomatic posture of neutrality. China has all along maintained that preservation of peace,

[22] Satyajit Mohanty, 'China and the Central Asian Republics: Towards Mutual Co-operation', *Journal of Peace Studies*, vol. 6, no. 2, March-April 1999, pp. 45-6.

[23] Bhartendu Kumar Singh, 'Chinese Views on the Kargil Conflict', available on the web-site www.ipcs.org (accessed on 3 November 1999).

tranquillity and regional stability along its borders is integrally linked with its internal stability and smooth economic development.

Hence, in the final analysis, it can be said that the various nuances of China's own external and internal security considerations shaped its response to the Kargil situation.

Sino-Indian Relations: Looking Beyond Kargil

At present, Sino-Indian ties are standing at a delicate crossroads. In the post-Pokhran II phase, India has emphasized upon building good relations with China and the US. China, on its part, realizes that India stands at an important geographical junction where the potentially hostile arc of countries along its eastern and south-eastern frontiers and/or the Green Crescent can converge. Hence, China's security considerations will increasingly have to take the 'India factor' into consideration. The 'Yogi' would do well to realize its increased importance in the strategic calculations of both the Eagle and the Dragon. Without either being pro-Washington or pro-Beijing, India can draw upon its diplomatic history of the 1950s and tilt the situation to its advantage. As far as the Sino-Indian relationship is concerned, the Kargil crisis has proved beyond doubt that China is willing to open a new chapter in bilateral relationships. India should move in quickly to seize the opportunity that China has provided in the context of Kargil to mend fences with China. Both countries can forge deep relationships, at first, in the non-conflictual 'low politics' areas such as increasing trade and economic ties and forging a common stand on certain global issues. Then both India and China could move beyond the twentieth century by trying to break the ice on the boundary disputes. The history of international relations is replete with cases where a crisis situation has acted as a trigger for providing new avenues in bilateral and multilateral relationships. The Kargil crisis has provided both India and China such an opportunity, and both countries should act immediately to open a new chapter in the Sino-Indian relationship.

8

The Kargil Crisis and the G-8

Mallika Joseph A.

The overwhelming international attention in its favour was a clear diplomatic victory that India achieved at Kargil. It underlined not only India's diplomatic finesse, but also a change in the attitude of the international community towards India. While it is essential to analyse this change, it is also important to examine why this change has come about. Additionally, it is pertinent to determine the degree to which it has been effected.

A CHANGE?

The G-8 communiqué relating to Kashmir released at Cologne on 20 June 1999 had a mixed response in the subcontinent. Both India and Pakistan claimed a diplomatic victory for themselves. While Pakistan maintained that 'the G8 has categorically endorsed Pakistan's stand . . . we have been vindicated',[1] Indian newspaper headlines cried out 'Clear support for India in G-8 statement'. Whereas the initial euphoria in Pakistan over the communiqué slowly died down as the media commenced strong criticism against the total diplomatic failure of the Pakistani Government, it has been established in India that the G-8 statement was in its favour.

The Cologne communiqué states:

> Kashmir: We are deeply concerned about the continuing military confrontation in Kashmir following the infiltration of armed intruders which violated the line of control. We regard any military action to change the status quo as irresponsible. We, therefore, call for the immediate end to these actions, restoration of the line of control and for the parties to work

[1] Amit Baruah, 'Pak Proclaims "Victory" at G-8 Summit', *The Hindu*, 22 June 1999.

for an immediate cessation of the fighting, full respect in the future for the line of control and the resumption of dialogue between India and Pakistan in the spirit of the Lahore declaration.

Missile and nuclear tests by India and Pakistan: one year after the nuclear tests by India and Pakistan, we reiterate our concerns and reaffirm our statement from the Birmingham communiqué. Recent missile tests have further increased tension in the region. We encourage both countries to follow first positive steps already undertaken by joining international non-proliferation and taking the steps set out in UN Security Council Resolution 1172.[2]

To determine whether there has been a change in the position of the G-8 towards India, one needs to take closer look at the position taken by the G-8 on earlier occasions, the most recent being in the wake of the nuclear tests. The G-8's Birmingham communiqué of 15 May 1998 strongly condemned the Indian tests, and, in addition, urged India to 'adhere unconditionally to the NPT and CTBT'. It also declared that 'India's relationship with each of us has been affected by these developments'.

The G-8 Foreign Ministers' communiqué of 12 June at London was more critical and further enlarged the sentiments expressed by their respective heads of governments. It emphasized its support for UN Security Council Resolution 1172 and had condemned the Indian and Pakistani nuclear tests, and urged 'India and Pakistan to resume the dialogue between them on all outstanding issues, particularly on all matters pertaining to peace and security, in order to remove the tensions between them and encourages them to find mutually acceptable solutions that address the root causes of those tensions, including Kashmir . . .'.[3] The Foreign Ministers' communiqué further stated that:

With a view to reducing tension, building confidence and encouraging peaceful resolution of their differences through dialogue, India and Pakistan should:

- Undertake to avoid threatening military movements, cross-border violations, including infiltrations or hot pursuit, or other provocative acts and statements
- Discourage terrorist activity and any support for it

[2] 'G-8 Condemns Violation of the LoC', *The Hindu*, 21 June 1999.
[3] S/RES/1172 (1998), 6 June 1998.

- Implement fully the confidence- and security-building measures they have already agreed and develop further such measures
- Resume without delay a direct dialogue that addresses the root cause of tension, including Kashmir. . . .

A cursory look at the Foreign Ministers' communiqué and the Cologne communiqué reveals that the former was stronger in its statements against infiltration, cross-border violation and abetting terrorism. However, absence of any mention of the 'root causes of tension, including Kashmir' in the Cologne statement seems to have made all the difference. The Indian response has been varied to both these communiqués, and will be discussed later.

It is interesting that the Cologne communiqué was hailed as a success by both India and Pakistan based on omissions in the statement rather than what it actually contained. Pakistan was happy that the statement restricted itself to demanding an immediate cessation of hostilities, mutual respect for the Line of Control, and the dialogue being resumed. It also made a plea for a cease-fire since India had commenced air strikes against the intruders. India on the other hand, was glad there was 'no hint in it of mediation or a third party role, apart from clear support to India on the genesis of the crisis . . .'.[4] There was some dissatisfaction, however, that the communiqué was ambiguous and did label Pakistan as the aggressor. Nevertheless, popular opinion held that in the statement on who the aggressor was: 'The communiqué is unambiguous in identifying the cause of the crisis, tracing its origin to the "infiltration of armed intruders which violated the Line of Control".'[5] Also, the public statements made by individual members of the G-8, particularly France and Russia, clearly stated Pakistan as the aggressor.[6]

Why did the G-8 not explicitly name Pakistan as the aggressor? While some see this as an obvious attempt to be neutral or that they were Pakistan's Cold War allies, it is important to note:

> Pakistan's political system might be under unsustainable pressure. If it is difficult to deal with Indo-Pakistan problems now . . . think what it would be like with a more fragmented Pakistan in which more extreme political elements held greater sway. This leads to an international willingness to go the extra mile in ensuring that Pakistan's economic problems and political

[4] K.K. Katyal, 'Clear Support for India in G-8 Statement', *The Hindu*, 22 June 1999.

[5] 'Time Pakistan Heeded the Call', *The Hindu* (editorial), 22 June 1999.

[6] Katyal, op. cit., n. 4.

pressure points do not intensify beyond the point that would cause the government—or the country—to collapse.[7]

WHY THE CHANGE?

The change in the G-8's position can be explained in the light of recent developments in the subcontinent and the planning of the Kargil intrusion. Among the multitude of reasons, three merit careful analysis.

First, the nuclearization of the subcontinent. Pokharan II and Chagai forced the global community to rethink its policies towards nuclear proliferation, but more particularly, in the subcontinent. While overt nuclearization reinforced the concept of Kashmir being a nuclear flashpoint, Kargil made it a reality. However, 'Contrary to the view of some Indian observers, the international community did not see this as an excuse to intervene. Rather, it was genuinely concerned about the implications of two nuclear-armed neighbours with major unresolved problems.'[8] Their concern has been consistent with the Birmingham Foreign Ministers' and Cologne statements, which made references to both India and Pakistan signing the NPT and the CTBT. The tone of the G-8's displeasure towards the antagonists in the region does seem to have mellowed down.

Second, the bus diplomacy and the Lahore Declaration. By its significant initiative of 'bus diplomacy', the BJP Government sent a signal to the world that it favoured peace, and, consequently, was taking the first step towards de-escalating tensions between the two neighbours. Vajpayee's friendly initiative was taken in the face of domestic reactions ranging from condemnation to ridicule. That a Hindu hardline party like the BJP could strive to do this was remarkable for many Western analysts and leaders of the OPEC community.[9] This laid the foundation for the subsequent change in Western reactions. In the light of the Pakistani intrusions, the preparations for which must have commenced before the Lahore Declaration, the popular perception was that Islamabad had betrayed New Delhi's trust: 'The personal trust and political commitment that were the essence of the Lahore Declaration have been

[7] Teresita C. Schaffer, 'A Changed Perspective', *The Outlook*, vol. V, no. 27, 19 July 1999, pp. 30-1.

[8] Ibid.

[9] 'OPEC Chief Hails Indo-Pak Talks', *Pioneer*, 26 February 1999.

badly undermined, and mistrust has deepened.'[10] Lack of vigilance apart, the world chose to support India only because it was sincere in its efforts to bring peace and was stabbed in the back. Notwithstanding the hypocrisy in international politics that masquerades as pragmatism, the international community could not accept this tactical act of betrayal that had lulled Indian military into complacency.

Third, the undeniable role of Pakistan in the entire Kargil operation. The first undeniable proof of the Government's involvement was the release of the taped conversation between Pakistan Chief of the Army Staff, Gen. Pervez Musharraf and the Chief of the General Staff Lt. Gen. Muhammed Aziz, which was perhaps handed over to Indian intelligence by the CIA. Whilst placing Pakistan's involvement in Kargil beyond the shadow of doubt, they also accentuated global disenchantment with Pakistan. What followed made clear who the aggressor was. Michael Krepon of the Stimson Centre, Washington, reaffirms this by saying:

> Pakistan's claims that this was the handiwork of 'mujahideen' have not been accepted here. Afghans and other jehadists may well be involved in this operation, but they could not, by themselves, have managed to seize the mountain ridges dominating the road to Ladakh and the base camps in Siachen. The scope and planning of this operation—as well as the equipment, logistics, artillery and communication support necessary to carry it out—all point to the direct involvement of the government of Pakistan, its army and the intelligence services. As a result, Washington has privately called on Pakistan to immediately cease this operation.[11]

Indian diplomacy also needs to be lauded for the confidence it could muster in the global community. What seemed interesting in this entire episode was the proactive diplomacy carried out by both India and Pakistan to influence international opinion in their favour. While it was expected that Pakistan would try its best to invite outside attention and intervention in the region, the Indian diplomatic moves by sending letters and emissaries soliciting a favourable international reaction, specially on an issue as sensitive as Kashmir, whilst stressing the need for bilateralism, is a new phenomenon. India has emphasized that 'in its reaction to the Cologne summit's stand, New Delhi does not project itself as the

[10] Schaffer, op. cit., n. 7.

[11] Michael Krepon, 'Pak's Pact with Blood', *Outlook*, vol. V, no. 24, 28 June 1999, p. 16.

seeker, even in a remote and an implicit manner, of intervention'.[12] How India will maintain the distinction between outside facilitation and intervention needs to be seen.

THE IMPLICATIONS

The G-8 statement, regardless of whether it favours India or Pakistan or remains neutral, has raised two pertinent questions—the LoC and the internationalization of the Kashmir issue.

The communiqué clearly state that:

1. The LoC was violated—by the infiltration of armed intruders.
2. The status quo needed to be restored.
3. Any military action to change the status quo was irresponsible and full respect was required in the future for the Line of Control.

By condemning any military action to alter the status quo of the Line of Control as 'irresponsible', the G-8 has admonished the Pakistani intrusion. This development has largely been in favour of India. Nonetheless, it did raise some apprehensions in some sections in India that the world community would not approve its actions even if India were to cross the LoC only to encircle the intruders and ensure their quick withdrawal. Another debate that has been sparked off is on the demarcation of the LoC. Pakistan has claimed that the LoC has not been clearly marked in many areas and the conflict in Kargil was, in effect, an offshoot of this ambiguity. It also suggested that, if the sanctity of the LoC was to be maintained, India would have to vacate its positions in Siachen. However, 'Washington is clear that the reference to the '72 status on the LoC in the Clinton-Sharif joint statement in no way requires India to vacate Siachen . . . because the designation of the LoC stops at Siachen.'[13]

While the first two components are Kargil-specific and have no relevance beyond the range of the Kargil conflict, the third aspect has significance beyond the conflict and requires a binding commitment from the parties concerned in the future. By advocating this, the G-8 has made the LoC inviolable like any international border. This is in line with the Simla negotiations, where Bhutto had

[12] Katyal, op. cit., n. 4.

[13] A. Mitra and Ramananda Sengupta, 'Us, Them and the US', *Outlook*, vol. V, no. 27, 19 July 1999, p. 28.

not only agreed 'to change the ceasefire line into a line of control . . . but also agreed that the line would be gradually endowed with the 'characteristics of an international border'.[14] However, will turning the LoC into an international border be a popular measure?

> There seems to be virtually no international interest in redrawing the lines of control which have separated India and Pakistan for upwards of 30 years. The logic here has nothing to do with who is right or wrong in '47 and much more to do with the presence of nuclear weapons on both sides. Since border adjustments can't be made peacefully, the implicit argument goes, they probably shouldn't be made at all. There is not yet an international consensus that the world should actively push India and Pakistan to formalize the LoC as a border, but that sentiment is being heard with increasing frequency.[15]

Selig S. Harrison carried the sentiment further by saying that an agreement on the basis of the LoC could 'eventually set the stage for a Trieste-type solution in which there would be a soft border between the two sides of Kashmir'.[16] The G-8 statement reflects this changing international opinion on the issue.

Pakistan has been averse to this proposal all along, even when it was proposed as early as 1948, because it shatters the very fundamentals of its claim to Kashmir. Also, 'there's the view that if Pakistan could not be persuaded in '72—when they were comprehensively beaten—to turn this line into a border, there's little reason for them to agree now'.[17]

In India, there has been an increase in the perception that the LoC can be turned into an international border. 'In private, politicians are increasingly veering around to this thinking. But they know it is politically incorrect, perhaps suicidal, to advocate it openly.'[18] In addition to this issue opening up a festering wound, there is a standing resolution passes unanimously in the Indian Parliament authorizing all means that need to be taken to take back Pakistan-Occupied Kashmir (POK).

The next feature that the G-8 statement and the Indian handling of the Kargil conflict brought to light is the internationalization of

[14] Sunil Narula, 'Bordering on the Impossible', *Outlook*, vol. V, no. 26, 12 July 1999, p. 42.

[15] Schaffer, op. cit., n. 7.

[16] Narula, op. cit., n. 14.

[17] Ibid.

[18] Ajith Pillai and Ishan Joshi, 'The Road Ahead', *Outlook*, vol. V, no. 26, 12 July 1999, p. 26.

the Kashmir issue. India has always maintained that Kashmir was a bilateral issue and third-party mediation of any kind would not be tolerated. In this particular instance, it welcomed the favourable international responses and even solicited attention by sending emissaries and letters. Despite such overt actions that secured US President Clinton's assurance of 'personal interest' in resolving the issue, the Government still maintains that there has been no internationalization of the Kashmir issue. None the less, doing the rounds is a host of synonyms for 'mediation', like 'facilitation', that hope to explain the increased international interest in the region and without jeopardizing the Government's insistence on bilateralism. Even so, it cannot be asserted that there has been no internationalization.

A year back, the Indian response to the London Foreign Ministers' communiqué as noted earlier was very critical. It said:

> India remains committed to developing a framework of peaceful relations with Pakistan through a broad based and sustained bilateral dialogue. This provides an effective means of identifying the possibilities of mutually beneficial cooperation and resolving outstanding issues through bilateral negotiations. . . . In this process of dialogue, there is no place for third party involvement of any kind whatsoever. . . . It is a matter of regret that the G-8 Foreign Ministers Joint Communiqué has not taken into account these proposals but has instead repeated unrealistic prescription, couched in the language of pressure. . . . The Government of India cannot consider any prescriptions which have the effect of undermining India's independent decision making. . . . The G-8 has professed an interest in the welfare and economic growth of the people of the region. These professions are inconsistent with the actions threatened in the Joint Communiqué.[19]

A few months later, at the NAM summit, Mr Vajpayee took extreme offence to the very mention of Kashmir. A year later, the same Prime Minster, Mr Vajpayee, sent letters and emissaries to Western capitals to influence world opinion in India's favour. What has brought about this change? We can only presume that India's objections to mediation and internationalization of Kashmir issue are contextual and tactical in nature.

New Delhi's reaction to the G-8's Birmingham communiqué and Western opinion on its nuclear tests has probably been sharp due to its tacit awareness of the fact that it had violated a global norm. This had much less to do with a threat of its sovereign decision making.

19 Statement by the Official Spokesperson of India on the G-8 communiqué, 13 June 1998.

India's justification for the tests, portraying a threatening security environment—like any other nuclear country earlier—had emerged after the tests and not before. In the context of the Kargil conflict, India has been the good guy who has been stabbed in the back after offering peace. This position of India has given it the confidence to solicit international attention openly only because it was sure that it would be favourable to it. The motivating factor behind this is only to place additional pressure from the international community on Pakistan, forcing it to withdraw its forces and restore the status quo ante.

> However, what has not been realized is that . . . earlier India could handle Pakistan on its own . . . this time the situation has to be viewed in the context of the increasing irrationality of the Pakistani establishment. . . . To deal with the current Pakistan reality, we must consider taking help even from its erstwhile friends. It will be wrong to assume that because of their past friendship they are not concerned about the present nature of Pakistani polity. Our own obsession with Pakistan should not blind us to the international security concerns about that country.[20]

If India could have acknowledged this reality, it could have derived mileage and resumed the dialogue with Pakistan without laying down impossible conditions. While securing the country militarily, diplomatically, with all the international support available, it could have bargained for an assurance on the non-occurrence of another Kargil in future. The impending elections in India might have deterred such an initiative. With the collapse of the civilian government in Pakistan, a resumption of talks, which could not have been possible earlier, might not be too easy now.

20 'Taming Pakistan', *Times of India* (editorial), 26 June 1999.

Conclusion
Indo-Pak Relations: Uncertain Future

P.R. Chari

Present Confusion

The present is an unsuitable juncture for prognosticating on the future of the adversarial Indo-Pak relationship, appreciating the charged atmosphere obtaining in both countries following the Kargil conflict. This has not heralded an end to violence in Kashmir either, since the proxy war continues. Several fedayeen suicide attacks upon the security forces and violence against civilians in Kashmir have taken a fresh toll of lives and further embittered Indo-Pak relations. It would take determined statesmanship on both sides to resume the Lahore process, which, in time, they must. Besides, the mood in Pakistan is one of resentment and bewilderment with its military and political leadership, which has only partly been alleviated by the military coup leading to the removal of the venal civilian government. The prosecution of political leaders on a variety of charges has also deflected attention from that misadventure.

Still, considerable resentment continues with the civilian and military leaderships for leading Pakistan into a profitless enterprise, which ended in the nation's discomfiture and isolation within the international system. Some part of this anger is also tinged with confusion, since the official media had assiduously promoted the myth that the militants were winning the conflict; consequently, it was incomprehensible why Nawaz Sharif should have succumbed to American pressure and agreed to withdraw them. The myth had also been assiduously promoted that only militants were involved in the fighting, whilst denying the major role of Pakistan's regular troops in the conflict. This fiction could hardly be maintained when the casualties and coffins began coming back from Kashmir.

The crumbling of this facade left unanswered several perplexing questions to further bewilder the people in Pakistan. For instance, why should the Director General of Military Operations in Pakistan have negotiated the disengagement of the *militants* in Kargil with his Indian counterpart? Why was the return of the prisoners-of-war captured by Indian troops and the bodies of Pakistani army personnel killed in Indian territory first refused, and then accepted by Pakistan? This contradicted the official reason given earlier by Pakistan that Indian shelling from across the border had caused these casualties. Several other key questions were identified:

> What was this operation all about? Who was its real mastermind? When was the operation planned and what kind of forces were used to take control of the strategic heights and ridges in the Kargil—Dras region? And, most importantly, was the diplomatic fallout, or for that matter the expected gains and losses, taken into account before embarking on this adventure.[1]

Pakistan's withdrawal of its forces under American pressure confused people in Pakistan greatly. In terms of the President Clinton–Prime Minister Sharif agreement of 4 July 1999, Pakistan agreed 'that concrete steps will be taken for the restoration of the Line of Control in accordance with the Simla Agreement. The President urged an immediate cessation of the hostilities once these steps are taken.'[2] Earlier, Pakistan had questioned the validity of the Line of Control, breached its sanctity, but then withdrew its forces without achieving any tangible military or political results; its diplomatic isolation was patent. Consequently, this disconcertment in Pakistan was entirely explicable.

A balance has always obtained in Pakistan between the civilian and military hierarchies. This was put to the test after its Kargil misadventure: both the civilian and military leaderships indulged in blaming on each other, covertly and publicly. The debacle provided the backdrop against which the attempted civilian coup and military counter-coup then unfolded. A comparison is possible with Prime Minister Bhutto's situation after the Pakistan Army's debacle in 1971. Bhutto's hold over Pakistan was complete in the beginning, but it steadily eroded with the passage of time. Ultimately, Gen. Zia's seizure of power in 1977 revealed the essential fragility of civilian power in Pakistan.

The financial pressures upon Pakistan are evident, with the likelihood of default in repayment of its external debts ever-present.

[1] Zafar Abbas, 'Whodunnit?', *Herald* (Karachi), August 1999, p. 65.

[2] The text of the Clinton–Sharif Statement of 5 July 1999 may be seen in *The Hindu*, 6 July 1999.

This required a bail-out in the past by international financial institutions or benevolent donors like Saudi Arabia. Will this continue in future? There is little indication that the IMF, for instance, would agree to defer the repayment of loans or sanctioning new loans unless Pakistan agrees to draconian conditions, which it would find politically difficult to accept.

The more difficult question relates to its internal polity, which is marked by sectarian strife between the Shias and Sunnis in Punjab, Sindhis and mohajirs in Sindh, disaffection with the federal government in Baluchistan and the NWFP, extensive drugs and arms smuggling, growth of religious militias, and the evolution of a Kalashnikov culture in the country. More ominously, a number of new militant organizations had mushroomed in Pakistan during the Kargil conflict, and an alliance of some fourteen such groups has been formed. The danger to Pakistan from these developments is that:

> Militant organizations currently involved in Kashmir may have come together for the time being in anticipation of some major military gains in the Indian occupied territory, but once it is obvious that there are no military solutions in Kashmir, they can easily turn upon each other: one should not forget that their sectarian loyalties take precedence over all other allegiances. If that happens, it will only be a matter of time before major cities in Pakistan turn into battlegrounds quite like the ones in Srinagar and Kabul.[3]

The empirical evidence reveals that countries in South Asia which have supported terrorism and militancy in their neighbours have discovered that these adventurous policies have ultimately recoiled upon themselves. Witness, for instance, the LTTE's depredations in South India: they were trained and equipped by India to challenge the Sinhala hegemony in Sri Lanka. Pakistan cannot be an exception to this empirical rule: this forebodes serious dangers to its polity.

Future of Indo-Pak Relations

The reality cannot be escaped that India and Pakistan are bound together by geography: their intertwined civilizational links comprise a shared history, culture, language, and religion. This verity must inform that instability in Pakistan would spill across the Indo-Pak border and manifest itself by refugee inflows, diffusion of sectarian

[3] Zaigham Khan, 'Unholy Dividends', *Herald* (Karachi), August 1999, p. 69.

violence, strengthened linkages between criminal elements on both sides of the border and so on. These instabilities would be exacerbated by the steady weaponization of Pakistan's and India's nuclear capabilities following their sequential nuclear tests in May 1998. Thereafter, India had tested its over-2,000-km range Agni II missile in April 1999;[4] Pakistan tested its Ghauri-II (1500 km) and Shaheen (600 km) missiles within days.[5] Both countries are believed to be further refining their nuclear warheads and developing longer-range missiles, which presages a nuclear-capable missile arms race in future. Growing instability and intransigence in a nuclearized Pakistan, which has constantly displayed aberrant behaviour, should greatly concern India.

It would be feckless for India to ignore this basic aspect of the Kargil conflict, despite the Indian debate on future relations with Pakistan getting completely polarized. The 'smash them' school prides itself on its 'realism', and would like India to punish Pakistan by:

1. Imposing heavy military costs through a process of attrition.
2. Withdrawing the most favoured nation trade status.
3. Raising India's defence expenditure to force a matching response to beggar Pakistan, as happened when the US forced the Soviet Union to enter a nuclear arms race.
4. Scrapping the negotiations to buy electricity and sugar from Pakistan.
5. Rigging the price of cotton to hurt Pakistan's major source of export earnings.
6. Refusing to accept the LoC as the divide, and claim the whole of Kashmir.[6]

The 'love them' school argues the contrary case, that instability would lead to Pakistan's polity falling into the hands of the Islamic fundamentalists: clearly, promoting instability in a nuclear neighbour is dangerous. This would also prejudice the international support received by India for its remarkable 'restraint' during the Kargil

[4] Details of the salient features of the Agni II missile may be seen in the Reuters Report, 'India Tests Missile, Ready to Face Threats', 11 April 1999.

[5] Details of these tests may be found in the Reuters Report, 'Text of Pakistan's Announcement of Missile Tests', 14 April 1999; and Associated Press of Pakistan Report, 'Pakistan Tests Surface-to-Surface Shaheen Missile', 16 April 1999.

[6] Vishal Thapar and Anita Kanungo, 'What Should We Do With Pakistan', *Hindustan Times Overview*, 10 July 1999.

conflict; besides, ruining Pakistan's economy by India would not be realistically possible, short of blockading Karachi.[7]

Using the economic weapon against Pakistan would have three other consequences.

First, it would deliver a body blow to SAARC, which is proceeding, steadily, albeit slowly, towards SAPTA and SAFTA, and a greater harmonization of political relations in South Asia. This could, in time, harmonize political relations in the region. SAARC has visibly lagged far behind other regional economic groupings, like ASEAN, NAFTA and MERCUSOR. Promoting economic warfare within SAARC would spell its early demise.

Second, raising India's defence expenditure to beggar Pakistan would be singularly ill-advised for a domestic reason. It plays into the hands of vested interests in India that profit from large arms transfers having little bearing on India's real or future security needs. Enhanced defence spending would have significant opportunity costs and lead to deprivation of funds for the social sectors of the economy that are equally significant for the maintenance of comprehensive national security. The raising of India's defence expenditure for the financial year 2000–1 by some 28 per cent over the budget for the previous year reveals that these vested interests have succeeded in their efforts. Quite apart from meeting the deficiencies in equipment revealed by the Kargil conflict, a large part of this expenditure is for procuring items in the wish list of the Army and Air Force. Some consternation has been caused in Pakistan, and it could be expected that it would place greater reliance on its nuclear deterrent to counter the enhanced threat from India.

Third, trade profits both parties. Importing sugar from Pakistan saves India the higher freight charges involved in procurement from distant suppliers. Buying electricity from Pakistan would enable India to increase power supply to its chronically deficient Northern Grid, establish industries in this region, promote its development and generate employment.

Therefore, taking punitive economic measures against Pakistan would really amount to hurting India to derive the satisfaction of hurting Pakistan. It cannot be anyone's case that India should either be negligent or credulous in its relations with Pakistan. Hence, the re-establishment of a dialogue with Pakistan does not mean that India should be complacent regarding the defence of its borders.

[7] Ibid.

Moreover, the Simla Agreement commits both countries 'to settle their differences by peaceful means through bilateral negotiations or by any other peaceful means mutually agreed upon between them'.[8] Similarly, the Lahore Declaration records the agreement of the two countries to 'intensify their composite and integrated dialogue process for an early and positive outcome of the agreed bilateral agenda'.[9] Refusing to enter a bilateral negotiatory process erodes the validity of the Simla Agreement, no less certainly than violation of the Line of Control in Kargil by Pakistan.

It would, of course, be purblind to ignore the prevailing mood of belligerence in India. It derives from a sense of betrayal by Pakistan, in that Prime Minister Vajpayee had undertaken his bus journey to Pakistan in good faith and signed the Lahore Declaration to establish a peace process and normalize Indo-Pak relations: this was destroyed by Pakistan's treachery in Kargil. The official position taken by India immediately after the conflict was that it expects Pakistan to restore trust in the bilateral relationship.[10] This requires the Kashmir issue to be settled through bilateral dialogue. For the dialogue to resume, however, India insisted upon some preconditions being met: they included the complete withdrawal of the Pakistan-supported insurgents from Jammu and Kashmir, acceptance of the inviolability of the LoC, and cessation of cross-border terrorism.[11] These preconditions were set by the BJP Government in a tactical move to delay the dialogue process, since the country was then in an election mode.

The insistence on these preconditions thereafter would seem to have secured the tacit support of the US, as became apparent from the careful wording of President Clinton's message to both countries during his recent visit to South Asia. Still, India perforce has to deal with its aberrant nuclear neighbour: the absence of dialogue cannot be forever sustained. Apropos, UN Security Council Resolution 1172 of 6 June 1999 urges 'India and Pakistan to resume the dialogue between them on all outstanding issues, particularly on all matters

[8] The text of the Simla Agreement may be seen in Michael Krepon and Amit Sevak, *Crisis Prevention: Confidence Building, and Reconciliation in South Asia* (Manohar, New Delhi, 1996), pp. 251-3.

[9] The text of the Lahore Declaration may be seen in *The Hindu* 22 February 1999.

[10] 'Restore Trust, PM Tells Pakistan', *The Hindu* 1 August 1999.

[11] Amit Baruah, 'Sartaj Contradicts Secy. on Talks with India', *The Hindu* 1 August 1999.

pertaining to peace and security . . .'.[12] Delay in resuming the dialogue would, in time, isolate India in the international community as comprehensively as Pakistan after its Kargil misadventure.

TOWARDS RESOLVING THE KASHMIR ISSUE

Proceeding further, there are two ways in which the Kargil conflict could be classified.

First, as a continuation of the proxy war in Kashmir, launched initially by Pakistan in 1989. This led to a low-intensity conflict ensuing, which has been steadily proceeding in the state over the 1990s decade, despite periodic claims being made by India that the situation was coming under control.

Second, as the fourth Indo-Pak war, fought in a limited sector, as part of a continuum of conflict, which includes the 1948-9 war, the September 1965 war (preceded by a side-show in Kutch), and the December 1971 war that resulted in the emergence of Bangladesh. This is apart from the several crises and near-war situations that have occurred in the intervening years.

The Kargil episode highlighted, once again, the centrality of the Kashmir issue in Indo-Pak relations. The contrary argument is well taken that Kashmir is merely symptomatic of a general malaise in Pakistan that requires an anti-India fixation to be promoted for maintaining its unity and integrity. The argument is valid that, even if the Kashmir dispute was somehow resolved, this would not relieve the adversarial Indo-Pak relationship of its inherent tensions and instabilities. The dominance of Kashmir over this relationship is therefore patent. Apart from being the chief bone of contention between them, Kashmir is the major unresolved internal security issue in India.

It cannot be denied that India has committed serious mistakes in dealing with Kashmir after its accession to India in September 1947. There is ample evidence to confirm that the central and/or state governments have systematically rigged practically all the elections held in Kashmir. Hence the argument that, since elections are being regularly held in Kashmir, it proves that its population has chosen to link its destiny with India cuts no ice outside the country: indeed the belief is rife that these elections are coercive exercises. The militancy in Kashmir and the resultant insurgency and terrorism cannot

[12] The text of the UN Resolution may be seen in *IPCS Newsletter* 11/98, pp. 6-7.

obviously yield to a military solution. Nor can it be resolved through Indo-Pak negotiations without reference to the indigenous population. A solution to the Kashmir issue, which encapsulates the Kargil conflict, must realistically be sought consequently at two levels.

First, India would perforce need to concede greater autonomy to the state. A special dispensation for Kashmir could be expected to have its repercussions in the country and lead to similar demands being raised by other states. But conceding greater autonomy to them has also become unavoidable with coalition governments becoming the norm at the Union and state levels. Regional parties, too, have become more assertive in seeking to control the affairs of the central government. Hence, conceding greater autonomy to the states would only strengthen the federal polity. This logic is especially applicable to Kashmir where the dominant National Conference party has shared power with several national and all-India parties at different points in time. Framing a clear Kashmir policy and seeking a national consensus is imperative, as with other security issues, on which the BJP Government has invested so heavily.

Second, at the Indo-Pak level, greater thought needs being given to imbuing the LoC with the imprimatur of an international border, and, if necessary, by making adjustments to ensure its greater rationalization and defensibility. In other words, the logic of Partition should be extended to Kashmir by bisecting the state along the LoC. This is by no means a novel suggestion: it was explored on at least three earlier occasions.

(a) When Pakistan's Governor General Ghulam Mohammed made this suggestion to Prime Minister Jawaharlal Nehru in 1954—the latter rejected this proposal outright.[13]

(b) In a major reversal of roles, India suggested formalizing the cease-fire line during the course of the Bhutto–Swaran Singh talks in Rawalpindi in 1963—on this occasion Pakistan rejected the proposal.[14]

(c) An understanding was reached by Zulfikar Ali Bhutto and Indira Gandhi to convert the Line of Control into an international border during negotiations on the Simla Agreement

[13] Kanti P. Bajpai, P.R. Chari, Pervaiz Iqbal Cheema and Stephen P. Cohem, *Brasstacks and Beyond: Perception and Management of Crisis in South Asia* (Manohar, New Delhi, 1995), p. 117.

[14] For a description of these talks, see Y.D. Gundevia, *Outside the Archives* (Sangam Books, Hyderabad, 1984), pp. 277-81.

in July 1972. Bhutto did not agree to incorporate this commitment into the agreement, but pledged to 'work towards its implementation in practice and over time'. [15] For reasons that need not detain us here, Bhutto could not deliver on his promise; in truth, Indira Gandhi, too, became lukewarm towards this solution in appreciation of the domestic opposition that she anticipated.

This question can be approached from different premises, viz., by reviewing the alternative solutions that have been advanced to resolve the Kashmir problem. They include: mediation by the international community; making Kashmir independent; or handing over the state to Pakistan. None of these solutions are acceptable to India. Hence, maintaining the status quo by conferring the status of an international border upon the LoC seems to be the only viable solution available to address this territorial dispute: naturally it would require India and Pakistan to extinguish their claims to that part of the state which is not in their possession. The difficulties in pressing this proposal upon Pakistan at the present juncture cannot be underestimated. It continues to harp on the UN resolutions and their reference to a plebiscite in the State, without appreciating the reality that some fifty years have elapsed since these resolutions were passed, hence they have become wholly irrelevant as a pragmatic approach to the Kashmir issue. Indeed, in terms of the UN resolutions, Pakistan would need to vacate that part of Kashmir now in its possession *before* the plebiscite was conducted.

There remains the perplexing conundrum as to whom India should deal with in Pakistan to negotiate an LoC solution or a broader Kashmir settlement. The reality remains that its military leadership is intransigent, and its civilian leaders cannot deliver on these issues. This situation aggravates the existing 'structural mismatch in South Asia that dooms Indo-Pakistani dialogue to failure. Powerful and responsible Indian politicians would not deal directly with the Pakistan army, the real power-holder in Pakistan. Pakistani civilians were afraid to deal with India, for fear of the response of their own army and security establishment.'[16] Moreover, following the Kargil

[15] P.N. Dhar, 'Kashmir: The Simla Solution', *Times of India*, 4 April 1995. Also see, P.R.Chari, *The Simla Agreement: An Indian Appraisal* (Manohar, New Delhi, 2001).

[16] Stephen P. Cohen, 'Another Last Chance for Pakistan', *Chicago Tribune*, 24 October 1999.

conflict, a coalition of interests is believed to have developed between the younger officers in its Armed Forces, leaders of extreme religious persuasions, and political parties drawing advantage from the conservative mood in the country. It would undoubtedly be difficult for India to establish a dialogue with these forces that are slowly converting Pakistan into a fundamentalist and national security state. Still, it requires better appreciation among the Indian elite that the military is a political force in Pakistan. This verity cannot be either ignored or wished away.

Besides, there are voices of moderation to be heard on both sides of the Indo-Pak divide. Many of them support a solution to the Kashmir issue by geopolitical partition along the LoC. In India, Farooq Abdullah has long urged the LoC solution despite strenuous opposition from several quarters. His logic is based on the realization that maintaining the status quo will indefinitely prolong the bloodbath in the Valley, a military solution would be dangerous for India and Pakistan in view of their nuclearization, but the division of the state along the LoC would be in the spirit of give-and-take and accept the situational reality.[17] In Pakistan, a respected supporter of human rights, civil liberties, and the improvement of Indo-Pak relations has advanced a similar solution. The formula suggested by him includes four settlements comprising: an agreement between India and Pakistan on major outstanding issues; an agreement between Pakistan and the political parties on its side of the LoC; an agreement between India and the political parties on its side of the LoC; and an agreement between political parties on both sides of the LoC.[18] It is a moot question whether these agreements should initially be sought through open or confidential negotiations.

These formulations suggest a composite solution being sought to the Kashmir problem. A six-point agenda for India has been suggested that envisages: ensuring the rule of law; initiating a dialogue with the political parties involved; making constitutional arrangements for providing 'maximum autonomy'; restoring the battered administration; rehabilitating the victims of violence and terrorism; and legislating the promotion of human rights.[19] India

[17] Cf. B.K. Karkra on Farooq Abdullah's 'Suggestion for LoC as Border', *Muslim India*, no. 193, January 1999, p. 25.

[18] Mubashir Hasan, 'The Kashmir Settlement', *Mainstream*, 7 August 1999.

[19] Frank G. Wisner, former U.S. Ambassador to India, made this proposal during a visit to Kashmir in February 1997. See, *Peace Initiatives* (editorial), vol. iii, no. ii, March-April 1997, p. xii.

could pursue several parts, if not the whole of this agenda, to its advantage. But Pakistan must also accept its legal commitments under the Simla Agreement regarding the inviolability of the LoC, which has also been endorsed by the US and China. This requires some expression of regret for the Kargil intrusions, and the cessation of material support to the militants in Kashmir—the latter proposition is supported by the US.

A space exists in this milieu for citizen's diplomacy to soften the edges of suspicion and mistrust between the two countries. This space has considerably enlarged after the Kargil conflict. It will eventually be necessary for the two countries to revive their dialogue, as envisaged by the Simla Agreement and the Lahore Declaration. Otherwise, it could be reasonably expected that the international community would mount pressure, and not inconceivably, initiate mediation efforts to resolve the Kashmir dispute. The nuclearization of South Asia imbues Indo-Pak tensions with an altogether new dimension: this will persuade the international community to intervene, lest they proceed to another conflict and escalate across the nuclear threshold. The interests of the international community lie in promoting an Indo-Pak peace process to engage the two countries. This would involve their negotiating Confidence-Building Measures (CBMs) to deflect them from hostile words and deeds.

Invigorating the CBM Modality

The empirical evidence informs that the CBM process has proceeded fruitfully between India and Pakistan after phases of tensions and/or hostilities in their antagonistic relationship. They have included the Tashkent (1966) and Simla (1972) Agreements that followed the Indo-Pak conflicts in 1965 and 1971, and the slew of military CBMs established in the early 1990s after the Brasstacks (1987) and the Kashmir-related Spring (1990) crises. These comprised an agreement not to attack each other's designated nuclear facilities and installations (1988); advance notification of military exercises and manoeuvres (1991); prevention of airspace violations and permitting overflights/landings by military aircraft (1991); upgrading hotline communications between the Directors General of Military Operations (1991); and a joint declaration not to use, produce, or stock chemical weapons, or transfer the related technology to others (1992).

There could, therefore, be cause for optimism that the end of the

Kargil conflict might ensure another slew of CBMs being emplaced between the two countries. Several were envisaged in the Memorandum of Understanding accompanying the Lahore Declaration. Several non-military CBMs were also listed in Article III of the Simla Agreement, envisaging that:

1. Steps shall be taken to resume communications, postal, telegraphic, sea, land, including border posts, and air links including overflights.
2. Appropriate steps shall be taken to promote travel facilities for the nationals of the other country.
3. Trade and cooperation in economic and other agreed fields will be resumed as far as possible.
4. Exchange in the fields of science and culture will be promoted.

Some desultory action has occurred on all these proposals, but they remain insignificant and hesitant considering the potential available, despite over a quarter century having elapsed since the agreement. The Wagah border was opened to road traffic between the two countries in February 1999 after Prime Minister Vajpayee's symbolic bus journey to Lahore (it had been closed in 1965). But communications between the Rajasthan and Sindh border post in Munabao continue to remain closed. Moreover, the problems confronting citizens in obtaining visas to visit the other country are legion; so is the difficulty in obtaining books, newspapers and periodicals. Scientific and cultural exchanges have taken place on a very restricted scale. Trade and cooperation proceeds at a glacial pace between India and Pakistan. Meanwhile, bilateral trade between India and Pakistan was computed at $950 million in 1995, of which official trade accounted for only $150 million.[20] The balance was ascribed to 'informal border trade', an euphemism for smuggling, that only profits anti-social elements on both sides of the border at the expense of state revenues.

Still, these salubrious clauses in the Simla Agreement do provide a modus vivendi for seeking a wide range of non-military CBMs to normalize Indo-Pak relations. The greatest significance must attach to widening interaction between professional groups in the two countries like doctors, lawyers, teachers, and legislators. The current

[20] *Observer of Business and Politics* (New Delhi), 26 September 1995. A.K. Rungta, President of the Indian Chambers of Commerce and Industry, made these estimates in his address to the Indo-Pak conference on SAPTA in Islamabad.

visa restrictions would need easing but, prior to that, the two leaderships must generate the political will to pursue the paths of peace; the Kargil conflict has clearly underlined the dangers and costs of war.

The CBMs process has acquired a new prescience since nuclear CBMs were prominently envisioned by the Lahore Declaration. The Memorandum of Understanding[21] therein envisages that the two countries would provide each other with 'advance notification in respect of ballistic missile flight tests'; notify any 'accidental, unauthorized or unexplained incident'; maintain a 'unilateral moratorium on conducting further nuclear test explosions'; 'conclude an agreement on prevention of incidents at sea'; 'review the implementation of existing confidence building measures'; and 'review existing communication links . . . with a view to upgrading and improving these links'. These measures, whenever implemented, would replicate the arrangements that were negotiated between the US and the Soviet Union over the long years of their nuclear confrontation.

The greatest effort must be invested in proceeding with the agreement in the Memorandum of Understanding to 'engage in bilateral consultations on security concepts, and nuclear doctrines, with a view to developing measures for confidence building in the nuclear and conventional fields, aimed at avoidance of conflict'. This has become imperative since India published its draft nuclear doctrine.[22] It makes high declarations on a host of controversial issues like no first use, credible minimum deterrence, command and control of nuclear forces, deterring nuclear states and 'entities', adopting a nuclear posture that provides an 'assured capability to shift from peacetime deployment to fully employable forces in the shortest possible time', and so on. Although this doctrine has been deprecated as only a draft document circulated for discussion,[23] the strategic direction in which India would proceed if it decides to weaponize and deploy its nuclear capabilities has been clearly spelt out therein. Pakistan could be expected to declare its nuclear doctrine

[21] The text of the Memorandum of Understanding accompanying the Lahore Declaration may be seen in *The Hindu*, 22 February 1999.

[22] The text of the Nuclear Doctrine may be seen at http://www.meadev.gov.in/govt/indnucld.htm

[23] The 'draft' aspect of the nuclear doctrine was stressed in an extensive interview given by Foreign Minister Jaswant Singh to *The Hindu*, 29 November 1999.

soon:[24] in its absence, some uncertainty obtains regarding the relevance of the measures suggested in India's draft doctrine like minimum deterrent and no-first-use declaration. The need for a dialogue to understand each other's approach to these seminal questions underlying nuclear deterrence cannot be overemphasized to stabilize the nuclear stand-off between India and Pakistan.

Both countries are cognizant of the danger of conflicts like the Kargil hostilities getting out of hand. For instance, the 'restraint' shown by India during that conflict by not transgressing the LoC or extending the conflict to its other sectors was partly influenced by diplomatic considerations, but largely by the realization that the conflict could have widened and acquired nuclear overtones. Prime Minister Vajpayee's diplomatic overtures that fructified in the bus journey to Pakistan and the Lahore Declaration were probably guided by an appreciation of the new dangers after the nuclear tests. Both countries should be interested, consequently, in formalizing the nuclear restraint they had displayed during the Kargil conflict.

It could, of course, be argued that their antagonism has not abated but only shifted into subterranean channels. Realism suggests that the alternate scenario cannot be ignored that an Indo-Pak dialogue may not be resumed very soon, consequent to the military coup in Pakistan, its chagrin following its failure to achieve its strategic objectives in Kargil, and the current mistrust in India with its peace overtures. Even if this bilateral dialogue is resumed under international pressure, it might proceed at a glacial pace for cosmetic purposes.

There are two other paradoxes that could affect the pursuit of the CBM modality, which require greater appreciation.

First, CBMs indubitably establish trust between adversarial states, but trust is needed before CBMs can be established. Hence, some limited confidence must exist between states before a CBM process could be initiated or revived. This does not exist currently between India and Pakistan.

Second, CBMs are easy to establish, but equally easy to disrupt, hence, they work admirably when not required, but fail during crises. The best example would be the hotlines established between the

[24] A preview of what could be expected therein maybe seen in a long article by three Pakistani establishment figures. See Agha Shahi, Zulfikar Ali Khan and Abdul Sattar, 'Securing Nuclear Peace', *News* (Islamabad), Internet version, 5 October 1999.

two militaries. The experience during the Brasstacks (1987) crisis showed that '... information shared through the hotline was deemed unreliable because of mutual suspicions; hence information supplied on Pakistani request was only minimally complied with'.[25] This was also true during other Indo-Pak crises.

In truth, there is considerable domestic opposition in both countries to resuming the dialogue. Since entrenched interests are opposed to normalizing bilateral relations, their resistance can be exaggerated and used by the political leadership to equivocate in this matter. Much depends on the political will of the two leaderships to explore the peace process, and how strongly international influence is exercised upon them to get serious.

Hopefully, the Indo-Pak leaderships would be mindful of the systemic factors that favour the generation of political will to proceed with the bilateral dialogue and peace process. These disparate but wide-ranging factors include: the several Track II efforts that are proceeding; attempts by common citizens to re-establish people-to-people contacts; and initiatives taken by SAARC and the chambers of commerce to enlarge bilateral trade relations. Besides, a new post-Simla generation is coming into positions of responsibility in both countries that is more largely concerned with economic betterment and less with dwelling on the stultifying memories of a bitter, conflictual past. A ray of hope emerges from the fact that the twice-weekly bus that plies between New Delhi and Lahore continued to operate at full capacity at the height of the Kargil conflict, and remained fully booked for over six weeks ahead.

The exploration of large, dramatic steps to normalize the estranged Indo-Pak relationship can also be suggested here. Three suggestions can be made.

First, the construction of pipelines linking Pakistan and India, besides other countries of South Asia, with oilfields in Turkmenistan and Eastern Oman via the land and sea routes. A deep suspicion obtains in India that Pakistan will interdict such oil supplies during an emergency. The contrary argument cannot be ignored, however, that Pakistan would lose, by such intransigence, the transit fees accruing to it, whilst incurring the wrath of the suppliers and other recipients like Nepal and Bangladesh.

Second, the agreement currently being negotiated for the sale of surplus power from Pakistan to India could be extended into a power

[25] Bajpai et al., op. cit., n. 13, p. 41.

generation and sharing arrangement by the construction of hydro-power projects in Tajikistan and Kyrgyzstan. Large schemes for power generation in Nepal and Bhutan are also possible, which could be shared by India and Pakistan.[26]

Third, the ambit of the Indus Waters Treaty (1960) could be further extended by comprehensively developing the rivers of the Indus basin in conformity with the principles of spatial planning; at present it only distributes the Indus rivers between the two countries, but does not optimize their exploitation.[27] This ambitious scheme would require extensive surveys and huge investment to be made, which could only be provided by international financial institutions, and they could be forthcoming.

All these schemes are massive, with long gestation periods. They would require serious political commitments being made by the two leaderships. But the very process of engagement in such visionary enterprises could lead to a muting of differences between the two countries. Hopefully, the realization will also accrue upon their ruling elite that regional cooperation is good international politics in the post-Cold War world, that it would catalyse their development, and enhance their relevance to the international community.

Three Underlying Questions

In conclusion, three questions need focusing upon that reflect on some aspects of the Kargil conflict of great relevance to future Indo-Pak relations.

1. Could a conflict of this nature occur again? Incautious leaders in both countries have warned that more Kargils could be engineered, which suggests they could seize unmanned areas on both sides of the LoC. This is not difficult considering the expanse, inhospitable climate and remote terrain in this region. Indian military and political leaders accept the impossibility of continuously patrolling all sections of the LoC. It had become a live border over the past few years due to frequent artillery firing by both countries across the LoC and persistent attempts by Pakistan to

26 Aurangzeb Z. Khan, 'India and Pakistan: Bilateral Cooperation in the Energy Sector', *Regional Cooperation in South Asia: Prospects and Problems*, ed. Sony Devabhaktuni, The Henry L. Stimson Centre, Occasional Paper no. 32, February 1997, pp. 74-5.

27 P.R. Chari, 'The Indus Waters Treaty-II', *The Hindu*, 10 March 1999.

infiltrate militants into this area. There are strident voices in India demanding that it should take retaliatory action on the Pakistani side of the LoC as a deterrent counter-measure; this however, would equate India with Pakistan in terms of adherence to norms of conduct.

The LoC was sanctified by the Simla Agreement, and both countries agreed to respect it 'without prejudice to the recognized position of either side'. Further, it affirmed that: 'Neither side shall seek to alter it [The LoC] unilaterally, irrespective of mutual differences and legal interpretations. Both sides further undertake to refrain from the threat or the use of force in violation of this Line.' The Lahore Declaration reiterated 'the determination of both countries to implementing the Simla Agreement in letter and spirit'. These solemn commitments were breached by Pakistan's intrusions in the Kargil sector. Pakistan's ill-considered attempt to erode the integrity of the LoC resulted in this conflict, when it was steadily acquiring the attributes of an international border.[28]

Creating new Kargils would be fraught with the same dangers of escalation that presented themselves during the recent conflict. The shooting down of a Breguet Atlantique naval reconnaissance aircraft over the Kutch region shortly thereafter suggests that the international border could also get activated by cross-border aerial or land incursions. Despite these dangers, India's ebullient Defence Minister, George Fernandes, has promoted a thesis that a limited conventional war is possible between India and Pakistan, although the danger of escalation was always there. The short answer to the question whether more Kargils are possible has, therefore, to be in the affirmative.

A bilateral declaration by the two countries, at this stage, to adhere by the Simla Agreement would go a long way towards alleviating the deep suspicions that obtain in India against Pakistan's bona fides; a reiteration of the existing provision in the Simla Agreement that they 'shall prevent the organization, assistance or

[28] This becomes clear from the intercepted telephone conversation between Pakistan's Chief of the General Staff, Lt. Gen. Mohammed Aziz and Chief of the Army Staff, Gen. Pervez Musharraf on 29 May 1999. In one place, Lt. Gen. Aziz says, '[The] Hint is that, given that the LoC has many areas where the interpretation of either side is not what the other believes. So, comprehensive deliberation is required. So, that can be worked out by DGMOs.' Gen. Musharraf agreed with this strategy. The text of the intercept can be seen in the *Hindustan Times*, 12 June 1999.

encouragement of any acts detrimental to the maintenance of peace and harmonious relations' would add immeasurably to the significance of this declaration.

2. How realistic is India's insistence on bilateralism in its relations with Pakistan? It would be churlish to deny the yeoman efforts and sacrifices made by the young officers and jawans that made it possible for India to retrieve much of its territory in the Kargil sector that had been forcibly occupied by Pakistan. But, ultimately, it was American pressure upon Pakistan that secured the precipitate withdrawal of its troops. This would undoubtedly have been achieved with the passage of time, but at considerably greater cost and loss of lives. India had the satisfaction that President Clinton consulted Prime Minister Vajpayee at several stages of the conflict, especially during his final talks with Prime Minister Nawaz Sharif in Washington which led to the withdrawal of Pakistan's forces from across the LoC. Consequently, it would be equally churlish to deny that American intercession played a major role in ending the Kargil conflict. According to the State Department's spokesman, 'We think we were quite helpful in the most recent situation, with respect to Kargil. Clearly the United States played a critical role in ensuring that the situation didn't spin out of control.'[29] The lukewarm response that Pakistan received to its frantic pleas for support from China further undermined its resolve to continue with the Kargil intrusions. This suggests that American intercession, if not intervention, coupled with China's helpful attitude, secured the Pakistani withdrawal from Kargil in a shorter time frame than what might have been possible by India's military forces; they were severely crippled in any case by the political decision taken not to cross the LoC under any circumstances.

Realism would also suggest that India be pragmatic and not make a fetish of bilateralism in conducting its foreign relations with Pakistan in the light of its Kargil experience. The results are important, not the modality. Not that India has been consistent about shunning mediation. It accepted the World Bank's intervention to arbitrate the Indus Waters Treaty (1960), and Soviet mediation to conclude the Tashkent Agreement (1966). India itself helped in mediating the Partial Test Ban Treaty between the United States and

[29] USIS, 'State Department Briefing August 9, 1999', *Wireless File*, 10 August 1999.

the Soviet Union in 1963, so its obsession with bilateralism being the cornerstone of its foreign relations with Pakistan is excessive.[30]

3. The question that needs to be raised now is: What have the nuclear tests succeeded in deterring. Ironically, the sequential nuclear tests conducted by India induced Pakistan to follow suit. Since Pakistan now possesses discrete nuclear capabilities and has revealed a penchant for irresponsible conduct, this strengthened India's resolve to restrain its forces from crossing the LoC. Hence, the unintended consequence of India's nuclear tests was to propel Pakistan's nuclear tests forward, after which India found itself deterred in crossing the LoC to attack Pakistan's operational bases in Skardu.

Historically, the belief has informed Pakistan that the deterrent value of its non-weaponized nuclear option deters India from crossing the LoC in pursuit of militants to destroy their camps in Pakistan-Occupied Kashmir despite vociferous calls by the BJP to do so, specially during the Kashmir-related Spring crisis in 1990. The deterrent value of Pakistan's nuclear option increased after its Chagai tests. Anxiety not to escalate the conflict to the nuclear level indubitably guided India in exhibiting restraint in not crossing the LoC, apart from ensuring that the conflict did not get internationalized. Not crossing the LoC when Pakistan had done so with impunity, severely hampered the operations of the Indian Army and the Air Force. It was contrary to military logic: indeed, flexibility in crossing the LoC when military necessity so demanded could have saved many lives. These constraints ensured, instead, that India was fighting a war in terrain and on terms dictated by Pakistan.

Proceeding further, nuclear weapons can, in theory, deter the use or threat of use of nuclear weapons; they are also believed to be capable of deterring large-scale conventional conflict. But the Kargil conflict revealed that nuclear weapons could not deter limited conventional conflicts or sub-conventional conflicts like proxy wars, or support to cross-border militancy and terrorism. On the contrary, the presence of nuclear weapons seems to have encouraged Pakistan to believe that it could, with impunity, indulge in 'salami slicing' to capture small pieces of territory under the rubric of nuclear deterrence, and in the confidence that India would not find it possible to escalate the conflict lest it approach the nuclear level. Comforted

30 This argument is made in P.R. Chari, 'Advantage of Third-Party Mediation Cited', *India Abroad* (New York), 30 July 1999.

by this logic, Pakistan could have been emboldened to undertake its intrusions across the LoC in Karg . An underlying paradox of nuclear deterrence is that nuclear weapons might confer stability at the uppermost hierarchical levels of conflict, but they make sub-conventional conflict, proxy wars, cross-border militancy and terrorism safer for the aggressor: this has been recognized as the 'Stability-Instability' paradox. The Kargil conflict provides the evidence to support this hypothesis, and is a major conclusion to be drawn from this episode.

This paradox also interrogates India's recently announced draft nuclear doctrine,[31] which distils the views of its National Security Advisory Board, a strategic enclave within the country that largely favours India's acquisition of nuclear weapons. The draft nuclear doctrine recommended the need for a triad of nuclear forces and the establishment of elaborate command and control arrangements. The investment of huge resources on these requirements would add very incrementally to India's national security from external threats. In any case, the major threats to its national security arise from internal and non-military threats: limited conventional war or sub-conventional war or proxy war would anyway not be deterred.

The Kargil conflict also highlighted another dilemma: How should the international community deal with the phenomenon of aberrant states like Pakistan that are not bound by norms of accepted international behaviour but have come into the possession of nuclear weapons? Moreover, these nuclear weapons are now under the control of a military regime, which has been primarily responsible for Pakistan's aberrant conduct in the past. This requires urgent discussion in appropriate bilateral and global forums. The conjoint influence of the international community may persuade Pakistan to re-evaluate its policy of supporting militancy and covert operations in Kashmir and entering into a serious dialogue with India to resolve the several issues in contention between them. An amelioration of its inimical relations with India will also allow Pakistan to address its domestic socio-political and economic crises that are threatening to destroy the fabric of the country. Should this occur, a Pax Atomica would be established in South Asia with the same certitude as obtained in Europe during the Cold War.

[31] The Draft Report of the National Security Advisory Board on the Indian Nuclear Doctrine may be seen at http://www.meadev.gov.in/indnucld.htm

So much is clear. The Kargil conflict has been variously classified as an 'undeclared war' or 'a kind of a war' or 'an unofficial war' and so on. Its fuller implications have yet to manifest themselves. But, it has been a major defining moment in the tortuous history of Indo-Pak relations, and will remain in their collective memory as permanently as their geography.

APPENDIX 1

CHRONOLOGY OF EVENTS DURING THE KARGIL CRISIS

Compiled by
D. Azhagarasu, Deepa Rajkumar and Anju Susan Alex

9 May 1999

After a long spell Pakistani rangers resorted to heavy shelling in Kargil.

14 May 1999

The Defence Ministry denied reports about the fall of an Indian post in the wake of Pakistani firing in Kargil, but said Pakistan Army regulars and trained mujahideens had infiltrated the area under the cover of fire. The Infiltrators, however, occupied some remote and 'unheld' areas.

16 May 1999

Elaborate operations undertaken by the Indian Army in Kargil had been successful in cutting off the infiltrators in Dras sector. The infiltrators from across the border were forced to flee from one of the ridge lines.

The Army was in the process of clearing up the rest of the infiltrators from this area. Meanwhile, the Zo Lila route was fully functional and the convoys were moving along this. In the Batalik sector as well, the operations had resulted in the infiltrators being forced to vacate one of the ridge lines after having suffered considerable casualties.

18 May 1999

In a major offensive, the Indian Army gunned down 52 heavily-armed Pakistan-backed militants and injured many others since 16 May in the Kargil sector of Jammu and Kashmir where they had infiltrated under heavy artillery fire by the Pakistan Army since 9 May. The Army lost 9 men in the operation that began on 17 May to flush out militants entrenched in 4 of the 7 ridges in the Kargil mountains.

20 May 1999

The Indian Army continued its operation against Pakistani infiltrators for the twelfth day. Pakistani troops resumed shelling and small arms firing that had spread to the Gurez sector, a relatively peaceful area.

The Indian Air Force (IAF) placed two fighter squadrons on high alert for possible strike operations in Kashmir's Dras-Kargil-Batalik region where an estimated 300-450 infiltrators continued to occupy about 46 sq. km of Indian territory.

21 May 1999

On the second day of the eviction operations launched against Pakistani soldiers and their militants, a senior South Block official said, 'If the Pakistanis are aiding and abetting the alteration of the LoC, there is no reason for us to let it be a localized issue. We too can make gains on the LoC and we may well exercise that option.'

22 May 1999

Pakistan claimed that India was concentrating aircraft and troops in Srinagar and said that it was 'alive to the situation and ready for all eventualities'.

23 May 1999

The situation along the international border in Punjab and Jammu and Kashmir was well under control despite unprovoked, intermittent firing from Pakistan.

The Pakistan Prime Minister, Mr Nawaz Sharif, held a 'strategic meeting' with the Army Chief and Chairman of the Joint Chiefs of Staff Committee (JCSC), Gen. Pervez Musharraf, on 22 May to discuss the latest situation on the LoC in Kargil and Dras sectors.

A Pakistani-based militant outfit, Tehrik-i-Jihad, had claimed responsibility for infiltrating its cadres into the Kargil-Dras sector on the Indian side of the LoC.

24 May 1999

Mr Atal Behari Vajpayee spent over an hour at the Operations Room in the Army Headquarters where the Director General of Military Operations (DGMO) made a presentation on the prevailing situation.

25 May 1999

Maj. Gen. J.J. Singh said, 'If it (Pakistan) decides to hold some portions on the Line of Control (LoC) or immediately across, it will be our strategy to see the viability (of retaking) on the ground.

Prime Minister Vajpayee said 'all possible steps', including air strikes, would be taken to clear the Kargil area. Calling the shelling in the region a 'new situation' and unacceptable to the nation, he said it was not infiltration but a move to occupy new territory.

26 May 1999

Operation Vijay is born out of the Army's failure to read the consistency with which Pakistan conducted its infiltration campaign in J&K, and RAW's inability to detect the training and movement.

The Directors General of Military Operations of the Indian and Pakistan Armies established contact on the hotline to discuss the developments in the Kargil sector of Jammu and Kashmir.

India said that the intrusion into the Kargil sector of Jammu and Kashmir had been 'obviously' undertaken 'with the full complicity and support of the Government of Pakistan. Pakistan issued a stiff warning to India following air strikes by Indian jet fighters against infiltrators in Kashmir saying, 'We will take necessary steps to defend ourselves. . . . We are retaliating and we will retaliate.'

27 May 1999

The Russians expressed serious concern at the infiltration by foreign militants into the territory of the state of Jammu and Kashmir. 'We appeal to India and Pakistan to manifest mutual restraint in connection with the incident and to continue to adhere to the Lahore agreement with a view to settling the problems between the two countries peacefully and on a bilateral basis.'

Mr Nawaz Sharif said that the nuclear tests had given Pakistan the confidence to counter 'any enemy attack'. 'They (people) are confident for the first time in their history that in the eventuality of an armed attack they will be able to meet it on equal terms.'

The US rejected Pakistan's claim that some Indian bombs fell on the Pakistani side of the (LoC). A State Department official added, 'To our knowledge, India has not struck over the Line of Control deliberately or accidentally.'

Urging the international community to take note of the situation, Mr Mushahid Hussain said, 'If the international community could act on Kosovo, they could do so in Kashmir as well. . . . Kashmir is a basic issue and must be resolved.'

The Vice Chief of the General Staff of the Pakistan Army, Maj. Gen. Anis Bajwa, claimed that it brought down two Indian MiG aircrafts with 'ground fire' inside Pakistan-controlled territory. Sqn. Ldr. Ojha (17 Squadron, Srinagar) piloting a MiG-21 was killed in the Pakistani attack while Flt. Lt. Nachiketa (No. 1135, 9 Squadron, Srinagar) flying a MiG-27 was taken prisoner.

28 May 1999

Britain said it had no plans to ask the UN Security Council to seek a report on exchange of artillery fire in the Kargil sector of Jammu and Kashmir, but expressed deep concern over the situation.

Voice of Russia, Russia's state-owned radio, had described the infiltrators holed up in Kargil as 'fundamentalists, extremists and separatists' receiving various kinds of support from across the border.

Mr Frank Pallone, the founder and former Co-Chairman of the Congressional Caucus on India, said he had no problems with New Delhi's 'hot pursuit' of the terrorists across the border like Israel's forays against terrorist camps in Lebanon. 'My view is that these infiltrations continue from Pakistan and that India has every right to defend against them and do what is necessary to prevent them.'

Mr Nawaz Sharif spoke to Mr Vajpayee, to inform him that the present crisis in relations between the two countries could be settled across the table and not by sending aircraft into Pakistani air space.

At the media briefing, radio transmission messages of the two IAF pilots were read out by AVM (Operations) S.K. Malik, to underline the fact that both of them were operating well inside the LoC on the Indian side when the MiG-21 was hit by a missile from across the border.

Pakistani infiltrators shot down a MiG-17 helicopter of the IAF, on the Indian side of the LoC. Two pilots and two crew of the helicopter lost their lives. The US-made, shoulder-fired Stinger missile of the type freely used in Afghanistan hit the helicopter.

29 May 1999

The Indian Finance Minister, Mr Yashwant Sinha, opined that the Kargil situation would not have any destabilizing effect on the economy. Mr Sinha conceded that initially there had been some impact of the Kargil situation on the stock markets, which normally react to any significant event.

The US ruled out any mediatory role in defusing tensions between India and Pakistan over Kashmir. The State Department Spokesman, Mr James, 'Our position on Kashmir is well known. At this time, there are no plans to send a U.S. envoy to the region.'

The GOC-in-C Northern Command, Lt. Gen. H.M. Khanna, admitted that the Pakistani soldiers and Afghan mercenaries of the Taliban had managed to breach the surveillance network of the Army and helicopter patrols in the unheld areas of the LoC in Kargil. 'There has been a certain amount of surveillance failure', he said when asked as to how such large scale infiltration had been allowed with the intruders managing to come halfway down the slope to the national highway at Dras.

A preliminary examination of the body of Sqn. Ldr. Ajay Ahuja showed bullet wounds: he was most probably shot dead after bailing out from his MiG aircraft that was downed by a Pakistani missile.

Mr Atal Behari Vajpayee rejected his Pakistani counterpart Nawaz Sharif's suggestion to stop the air strikes in Kargil to pave the way for talks with Islamabad to resolve the present crisis.

Four permanent members of the UN Security Council assured India that they would not raise the Kargil issue in the Council.

30 May 1999

The IAF intensified its air campaign against armed intruders in the Kargil sector by inducting its state-of-the-art Mirage-2000 planes in Operation Vijay. The Pakistan Foreign Minister, Mr Sartaj Aziz, said that the 'urgent' priority for both countries was to 'defuse the situation' along the LoC.

The US supported India's military action against infiltrators in the Kargil sector of Kashmir saying that the intruders who had seized Indian territory along the LoC would have to go. The US Assistant Secretary of State for South Asia, Karl Inderfuth, said, 'Clearly the Indians are not going to cede this territory. They (infiltrators) have to depart, and they will depart, either voluntarily or because the Indians take them out.'

Mr Kofi Annan, the UN Secretary General, admitted, 'Pakistan is violating the Line of Control' and volunteered to send its observers to the two countries.

31 May 1999

The Pakistan Foreign Secretary, Mr Shamshad Ahmad, warned, 'We will not hesitate to use any weapon in our arsenal to defend our territorial integrity.'

1 June 1999

Militants blew up a vital bridge cutting off Lolab Valley in Kupwara district from the rest of Kashmir.

The Defence Minister, Mr George Fernandes, said India was prepared to consider a 'safe passage' for the armed intruders to sneak back into Pakistan as diplomatic efforts to defuse the Indo-Pak tensions entered a delicate stage.

2 June 1999

The UN Secretary General Kofi Annan said that the LoC in Kashmir must be respected.

France issued a thinly-veiled warning to Pakistan to desist from increasing tensions along the LoC in Jammu and Kashmir.

3 June 1999

The Pakistan Army shelled the Akhnur sector along the LoC. Simultaneously, intense engagements began along the Chorbatla–Turtok alignment, north-east of Batalik in Ladakh where key segments along the entire stretch of the LoC were affected by varying degrees of firing. Shelling was also reported from the Keran, Uri, Poonch and Naushera sectors.

Pakistan brought Flt. Lt. K. Nachiketa, the detained IAF pilot, to the Foreign Office in what was seen as a prelude to his release after eight days in captivity. The pilot was reportedly being handed over to the International Committee of the Red Cross several hours after Pakistan was to have handed him over to the Indian High Commissioner, Mr. G. Parthasarathy.

4 June 1999

US President Clinton wrote to Mr Nawaz Sharif calling upon Pakistan to 'take steps to defuse the crisis and respect the Line of Control (LoC)' in Jammu and Kashmir.

Mr Sharif said Pakistan proved its 'sincerity' by releasing the pilot as a 'goodwill gesture', and added, 'It was now India's turn to respond positively to defuse the situation by halting massive shelling on the LoC.'

5 June 1999

The Chief of the Naval Staff, Adm. Sushil Kumar, said the Indian Navy was well equipped to face any nuclear strike by the Pakistan Navy.

Mr James Rubin, the State Department Spokesman, said, 'We strongly support talks between India and Pakistan to resolve this latest dispute and believe these talks should take place as soon as possible. Ending the fighting in the Kargil area can only be accomplished through direct engagement by India and Pakistan. We remain in touch with the Indian and Pakistani Governments to express our strong concern, to urge them to show restraint and to prevent the fighting from spreading and to urge both countries to work together to reduce tensions.' The Indian President, Mr K.R. Narayanan, blamed Pakistan for spreading 'disinformation' and 'hoodwinking' the world by claiming that the Line of Control was vague and had no sanctity.

India deferred the visit of the Pakistan Foreign Minister, Mr Aziz, to New Delhi as the 'date was not convenient'.

6 June 1999

Russia calls for restoration in the status quo on the LoC in Kashmir that existed before the intrusion of Pakistan-backed militants and asks for the Kashmir issue to be resolved through political dialogue between New Delhi and Islamabad.

Mr Nawaz Sharif said that Pakistan was not in favour of developing the current situation into a full-scale war.

7 June 1999

Hafiz Muhammad Sayeed, chief of the Lashkar-e-Toiba, one of the front-ranking organizations engaged in fighting Indian troops in Kargil–Dras sector, said, 'we are not going to withdraw even an inch from Kargil and Drass at the request of United States or Pakistan'.

Pakistan Foreign Minister Sartaj Aziz had said he was ready to visit New Delhi 'any time' to hold talks with his counterpart .

10 June 1999

The Group of Eight industrialized nations (G-8) called upon India and Pakistan to respect the LoC, to work for an immediate cessation to fighting and return to the negotiating table in the spirit of the Lahore Declaration.

India received from Pakistan the 'mutilated and disfigured' bodies of 1 officer and 5 jawans, but deferred fuller comment till the post-mortem examinations were conducted.

Mr Vajpayee declared that there would be no let-up in action by the Armed Forces in Kargil till all the territory occupied by the intruders was reclaimed.

11 June 1999

Indian troops recaptured the prime 'Batalik Top' from infiltrators.

Pakistan described as 'absurd' the Indian statement that bodies of 6 soldiers returned to New Delhi had been mutilated.

12 June 1999

The Clinton Administration said that reports of Pakistan handing over 6 mutilated bodies of Indian soldiers were 'disturbing', and that it was seeking more information.

Pakistan Foreign Minister Sartaj Aziz said the taped conversation between the Pakistan Army Chief and Chief of the General Staff on operations in Kargil, produced by India, could be 'doctored and distorted', a charge denied by New Delhi.

13 June 1999

The hard-line Jamaat-e-Islami said Pakistan was in the grip of chaos as it stood isolated internationally over the Kargil developments and there was a possibility of war following the failure of Foreign Ministerial-level talks in New Delhi.

The Indian Army secured the strategic Tololing peak in the Dras sector. The capture of Tololing (around 4,500 m high) opened up some major operational opportunities for the Indian troops.

Mr Nawaz Sharif telephoned his Indian counterpart, Mr Vajpayee and reiterated Islamabad's 'desire' to defuse the situation along LoC. This was the third telephone contact between the Prime Ministers since the Kargil situation developed into a full-blown crisis.

14 June 1999

The Army said it recovered gas masks from soldiers of the Pakistani Northern Light Infantry (NLI) in the Tololing heights in the Dras subsector.

The US President, Mr Clinton, spoke to the Prime Minister, Mr Vajpayee on the telephone and appreciate India's restraint in Kargil where troops were fighting to flush out Pakistan-backed infiltrators.

The Indian Army notched up another kill in the Dras subsector with the Pakistani intruders being evicted from two key positions north of Tololing.

15 June 1999

India rejected a US proposal for talks with Pakistan, saying there could be no 'meaningful dialogue' till the infiltrators vacated the occupied land.

The Clinton administration said that it was disappointed that the talks between India and Pakistan on defusing tension on the LoC were not more productive, and was of the view that the issue had to be resolved bilaterally.

Pakistan accused the US of being biased and prejudiced against Islamabad for not asking India to respect the LoC.

The US President, Mr Clinton asked the Pakistani Prime Minister, Mr Sharif to remove his forces from the Indian zone of Kashmir, saying that such deployment would hold up efforts to end the fighting.

The Pakistan Army had planned the invasion of the Kargil-Dras region fourteen years earlier to cut off India's road connection to Siachen, said *Takbeer*, a weekly brought out by the pro-Army Jamaat-e-Islami.

17 June 1999

Russia issued a stern warning to Pakistan to withdraw militants from the Indian side of Kashmir and not to attempt to alter the LoC.

Mirage-2000 planes of the IAF were inducted to bombard a key enemy supply base in the Batalik sector in Operation Vijay.

20 June 1999

Leaders of the Group of Eight countries condemned the violation of the Line of Control in Jammu and Kashmir, called for an immediate end to fighting in the region and termed as 'irresponsible' any military action to change the status quo of the LoC.

Nawaz Sharif threatened more Kargil-like situations if the Kashmir issue was not resolved. Indian troops flushed out Pakistani invaders from Point 5140, one of the strategic heights overlooking the Srinagar-Leh national highway.

21 June 1999

The Indian forces shifted focus from Dras to the Batalik sector and managed to evict Pakistani troops from the north-west spur of Point 5203.

23 June 1999

Gen. Anthony Zinni, C-in-C, US Central Command, accompanied by Mr Gibson Lanpher, Deputy Assistant Secretary of State, arrived in Islamabad.

A Pakistani military spokesman admitted that 76 soldiers had been killed and 80 wounded in the fighting with India since early May. The figure of 76 dead was up from the one of 47 announced earlier. In the same period, India had suffered 400 dead and 750 wounded. The Indian Army recaptured the strategic height, Point 5203, and engaged Pakistani infiltrators in a fierce gun-battle to gain control over Jubar Hills, Kokarthang and Barso peaks on the forty-first day of Operation Vijay.

'If necessary we can cross the LoC in the supreme national interest but the decision lies with the cabinet', Gen. Malik, the Indian Army Chief, said in response to questions at a press conference.

26 June 1999

Mr Vajpayee warned Pakistan that India would neither run away from war nor would it return the land it would capture if war was imposed on it this time.

27 June 1999

A former ISI chief, Lt. Gen. Javed Nasir, said that mercenary militants occupied the 'vacant' heights in the Kargil-Dras sectors as early as January-February that year (1999), and at the same time Mr Nawaz Sharif was receiving his Indian counterpart, Mr Vajpayee at Wagah.

'The Lashkar-e-Toiba chief, Hafiz Mohammed Saeed, declared that whether the American Gen. Zinni or even President Clinton went to Pakistan, the mujahideen would not withdraw from their posts in Dras and Kargil sectors.

Gen. Musharraf said, 'It is too early to say (but) it's a government decision. It is the prime minister's decision. We will not withdraw unilaterally', when asked whether Pakistan would withdraw its forces from the embattled Kargil.

28 June 1999

The former Pakistan Foreign Secretary, Mr Niaz A. Naik, had left for New Delhi by a special aircraft for talks with Indian authorities on the Kargil situation.

The IAF intensified operations by beginning round-the-clock bombardments of enemy positions in Batalik and Dras even as Pakistan was engaged in deepening its defences, which could discourage movement by the Indian Armed Forces across the LoC.

29 June 1999

The Chinese Premier, Mr Zhu Rongji, urged Pakistan and India to resume peace talks to end the fighting in Kashmir during talks with his visiting Pakistani counterpart, Mr Nawaz Sharif. He said, 'This is an issue left over from history concerning territory, ethnic nationalities and religion and can only be resolved through peaceful methods.'

Mr Vajpayee said that the Government was not making any 'secret deals' with Pakistan on ending the Kargil conflict, and asserted that no proposals or third party mediation would be accepted.

Mr Vajpayee said the Government agreed to receive Mr Naik to allow Islamabad one chance to explain its position. 'We wanted to hear from them their willingness to withdraw the intruders, without conditions and in a specified time-frame. This we did not hear. We are clear that there will be no further dialogue so long as the incursion continues.'

30 June 1999

The Army had taken two major peaks close to the Tiger Hill area.

Pakistan confirmed that the former diplomat had actually gone to India. However, a senior Pakistani official also claimed that Mr R.K. Mishra, editor of the *Observer of Business and Politics*, had visited Lahore as an Indian emissary eleven days earlier and met Mr Nawaz Sharif and the Foreign Secretary, Mr Ahmad.

1 July 1999

Indian troops recaptured two major heights on Jubar Hills, some two kilometres from the LoC in the Dras subsector.

2 July 1999

Russia rejected Pakistan's request for mediation in the normalization of relations between India and Pakistan. The issue was raised by Mr Nawaz Sharif's special envoy, Khursheed Mehmood, during talks with his Russian counterpart, the Foreign Ministry's Secretary General Alexander Losyukov.

3 July 1999

A US Congressional panel rejected a plebiscite as a possible solution to the Kashmir problem. By a vote of 20 to 8, the House International Relations Committee defeated an amendment sought by the Republican Congressman, Mr Dana Rohrabacher.

The Defence Committee of the Pakistan Cabinet declared that it wanted to resolve the 'current crisis' in Kashmir through 'negotiations in the spirit of the Lahore Declaration' while regretting that India had 'failed to respond' to positive initiatives taken by Prime Minister Sharif.

5 July 1999

Mr Vajpayee expressed his inability to accept US President Clinton's invitation to Washington to discuss the Kargil situation during their telephone talk.

The Indian Army recaptured the strategic Tiger Hill, capping its operations in the Dras sector to secure the most vulnerable stretch of road, which links Kashmir Valley to Ladakh.

6 July 1999

A joint statement issued at the end of a three-hour meeting between Mr Clinton and the Prime Minister of Pakistan, Mr Nawaz Sharif, said the two leaders 'agreed that it was vital for peace of South Asia that the Line of Control in Kashmir be respected by both parties in accordance with their 1972 Shimla Accord'.

8 July 1999

Pakistan-backed intruders counter-attacked in the Dras sector and stepped up shelling north of Jammu, even as the Indian Army continued to advance in the Batalik sector. The western spur leading from Tiger Hill was the focus of one such counter-attack.

In the fighting at two points ('India Gate' and 'Helmet') on the spur, 17 Pakistani regulars were killed. India lost 3 JCOs (Junior Commissioned Officers) and 11 jawans. A battalion of Sikh troops repulsed the attack. Found abandoned in shallow pits in the area, were 7 Pakistani bodies.

Jat and Jammu and Kashmir Rifles battalions repulsed another counter-attack at Point 4875 and Twin Bump, south-west of Tiger Hill, killing 46 enemy soldiers.

9 July 1999

The Indian Army cleared the Pakistani intrusion in the strategic Batalik sector and further consolidated its position in Dras. According to the Indian

Army spokesman, 99 per cent of Batalik was cleared of the Pakistani incursion. With the Jubar height as the hub, Indian troops fanned out in all directions and advanced to the LoC in this area.

Pakistan's Defence Committee of the Cabinet (DCC) decided to 'appeal to the Mujahideen' to 'help resolve the current Kargil situation'.

10 July 1999

The Indian troops recovered the last major peak, Rocky Knob, in Mushkoh valley.

11 July 1999

The Indian Army made advances in the Mushkoh valley with the recapture of two more positions. Batalik came completely under the control of the Indian Army, with no resistance from the intruders.

The bodies of 2 Pakistani officers, which were recovered on 8 July, were shown to press persons as more proof of Pakistan's involvement in the Kargil intrusions.

The DGMOs of the Indian and Pakistan Armies met at Attari on the Indian side of the international border in Punjab.

Mr Aziz stated that the DGMOs of India and Pakistan could meet again to review the progress of 'disengagement', which had proceeded satisfactorily in the Kaksar sector.

12 July 1999

India set a deadline of 16 July for the intruders to withdraw. The official statement said 'Operation Vijay is still continuing', and there was no question of the pull-out of Indian forces from the Kargil sector.

13 July 1999

Pakistani troops continued to withdraw from most sectors, but Indian artillery had to force them out from other places.

Even as the peaks were cleared of infiltrators, the Army began permanent deployment of troops in the vacated areas.

The Chief of the Naval Staff, Adm. Sushil Kumar, said the Indian Navy would remain on a state of alert till normalcy was restored in the Kargil sector.

The Pakistan High Commission contacted the Ministry of External Affairs (MEA) and the Indian Army HQ, saying that they wanted to discuss the burial of 3 men who India said were Pakistan Army officers from Pakistan's Northern Light Infantry Regiment (NLI) killed on Indian soil.

India spelt out three conditions for the resumption of the Lahore peace process, in response to Mr Sharif's fresh offer for talks. New Delhi said that

Islamabad should, besides completely pulling out its troops from Kargil, reaffirm the sanctity of the LoC and stop sponsoring cross-border terrorism before any meaningful talks could be resumed.

14 July 1999

Pakistan accused India of indulging in propaganda by 'refusing' to hand over 3 bodies of Pakistani officers—reportedly of Capt. Imtiaz, Capt. Karnal Sher and Maj. Iqbal—to the Pakistan High Commission in New Delhi.

India said it was firm about the 16 July deadline for the pull-out of Pakistani intruders from Kargil, and reiterated that the date had been fixed by the top military officers of the two sides, dismissing the Pakistani assertion that no such deadline had been fixed.

15 July 1999

With hours to go for the expiry of the deadline for withdrawal of Pakistani intruders from Kargil, Indian troops occupied dominating heights along the LoC in Batalik, Kaksar and Dras sectors, and were inching forward in the Mushkoh valley.

India extended Friday's deadline 'by [a] day or two' for the withdrawal of Pakistani intruders in Kargil, but asserted that it would resume military operations if warranted.

16 July 1999

As Pakistan continued to pull back its forces from across the LoC in the Kargil sector, India extended the deadline for withdrawal that expired on 16 July. Assessing that the Pakistani retreat was in progress and the delays were not deliberate, India decided to give Pakistan a little more time.

17 July 1999

India said that the Pakistani intrusion in Kargil had practically ended and that its forces had already advanced to the LoC in three out of the four subsectors in the combat zone.

The Pakistan Government agreed to take back the bodies of 2 of its Army officers killed in action against Indian troops.

India handed over the bodies to the International Committee of the Red Cross (ICRC) that evening, hours after Pakistan Army Chief Gen. Pervez Musharraf's admission that Pakistani soldiers were involved in the Kargil conflict.

In connection with the bodies of Pakistani soldiers found in the Kargil sector during Operation Vijay, Army spokesman Col. Bikram Singh said that 249 bodies hade been recovered till then. Of these, 150 were killed in the Dras and Mushkoh valley sectors. The maximum bodies (35) were retrieved from a position named 'Helmet' in Dras, while 27 were buried as per military custom by Indian troops at Point 4812 in the Batalik sector, where 99 bodies were found; 20 bodies were recovered on Pimple II in Dras and 20 each in point 5140 and south of point 5287 in the Batalik sector. Except for the bodies that had been handed over, the remaining 244 had been buried by Indian troops.

18 July 1999

India said resumption of bilateral talks would depend on 'tangible steps by Pakistan on the ground' on ending cross-border terrorism and maintaining the sanctity of the LoC.

The infantry made significant progress, having touched the LoC in Dras, Kaksar and parts of the Mushkoh valley. However, it faced stiff resistance in a few pockets in Mushkoh where the intruders had not withdrawn.

19 July 1999

The Chief of the Army Staff, Gen. V.P. Malik, said the Army would increase surveillance on the LoC in Kargil and Dras to prevent any further intrusions by Pakistan.

The progress of the troops, who were moving forward to occupy the heights, had been slowed down by bad weather. The going was also slow due to anti-personnel mines.

20 July 1999

Pakistani intruders continue to hold strategic positions on the Indian side of the LoC, despite the expiry of time for their withdrawal as agreed by the top military officers of the two sides. Indian sources said that the Pakistani forces had not moved out of their bunkers near Point 5060 in Mushkoh valley, the base of Marpola in Dras and the Shangruti Top in Batalik sector. The intruders were getting cover from Pakistani artillery fire. India said it was ready for an early renewal of talks with Pakistan, but hoped that Islamabad would take concrete confidence building measures and quickly resolve its internal contradictions to push the Lahore process forward.

The US has expressed 'understanding' for India's position that Pakistan had to take specific steps to reaffirm the sanctity of the LoC, including cessation of cross-border terrorism. This American 'understanding' was conveyed to India during a twenty-minute conversation that evening between Mr Clinton and Mr Vajpayee.

21 July 1999

The Indian Army hardened its stance towards Pakistani intruders, numbering 50-70, who continued to occupy three positions in the Kargil sector even as both sides exchanged fire. Pakistan rejected the three measures set out by India for early resumption of bilateral dialogue to resolve all outstanding issues including Jammu and Kashmir.

22 July 1999

Germany expressed deep appreciation over the exemplary restraint shown by India while dealing with the Kargil conflict. Joschka Fischer conveyed this during a meeting with India's visiting National Security Adviser, Brajesh Mishra. Mr Mishra was also told about Germany's understanding of India's position that withdrawal of militants from the Indian side of the LoC by Pakistan-backed intruders was a prerequisite for defusing tension in the region. The group of seven industrialized countries and Russia (G-8) and the 15-member European Union (EU) also shared Germany's views appreciating New Delhi's handling of the situation, Fischer told Mishra.

23 July 1999

The Batalik sector witnessed a fierce battle as the Pakistan Army did not keep its commitment of withdrawal and continued to hold peaks inside the Indian side of the LoC.

Firing and artillery exchanges were also reported from Dras, Kaksar and the Mushkoh valley areas where discord was again over the delineation of the LoC. Pakistani soldiers continued to hold stray pockets on some peaks in the sectors, refusing to budge.

The Indian Army blasted at least six enemy bunkers in the Mushkoh valley in a bid to oust the intruders from certain positions they were still holding on to, even as the Pakistan Army shelled civilian areas of Kargil, Dras and Batalik, official sources said.

The Indian Army exchanged small-arms fire with the intruders, an estimated 60 of whom were holed up on a few heights in the Mushkoh valley, Dras and Batalik.

Pakistan is reported to have lost about 25 soldiers in the previous night's operations.

Pakistan alleged that Indian troops had 'violated' the 'cease-fire' agreed to by the two countries when they targeted Pakistani positions across the LoC with artillery, mortar and automatic weapons.

Mr Nawaz Sharif said that bilateral talks with India could produce results only if India demonstrated sincerity and readiness in holding a meaningful dialogue on all outstanding issues.

The Clinton Administration said that while it was not in a position to determine who was responsible for the killing of civilians in Jammu and Kashmir, it, however, believed that 'militant groups, with leaders and infrastructure in Pakistan, were among those connected with the killings'.

Britain condemned the incursion of militants into Kashmir, and accused them of human rights abuses. Speaking in the House of Commons, the Minister in the Foreign Office dealing with the subcontinent, Mr Geoff Hoon, called for an end to the support the militants were receiving from outside.

24 July 1999

Mr Nawaz Sharif called for early and unconditional talks with India on the Kashmir dispute.

The Association of South East Asian Nations (ASEAN) urged India and Pakistan to adhere to a process of dialogue to resolve 'the dispute' that was central to the latest hostilities along the LoC.

The Indian Government ordered a probe into the events leading to the Pakistani aggression in Kargil.

25 July 1999

Intense fighting was going on in the Mushkoh valley and Batalik even as the Indian Army finally cleared the Dras sector of Pakistani intruders, Defence Ministry officials said.

A total of 21 Indian soldiers died in the assaults in Dras and Batalik while 60 Pakistani intruders were killed.

Mr Nawaz Sharif said that India should refrain from putting forward any 'conditions' for the resumption of dialogue.

The US told Pakistan to withdraw all its troops from the remaining areas of Kargil and push for the Lahore process, as India made it clear that the resumption of Indo-Pak dialogue depended on the stoppage of cross-border terrorism by Pakistan.

26 July 1999

India declared that its territory was completely free from Pakistani intruders along the entire alignment of the LoC, though military tension in the area had not completely eased.

India's diplomatic campaign for a revival of the 'Lahore process' and an equitable global order of nuclear disarmament was endorsed by the ARF (the Association of South East Asian Nations' Regional Forum) at its sixth annual meeting.

An international conference on nuclear non-proliferation and disarmament dropped from its final document a 'call for China to become involved in a three-way effort to eliminate the threat posed by ongoing tensions between India and Pakistan'. China's role in the India–Pakistan dispute settlement was earlier suggested by the US and strongly backed by Japan and Australia at the third meeting of the 'Tokyo Forum' in New York in April.

27 July 1999

India and Pakistan discussed steps to ease tension along the 740-km LoC. DGMOs of the two sides discussed CBMs which could be undertaken to de-escalate tension along the LoC.

Gen. V. P. Malik claimed the action in Kargil was 'far from over' and said firing was continuing along the LoC despite the eviction of Pakistani intruders as there was neither political nor military understanding between the two countries.

Pakistan accused India of trying to avoid bilateral talks by 'raising extraneous and marginal issues' and appealed to the international community to facilitate resumption of 'meaningful and result-oriented dialogue' to resolve the Kashmir issue.

In a bid to counter Pakistani propaganda in Jammu and Kashmir, on Tuesday the Union Cabinet approved a Rs. 43 crore package for upgrading Doordarshan and All India Radio services in the state.

The Indian Space Research Organisation moved an Indian Remote Sensing satellite over the Jammu and Kashmir theatre of operations to scan the landscape for intruders.

28 July 1999

When Pakistani troops resorted to artillery fire and mortar shelling in Batalik and other subsectors along the LoC, 1 Indian soldier was killed.

Pakistan made it clear it would 'man' the peaks on the LoC overlooking the Dras–Kargil road on the Indian side throughout the year.

29 July 1999

Mr Nawaz Sharif renewed his offer of talks with India to settle the Kashmir issue.

30 July 1999

India summarily rejected Pakistan's demand that it first commit itself to solving the Kashmir issue rather than insisting on a composite dialogue process on all the outstanding issues. India also reiterated that no dialogue with Pakistan was possible until cross-border terrorism promoted by the latter was stopped forthwith and the relevant infrastructure dismantled.

31 July 1999

Mr Sartaj Aziz contradicted his Foreign Secretary, Mr Shamshad Ahmad's statement that Pakistan would talk only Kashmir with India. Mr Aziz said whenever the Lahore process was restored, all eight issues identified for discussion by the two countries, including Kashmir, would come up for discussion.

1 August 1999

Kargil town, including the area around its hospital, had been severely shelled by Pakistan.

The Army scuttled an infiltration attempt by Pakistan to send armed militants into Kashmir Valley when they shot dead 6 intruders in Nowgam sector of Kupwara, official sources said.

2 August 1999

Army troops gunned down 5 foreign mercenaries who had sneaked 10 km inside Indian territory in the Kupwara sector of north Kashmir.

3 August 1999

India asserted that it was incumbent upon Pakistan to cease sponsorship and instigation of cross-border terrorism in Jammu and Kashmir to facilitate the creation of a 'conducive atmosphere' for the resumption of the composite dialogue process.

6 Augst 1999

In a pre-dawn attack, militants stormed an Army camp and engaged the troops in a fierce hand-to-hand encounter.

10 August 1999

The IAF shot down a Pakistani naval anti-submarine and surveillance aircraft which intruded 10 km into Indian territory in the Kori Creek area in Gujarat. Pakistan said all 16 personnel on board were killed.

The Indian Government protested strongly against the provocative intrusion by Pakistani military aircraft into Indian airspace.

APPENDIX 2

TEXT OF THE LETTER ADDRESSED TO LORD MOUNTBATTEN, THE GOVERNOR GENERAL OF INDIA CONTAINING THE DECISION OF THE MAHARAJA OF JAMMU AND KASHMIR STATE REGARDING ACCESSION OF THE STATE[1]

26 October 1947

My dear Lord Mountbatten,

I have to inform Your Excellency that a grave emergency has arisen in my State and request immediate assistance of your Government.

As your Excellency is aware the State of Jammu and Kashmir has not acceded to either the Dominion of India or to Pakistan. Geographically my State is contiguous to both the Dominions. It has vital economical and cultural links with both of them. Besides my State has a common boundary with the Soviet Republics and China. In their external relations the Dominions of India and Pakistan cannot ignore this fact.

I wanted to take time to decide to which Dominion I should accede, whether it is not in the best interest of both the Dominions and my State to stand independent, of course with friendly and cordial relations with both.

I accordingly approached the Dominions of India and Pakistan to enter into a standstill agreement with my State. The Pakistan Government accepted this arrangement. The Dominion of India desired further discussion with representatives of my Government. I could not arrange this in view of the developments indicated below. In fact the Pakistàn Government under the standstill agreement are operating Post and Telegraph system inside the State.

Though we have got a standstill agreement with the Pakistan government, that Government permitted steady and increasing strangulation of supplies like food, salt and petrol to my State.

Afridis, soldiers in plain clothes, and desperadoes, with modern weapons, have been allowed to infilter into the State at first in Poonch area, then in Sialkot and finally in mass in the area, adjoining Hazara district on the Ramkot side. The result has been that the limited number of troops at the

[1] Balraj Madhok, *Kashmir Divided*, Rasthra Dharam Prakashan, Lucknow, 1949 pp. 192-5.

disposal of the State had to be dispersed and thus had to face the enemy at several points simultaneously that it has become difficult to stop the wanton destruction of life and property and looting. The Mahoora Power House which supplies the electric current to the whole of Srinagar has been burnt. The number of women who have been kidnapped and raped makes my heart bleed. The wild forces thus let loose on the State are marching on with the aim of capturing Srinagar, the summer capital of my Government, as a first step to overrunning the whole State.

The mass infiltration of tribesmen drawn from the distant areas of the N.W.F. Province coming regularly in motor trucks using Mansehr–Muzaffarabad road and fully armed with up-to-date weapons cannot possibly be done without the knowledge of the provincial government of the N.W.F. Province and the Government of Pakistan. In spite of repeated appeals made by the government no attempt has been made to check these raiders or stop them from coming to my State. In fact both the Pakistan Radio and press have reported these occurrences. The Pakistan Radio even put out a story that a provisional Government has been set up in Kashmir. The people of my State both the Muslim and non-Muslims generally have taken no part at all.

With the conditions obtaining at present in my State and the great emergency of the situation as it exists I have no option but to ask for help from the Indian Dominion. Naturally they cannot send the help asked for by me without my State acceding to the Dominion of India. I have accordingly decided to do so and I attach the Instrument of Accession for acceptance by your Government. The other alternative is to leave my State and my people to freebooters. On this basis no civilised Government can exist or be maintained. This alternative I will never allow to happen so long as I am the Ruler of the State and I have life to defend my country.

I may also inform Your Excellency's Government that it is my intention at once to set up an Interim Government and ask Sheikh Abdullah to carry the responsibilities in this emergency with my Prime Minister.

If my State has to be saved immediate assistance must be available at Srinagar. Mr. Menon is fully aware of the situation and he will explain to you if further explanation is needed.

In haste and with kindest regards.

(Sd.) Hari Singh

APPENDIX 3

UN RESOLUTION DATED 13 AUGUST 1948[1]

PART I

CEASE-FIRE ORDER

The Governments of India and Pakistan agree that their respective High Commands will issue separately and simultaneously a cease-fire order to apply to all forces under their control in the State of Jammu and Kashmir as of the earliest practicable date or dates to be mutually agreed upon within four days after these proposals have been accepted by both Governments.

The High Commands of the Indian and Pakistan forces agree to refrain from taking any measures that might augment the military potential of the forces under their control in the State of Jammu and Kashmir. (For the purpose of these proposals 'forces under their control' shall be considered to include all forces, organised and unorganised, fighting or participating in hostilities on their respective sides.)

The Commanders-in-Chief of the Forces of India and Pakistan shall promptly confer regarding any necessary local changes in present dispositions which may facilitate the cease-fire.

In its discretion and as the Commission may find practicable the Commission will appoint military observers who under the authority of the Commission and with the co-operation of both Commands will supervise the observance of the cease-fire order.

The Government of India and the Government of Pakistan agree to appeal to their respective peoples to assist in creating and maintaining an atmosphere favourable to the promotion of future negotiations.

PART II

TRUCE AGREEMENT

Simultaneously with the acceptance of the proposal for the immediate cessation of hostilities as outlined in Part I, both Governments accept the following principles as a basis for the formulation of a truce agreement, the details of which shall be worked out in discussion between their Representatives and the Commission.

[1] Study Group HQ Northern Command, 'Solders Role in Jammu and Kashmir (HQ Northern Command, Delhi, 1984), pp. 121-2.

As the presence of troops of Pakistan in the territory of the State of Jammu and Kashmir constitutes a material change in the situation since it was represented by the Government of Pakistan before the Security Council, the Government of Pakistan agrees to withdraw its troops from that State.

The Government of Pakistan will use its best endeavour to secure the withdrawal from the State of Jammu and Kashmir of tribesmen and Pakistan nationals not normally resident therein who have entered the state for the purpose of fighting.

Pending a final solution, the territory evacuated by the Pakistan troops will be administered by the local authorities under the surveillance of the Commission.

When the Commission shall have notified the Government of India that the tribesmen and Pakistan nationals referred to in Part II A-2 thereof have withdrawn thereby terminating the situation which was represented by the Government of India to the Security Council as having occasioned the presence of Indian forces in the State of Jammu and Kashmir, and further, that the Pakistan forces are being withdrawn from the State of Jammu and Kashmir, the Government of India agrees to begin to withdraw the bulk of their forces from that State in stages to be agreed upon with the Commission.

Pending the acceptance of the conditions for a final settlement of the situation in the State of Jammu and Kashmir, the Indian Government will maintain within the lines existing at the moment of the cease-fire those forces of its Army which in agreement with the Commission are considered necessary to assist local authorities in the observance of law and order. The Commission will have observers stationed where it deems necessary.

The Government of India will undertake to ensure that the Government of the State of Jammu and Kashmir will take all measures within their power to make it publicly known that peace, law and order will be safeguarded and that all human and political rights will be guaranteed.

Upon signature, the full text of the Truce Agreement or a communiqué containing the principles thereof as agreed upon between the two Governments and the Commission, will be made public.

PART III

The Government of India and the Government of Pakistan reaffirm their wish that the future status of the State of Jammu and Kashmir shall be determined in accordance with the will of the people and to that end, upon acceptance of the Truce Agreement both Governments agree to enter into consultations with the Commission to determine fair and equitable conditions whereby such free expression will be assured.

APPENDIX 4

THE INTER-SERVICES INTELLIGENCE OF PAKISTAN, PAKISTAN-SPONSORED MILITANCY IN J&K AND ITS NEXUS WITH ISLAM

THE ISI

When infiltration occurs in Jammu and Kashmir (J&K), or bomb blasts are reported in Delhi, Mumbai (Bombay) or Coimbatore, or anywhere else in India, Government organizations and the media point a finger of suspicion at Pakistan's Inter-Services Intelligence (ISI). India has indeed been the prime target of this organization's external activities. It is, therefore, essential to comprehend the aims and manner of functioning of the ISI to see how it threatens the security of India.

The ISI is headed by a Director General (DG) of the rank of Lt. Gen./ Maj. Gen., he has hitherto been a serving officer seconded from the Army. The ISI coordinates the functioning of the intelligence directorates of the Armed Forces and is the sole organization for collection of military and external intelligence. The DG, although under the Ministry of Defence, is also the adviser to the Prime Minister on intelligence matters. The DG being the Army Chief's man only disseminates what the Army Chief wants the politicians to know. The Army Chief draws his power from the Army, which has the final say in Pakistan on matters of national security: any political interference or opposition is not countenanced. The plans of the ISI are really the plans of the Pak Army. The ISI is, therefore, an organ of the Army, not an organ of the State. Whenever Prime Ministers have tried to use the ISI as informers and hatchet men, they normally have got a severe rap on their knuckles from the GHQ (General HQ, i.e. Army HQ).

The ISI combines in itself all the functions carried out in India by the Research and Analysis Wing, the Intelligence Bureau, the Special Intelligence Bureau, the Central Bureau for Investigation, the various specialist agencies under the Home Ministry, the Intelligence Directorates of the Armed Forces and paramilitary forces, and the Joint Intelligence Committee. The ISI has been working towards the dismemberment of India ever since the time of its raising in 1949. Pakistan is not comfortable with an India seven times its size and would like India's northern, eastern, and southern wings to be severed, so that what remains of India approximates Pakistan's size. Prior to 1971, the ISI aided and abetted insurgencies in eastern India, and, in the post-1971 period it enlarged its activities to encompass Punjab and J&K and later Tamil Nadu.

Kashmir and its annexation or liberation would continue to be the prime objective of the Pak Army and hence the basic aim of the ISI. Pakistan would not be happy with an independent Kashmir as it could be under the sway of other countries. The origin of the current wave of terrorism in J&K has been traced to the loss of Siachen in 1984 and the Movement for the Restoration of Democracy (MRD) in Pakistan directed against Gen. Zia-ul-Haq's military dictatorship. To divert attention from this military setback and domestic problems, the military regime chalked out a strategy to create trouble in Punjab and J&K.

The ISI spends nearly Rs. 100 crore every year to run its proxy war in J&K. Each militant is paid between Rs. 2,000 and Rs. 3,000 per month depending upon his experience and status in the terrorist outfit. In case a militant dies in action, his or her family gets compensation ranging from Rs. 20,000 to Rs. 30,000. ISI agents active in Kashmir receive between Rs. 50,000 and Rs. 1,00,000 (one lakh) a month as emoluments. They are accorded five-star facilities during their visits to Rawalpindi. Some Islamic organizations are also funding the militants in J&K.

About 90 militant training camps are running in Pakistan and Pakistan-Occupied Kashmir (POK). These camps are controlled from headquarters in Muzaffarabad and Kotli. The ISI is assisted in its activities by the Harkat-ul-Ansar (HuA), a group declared to be terrorist by the US State Department in 1997. Since then, this organization is using its earlier name, Harkat-ul-Mujahideen (HuM). The HuA has close links with Osama Bin Laden, the dissident Saudi millionaire blamed for the bombing of two US embassies in Africa in 1998. The HuA's two militias (Harkat-ul-Mujahideen and the more extreme Harkat-ul-Jihad) provide shelter, food and clothing for the trainees at these camps, while the ISI provides weapons, ammunition and transport, along with specialist instructors for training. The ISI has been training Afghan mujahideen, Kashmiris and Punjabis from Pakistan at these camps. The fanatic trait of the trainees is evident from the fact that they are now seeking to change the basic ideology in Kashmir from *azadi* (freedom) to jihad (Islamic uprising). Hired soldiers from several countries (Iran, Yemen, Chechnya, Kazakhstan, Sudan, Bahrain, Turkey, Saudi Arabia and Afghanistan) have also been employed by Pakistan in J&K. They are paid much more than those recruited from J&K, POK or Pakistan. Pak Army personnel disguised as militants or civilians, apart from aiding infiltration and terrorism, are also operating in J&K for collecting intelligence about Indian Army and Indian Air Force movements, identifying targets for attack in case of war, and directing artillery fire on Indian locations from vantage points.

Elsewhere in India, the ISI offers monetary rewards, sex, and other attractions to cultivate agents. One of their tactics is to form cells near military cantonments. Using its old contacts in Bangladesh, reportedly with some cooperation from the Bangladesh intelligence services, the ISI has activated its networks, and established contact with every insurgent group in the north-eastern region and in Assam. It is also using Nepal for opening new areas to infiltrate and ex-filtrate agents and material into eastern India.

The success of the peace process between India and Pakistan depends to a very large extent on the ability of the Pakistan Government to rein in the Pak Army (and hence, the ISI), and equally, on how effectively India defeats their plans in J&K and in other parts of India.

Fundamentalist Parties and Terrorist Outfits

About a dozen Pak-based militant outfits have made the wresting of Kashmir from India their primary aim. Among the leading terrorist groups are the Lashkar-e-Toiba (LeT) and the Harkat-ul-Ansar, which are funded through local jihad collections as well as by Arab countries. Details of some of the fundamentalist parties and terrorist outfits of Pakistan are as follows.

1. *Jamaat-e-Islami (JI)*: A fundamentalist religious party which is led by Qazi Hussain Ahmed. It comprises three major wings.
   (a) *Islami Jamaat-e-Tulba*: It is the student wing of the JI and enrols members from various colleges in Pakistan.
   (b) *Jamaat-Tulba-e-Arabia*: Its members are drawn from religious schools (madrassas).
   (c) *Hizbul Mujahideen (HM)*: This militant outfit is effectively supported by the JI and is most active in Kashmir Valley. The HM, unlike other organizations, operates only in Kashmir. Founded in 1989, its popularity increased once the pro-independence groups of Kashmir fell out of Pakistan's favour. The HM has strong links with the Jamaat-e-Islami of Pakistan and most of the members of the HM are from the Islami Jamaat-e-Tulba, the student wing of the JI. Though the HM claims that its members are from Kashmir, there is a sizeable population of Afghans and Pakistanis. The HM, unlike the LeT (Lashkar-e-Toiba) and the HuM, does not have any bases for training in Afghanistan, because of its closeness to the JI. (The Jamaat-e-Islami has close links with Gulbuddin Hekmatyar, who is fighting against the Taliban in Afghanistan. Contrary to popular belief, the JI does not support the Taliban's influence inside Pakistan.) Though supported by the ISI, the HM today is not under its full control, as it receives its orders from Qazi Hussain Ahmed, the Amir of the JI. About 800 Hizbul Mujahideen are active in Kashmir.

2. *Markaz-Dawa-Wal-Irshad (Centre for Preaching)*: A religious organization, founded in 1987, it has its headquarters at Muridke, a small town 48 km north of Lahore. Its twin objectives are preaching and

preparing the mujahideen for jihad around the world. The 190-acre Muridke centre was set up after a meeting between Saudi millionaire Osama Bin Laden and a professor of Lahore's University of Engineering and Technology. Initially funded by the Arabs and Pakistanis, the Markaz generates its own income from iron and garment factories which it owns and the like. There are about 30 schools run by the Markaz, in which 5,000 students are studying. All the students do not become fighters, but those who wish to are given special military training in Pakistan and Afghanistan. On completion of training, in which a mujahideen is taught guerrilla warfare and the use of weapons, he is also given a new name after a mythical hero. Though the Markaz fighters are products of these 30 schools and the majority of them are from Pakistan, there are also others from other organizations. Most of them are educated and come from the middle class. The Markaz was initially helped by the ISI, but the organization and the fighters it trains are not wholly under control of either the ISI or the Pakistan Government: they have succeeded in generating their own independent income. The militant wing of the Markaz is known as the *Lashkar-e-Toiba (LeT)* or the 'Army of the Pure'. This militant outfit is backed by the ISI and operates from POK. Its Kashmiri wing is headed by Abdul Rehman ul-Dakhil. About 300 Markaz Lashkars are active in the Valley, Poonch, Rajouri and Doda.

3. *Harkat-ul-Ansar (HuA)*:

   (a) It was started in the early 1980s as the *Harkat-ul-Mujahideen (HuM)*. This organization draws support from the *Tablighi Jamaat Movement* now headed by Lt. Gen. (retd) Javed Nasir, former Director General of the ISI. In October 1993, the *Harkat-ul Ansar (HuA)* came into being with the merger of two Pakistani political activist groups, the *HuM* and the more extreme *Harkat-ul-Jihad*. The HuA is an Islamic militant group based in Muzaffarabad in POK which seeks Kashmir's accession to Pakistan. According to the leader of the alliance, Maulana Saddatullah Khan, the group's objective is to continue the armed struggle against non-believers and anti-Islamic forces. The HuA is open to all who support its objectives and are willing to take the group's forty-day training course during which they are taught to use assault rifles, light and heavy machine guns, mortars, explosives and rockets. It has a core militant group of about 300, mostly Pakistanis and Kashmiris, but includes Afghans and also veterans of the Afghan war trained by the ISI and the CIA to fight the Soviets in Afghanistan. When the Najibullah regime collapsed in Afghanistan, HuA personnel were sent to other parts of the world from Algeria to Bosnia to Kashmir. Of an estimated total of 5,000 volunteers, around 350 are fighting in Kashmir.

(b) When the HuA was declared a terrorist organization by the US in 1997, it reverted to its old name, the HuM. The HuA had had close links with Osama Bin Laden, who was held responsible for the bombing of two US embassies in Africa in 1998.

(c) The HuM belongs to the Deobandhi–Wahabi faith and is closely linked to the Maulana Samiul Haq faction of the Jamaat-e-Ulama-e-Islam (JUI). Unlike the LeT, the HuM does not have an organizational structure from which it can recruit its members. Most of its intake is from other organizations, specially from the Tablighi Jamaat. The President of Pakistan, Rafiq Tarar, is associated with the Tablighi Jamaat.

4. *Binnot Town Madrassa*: This centre for Sunni learning in Karachi has produced some of the Taliban's top military commanders. Madrassa graduates wait in Kabul for military assignments and weapons. The bulk of them have been trained at the Darul Uloom Haqqania near Nowshera in the North West Frontier Province and the Jamia Uloomul Islamiya in Karachi.

There are differences among these groups regarding their objectives. Whereas the HM's objective is focused only on the 'liberation of Kashmir from Indian occupation', the objectives of the LeT and the HuM are broader. Both aim to use Kashmir as a stepping stone towards a larger goal to unite the entire Muslim community in the subcontinent and elsewhere. It is not merely Kashmir but 'The 'jihad' which they want to promote. For these 'jihadis', Kashmir is only a gateway to establish the 'rule of Allah throughout the world'. For them, Kashmir is not the end but only a means. The ultimate aim of these 'jihadi' groups is 'to revive the tradition of Jihad among Muslims everywhere in order to win back the lost glory of the Muslim world'.

Apart from the groups mentioned above, there are a number of minor groups operating in J&K. Some of these are: Tehrik-ul-Mujahideen, Al Badr, Al Barq, Al Jihad, Jamait-ul-Mujahideen, Islami-Inqualabi-Mahaz, Bait-ul-Islam, Ishkwan-ul-Muslimeen, Janbaaz Force, Allah Tigers, Tehrik-ul-Jihad-e-Islami, Pasdaran-e-Islam-Ansarullah and the Jammu and Kashmir Liberation Force (JKLF); the Amanullah Khan faction has its headquarters in Pakistan.

Pakistan-Sponsored Militancy and its Nexus with Islam

Since the time of India's partition in 1947, Pakistan has consistently used overt and covert means to annex the state of J&K. It has made every effort to internationalize the Kashmir problem and to gain the sympathy of the world community in general, and the Islamic world in particular. The Pakistan military has been playing the Islamic card to motivate its own forces, the ISI, as well as the large number of mercenaries who serve Pakistan-sponsored militant organizations. In addition to the militants and terrorists operating in J&K, a large number of Pak Army personnel disguised as militants are also operating in the state as part of various militant outfits. This is clear proof of the military and ideological nexus between Pakistan's regular army and Islamic militants.

Militants do not hold ground and are not capable of fighting pitched, regular battles. Their philosophy is to melt into the inner areas of their choosing in small groups, terrorize the local populace, discredit the local government, and try and move to other areas before being liquidated. The recent attacks on some posts of the Indian security forces along the LoC—and in some interior areas—is further indication that the militants have been emboldened by the presence of Pak Army personnel in disguise in their midst, enabling them to feel strong enough to alter their tactics. The increasing involvement of the Pak Army has given the impetus to the militants to shift their terrorist activities from the Kashmir region to the areas of Doda, Rajouri, Poonch and Surankot in the Jammu region.

Islamization of the Pakistan Army

Ever since President Ayub Khan was overthrown and Zulfikar Ali Bhutto made Yahya Khan the Army Chief, the Pakistan Army has steadily been Islamized with Koran Kwani being introduced into the Armed Forces. Pakistani military leaders quote frequently from the Koran and Sunnah and continue to urge their Muslim troops to fight the anti-Islamic 'Kafir army'.

During the Afghan struggle against the Soviets, Islamization received an impetus. The ISI tried to whip up Islamic passions amongst the Afghan mujahideen, and in the process, they became Islamic fanatics. It is well known that the ISI has always sought the help of fundamentalist parties like the Jamaat-e-Islami, and organizations like the Tablighi Jamaat and Markaz-Dawa-Wal-Irshad, to serve their anti-India cause. The state has also been responsible for Islamization of the Army. Pakistan Army officers like Hamid Gul and Javed Nasir, who headed the ISI, are well known for their fanaticism. These two officers in particular were responsible for focusing the efforts of the Pakistan Army and the ISI towards a common goal. Consequently, the ISI and the Army are two sides of the same coin: the same mission, the same leadership and the same funding.

President Zia was regarded as the major initiator of Islamic fundamentalism in the Army. Today, most major generals and below are radical fundamentalists. Islamization of the Pakistan Army personnel begins from the day the recruits take the oath or swear on the sharia. This is systematically followed by periodic motivation on the tenets of Islam. Such steady indoctrination provides fertile ground to Islamic fundamentalist parties in Pakistan to extend their influence over personnel of the Armed

Forces. Besides, Pakistani troops are regularly subjected to religious tests, which are based on the fundamentals of Islam as perceived by the majority Sunnis. These tests are intended to raise the level of religious awareness among Pakistani troops and ensure indoctrination.

Apart from its identity and ideology being anchored in Islam, the Pakistan Army has gone a step further than other armies by playing a pan-Islamic role. Personnel of the Pakistan Armed Forces participated in the 1967 and 1973 Arab-Israeli wars. Pakistan Army personnel have fought alongside the fundamentalist groups in Kashmir in 1965, viz., Operation Gibraltar and again since 1988 in the proxy war against India. Personnel of Pakistan's Armed Forces fought in Afghanistan and Zia even offered to send troops to Syria in 1982. In this context, it should be noted that Pakistan's response to serve in conflict situations like Somalia and Bosnia under UN auspices was due to these situations being perceived as Muslim causes.

Export of Terrorism by Pakistan

Che Guevara's 'foco' theory was the world's first attempt to export terrorism and revolution. Focoism was based on the premise that a passive population could be aroused to revolutionary fervour by the armed struggle of mercenaries. Notwithstanding the failure of the idea of exporting revolution, Pakistan has now taken on this responsibility. They learnt their basic lessons in Afghanistan and have trained about 25,000 terrorists/militants from eight different nationalities and have organized them into various '*tanzeem*'. These militants pose a serious threat not only to India, but to neighbouring countries as well.

Sponsoring international terrorism and separatist subversion and insurgency is not new to Pakistan. Since 1970, Islamabad has been training Sikh ultras and personnel of other Indian separatist movements as part of Zulfikar Ali Bhutto's strategy of Forward Strategic Depth. The thrust of Sikh fundamentalism increased after the assassination of Mrs Indira Gandhi, and some Sikhs were reportedly killed in Soviet raids in Paktia (Afghanistan) and their documents seized.

By 1985, the ISI had put into place a vast training infrastructure for the Afghan resistance movement. Afghan militants trained by the ISI (and the CIA) were smuggled into India with the purpose of organizing acts of terrorism against members of the Indian Government and foreign diplomatic representatives. A similar brand of terrorism was exported to Kashmir on the bogey that 'Islam was in danger'.

These activities transformed themselves into an active ISI programme. Initially, the emphasis of this programme was on using the Afghan support infrastructure in Pakistan to support Kashmir militants. At times, ISI assistance to Kashmiri Islamists was even funnelled through the Afghan rebel leader Gulbuddin Hekmatyar's Hizb-i-Islam group, thus providing Islamabad with deniability.

The rise of Islamist ideology in Kashmir facilitated the development of a tight link between Kashmiri insurgents, their supporters and Islamabad. Consequent upon the spread of the Islamist ideology, Kashmiri militants and their supporters now sought ideological sustenance from a transnational Islam, while simultaneously basking in the guaranteed patronage of their nefarious activities from across the border.

K-2 PROGRAMME

The Pakistan ISI political chief, Brig. Imtiaz, developed a long-term programme for Kashmir and Punjab, called the K-2 Programme. In this programme, Kashmiris, Sikh extremists and Muslim fundamentalists were trained and motivated to destabilize India's border states, and intensify acts of violence in the Terai region of Uttar Pradesh.

NEXUS OF ISLAMIC FUNDAMENTALIST GROUPS

The nexus between the Islamic fundamentalist groups operating in Kashmir and Pakistan has been well established. The Hizbul Mujahideen (HuM) was supported by the Jamaat-e-Islami (JI) in terms of funds, weapons and training assistance. Such assistance was in addition to the support they received from the ISI. The ISI established the Janbaaz Mujahideen Force to give training in subversion to Kashmiri militants in POK to carry out subversive activities on behalf of Islamabad.

In addition to established Muslim fundamentalist organizations, Pakistan's ISI runs its own Kashmiri organizations like the Hizb-i-Islam. The ISI has also established a force made up of a Pakistan special force, dressed in Indian Army uniforms, to assist Pakistan-trained Kashmiris in dealing with major crises. Pakistan trained and armed thousands of Kashmiri youth in the period from 1988 to the mid-1990s, till the Kashmiris realized that they were being used as pawns in a bigger game. This disenchantment led to the Kashmiris disassociating themselves from Pakistan's activities. The ISI then renewed its process of Islamic indoctrination and its training facilities, but this time with very limited success.

A paper on 'Defence Planning in the Era of Strategic Uncertainty' was presented on behalf of Gen. Aslam Beg, erstwhile COAS, Pakistan Army, at a conference on 'Asian Security in the 21st Century' at New Delhi on 27-8 January 1999. In the paper, Gen. Aslam Beg stated:

> Afghanistan war of liberation experience provides the strength for the Kashmiri freedom fighter in the wider dimension of the conflict and should peace come to the war ravaged Afghanistan, the Mujahiddin would like to pay back the gratitude they owe to their Kashmiri brothers for joining them in their struggle against the Soviet aggressor.

SOME FACTS AND FIGURES

The number of Pakistan-run terrorist camps is approximately as under.

(a) In Pakistan 37
(b) In POK 49
(c) In Afghanistan 22

In 1999, the number of hardcore terrorists operating in J&K was assessed to be about 2,300 of which 900 were foreign mercenaries. In the gory decade of violence since 1990, Pakistani terrorists have killed more than 29,000 Indian civilians and 3000 personnel of the security forces in J&K. The number of Pakistani terrorists killed by Indian security forces stood at about 12,000. The number of firearms recovered from Pakistan-trained terrorists in India was approximately 47,000, while the amount of explosives recovered was about 60 tons (60,000 kg). The number of explosions carried out by the terrorists was in the region of 4,730.

Nearly 3,00,000 Kashmiri Pundits (original Hindu inhabitants of Kashmir Valley) were driven out of their ancestral homeland by Pakistan-supported terrorists.

APPENDIX 5

PAKISTAN'S NORTHERN LIGHT INFANTRY

HISTORICAL BACKGROUND

During the 1880s, following the annexation of the North Western Frontier Province (NWFP) and extension of the British military control up to the Durand Line, the British were required to manage the tribals in the NWFP. Due to manifold problems (including ignorance of terrain, language, customs and habits of the hostile tribal people), the Indian and British units could not be used in isolation. The Militia and Scouts units were, therefore, raised by recruiting local tribal people. These units were employed in front of and on the flanks of regular units, for reconnaissance and protection. Later, the role of the Militia/Scouts was changed to picqueting and guarding of communications prior to the launching or employment of the military force.

Consequent upon the creation of Pakistan in 1947, the Militia and the Scouts were gradually reorganized and equipped with modern weapons. Army units were withdrawn and Militia/Scouts deployed in POK, NWFP and Baluchistan. The DIG Northern Areas was located at Gilgit and the Scouts were deployed as follows in POK:

(a) Gilgit Scouts: For North Gilgit, with headquarters at Gilgit.
(b) Northern Scouts: For South Gilgit, with headquarters at Gilgit.
(c) Karakoram Scouts: For Baltistan, with headquarters at Skardu.

During 1973, units with HQ Northern Areas along with its Scouts wings (Gilgit Scouts, Northern Scouts and the Karakoram Scouts) were re-organized as Northern Light Infantry (NLI) battalions. On raising, the NLI battalions were placed under control of the Pakistan Ministry of Defence (MOD). As a result of a study undertaken in 1993, NLI battalions were reorganized into regular battalions. The Regimental Centre of the NLI units was located at Bunji near Gilgit.

ETHNIC COMPOSITION

The sectarian break up in the Northern Areas consists of eight major ethnic groups (the Baltis, Shins, Yashkuns, Mughals, Kashmiris, Pathans, Ladakhis and Turks) who speak dialects of Balti, Shina, Brushaki, Wakhi, Turki, Tibetan, Pushto, Urdu and Persian. The Northern Areas, despite having a very small population, presents a very diverse sectarian picture, with the presence of four Muslim sects—Shia, Sunni, Ismailis and Noor

Bakshis. The ethnic composition of NLI battalions with their sectarian affiliations as documented in 1993 were as follows.

(a) Area-wise proportion of recruitment in NLI battalions
  - (i) Gilgit - 55%
  - (ii) Baltistan - 35%
  - (iii) Other areas (Gircha, Chilas and POK) - 10%

(b) Ethnic composition of NLI battalions
  - (i) Sunnis - 18%
  - (ii) Shias - 49%
  - (iii) Ismailis - 23%
  - (iv) Noor Bakshis - 10%

(c) The ethnic pattern in NLI mortar batteries is in similar proportion for Sunnis, Shias and others.

ORBAT AND ORGANIZATION

Regarding the Order of Battle (Orbat), consequent upon the reorganization of 1973, ten NLI battalions numbering 1 to 10 along with three (independent) NLI batteries were raised. Four additional NLI battalions were raised in 1985, for employment in the Siachen sector. The organization of an NLI battalion and an independent NLI battery are given as follows.

NORTHERN LIGHT INFANTRY BATTALION

BATTALION HEADQUARTERS
- Anti-Aircraft Section (4 x 12.7 mm AAMG)
- General Duty Section (Sec)
- 4 × Company (Coy) (112)
  - Coy HQ (20)
    - Weapon Sec (11)
      - 2 × 60 mm Mortars
      - 1 × 75 mm Recoilless Rifle
    - 3 × Pl (37)
      - Pl HQ (7) 1 × 3.5 Rocket Launcher
        - Sec (10) 2 × 7.62 Light Machine Guns
        - Sec
        - Sec
- HQ Company
  - Pioneer Pl (20)
    - Sec
    - Sec
    - Sec
  - Mortar Pl (39)
    - Sec
    - Sec 4 × 81mm Mor
  - Medical Pl
  - Signal Pl
  - Mechanical Transport Pl
  - Administration Pl
- Intelligence Section
- Regimental Police Section
- Animal Transport Section

WEAPONS

9 mm. Pistol	-	73	81 mm Mor	-	8
Sten Machine Carbine	-	102	60 mm Mor	-	8
Rifle	-	528	12.7 mm AAMG	-	4
7.62 LMG/MG	-	*72	HE 36 Hand Gren	-	743
75 mm RR	-	4			
3.5 RL	-	12			

* Including 12 x MG

EQUIPMENT

(a) *Night Vision.* Night Vision Goggles/Binoculars, Night Vision Sight for 75 mm RR based on sectoral profile.

(b) *Radio Sets*
   (i) 37 x Radio Sets RS PRC-77.
   (ii) 16 x Radio Sets RS 884.

NORTHERN LIGHT INFANTRY MOUNTAIN BATTERY (NLI BTY)

1. Organization

HQ (I) NLI BTY

2 x Dets
3 x 105 mm How (Pack)/25 pdr/122 mm Field Guns with each det

2. Personnel

Officers	-	5
Junior Commissioned Officers	-	7
Gunners	-	37
Technical Assistants	-	9
Drivers and Operators	-	60
	Total	118

Note: 452 (I) NLI Bty is also holding unspecified numbers of 122 mm Multi-Barrel Rocket Launchers/Single-Barrel Rocket Launchers as sector stores.

TRAINING

Personnel of NLI battalions are specially trained for snow warfare, commando operations and anti-heliborne operations. Trained commando personnel are also deputed to the Special Services Group (SSG).

OPERATIONAL ASPECTS

Mission

To defeat the hostile force by skilful use of firepower and manoeuvre by day and night, in any type of weather and terrain.

Capabilities

The NLI battalion is expected to perform the following tasks.

(a) Closing with the enemy by means of fire and manoeuvre in order to destroy him.
(b) Repulsing enemy attack by fire and counter-attack.
(c) Providing a base for fire and manoeuvre elements.
(d) Seizing and holding ground.
(e) Conducting independent operations on a limited scale.
(f) Participating in air landing operations when provided with sufficient air transportation.
(g) Taking part in different types of operations by day and night.
(h) Conducting operations in all types of terrain and climatic conditions.
(j) Moving by any method cross-country, road, sea and air.
(k) Providing anti-tank protection.
(l) Internal security and civil defence.

By virtue of their training and because the men are drawn from the Northern Areas, the NLI battalions are more effective in high altitude warfare than other regular units of the Pakistan Army.

APPENDIX 6

DETAILS OF THE INITIAL INDIAN RESPONSE TO THE KARGIL INTRUSIONS[1]

The intrusions in the Kargil sector were first noticed on 3 May 1999 by two shepherds (both occasional sources of 121 Infantry Brigade), in the general area of Banju in the Batalik sector. This information was reported to 3 PUNJAB, the battalion responsible for the security of that area. The sequence of actions thereafter in the various subsectors was as follows.

1. *Batalik Sector.* 3 PUNJAB sent two patrols on 4 and 6 May 1999 to investigate the reported intrusion. The intrusion was confirmed by a 3 PUNJAB patrol on 7 May. One company each of 10 GARH RIF and 16 GRENADIERS was immediately moved to contain the intrusion. Soon thereafter, two battalions (1/11 GR and 12 JAK LI) which had just been deinducted from the Siachen sector and were readily available, were moved on 9 May and positioned in the Batalik sector by 10 May. Subsequently on 11 May, HQ 70 Infantry Brigade, which was then at Dras, was moved and made responsible for this sector.

2. *Dras and Mushkoh Sectors.* Enemy intrusions in the Dras sector were detected on 12 May 1999 by a patrol of the LADAKH SCOUTS and in the Mushkoh sector by Army Aviation helicopters on 14 May. The diversion to Dras of 1 NAGA (which had been moved from the Valley on 9 May) was ordered soon after the detection of the intrusion in the Batalik sector, and it was employed there from 12 May onwards to contain the intrusion in that area. The 8 SIKH and 28 Rashtriya Rifles (RR) battalions were moved in on 14 May.

3. *Kaksar Sector.* The enemy intrusion was detected on 14 May by a patrol of 4 JAT in the area of the south-west spur of Point 5299, commonly known as 'Bajrang Post'. This was the only post that was vacated by Indian troops on 2 March 1999 in the face of extreme snow conditions. Initially, one company of 28 RR was released to contain the intrusion and subsequently, on 21 May, 14 JAK RIF moved for deployment in the Kaksar sector.

4. *Subsector Haneef (Turtok).* During the last week of April 1999, seven Pakistani helicopters were observed flying with underslung loads in the area.

[1] This appendix is based on the Kargil Committee report.

A patrol of 12 JAT sent to monitor activity along the LoC was ambushed on 6 May. Subsequent patrols sent on 16 and 19 May confirmed that the enemy had occupied the ridge line along and across the LoC at five locations. The 11 RAJ RIF and 9 MAHAR battalions were tasked to occupy defences, and the enemy was subsequently evicted by physical assault.

5. *Chorbat La Sector.* Once the enemy intrusions in the Kargil sector and the Haneef subsectors were established, five companies of LADAKH SCOUTS were moved to reinforce the Chorbat La sector. They occupied defences along the LoC during the period 18-31 May 1999, and foiled all enemy attempts to intrude into the area.

With a view to ensuring expeditious eviction of the intruders, the following formations/headquarters, which were deployed for counter-insurgency operations in the Valley, were moved to Kargil during the period 15 May 1999 to 1 June 1999.

(a) 56 Mountain Brigade to Dras sector on 15 May 1999.
(b) 79 Mountain Brigade to Mushkoh sector on 29 May 1999.
(c) HQ 8 Mountain Division moved to the Kargil sector on 29 May 1999 and took over operational control of the Dras-Mushkoh sector from 1 June 1999.

Once confirmed reports regarding major intrusions in the Batalik sector had become available, HQ Northern Command placed all troops in J&K in a state of high alert on 12 May 1999. Soon thereafter, certain other moves were also ordered within and into Northern Command to maintain operational balance.

Progressively, defensive and offensive formations of the Army in the Western and Southern Commands were also moved forward closer to the border to ensure a balanced posture at the strategic level to deter Pakistan from escalating the conflict and preventing it from focusing solely on Kargil.

APPENDIX 7

CITATIONS OF THE RECIPIENTS OF THE PARAM VIR CHAKRA AND MAHA VIR CHAKRA—OPERATION VIJAY AND NAMES OF VIR CHAKRA RECEIPIENTS

The citations given below have been extracted from the Gazette of India of 11 March 2000.

PARAM VIR CHAKRA

1. *Lieutenant Manoj Kumar Pandey* (IC-56959) 1st Battalion the 11th Gorkha Rifles (Posthumous)
   (Effective date of the Award: 2 July 1999)

Lt. Manoj Kumar Pandey, a young officer of 1/11 GR, took part in a series of boldly-led attacks during Operation Vijay, forcing back the intruders with heavy losses in Batalik including the capture of Jubar Top.

His finest hour was during the advance to Khalubar, when he was Number 5 Platoon Commander. On the night of 2/3 July 1999, as the platoon approached its final objective, it came under heavy and intense enemy fire from the surrounding heights. The officer was tasked to clear the interfering enemy positions, so as to prevent his battalion from getting daylighted, being in a vulnerable position. The officer quickly moved his platoon to an advantageous position under intense enemy fire and sent one section to clear the enemy positions on the left. Fearlessly assaulting the first enemy position, he killed two enemy personnel and proceeded to assault the second and destroyed it by killing two more enemy personnel. Lt. Manoj Kumar Pandey was injured on the shoulder and legs by enemy fire while clearing the third position. Undaunted and without caring for his grievous injury, he led the assault on the fourth position, urging his men on and destroyed the same with a grenade, even as he got a fatal medium machine gun burst on his forehead. It is this singular daredevil act of the officer, which provided the critical firm base for the companies, which finally led to capture of Khalubar.

Lieutenant Manoj Kumar Pandey, thus showed most conspicuous bravery, indomitable courage, exemplary personal valour, outstanding leadership and devotion to duty of an exceptionally high order, in the face of enemy and made the supreme sacrifice in the highest traditions of the Army.

2. *Grenadier Yogendar Singh Yadav* (2690572) 18th Battalion the Grenadiers Regiment (Mechanised Infantry)
(Effective date of the Award: 3 July 1999)

Gdr. Yogendar Singh Yadav was part of leading team of Ghatak Platoon tasked to capture Tiger Hill on night 3/4 July 1999. The approach to the top, at a height of 16,500 ft was steep, snow bound and rocky. He volunteered to be in the lead and fixed a rope for his team to climb up, unmindful of the risk involved.

The enemy, on seeing his team approach the area top, opened intense automatic, grenade, rocket and artillery fire. His team commander and two of his colleagues fell to murderous enemy fire. The further advance of Ghatak Platoon was stalled. Knowing the gravity of the situation, he crawled up to the enemy position to silence it, but sustained multiple bullet injuries. Unmindful of his injuries and the hail of enemy bullets, he continued towards the enemy positions, lobbed grenades inside and fired from his weapon, killing four enemy soldiers in close combat and silenced the automatic fire.

During the charge, he again sustained multiple bullet injuries but refused to be evacuated even in a critical condition. Inspired by his gallant act, the rest of the Ghatak Platoon charged on to the other positions, and captured Tiger Hill Top, a National Objective.

Grenadier Yogender Singh Yadav, thus, displayed most conspicuous courage, indomitable spirit, grit and determination under an extremely difficult situation beyond the call of duty.

3. *Rifleman Sanjay Kumar* (13760533) 13th Battalion the Jammu & Kashmir Rifles
(Effective date of the Award: 4 July 1999)

Rfn. Sanjay Kumar volunteered to be the leading scout of the attacking column tasked to capture area Flat Top of Point 4875 in the Mushkoh valley on 4 July 1999.

As the attack progressed, enemy automatic fire from one of the *sangars* posed stiff opposition, thereby stalling the column. Rfn. Sanjay realizing the gravity of the situation, displayed indomitable spirit and unadulterated courage when he charged the enemy *sangar* with utter disregard to personal safety. In the ensuing hand-to-hand combat, he killed three of the intruders and was himself seriously injured. Despite being injured, he charged on to the second *sangar*. The enemy was taken totally by surprise and they left behind one universal machine gun and started running. Rfn. Sanjay Kumar picked up the weapon left behind by the enemy and killed the fleeing enemy. Although Rfn. Sanjay was bleeding profusely from his wounds, he refused to be evacuated. This superhuman act of Rifleman Sanjay Kumar motivated his comrades, who took no notice of the treacherous terrain and charged on to the enemy, thus wresting the area Flat Top from the hands of the enemy.

Rifleman Sanjay Kumar, thus, displayed most conspicuous and extraordinary gallantry, cool courage and devotion to duty of an exceptionally high order in the face of the enemy.

4. *Captain Vikram Batra* (IC-57556) 13th Battalion the Jammu & Kashmir Rifles (Posthumous)
(Effective date of the Award: 7 July 1999)

In Dras sector, the enemy held strong fortified positions, heavily reinforced with automatic weapons, with treacherous approaches dominating the Srinagar–Leh road, the lifeline of supplies to Leh.

On 20 June 1999, Capt. Vikram Batra, Commander Delta Company, was tasked to attack Point 5140 during Operation Vijay. Capt. Batra with his company skirted around the feature from the east and maintaining surprise reached within assaulting distance. The officer reorganized his column and motivated his men to physically assault the enemy positions. Leading his men from the front, the officer, in a daredevil assault, pounced on the enemy and killed four intruders in a hand-to-hand fight.

On 7 July 1999, in yet another operation in the area of Point 4875, the company of the officer was tasked to clear a narrow feature with sharp cuttings on either side, and heavily fortified enemy defences, that covered the only approach to it.

In order to speed up the operation, the officer decided to assault the enemy positions along a narrow ridge. Leading the assault, he engaged the enemy in a fierce hand-to-hand fight and killed five enemy soldiers at point blank range. In this action, Capt. Batra sustained grievous injuries. Despite the serious injuries, he crawled towards the enemy and hurled grenades, clearing the position. Leading from the front, he rallied his men and pressed on the attack and achieved a near impossible military task in the face of heavy enemy fire with utter disregard to personal safety. The officer, however, succumbed to his injuries.

Inspired by this display of extraordinary junior leadership, the troops fell upon the enemy with vengeance and annihilated them, finally capturing Point 4875.

Captain Vikram Batra thus displayed the most conspicuous personal bravery and junior leadership of the highest order in the face of enemy and made the supreme sacrifice in the highest traditions of the Army.

MAHA VIR CHAKRA

5. *Major Sonam Wangchuk* (IC-45952) The Ladakh Scouts (Indus Wing)
(Effective date of the Award: 30 May 1999)

On 30 May 1999, Maj. Sonam Wangchuk of Indus Wing, LADAKH SCOUTS, as a part of ongoing Operation VIJAY in the Batalik sector, was leading a column for occupation of Ridge Line on the Line of Control in a glaciated area at a height of about 5,500 m: This was essential so as to pre-empt its occupation by the enemy and any subsequent infiltration.

While moving towards the LoC, the enemy ambushed the column by firing from a vantage position. In the process, one NCO (Non-Commissioned Officer) of LADAKH SCOUTS was killed. Maj. Wangchuk held his column together and in a daring counter-ambush, led a raid on the enemy position from a flank, killing two enemy personnel. The officer also recovered one heavy machine gun and one universal machine gun, ammunition, controlled stores and also three dead bodies of the enemy personnel.

Thereafter, the officer took stock of all forces along the Chorbat La axis in the Batalik sector and cleared the axis up to the LoC of all enemy intrusions at a great risk to his life.

Major Sonam Wangchuk displayed exceptional bravery and gallantry of the highest order in the presence of enemy fire and in extreme climatic conditions in the glaciated area.

6. *Major Rajesh Singh Adhikari* (IC-52574) 18th Battalion the Grenadiers Regiment (Mechanised Infantry)
(Posthumous)
(Effective date of the Award: 30 May 1999)

On 30 May 1999, as a part of battalion operations to capture the Tololing feature, Maj. Rajesh Singh Adhikari was tasked to secure the initial foothold by capturing its forward spur where the enemy held a strong position. The enemy position was located in a treacherous, mountainous terrain covered with snow at a height of about 15,000 ft.

While Maj. Adhikari was leading his company towards the objective, he was fired at from two mutually supporting enemy positions with universal machine guns. The officer immediately directed the rocket launcher detachment to engage the enemy position and without waiting, rushed into the position and killed two enemy personnel in close-quarter combat.

Thereafter, the officer, displaying presence of mind under heavy fire, ordered his medium machine gun detachment to take position behind a rocky feature and engage the enemy. The assault party continued to inch their way up. While so advancing forward, Maj. Adhikari suffered grievous bullet injuries, yet he continued to direct his subunit. Refusing to be evacuated, the officer charged at the second enemy position and killed one more occupant, thus capturing the second position at Tololing which later facilitated the capture of Point 4590. The officer, however, later succumbed to his injuries.

Major Rajesh Singh Adhikari displayed exceptional valour, outstanding leadership in the presence of the enemy and laid down his life in the highest traditions of the Indian Army.

7. *Major Vivek Gupta* (IC-51152) 2nd Battalion the Rajputana Rifles (Posthumous)
(Effective date of the Award: 13th June 1999)

Maj. Vivek Gupta was in command of the leading Charlie Company, when 2 RAJ RIF launched a battalion attack on Tololing Top, in Dras Sector on 13 June 1999.

In spite of heavy artillery and automatic fire, the company, under the inspiring leadership of Maj. Gupta, was able to close in with the enemy. As soon as the company emerged in the open, they came under multidirectional intense fire. Three personnel of the leading section of the company were hit and the attack was temporarily stalled.

Knowing fully well that staying any longer in the open under the murderous enemy fire would lead to more losses, Maj. Gupta reacted immediately and fired a rocket launcher at the enemy position. Before the shocked enemy could recover, Maj. Gupta charged on to the enemy position. While so charging, he was hit by two bullets, despite which he kept moving towards the position. On reaching the position, he engaged the enemy in fierce hand-to-hand combat and managed to kill three enemy soldiers despite his own injuries.

Taking inspiration from the gallant deed of the officer, the rest of the company charged onto the enemy position and captured it. However, in the ensuing combat, Maj. Vivek received another direct hit from enemy bullets and finally succumbed to his injuries.

Major Vivek Gupta displayed conspicuous gallantry and inspiring leadership in the face of the enemy, which ultimately led to the capture of Tololing Top.

8. *Naik Digendra Kumar* (2883178) 2nd Battalion the Rajputana Rifles
(Effective date of the Award: 13 June 1999)

Nk. Digendra Kumar was commander of the light machine gun group during his company's assault on Tololing feature in Dras sector. The objective was to capture a well-fortified enemy position.

On 13 June 1999, when the assault group was nearing its objective, it came under effective enemy fire of well-concealed universal machine gun, heavy machine gun and other small arms leading to heavy casualties in the assault group. Nk. Digendra was hit by a bullet in his left arm. Undaunted and unmindful of his own injury, he kept firing with one hand and brought down effective and accurate light machine gun fire on the enemy. His accurate fire kept the enemy's head down while his own men advanced towards the objective. Finally, under his effective covering fire, own troops physically assaulted the enemy position and cleared it after a fierce hand-to hand fight.

Despite being seriously wounded, it was due to his courageous action that the assault group could finally capture the objective. Naik Digendra Kumar displayed conspicuous gallantry, courage and grit in the face of the enemy.

9. *Major Padmapani Acharya* (IC-55072) 2nd Battalion the Rajputana Rifles
   (Posthumous)
   (Effective date of the Award: 28 June 1999)

On 28 June 1999, Maj. Padmapani Acharya, as a company commander, was assigned the formidable task of capturing an enemy position which was heavily fortified, strongly held and covered with mines and sweeping machine gun and artillery fire.

The success of the battalion and brigade operations hinged on the early capture of the position. However, the company attack almost faltered at the very beginning when the enemy's artillery fire came down squarely on the leading platoon, inflicting large numbers of casualties.

With utter disregard to his personnel safety, Maj. Acharya took the reserve platoon of his company and led it through intense artillery shelling. Even as his men where falling to the murderous enemy fire, he continued to encourage his men and charged at the enemy up the steep rock face with his reserve platoon.

Unmindful of the hail of bullets from the enemy's position, Maj. Acharya crawled up to the enemy position and lobbed grenades. In this daring assault, Maj. Acharya was seriously injured. Despite being severely injured and unable to move, he ordered his men to leave him and charge at the enemy while he continued to fire at the enemy. The enemy position was finally overrun and the objective was captured.

After completion of the mission, the officer, however, succumbed to his injuries. Major Padmapani Acharya displayed exceptional courage, leadership and spirit of self-sacrifice in the face of the enemy.

10. Captain Neikezhakuo Kenguruse (IC-58396) Army Service Corps
    (attached to the 2nd Battalion the Rajputana Rifles)
    (Posthumous)
    (Effective date of the Award: 28 June 1999)

Capt. Neikezhakuo Kenguruse was the Ghatak Platoon Commander during the attack on Area Black Rock in the Dras sector on the night of 28 June 1999 during Operation Vijay.

He volunteered to undertake a daring commando mission of attacking a well-sited enemy machine gun position, on a cliff face, which was interfering very effectively with all the approaches to the main objective of the battalion. As the commando team scaled the cliff face, it came under intense mortar and automatic fire, which caused heavy casualties.

The officer sustained a splinter injury in his abdomen. Bleeding profusely yet undeterred, he urged his men to carry on with the assault. On reaching the final cliff face, the commando team was halted by a sheer rock wall that separated them from the enemy machine gun post. The officer took off his shoes to get a good grip and scaled the rock wall carrying with him a rocket launcher, which he fired at the enemy position.

Unmindful of his personal safety, the officer thereafter charged at the enemy position and personally killed two men with his rifle and another two with his commando knife in hand to hand combat before succumbing to his injury.

By his daredevil act, Capt. Kenguruse single-handedly neutralized the enemy position, which had held up the battalion's progress.

Captain Neikezhakuo Kenguruse displayed conspicuous gallantry, indomitable resolve, grit and determination beyond the call of duty and made the supreme sacrifice in the face of the enemy, in the true traditions of the Indian Army.

11. *Lieutenant Keishing Clifford Nongrum* (SS-37111) 12th Battalion the Jammu & Kashmir Light Infantry
    (Posthumous)
    (Effective date of Award: 30 June 1999)

On the night of 30 June/1 July 1999, in the operations to capture Point 4812 in the Batalik sector, Lt. Keishing Clifford Nongrum was tasked to assault the feature from the south-eastern direction. Lt. Nongrum led his column over the near impossible vertical cliff feature. On reaching the top, his column encountered strong enemy opposition. The enemy was well-entrenched in interconnected positions carved out of boulders and remained immune even to artillery fire.

The enemy pinned down the column of Lt. Nongrum with heavy and accurate automatic fire for about two hours. On seeing the futility of own fire against the fortified enemy positions, Lt. Nongrum, with utter disregard to his personal safety, charged through the fire zone. Closing in with the first position, he threw grenades into it and killed six enemy soldiers. He then tried to snatch the universal machine gun of the enemy from the second enemy position and received a volley of bullets.

The audacious action of Lt. Nongrum stunned the enemy, giving valuable reaction time to his troops to close in and finally clear the position. Though severely wounded, Lt. Nongrum refused to be evacuated and fought valiantly till he succumbed to his injuries. This act resulted in the ultimate capture of Point 4812.

Lieutenant Keishing Clifford Nongrum displayed conspicuous bravery, dogged determination and raw courage in the face of the enemy and made the supreme sacrifice in the highest traditions of the Indian Army.

12. *Lieutenant Balwan Singh* (SS-37691) 18th Battalion the Grenadiers Regiment (Mechanised Infantry)
(Effective date of the Award: 3 July 1999)

On 3 July 1999, Lt. Balwan Singh with his Ghatak Platoon was tasked to assault the Tiger Hill Top from the north-eastern direction as part of a multipronged attack. The route to the objective, situated at a height of 16,500 ft, was snowbound and interspersed with crevasses and sheer falls.

The officer, with just three months service, set about his task with single-minded determination. The team, led and exhorted by him, moved for over twelve hours along a very difficult and precarious route and under intense artillery shelling to reach the designated spur.

The move took the enemy by complete surprise as his team used cliff assault mountaineering equipment to reach the top with stealth. On seeing the Ghataks, the enemy panicked and in a desperate firefight attempted to repulse the Ghataks. In the ensuing firefight, Lt. Singh was himself seriously injured. Though injured, his resolve to finish the enemy remained unshaken. He refused to be evacuated, and unmindful of his injury, moved swiftly to encircle the enemy and engaged them in close combat and he single-handedly killed four enemy soldiers. The remaining enemy personnel opted to flee rather than face the fury of the fierce officer.

The officer's inspirational leadership, conspicuous courage and bravery were instrumental in the capture of Tiger Hill, which was operationally one of the most important objectives in the Dras sector.

13. *Captain Anuj Nayyar* (IC-57111) 17th Battalion the Jat Regiment (Posthumous)
(Effective date of the Award: 6 July 1999)

On 6 July 1999, Charlie Company was tasked to capture an objective which was a part of the Pimple Complex on the Western Slopes of Point 4875, in the Mushkoh valley. At the beginning of the attack, the company commander got injured and the command of the company devolved on Capt. Nayyar.

Capt. Nayyar continued to command his leading platoon into the attack under heavy enemy artillery and mortar fire. As the platoon advanced, the leading section reported the location of three to four enemy positions. Capt. Nayyar moved forward towards the first enemy position, fired a rocket launcher and lobbed grenades into it.

Thereafter, the section, along with Capt. Anuj, physically assaulted and cleared the position. The enemy, who was well-entrenched, brought a heavy volume of automatic fire. Capt. Nayyar, unmindful of his personal safety, motivated his men and cleared two more enemy positions. While clearing the fourth position, an enemy rocket-propelled grenade hit the officer, killing him on the spot.

This action led by Capt. Anuj resulted in the killing of nine enemy soldiers and the destruction of three medium machine gun positions of the enemy. The success of this operation, after a brief setback, was largely due to the outstanding personal bravery and exemplary junior leadership of this daring officer.

Capt. Anuj Nayyar displayed indomitable resolve, grit and determination and motivated his command by personal example, acting beyond the call of duty and made the supreme sacrifice in the true traditions of the Indian Army.

14. *Sepoy Imliakum* (147002937) 2 Naga
(Effective date of the Award: 8 July 1999)

On 8 July 1999 Sepoy Imliakum volunteered to raid an enemy mortar position at a height of 15,000 ft. in Mushkoh Valley in Jammu and Kashmir.

Sepoy Imliakum formed part of the Assault Group and was tasked to stealthily silence the enemy sentry who was on duty on the outer perimeter of enemy mortar position. Sepoy Imliakum approached the enemy sentry during broad day-light and killed him. Thereafter, he kept moving forward and killed one more sentry and subsequently stormed the mortar position along with the Assault Group.

Sepoy Imliakum showed exemplary courage and determination in personally killing two enemy soldiers. All through, it was his determination, grit, cool confidence and raw courage in the face of enemy which was instrumental in eliminating the enemy from the almost indomitable mortar position.

The elimination of the enemy personnel by Sepoy Imliakum was a big success wherein three 120mm and two 81mm mortars were captured along with a huge stockpile of ammunition. The valiant action by Sepoy Imliakum, which was a true demonstration of valour, in the presence of a well entrenched enemy was the sole factor which paved the way for a successful raid on the enemy mortar position which led to the destruction of the enemy dump.

Sepoy Imliakum, thus showed exemplary courage in the face of enemy, sustained and successful performance in storming the enemy mortar position and killing two enemy soldiers.

VIR CHAKRA RECEPIENTS

1. Col. Umesh Singh Bawa, 17 Jat
2. Col. Lalit Rai, 1/11 Gorkha Rifles
3. Col. Magod Basappa Ravindranath, 2, Rajputana Rifles

4. Lt. Col. Yogesh Kumar Joshi, 13 J&K Rifles
5. Lt. Col. Ramakrishnan Vishwanathan, 18 Grenaiders (posthumcus)
6. Wing Commander Anil Kumar Sinha, Flying Pilot
7. Maj. S. Vijay Bhaskar, 13 J&K Rifles
8. Maj. Deepak Rampal, 17 Jat
9. Maj. Vikas Vohra, 13 J&K Rifles
10. Maj. Amrinder Singh Kasanam, 41 Field Regiment
11. Maj. Rajesh Sah, 18 Garhwal Rifles
12. Maj. Mohit Saxena, 2 Rajputana Rifles
13. Maj. M. Saravanan, 1 Bihar (posthumous)
14. Squadron Leader Ajay Ahuja, Flying Pilot (posthumous)
15. Maj. K.P.R. Hari, 1 Bihar
16. Maj. Gautam Shasikumar Khot, Army Aviation, 23 Reconnaissance and Observation Flight
17. Maj. Prabhu Nath Prasad, SM, Army Aviation, 32 Reconnaissance and Observation Flight
18. Capt. Shalamal Sinha, Kumaon, attached to 27 Rajput
19. Capt. Amol Kalia, 12 J&K Light Infantry (posthumous)
20. Capt. Sachin Annarao Nimbalkar, 18 Grenadiers
21. Capt. Sanjeec Singh, ASC attached to 13 J&K Rifles
22. Capt. Haneef Uddin, 11 Rajputana Rifles (posthumous)
23. Capt. Summet Roy, 18 Garhwal Rifles (posthumous)
24. Capt. Maridhvodan Veetil Sooraji, 18 Garhwal Rifles
25. Capt. Jintu Gogoi, 17 Garhwal Rifles (posthumous)
26. Capt. R. Jery Prem Raj, 158 Medium Regiment (SP) (posthumous)
27. Capt. Vijyant Thapar, ASC attached to 2 Rajputana Rifles (posthumous)
28. Capt. Shasi Bhushan Gildiyal, 315 Field Regiment
29. Capt. Rupesh Pradhan, 2 Engr Regiment
30. Capt Baleyada Muthana Cariappa, SM, 5 Para
31. Lt. Praveen Kumar, 14 Sikh
32. Lt. Deepankar Kapoor Singh Sharawat, 2 Naga
33. Sub. Chhering Stobdan, Ladakh Scouts (Indus Wing)
34. Sub. Bahadur Singh, 12 J&K Light Infantry (posthumous)
35. Sub. Lobzang Chhotak, Ladakh Scouts (Indus Wing) (posthumous)
36. Sub. Bhawar Lal, 2 Rajputana Rifles (posthumous)
37. Sub. Raghunath Singh, 12 J&K Rifles
38. Sub. Randhir Singh, 18 Grenadiers (posthumous)
39. Sub. Niramal Singh, 8 Sikh (posthumous)
40. Naib Sub. Mangej Singh, 11 Rajputana Rifles (posthumous)
41. Naib Sub. Karnail Singh, 8 Sikh (posthumous)
42. Naib Sub. Tashi Chhepal, Ladakh Scout (Indus Wing)
43. Comany Hav. Maj. Yashwir Singh, 2 Rajputana Rifles (posthumous)
44. Hav. Sultan Singh Narwaria, 2 Rajputana Rifles (posthumous)

45. Hav. Sis Ram Gill, 8 Jat (posthumous)
46. Hav. Udham Singh, 18 Grenaiders (osthumous)
47. Hav. Tsewang Rigzin, Ladakh Scouts (Indus Wing)
48. Hav. Joginder Singh, Kumaon, attached to 27 Rajput
49. Hav. Madan Lal, 18 Grenadiers (posthumous)
50. Hav. Kumar Singh, 17 Jat (posthumous)
51. Hav. Satish Chander, 12 J&K Light Infantry
52. Hav. Bhim Bahadur Dewan, 1/11 Gorkha Rifles (posthumous)
53. Lance Hav. Ram Kumar, 18 Grenadiers (posthumous)
54. Naik Ganesh Prasad Yadav, 1 Bihar (posthumous)
55. Naik Dev Prakash Yadav, 13 J&K Rifles
56. Naik Kashmir Singh, 18 Garhwal Rifles (posthumous)
57. Naik Shatrughan Singh, 1 Bihar
58. Naik Kaushal Yadav, 9 Parachute (SF) (posthumous)
59. Naik Brij Mohan Singh, 9 Parachute (SF) (posthumous)
60. Lance Naik Khushiman Gurung, 1 Naga
61. Lance Naik Ghulam Mohd Khan, 12 J&K Light Infantry (posthumous)
62. Lance Naik Gyanendra Kumar Rai, 1/11 Gorkha Rifles
63. Sepoy Tsering Dorjay, Ladakh Scouts (Indus Wing)
64. Sepoy A. Ashuli, 1 Naga (posthumous)
65. Sepoy Satpal Singh, 8 Sikh
66. Sepoy Tsewang Morup, Ladakh Scouts (Kaarakoram Wing)
67. Gunner Sanjeev Gopala Pillai, 4 Field Regiment (posthumous)
68. Rifleman Jai Singh, 2 Rajputana Rifles
69. Rifleman Anusuya Prasad, 18 Garhwal Rifles (posthumous)
70. Rifleman Kuldeep Singh, 18 Garhwal Rifles(posthumous)
71. Rifleman Shyam Singh 13 J&K Rifles (posthumous)
72. Rifleman Mehar Singh, 13 J&K Rifles.

APPENDIX 8

TEXTS OF THE G-8 STATEMENT ON THE KARGIL CRISIS

Kashmir

We are deeply concerned about the continuing military confrontation in Kashmir following the infiltration of armed intruders which [*sic*] violated the line of control.

We regard any military action to change the status quo as irresponsible.

We, therefore, call for the immediate end of these actions, restoration of the line of control and for the parties to work for an immediate cessation of the fighting, full respect in the future for the line of control and the resumption of the dialogue between India and Pakistan in the spirit of the Lahore declaration.

Missile and Nuclear Tests by India and Pakistan

One year after the nuclear tests by India and Pakistan, we reiterate our concerns and reaffirm our statement from the Birmingham communiqué.

Recent missile tests have further increased tension in the region. We encourage both countries to follow first positive steps already undertaken by joining international non-proliferation and taking the steps set out in U.N. Security Council resolution 1172.

Source: The Hindu, 21 June 1999.

APPENDIX 9

TEXT OF THE CLINTON–SHARIF STATEMENT, 5 JULY 1999

President Clinton and Prime Minister Sharif share the view that the current fighting in the Kargil region of Kashmir is dangerous and contains the seeds of a wider conflict. They also agreed that it was vital for the peace of South Asia that the Line of Control in Kashmir be respected by both parties, in accordance with the 1972 Simla accord.

It was agreed between the President and the Prime Minister that concrete steps will be taken for the restoration of the Line of Control in accordance with the Simla Agreement. The President urged an immediate cessation of the hostilities once these steps are taken.

The Prime Minister and President agreed that the bilateral dialogue begun in Lahore in February provides the best forum for resolving all issues dividing India and Pakistan, including Kashmir. The President said he would take a personal interest in encouraging an expeditious resumption and intensification of those bilateral efforts, once the sanctity of the Line of Control has been fully restored.

The President reaffirmed his intent to pay an early visit to South Asia.

Source: The Hindu, 6 July 1999.

APPENDIX 10

THE MUSHARRAF TAPES

CONVERSATION OF 26 MAY 1999

What follows is the verbatim record of the full telephone conversation on 26 May—the day the Indian air strikes began—between Lt. Gen. Mohammed Aziz, Chief of the General Staff, calling from Pakistan, and Gen. Pervez Musharraf, Chief of the Army Staff, who was on an official tour of China. The conversation was in Urdu and English. The portions translated into English are in italics.

China end: I am sorry the line is busy now.
Pakistan end: Can I hold? . . . Salam-ale-qum Sir.
Gen. Musharraf: Wale-Qum-Salam.
Pakistan end: Sir, there is a call from Pakistan for Gen. Pervez Musharraf.
China end: Yes, Sir.
Pakistan end: Gen. Aziz Khan will speak.
China end: *Yes.*
Pakistan end: Sir, Col. Hassan.
Gen. Musharraf: Yes, Hassan.
Pakistan end: Sir, how are you?
Gen. Musharraf: Grace of God.
Pakistan end: Sir, please speak, Hello?
Gen. Musharraf: Thank you.
Lt. Gen. Aziz: Sir, Salam-ale-qum.
Gen. Musharraf: Yes Aziz, how are you?
Lt. Gen. Aziz: Very fine, Sir. How is the visit going?

Gen. Musharraf: Yes, very well. OK. And, what else is the news on that side?

Lt. Gen. Aziz: Ham-dul-ullah. There is no change on the ground situation. They have started rocketing and strafing. That has been upgraded a little. It had happened yesterday also and today. Today high altitude bombing has been done.

Gen. Musharraf: On their side, in those positions?

Lt. Gen. Aziz: In those positions, but in today's bombing about 3 bombs landed in our side of Line of Control. No damage, Sir.

Gen. Musharraf: Is it quite a lot?

Lt. Gen. Aziz: Sir, about 12-13 bombs were dropped, from which 3 fell on our side, which does not appear to be a result of inaccuracy. In my interpretation, it is a sort of giving of a message that if need be we can do it on the other side as well. It is quite distance apart. Where the bombs have been dropped, they have tried to drop from a good position where they are in difficulty, from behind the LoC but they have fallen on our side of the LoC. So I have spoken to the Foreign Secretary and I have told him that he should make the appropriate noises about this in the Press.

Gen. Musharraf: They (Indians) should also be told.

Lt. Gen. Aziz: That we have told, Foreign Secretary will also say and Rashid will also say. He will not, generally speaking, make any such mistake about those other bombs falling on the other side, our stand should be that all these bombs are falling on our side. We will not come into that situation. The guideline that they have given, we have stressed that we should say that this build-up and employment of air strike which has been done under the garb of . . . us [?], actually they are targeting our position on the LoC and our logistic build-up, these possibly they are taking under the garb having intention for operation the craft [?] Line of Control, and this need to be taken note of and we should retaliate in kind . . . is what happened? So, the entire build up we want to give this colour.

Gen. Musharraf: Absolutely OK. Yes, this is better. After that, has there been any talk with them? And meetings etc?

Lt. Gen. Aziz: Yesterday, again, in the evening.

Gen. Musharraf: Who all were there?

Lt. Gen. Aziz: Actually, we insisted that a meeting should be held, because otherwise that friend of ours, the incumbent of my old chair, we thought lest he give some interpretation of his own, we should do something ourselves by going there.

Gen. Musharraf: Was he little disturbed? I heard that there was some trouble in Sialkot.

Lt. Gen. Aziz: Yes. There was one in Daska. On this issue there was trouble. Yes, he was little disturbed about that but I told him that such small things keep happening. . . . [?] and we can reply to such things in a better way.

Gen. Musharraf: Absolutely.

Lt. Gen. Aziz: There is no such thing to worry.

Gen. Musharraf: So that briefing to Mian Saheb that we did, was the forum the same as where we had done previously? There, at Jamshed's place?

Lt. Gen. Aziz: No. In Mian Saheb's office.

Gen. Musharraf: Oh I see. There. What was he saying?

Lt. Gen. Aziz: From here we had gone—Choudhary Zafar Saheb, Mehmood, myself and Tauqir. Because before going, Tauqir had spoken with his counterpart. We carried that tape with us.

Gen. Musharraf: So, what was he (Indian counterpart) saying?

Lt. Gen. Aziz: That is very interesting. When you come, I will play it for you. Its focus was that these infiltrators who are sitting here, they have your help and artillery support, without which they could not have come to J&K. This is not a very friendly act and it is against the spirit of the Lahore Declaration. Then Tauqir told him that if your boys tried to physically attack the Line of Control and go beyond it . . . and that the bombs were planted on the Turtok bridge and the dead body received in the process was returned with military honours and I said, I thought that there was good enough indication you would not enter into this type of misadventure, and all this build-up that you are doing—one or more brigade strength and 50-60 aircraft are being collected, these are excuses for undertaking some operations against the various spaces, so I had put him on the defensive.

Then he said the same old story. He would put three points again and again that they (militants) should not be supported, and without your support they could not be there, they have sophisticated weapons and we will flush them out, we will not let them stay there. But this is not a friendly act.

Gen. Musharraf: So, did they talk of coming out and meeting somewhere?

Lt. Gen. Aziz: No. No, they did not.

Gen. Musharraf: Was there some other talk of putting pressure on us?

Lt. Gen. Aziz: No. He only said that they (militants) will be given suitable reception. This term he used. He said, they will be flushed out, and everytime Tauqir said that please tell us some detail, detail about how many have gone into your area, what is happening there? Then I will ask the concerned people and then we will get back to you. So whenever he asked these details, he would say, we will talk about this when we meet, then I will give details. This means, they are possibly looking forward to next round of talks, in which the two sides could meet. This could be the next round of talks between the two PMs which they are expecting it. . . . Sir, very good thing, no problem...

Gen. Musharraf: So, many times we had discussed, taken your [PM's?. . .] blessings and yesterday also I told him that the door of discussion, dialogue must be kept open and rest, no change in ground situation.

Lt. Gen. Aziz: So, no one was in a particularly disturbed frame of mind.

Gen. Musharraf: Even your seat man?

Lt. Gen. Aziz: Yes, he was disturbed. Also, Malik Saheb was disturbed, as they had been even earlier. Those two's views were that the status quo and the present position of Gen. Hassan [?] no change should be recommended in that. But he was also saying that any escalation after that should be regulated as there may be the danger of war. On this logic, we gave the suggestion that there was no such fear as the scruff (*tooti*) of their (militants) neck is in our hands, whenever you want, we could regulate it. Ch. Zafar Saheb coped very well. He gave a very good presentation of our viewpoint. He said we had briefed the PM earlier and given an assessment. After this, we played the tape of Tauqir. Then he said that what we are seeing, that was our assessment, and those very stages of the military situation were being seen, which it would not be a problem for us to handle. Rest, it was for your guidance how to deal with the political and diplomatic aspects. We told him there is no reason of alarm and panic. Then he said that when I came to know 7 days back, when Corps Commanders were told. The entire reason for the success of this operation was this total secrecy. Our experience was that our earlier efforts failed because of lack of secrecy. So, the top priority is to accord confidentiality, to ensure our success. We should respect this and the advantage we have from this would give us a handle.

Gen. Musharraf: Rest (*baki*), is Mian Saheb OK?

Lt. Gen. Aziz: OK. He was confident just like that but for the other two. Shamshad as usual was supporting. Today, for the last two hours the BBC has been continuously reporting on the air strikes by India. Keep using this—let them keep dropping bombs.

As far as internationalisation is concerned, this is the fastest this has happened. You may have seen in the Press about UN Secretary General Kofi Annan's appeal that both countries should sit and talk.

Gen. Musharraf: This is very good.

Lt. Gen. Aziz: Yes, this is very good.

Gen. Musharraf: OK, Bye.

CONVERSATION OF 29 MAY 1999

WHAT follows is the verbatim record of the full telephone conversation between Lt. Gen. Mohammed Aziz, Chief of the General Staff, at the Pakistan end, and his boss, Gen. Pervez Musharraf, Pakistan's Chief of the Army Staff, who was then on a tour of China. The conversation took place on 29 May 1999.

The conversation took place in Urdu and English. The portions translated into English are in italics:

(Pakistan end) Lt. Gen. Aziz: This is Pakistan. Give me room No. 83315 [the same room number]. Hello?

(China end) Gen. Musharraf: Hello Aziz.

Lt. Gen. Aziz: The situation on ground is OK, no change, this area but it is not brought down by attack. One of their MI-17 arms [?] was brought down. *Further, the position is*, we had approached to our position, *it was brought down*. Rest is OK. Nothing else except, there is a development. Have you listened to yesterday's news regarding Mian Saheb speaking to his counterpart? He told him that the spirit of Lahore Declaration and escalation has been done by your people. Specially wanted to speak to me thereafter. He told Indian PM that they should have waited instead of upping the ante by using Air Force and all other means. He (Nawaz) told him (Indian PM) that he suggested Sartaj Aziz could go to New Delhi to explore the possibility of defusing the tension.

Gen. Musharraf: OK.

Lt. Gen. Aziz: Which is likely to take place, most probably tomorrow.

Gen. Musharraf: OK.

Lt. Gen. Aziz: Our other friend [Lt. Gen. Ziauddin, DG ISI . . . ? . . . or could be United States] might have also put pressure on. For that, today they will have a discussion at Foreign Office about 9.30 and Zafar Saheb (Lt. Gen. Saeed uz Zaman Zafar, GOC 11 Corps & Acting Chief) is supposed to attend.

Gen. Musharraf: OK.

Lt. Gen. Aziz: Aziz Saheb (Sartaj Aziz, Foreign Minister) has discussed with me and my recommendation is that dialogue option is always open. But in their first meeting, they must give no understanding or no commitment on ground situation.

Gen. Musharraf: Very correct. You or Mehmood (GOC X Corps, Rawalpindi) must have to go with Zafar. Because, they don't know about the ground situation.

Lt. Gen. Aziz: This week, we are getting together at 8 O'clock because meeting will be at 9.30, so Zafar Saheb will deliberate it. We want to suggest to Zafar that they have to maintain that they will not be talking about ground situation. All that you say.

So far as the ground situation is concerned. Subsequently, DGMOs can discuss with each other and work out the modus operandi.

Gen. Musharraf: Idea on LoC.

Lt. Gen. Aziz: Yes. Hint is that, given that the LoC has many areas where the interpretation of either side is not what the other side believes. So, comprehensive deliberation is required. So, that can be worked out by DGMOs. If they are assured that we are here from a long period. We have been sitting here for long. Like in the beginning, the matter is the same—no post was attacked and no post was captured. The situation is that we are along our defensive Line of Control. If it is not in his (Sartaj Aziz's) knowledge, then discuss it altogether. Emphasise that for years, we are here only.

Gen. Musharraf: Yes, this point should be raised. We are sitting on the same LoC since a long period.

Lt. Gen. Aziz: This is their weakness. They are not agreed on the demarcation under UN's verification, whereas we are agreed. We want to exploit it.

Gen. Musharraf: This is in Simla Agreement that we cannot go for UN intervention.

Lt. Gen. Aziz: Our neighbour does not accept their presence or UNMOGIP arrangement for survey for the area. So, we can start from the top, from 9842 (NJ 9842) . On this line, we can give them logic but in short, the recommendation for Sartaj Aziz Saheb is that he should make no commitment in the first meeting on military situation. And he should not even accept cease-fire, because if there is cease-fire, then vehicles will be moving (on Drass-Kargil highway). In this regard, they have to use their own argument that whatever is interfering with you. That we don't know but there is no justification about tension on LoC. No justification. We want to give them this type of brief so that he does not get into any specifics.

Gen. Musharraf: Alright.

Lt. Gen. Aziz: In this connection, we want your approval and what is your programme.

Gen. Musharraf: I will come tomorrow. We are just leaving within an hour. We are going to Shenzhen. From there, by evening, we will be in Hong Kong. There will be a flight tomorrow from Hong Kong. So, we will be there at Lahore in the evening, via Bangkok flight.

Lt. Gen. Aziz: Sunday evening, you will be at Lahore. We will also indicate that, if there is more critical situation then it (Sartaj visit) should be deferred for another day or two. We can discuss on Monday and then do.

Gen. Musharraf: Has this MI-17 not fallen in our area?

Lt. Gen. Aziz: No, Sir. This has fallen in their area. We have not claimed it. We have got it claimed through the mujahideen.

Gen. Musharraf: Well done.

Lt. Gen. Aziz: But topwise side, crashing straight before our eyes.

Gen. Musharraf: Very good. Now are they facing any greater difficulty in flying them? Are they scared or not? This also you should note. Are they coming any less nearer?

Lt. Gen. Aziz: Yes. There is a lot of pressure on them. They were talking about greater air defence than they had anticipated. They can't afford to lose any more aircraft. There has been less intensity of air flying after that.

Gen. Musharraf: Very good. First class. Is there any build up on the ground?

Lt. Gen. Aziz: *Just like that* but the movement is pretty sluggish and slow. *One or two are coming near* No. 6. Till now only one call sign in which one has not reached the valley so far. Now the air people and the ground people will stay back and then the situation will be OK.

Gen. Musharraf: See you in the evening

Source: Hindustan Times, 12 June 1999.

APPENDIX 11

INDIAN PRIME MINISTER VAJPAYEE'S ADDRESS TO THE NATION, 7 JUNE 1999

My dear countrymen,

You are well aware of the situation which has developed in Kargil.

It is a serious situation; it is a situation fraught with danger; it is a situation that has arisen from one simple fact: the decision of Pakistan to cross the Line of Control, to send its men and materials to occupy our territory.

No government can tolerate such an incursion—our Government certainly will not.

Countries the world over have recognized that we have the full right to evict these intruders from our soil. But for me, and for my Government this is not just a matter of our having a right. It is our duty to rid our sacred Motherland of every single intruder.

For this reason, as you have seen, our armed forces have launched a major operation to drive them back. No one should entertain the slightest doubt: they shall not stop till they have completely attained their objective. No one shall stop them till they have done so.

You know well that our relations with Pakistan, as with all our neighbours, were improving rapidly; the Prime Ministers and other ministers of the two countries were in regular contact; dialogue among officials of the two countries was proceeding constructively, and satisfactorily; areas of cooperation had been identified, and, at various levels, plans were afoot to work together on each of them.

Most important, people-to-people contacts and exchanges had opened up as never before in fifty years—there had been an outpouring of goodwill on both sides.

In the midst of all this, regulars of the Pakistan Army and infiltrators have been sent across. Fomenting insurgency here was heinous enough. But this time Army regulars have been sent. They have been sent to occupy our territory. And, having occupied it, to choke off our links with other parts of our country—in particular with Siachin and Ladakh.

This step has been taken after a great deal of preparation. It was a preplanned operation.

It is a repudiation of the letter and spirit of the Lahore Declaration. It is a violation not just of one article of the Simla Agreement, but an eightfold violation of that solemn Agreement.

The Simla Agreement binds each side to respect the territorial integrity, sovereignty, and independence of the other. The Clauses repeatedly enjoin that neither side shall use the threat of force or force to affect the territorial integrity of the other.

The Agreement deals specifically with the Line of Control. It lays down that the Line of Control resulting from the cease-fire of December 17, 1971 shall be respected by both sides. Furthermore, that 'Neither side shall seek to alter it unilaterally'. The Agreement goes a step ahead and specifies, 'Both sides further undertake to refrain from the threat or the use of force in violation of this Line.'

And yet that is exactly what Pakistan has done: it has used force in an attempt to unilaterally alter the Line of Control.

This having been done, it has now been said that the Line of Control is vague. This is nothing but an ex post artifice to justify aggression. After [the] Agreement in Simla in 1972, the military authorities of the two sides went over the Line of Control—section by microscopic section. The salients, the locations, the coordinates were marked out on detailed maps. The exercise was done thoroughly: five months were expended on delineating the maps so that no ambiguity may remain.

Not just that, at no time in the last 27 years has the Line of Control been called in question—not once, not on a single occasion.

The new assertion, therefore, is just a contrivance to explain away the aggression. It will fool no one. And I do want to make it plain: if the stratagem now is that, the intrusion should be used to alter the Line of Control through talks, the proposed talks will end before they have begun.

India is always open to talks. But the talks must have a definite, specific purpose. In the present instance, the subject is one, and one alone: the intrusion, and how Pakistan proposes to undo it. To discuss this, our doors are always open, and all dates are convenient to us.

India wants peace. We are at peace with all other neighbours of ours. We were taking major steps with Pakistan also towards undoing the fifty-year history of bitterness. Our people desire it. Our Government is committed to it. We have travelled quite some distance for it.

I remain confident that the people of Pakistan too yearn for peace and harmony. They know the possible costs of hostilities—of how these will push economic gains even further beyond the horizon. They know that in today's world whosoever launches aggression of any kind will get isolated in the international community.

Moreover, both India and Pakistan are nuclear powers. Our responsibilities in this regard are all the greater.

Therefore, I once again urge the Government of Pakistan: undo the armed intrusion.

We must hope, my countrymen, that even now reason will prevail, that those within Pakistan who see the folly of aggression will have their way.

But till that happens, we have a job on our hands.

Our first thought, and our last thought must be for our jawans, for our airmen and our officers who are fighting back the intruders. I want each one of them to know: the entire country stands with you, every Indian is grateful to you. The whole operation has been thrust upon us. To ensure victory, you would not be wanting in your requirements.

Our jawans and officers are laying down their lives. Should we be continuing our petty squabbles at such a time? We should stand by them and avoid unnecessary debates.

Let us use this occasion to learn from our defence forces: let us translate into our own conduct some of the discipline for which they are renowned.

The whole world is watching how our brave armed forces are defending the Motherland in inhospitable hilly terrain and at grave risks to their lives. In this hour of crisis, we must maintain an equanimity and act with confidence.

We should not be disheartened by some momentary mishap. We must realise the gravity of the situation and emulate the fortitude with which our fighting men take such events in their stride.

Have confidence in the ability of our armed forces.

The armed forces shall accomplish this task and ensure that no one dares to indulge in this kind of misadventure in future.

Jai Hind.

Source: Web-site: http://www.meadev.gov.in/speeches/pm-jun.htm

APPENDIX 12

PAKISTAN PRIME MINISTER NAWAZ SHARIF'S ADDRESS TO THE NATION, 12 JULY 1999

My dear Countrymen, not everyone will know of the tensions that we have gone through and the circumstances we have braved during the last month and a half. It is a fact and no secret anyway that the deterioration in Pakistan-India relations brought our two countries to the brink of war. While there is no doubt that the Kashmiri Mujahideen through their sacrifices and battle successes wrote out a new chapter in their freedom struggle, the situation on the diplomatic front became so complicated that it was no easy task to straighten it out or control its adverse fallout.

Dear brothers and sisters by the grace of God, Pakistan is not a wall of sand or a child's plaything. We have the ability to deal befittingly with aggression. Had war been imposed on us, the invader would have lived to regret the day. However, we do not wish to make war, nor have we looked for it. We know that in a nuclear conflict there can be no victors.

It is my considered opinion that by going to war Pakistan and India can only multiply their problems without solving even one of them. I have repeatedly said that the Kashmir dispute should be resolved amicably. I am also aware of the record of those who vowed to fight for a thousand years. I know what their aims were. Their only gift to the nation was ignominy and lasting regret.

After taking stock of past events and making an objective study of history, I have come to the conclusion that our principal national priority should be making Pakistan a great self-reliant economic power. Only then can we achieve our supreme national objectives.

After the Lahore Declaration in February this year, not only the people of Pakistan and India but the international community as well had begun to hope that after their long history of discord, our two countries had chosen the path of peace. Prime Minister Vajpayee of India visited the Minar-i-Pakistan in Lahore and what he said on the occasion was a good augury for the future since it showed that he wanted to begin a new chapter in our relations, with the bitterness of the past forgotten and old attitudes abandoned. I welcomed this. While we were preparing for negotiations in line with the Lahore Declaration, the Indian Lok Sabha was dissolved and fresh elections were announced. On the other hand, the Kashmir freedom struggle which has been underway for the last eleven years entered a new and intensified phase with the freedom fighters gaining control of the Kargil mountains.

Prime Minister Vajpayee phoned me, expressing his concern at these developments. I suggested a meeting between local commanders while pointing out that we should resolve this matter at a local level, as in the past so that there should be no escalation. He agreed with me and the next day the two local commanders met but, simultaneously, India turned its heavy guns on us, while the Indian air force began to pound the Mujahideen-held positions. This sudden escalation was unexpected. It is true that the Mujahideen were present on several Kargil heights but it was part of their long freedom struggle and inseparable from it. For example, you all know that the Mujahideen took control of the Hazratbal shrine in Srinagar once. Now there is no way in which Pakistan could have come to their aid there. The shrine was surrounded by Indian troops and yet the Mujahideen took it over and held it for several days. Once the world took notice of what their action and the unresolved question of Kashmir became duly highlighted, they vacated their occupation of the shrine. It is for the same reasons that the Mujahideen must have occupied those heights in Kargil. Once the Mujahideen had succeeded in drawing world attention to Kashmir, it is understandable that they would wish to disengage.

Had we tried, this matter could have been resolved peacefully; but India set the fires of war alight instead of dealing with the situation through negotiations. It also chose to engulf the entire country in a war frenzy. However, Pakistan remained unprovoked and we saw to it that there was no war hysteria in the country. We also ensured that there would be no break in mutual contacts. Since the start of the crisis in Kargil, up to this day, I have spoken to Prime Minister Vajpayee on the phone several times. I also sent my Foreign Minister over though his visit proved fruitless. Given all this, it is unfair to allege that we stabbed anyone in the back. It has been my constant effort that our countries be spared the horror of a nuclear war. Only a desire for collective suicide can prompt us to take such a step. I have no such intention. I believe Prime Minister Vajpayee has no such intention either. However, going by the attitude of India, it did seem to us that New Delhi was rapidly moving towards war. The use of air and land power in Kargil by India was on a scale associated with a large and regular war only. Pakistani positions were shelled from across the Line of Control resulting in the death of innocent civilians and armed forces personnel who were merely defending themselves.

The number of troops deployed by India on our borders was again warlike. Its naval power was moved close to our shores and its nuclear missiles turned towards us. The Indian air force was put on red alert. I salute the armed forces of Pakistan which took all necessary steps to deal with the expected Indian attack with exemplary efficiency and speed. I also wish to pay tribute to all those innocent citizens who fell victim to Indian shelling. Those who suffered material loss as a result of Indian actions have my full sympathy. The government will soon take steps to give them due compensation. I also salute those mart;, s of the Pakistan army who fell while performing their duties on the Line of Control. Those who suffered injury also have my heartfelt sympathies. Their courage, valour and resoluteness will serve as an example to the world. They surprised a military power several times their size on the world's most inhospitable and difficult front by dint of their grit and determination. They resisted the unrelenting attacks of the Indian air force and infantry in an admirable manner. They proved that they were prepared to go to any extent for the sake of their freedom. I take this occasion to pay tribute to the gallant freedom fighters of the All Parties Hurriyat Conference.

My dear Countrymen, we have decided to give diplomacy another chance. This decision is neither hasty nor has it been taken under pressure or out of nervousness. It has been said that it takes more courage to extricate oneself from war than to start one. For many years and with time it has gained in intensity and strength. Kargil has been a part of that struggle. We were constantly in consultation with our friends as the fighting continued. When the clouds of war began to draw closer, we intensified our contacts. At the same time, we did not snap contact with the Indian government. I was busy trying to press every entity, every individual, in aid of our cause and its furtherance. I was in touch with President Clinton. When American representatives came to Pakistan, we made it clear to them that the problem would not be solved by putting out the fires in Kargil but to get to the heart of the problem. We argued that, the Kashmiri urge for freedom was like molten lava in the belly of the earth which would always find other points of eruption.

Even if we succeeded in capping the fire-spitting mountains of Kargil, unless the basic problem was addressed, there will be outbreaks elsewhere. If the Kashmiri people were not given their right of self-determination, there would be other Kargils. Neither we, nor India, would be able to stop that. The only way to stop more Kargils from happening was to do justice to the Kashmiris. The promises made to them had to be fulfilled. That was the message I carried to America and I am glad that President Clinton agreed that unless the basic issue of Kashmir was resolved, the clouds of war would continue to hover over the Subcontinent. This was the backdrop of the joint statement issued in Washington. The statement clearly stated that as soon as the situation on the Line of Control returned to normal, negotiations between India and Pakistan would begin in order to resolve all outstanding issues, including Kashmir. President Clinton extended the assurance that he would not only encourage all moves aimed at settling all outstanding disputes through dialogue, but he would take a personal interest in these efforts in order to ensure that they were intensified.

This assurance, coming from the head of a great power like the United States is no ordinary matter. It is clear that after this unequivocal commitment from President Clinton in particular and the international community in general, the world will pay serious attention to Kashmir, being now aware of its importance and sensitivity. That is why we appealed to the Mujahideen to come down from the heights they were occupying in Kargil and give diplomacy a chance so that it could carry forward and complete the mission for which they had made so many sacrifices. I am grateful to the Mujahideen for having accepted our appeal. The outcome of every war leads to negotiated decisions which is the route we have also taken and I am sure that truth and justice will prevail in the end.

My dear Countrymen, true leadership is that which is not interested in merely staying in office but in ensuring national security and public welfare. True leadership does not hesitate from sacrificing office or popularity if it is the security of the country and the people which is at stake. You will recall that in my first term as Prime Minister, the shadows of the Gulf war lay across this region. Kuwait had been occupied and the Allied forces were preparing to invade Iraq, at that time, many of our political parties, leaders and even individuals in the service of the state tried to gain cheap popularity by inciting the people and playing with their sentiments. They kept the facts hidden from the masses in order to advance their own political careers. They led processions and felt no hesitation in jeopardizing the national interest as long as it won them popular following. You know well that had I allowed myself to be swept away by emotion and begun to raise sentimental slogans to please the masses, the consequences for my country and its people would have been grave. Those who conspire to attain power and advance their political careers are the very same people who end up pushing their country and their nation over the precipice. Whatever decision I took, I took to protect the interest of my country and my people. During the Gulf war I chose what in my view was the right course. I was not swayed by considerations of personal power.

I did not follow the popular upsurge, if you recall. The results are there for everyone to see. If you have faith, you should only take those decisions which in your judgment are correct.

Dear Countrymen, I want to declare that the Kashmiri urge for freedom cannot be stifled by force. The Kashmiri people's struggle will continue. Freedom is their fundamental right and unless they win that right, the people of Pakistan will continue to be with them, shoulder to shoulder. We will never abandon the Kashmiris.

My dear Countrymen, it has always been my dream to take Pakistan to the highest pinnacle of glory and in the pursuit of this dream, I have not been held back by fear or self-interest. You will recall that when India was firing off its missiles and the world instead of restraining that country was putting every possible pressure on Pakistan not to join the race, I resisted and went on to test the Ghauri and Shaheen missiles. There were many other pressures on us subsequently but I refused to buckle under them. Can anyone forget the crass Indian bid to establish its overlordship over this region after detonating nuclear bombs on 11 and 13 May 1998! Highly provocative statements were issued and it was said that Pakistan would have to come to terms with its reduced statu While we were being subjected to intense external pressure and threats, inside the country there were some to whom the lure of dollars was more attractive than the attainment of self-sufficiency and freedom. They were terrified of sanctions but it was I who stood firm and went ahead to conduct our nuclear tests. Thereafter, sanctions were indeed imposed on us but I stood my ground. Such hard decisions can only be taken by a person who has the supreme interest of his people and the fear of God at heart. You know that whatever Nawaz Sharif does, he does in order that you and your children live in peace and security, enjoy prosperity and walk with honour. For me my country always comes first. Pakistan and Nawaz Sharif are one. Pakistan is a part of my being and I am part of Pakistan. Each breath that I take is like a prayer for the security of Pakistan and the progress and well-being of my people.

My dear Countrymen, I want to thank you today because at this most delicate point in our history, you have not fallen into the emotional traps laid out for you and you have not allowed yourselves to be fooled by any political party. You have refused to hit the streets for the sake of those who have chosen the path of negativism. You have demonstrated that the Pakistani nation is not willing to act frivolously when the questions involved carry grave national consequences. You have shown that you have complete trust in your elected leadership.

Let me assure you that given the help of God, I will never betray your trust.

My dear Countrymen, during the Lahore summit, I told Indian Prime Minister Vajpayee that we had gained nothing by fighting wars. Every war had led to the next one. I say again today that in the last fifty years, Pakistan and India, despite having fought several wars, despite having put their armies in direct face-to-face confrontation with each another, despite spending billions of rupees on armaments, and despite having trained their nuclear weapons at each another, have failed to resolve any of their disputes through conflict. Is that not a pity!

Because of the failure to resolve the Kashmir dispute, we have not been able to give the people of the Subcontinent a single day of peace. Can we not solve this problem and thereby guarantee a peaceful, tranquil and secure future to the one billion people who live here! How many more Kashmiris have to die at the hands of India before this reality dawns upon that country! How many more Kashmiri homes have to be laid waste! How many more Indian soldiers have to die pursuing an unjust war! How many more Kashmiri youth have to perish! How many more Kashmiri women still need to be outraged! How any more mothers in Indian cities are fated to shed tears over the dead bodies of their sons!

My dear Countrymen, world opinion will have to decide how long this drama of blood and fire is to be played in Kashmir. Why the delay in resolving the Kashmir problem! The United Nations conferred the right of self-determination on the Kashmiris over fifty years ago. India promised to implement those resolutions. It was not Pakistan which passed those resolutions: it was the United Nations. India neither implements those resolutions nor does it enter into any meaningful or result-oriented discussions with Pakistan. Is this how problems are resolved in this world! Where lies the gain in sticking to a single recalcitrant position! How can anything be resolved amicably if such diehard attitudes are allowed to prevail! Because of its intransigence, India has suffered. It has been left behind, and so have we. It is in the interest of both India and Pakistan to give up the old, obstinate, unbending attitudes of the past and make an honest attempt to settle the Kashmir dispute amicably through negotiations.

How long can we snatch food from the mouths of our people to buy guns?

How long will we go on jeopardizing the future of our children by buying the shells that go into these guns?

How long will we allow our resources to go up in gun smoke and add to the number of our unemployed?

India should learn a lesson from history. No liberation movement has ever been crushed through the use of military force. Bullets do indeed draw blood but in the process become blood drenched themselves. How long will India continue to tell the world that it is Pakistan which is interfering in Kashmir! No outside power can sustain a movement for eleven years through the use of infiltrators.

My dear Countrymen, you will remember that during my election campaign I had promised to end all disputes with India and establish good relations with that country. I want that the mandate which the people have given me should be used for their welfare. I want to settle the long-standing question of Kashmir so that I can forever secure the future of my country and its people. The people of India also need peace. India too has to move ahead. I ask Prime Minister Vajpayee to step forward and talk to us. Let's save our people from the scourge of war and give them peace and security. Let us sit across the negotiating table and begin our search for a better future for our people. A great deal of time has passed. Let no more time pass.

In the end, I pray for the solidarity, strength and well-being of Pakistan and its people. May God be our strength and our support.

Long live Pakistan.

Source: Web-site: www.stimson.org/cbm/sa/nwazspch.htm

Contributors

P.R. CHARI is a former member of the Indian Administrative Service (1960 batch/Madhya Pradesh Cadre). During the course of his official career he served two spells (1971-5 and 1985-8) in the Ministry of Defence. His last position there was Additional Secretary. He was Director of the Institute for Defence Studies and Analyses, New Delhi (1975-80), International Fellow, Centre for International Affairs, Harvard University (1983-4), and Research Professor, Centre for Policy Research (1992-6). Currently he is Visiting Professor at the Centre for the Study of Developing Societies and Director of the Institute of Peace and Conflict Studies.

He has worked extensively on nuclear disarmament, non-proliferation and Indian defence issues. He has published over 900 op-ed articles in newspapers, and over 100 monographs and major papers in learned journals/chapters in books in India and abroad. His publications include *Indo-Pak Nuclear Stand off: Role of the United States* (1995); co-author, *Brasstacks and Beyond: Perception and Management Crisis* (1995); co-author and co-editor, *Nuclear Non-Proliferation in India and Pakistan: South Asian Perspectives* (1996); editor, *India: Towards Millennium* (1998); and editor, *Perspectives on National Security in South Asia: In Search of a new Paradigm* (1999).

MAJ. GEN. ASHOK KRISHNA, AVSM was commissioned into 4/8 Gorkha Rifles in 1957 and he commanded the battalion in the 1971 war in the western sector. In 1974 he commanded 1/8 Gorkha Rifles, now 3 Mechanized Infantry. In 1988, he was appointed Colonel 8 Gorkha Rifles.

He has commanded a brigade actively engaged in counter-insurgency operations and a division in high altitude. He has held various staff appointments including in the Military Operations Directorate, Army Headquarters. He was Commander, Higher Command Wing, College of Combat, Mhow at the time of his retirement in 1994. Thereafter, he was with the Institute of Defence Studies and Analyses as Senior Fellow, and in 1999 he joined the Institute of Peace and Conflict Studies as Deputy Director.

He has written several articles on insurgency and terrorism and he has authored *India's Armed Forces: Fifty Years of War and Peace.*

ANJU SUSAN ALEX and DEEPA RAJKUMAR are M. Phil students at the School of International Studies, Jawaharlal Nehru University, New Delhi. AZHAGARASU D. is a freelancer.

BHARTENDU K. SINGH and SATYAJIT MOHANTY are pursuing their doctoral thesis at the School of International Studies, Jawaharlal Nehru University, New Delhi.

MALLIKA JOSEPH A. is a Research Officer at IPCS. She has co-authored with Suba Chandran *Lethal Fields: Landmines and IEDs in South Asia* (2001) and with Maj. Gen. Dipankar Banerjee *Anti-Personnel Landmines: A South Asian Regional Survey* (1999). Ms. Joseph has also contributed to *Landmine Monitor Report 2000* (2000).

SUBA CHANDRAN is a Research Officer at IPCS. He has contributed a chapter 'Meeting the Demand: Illegal Domestic Production of Small Arms in India' in Dipankar Banerjee (ed), *South Asia at Gun Point* (2000); co-authored *Lethal Fields: Landmines and IEDs in South Asia* (2001) and contributed to *Landmine Monitor Report 2000* (2000).

ARPIT RAJAIN is a Research Officer at IPCS. He is currently writing a monograph on *Deterring Nuclear Conflict in Southern Asia.* He has published in *South Asian Survey* (Sage).

Index